YOUR
CHILD'S
MIND

YOUR CHILD'S MIND

The Complete Book of
Infant and Child
Mental Health Care

Herman Roiphe, M.D.
Anne Roiphe

ST. MARTIN'S PRESS
New York

YOUR CHILD'S MIND: THE COMPLETE BOOK OF INFANT AND CHILD MENTAL
HEALTH CARE. Copyright © 1985 by Herman Roiphe, M.D., and Anne
Roiphe. All rights reserved. Printed in the United States of America. No
part of this book may be used or reproduced in any manner whatsoever
without written permission except in the case of brief quotations embodied
in critical articles or reviews. For information, address St. Martin's Press,
175 Fifth Avenue, New York, N.Y. 10010.

Library of Congress Cataloging in Publication Data

Roiphe, Anne Richardson, 1935–
    Your child's mind.

    1. Child psychology.   2. Child psychopathology.
I. Roiphe, Herman, 1924– .   II Title.
BF721.R636 1985   155.4   85-1742
ISBN 0-312-89783-9
ISBN 0-312-89784-7 (pbk.)

Design by Doris Borowsky

First Edition
10 9 8 7 6 5 4 3 2 1

I wish to acknowledge my debt to Dr. Eleanor Galenson, my co-director at The Infant Intervention Center at Mt. Sinai Hospital, New York. Through our eighteen years of research and work together, she has remained a challenging colleague and a dear friend.

Herman Roiphe, M.D.

Contents

CONTENTS

PART TWO: THREE TO SIX

Part Two, Section I

Part Two, Section II

PART THREE: SIX TO TEN

Part Three, Section I

Part Three, Section II

CONTENTS

PART FOUR: SPECIAL SITUATIONS

YOUR
CHILD'S
MIND

Preface

For many years I followed my husband to meetings and read the professional papers he was writing and discussing. Sometimes I would find a book on my own and we would share it. Each year when the enormous annual volume of the *Psychoanalytic Study of the Child* arrived, I would rush off with it. I had a true amateur's interest in child development and a wife's affection for her mate's field of interest. During all those years I was writing novels and journalistic pieces, and changing diapers and picking up children at school, and making dentist appointments and planning birthday parties, and both of us were working very hard at putting together our combined family. At the time we met, he had two children and I had one, and then we had two together.

Now, after seventeen years of remarriage, it seems like a perfect blend of all the themes in my life to write this book with my husband, combining his professional knowledge, my writing experience, and both our personal lives that have been so constantly filled with children. We took three on our honeymoon and once figured out that we were destined to endure twenty years of living with adolescents. We have almost survived it all. Survival does not in itself make anyone an expert, but it helps to be close to the other shore, looking up and down the surging river with the calm of one whose swim is nearly over.

1

Herman is a graduate of Physicians and Surgeons, Columbia Medical School. He did his internship and residency at New York Hospital and Yale University, and received his analytic training at the New York Psychoanalytic Institute. He has a private practice of adult and child patients in psychotherapy and psychoanalysis. He is an associate professor at Mt. Sinai Medical School in New York City, and with his colleague Dr. Eleanor Galenson, runs a nursery there for babies at risk of developing emotional problems. They have published a book for professionals on their work with infants and have written over twenty-five articles for medical journals on various aspects of child development.

When we first thought of doing this book together, I felt concerned because we are not perfect parents. Our children have suffered from our divorces and from other mistakes that we, despite all good intentions, could neither foresee nor avoid. Some of our children have had a harder time than others and some will never be the people we had hoped and others will be more than we had ever dared to expect. We have been through some bad times that temper our memories of the glorious and triumphant occasions. When we were thinking about this book, we decided together that we were experts of sorts, but not the kind of experts who watch the play from the sidelines. We have been bruised in the fray—and that has made us wiser and possibly better able to combine our intellectual knowledge and our skills in a way that might be meaningful to other parents.

We are writing out of a Freudian viewpoint. But this does not mean that all opinions were formed in turn-of-the-century Vienna, or that the discoveries and social changes of the last few decades have not profoundly influenced our thought. There is of course no way to avoid cultural prejudices and limitations. Freud could not see the sexism in his own society and there must surely be blind spots in our vision that we ourselves cannot identify. Psychology is a science that blends with art and can take on life and meaning only within a culture. Like the soul in the body, the culture must influence the shape of things. We have used the work of Anna Freud, D. W. Winnicott, Erik Erikson, and John Bowlby, as well as the advances made by the pioneers in family therapy and self-psychology. We have worked as well with the new discoveries of Margaret Mahler and her colleagues. We do not believe there is a single correct truth, and so we have presented alternatives wherever possible.

In this book we describe the psychological growth of the child through a normal childhood. We have tried to place the small problems, such as thumb-sucking or stalling at bedtime, in the context of how the child feels and what challenges he is meeting each day at each age of his life. We expect that the parent of a normal child will then be able to see the reasons behind the odd bits and pieces of puzzling behavior. While we offer suggestions here and there of ways to handle some common shared problems, we expect that the understanding itself of the child's mind will enable many parents to survive the inevitable rough spots in better humor. A separate section also describes the psychological symptoms and illnesses, from the mildest to the most severe, that do affect some children. In this way we hope to help parents distinguish between those problems that are passing and normal, part of the sweat of human growth, and those that really do signal trouble—trouble that might be helped or that must be faced.

We believe that the entire portrait of a child's mind, including the illnesses that affect only a few, will help parents to know their own children better. By examining what has gone wrong, we can learn what is happening when things are right. We can see from the disturbed child what the normal has accomplished. We do not discuss physical illness or normal physical growth except where these issues overlap or are affected by the child's state of mind. While of course mind and body cannot be separated, we are approaching the child from the discipline of psychiatry, not pediatrics.

We hope that parents reading through this book will see that the annoyances and aggravations of child care are necessary detours along a fascinating and incredible journey. As parents, we experience our best moments when we watch our children make their way through the world, when we hold them close, when we tell them stories, when we listen to their stories, when they tell us a joke or a secret, when we share with them everything we have. We hope that this book will enhance this pleasure while providing a guide to the sometimes hidden forces that affect the growing years. We hope to express our respect for the human mind. The more we understand, the more we can appreciate and enjoy our children.

The other night my stepdaughter, who is herself a doctor and a resident in psychiatry, came over for dinner. I listened to the two doctors arguing some medical point and watched their pleasure and pride in each other. It seemed natural. We are not birds that cast our young out of the nest and then fly off to the next adventure. We are a part of the human future because the next generation carries so much of our investment, our love. The next generation matters.

ANNE ROIPHE

Introduction

Every parent is a dreamer. We all hold our newborn infants in our arms and envision a child rich in happiness, strong in intelligence, beautiful in body and mind, and we have intentions, good intentions, to nourish in our children grand capacities for joy and success. We intend to create in them our "letter to the world," our connection to the future, our brave immortality. But all parents find that the dream was a little too large; reality and its daily frustrations expose the limits and flatten the expectations. Eventually, we learn to love and respect our children, imperfect as they are. We learn to recognize the outside edges of our control, and to appreciate their individuality, their uniqueness, their right to be themselves.

When the grizzly bear is born, it can fit in the palm of a man's hand. It is like the human baby, helpless, weak, and totally dependent on the parent for survival. The difference is that the bear's parents do not wonder what their infant is thinking. They do not ask, How do I best take care of this child? What part of my life still belongs to me and what to the baby? The human parent alone among the earth's species worries about the effect of the present on the future, wonders if he or she feels the right kind of love, enough love, is like or unlike other parents. These are perfectly natural concerns and are shared

5

by most parents facing with great delight and some terror their own new babies.

As human parents, we all soon dig furrows in which to plant the seeds of regret and guilt as well as pride and love. The bear grows up quickly, becoming a massive creature that sleeps, eats, eliminates, kills, and mates at will. The human baby journeys slowly—with many backward slides—toward maturity, continually fighting the necessary demands of civilization to control natural instincts, to postpone satisfaction, to stall and spoil pleasure. However, along the way, wisdom, sensitivity, knowledge, creativity, laughter, and love will become a part of our children as they join us in the human community.

The child must learn to create a self, a self that exists separate from mother, father, and friend. The child must learn to be apart from others and yet to sometimes be together with others. If our task as parents is done well enough, the child will have a moral center. The baby will become a person rich in the many textures and nuances of feeling and wise in the means to control, use, and enjoy those feelings. The human child must become comfortable with its gender, using maleness or femaleness not as a prison in which to play out stereotyped roles but as true biology—a source of happiness, a major piece of the puzzle of identity.

For most parents and most children this is an entirely natural process. The growth we ourselves experience while taking care of our children is a mirror image of the growing they do. Although we are psychologically complex, although amazing chemical reactions occur in our brains even in sleep, we have produced without any particular specialized knowledge generations of fine people following one after the other. Experts come and go, and they seem to change their advice every decade or so. They fall victim to the prejudices and the limitations of their own culture, their own conceptual frames. They pull parents around like so much taffy in the making. They told the mother of the thirties that she would spoil her offspring if she picked her up when she cried. They told the parent of the forties that need was all-important and that control was the nasty idea of totalitarian minds.

We write now taking the risk of making our own mistakes, because changes in the culture have brought about new and sensible balances between the old extremes, while observations of infants and children have given us some new insights into the workings of the young mind. We feel that those truths that have become self-evident among professionals should be shared; but take us with many grains of salt.

How do we define mental health? Is it merely conformity to the demands of society, or is it some kind of mysterious, unattainable state of mind, granted only to the lucky few who seem always successful, content, rewarded by self-love and the love of others?

Yes, the mentally healthy child will be able to conform to most of the reasonable requests of the society around him. Yes, he will be able to get along with his age mates and have friends. Yes, he will be able to be alone sometimes without panic or anxiety. He will be able to sleep reasonably well at night despite some bad dreams and occasional nightmares. Yes, he will not eat everything, but he will eat enough of a sufficient variety of foods to enable his body and mind to grow. Yes, he will like himself, but he will gradually increase his capacity for empathy with others. He will not think he is king of the castle all of the time. He will learn what his parents and the world around him call right and wrong. He will love, and in loving sometimes be hurt; he will hurt without falling into little pieces. He will feel pulled back toward his babyhood and he will sometimes permit himself baby behavior, but he will steadily take on more of the responsibilities for his own care, and he will see his destiny as an adult of a particular sex. He will not be frightened as each birthday brings him closer to maturity.

The healthy child will be proud of his achievements and eager for the next step. He will be frightened of change, but not so frightened that he doesn't move forward. He will learn everything from riding a bike to long division, and mastery, creativity, will keep him steady when the going gets hard. This is considerably more than conformity and a lot less than miraculous. Mental health is very ordinary, and yet it permits us to be different from each other, to be varied and complicated and playful. Mental health is contagious. It passes easily from parent to child.

Part One

BIRTH to THREE

Section I

Pregnancy

Pregnancy is the beginning and the end. It is the end of a way of life, of a stage of marriage. It is the final goodbye to those days in which you were responsible only for your own body and emotionally vulnerable only to events that brought direct pain or pleasure. Pregnancy is the beginning of fulfillment of a biological purpose and the beginning of a new social purpose—the first moments of a new self, one that will be connected ever after to another life. There is no divorcing a child. There is no annulment of birth.

Of course, we risk failure. Each parent is in some way judged and judges himself by the well-being and success of his child. We feel guilt, we feel hope. We feel great pride in the simplest of acts achieved by our children, a blob of paint on paper, a note on the piano, a new word; but we also feel shame if our child doesn't measure up, loses in comparison with others, or fails in some life task. The child might be physically damaged. We might expose our own psychological weaknesses. We might be bad parents.

Once pregnancy has begun, the happiness, the well-being of every concerned parent is hostage to that child's future. If the child suffers, the parent will suffer. The parent in taking that risk has become a full member of the human species, a part of the generational work of survival, a creator of life. If some of us prove to be false gods, the fault lies not in our daring. Don't be misled by how commonplace it seems—having a child, committing oneself to the long period of nurturing that the human infant requires, is without question a brave act. Some adults are too scared to try it. Their lives may be simpler, safer, but because of their caution they miss the exhilaration, the excitement, the intense pleasure to be found in the adventures and accomplishments and affections of children. The timid do not gain.

Whether the pregnancy was planned or accidental, whether it was long awaited or prompted a couple to decide to get married, are important factors in setting the emotional mood that follows the birth. Each of us brings along to the delivery room a set of conscious and unconscious feelings and attitudes toward the new baby. These feelings play a significant role in the way we will relate to our children, handle their bodies, their needs, their troubles.

Some parents have a strong preference for a child of one sex or another. This is revealed in the commonplace difficulty of thinking of a girl's or a boy's name. Strong and passionate hopes that a child will be of one sex or another usually indicate that the parent may be disappointed over his or her own sexuality or has experienced some grave misfortune at the hands of the undesired sex. Some parents may consciously or unconsciously identify the new baby with a brother or sister they either hated or admired. One woman from a very large family had wished throughout her childhood that she had been an only child. She was blissfully happy at the birth of her own daughter. But when she got pregnant for the second time, she became depressed. She felt no joy at seeing the second child; only with time was she able to prevent herself from experiencing the new infant as an unwanted intruder.

During pregnancy, most of us begin to work out the details of our fantasy of redoing our own childhood. In other words, we plan revenges on the past or alterations on the way it was that will make our children's lives different from our own. We plan to do everything better than our parents did, and we begin this redoing of our own past as we plan our children's future. We say we will be stricter or not as strict as our parents. We will be more sexually open or more reserved. We intend to be better companions or better nurturers. We plan to undo our own hurts by not doing to our children as was done to us. One woman might feel that if her mother worked, she will certainly stay home. Another will see her housewife mother as an oppressed oppressor and decide to leave for the office the day the baby's umbilical cord dries.

These plans—some of them unconscious—of revising the past by altering the future can bring about their own distortions. We carry our childhood experiences with us and they affect us profoundly, no matter how we twist and turn. We also intend to do those things for our children that we remember with particular pleasure. We will try to go back to the same cottage in the mountains where our parents spent their vacations. We will try to share fishing or baseball or stamp collecting with our children as they were shared with us. We hope to recreate our closeness to our parents, to relive our happiest moments by redesigning them into our children's lives.

During pregnancy, a common fear for both parents is that the child will be born with a severe defect of mind or body. This is a fear that holds a small kernel of reality. One out of every one thousand births reveals genetic error. Some of these are easily correctable; others are truly tragic. But considering how heavily the odds are in favor of any one of us producing a healthy, normal child, it is certainly not necessary for a parent to dwell persistently and intensely on the possibilities for disaster. When parents do have enormous concerns and constant dreads, these fears can reflect the parents' own bad feelings about themselves. Such mothers- or fathers-to-be probably experience their own bodies or minds as in some way defective, inadequate, or ruined. This is perhaps the first example of how hard it is for us not to confuse our own internal psychological climate with the baby's reality. But, of course, the baby's health does not depend on our own sense of self-esteem, and biology works either for or against us, without judgmental or moral implications.

Natural Childbirth

We do not take too seriously the exact method of childbirth a parent may use. Certainly, natural childbirth offers many advantages for mother, father, and infant. But the overall life of the child, and the nurturing that will come, are not dependent on the first seconds or moments of breath. Many parents trained in natural childbirth methods have experienced disappointment and felt as if they have failed if the mother has to have a caesarean, has a long and difficult labor, or is among those who really need anesthetic help. This is another one of the ways in which we can set up arbitrary and silly tests for ourselves. The profound commitment of mother, father, and child is like a river that flows across an entire continent rather than a fountain that appears in one spot. It is an experience lived out in the thousands of little daily events that follow delivery and last a lifetime through. The first moments are no more than first moments.

Bonding

We don't know a great deal about the maternal instinct or the parenting instinct, but we do know that the first sight of the baby probably provokes along with excitement and wonder a certain amount of fear and awe. We are not capable of instant love, and we certainly do not have an instinctive natural knowledge of what to do. Most of us raised in small nuclear families have not had experience with newborns. They look so strange. Human babies appear so fragile, so unlike us. We know that they are ours, and yet they look alien, wrinkled, out of proportion, unspeaking, oozing substances we have been taught to dislike. We are euphoric, thrilled to have delivered a healthy baby, yes, but most of us are also somewhat afraid. We learn slowly how to hold, how to comfort, how to listen to the baby's cues.

Some parents find the challenge of taking care of a newborn less difficult than others, but for all of us it is a time of major adjustments and a calling up of new resources. This is the right time to be patient with imperfections of soul and physical frailties. There are indications that mothers who are permitted more time with their new babies while they are in the hospital overcome their initial shyness and discomfort faster. We certainly feel that the more flexible lying-in plans offer the mother the best path toward gaining in confidence and strength.

The First Weeks

Nothing but experience can adequately prepare a new parent for the shock of the first post-delivery weeks. The fatigue of caring for a baby that wakes every several hours, sleeps in irregular patterns, and is sometimes distressed for no apparent cause can seem overwhelming. Without sufficient sleep, in a state of insecurity and anxiety, most new parents begin to will their children to become persons. Each time they feed, each time they change a diaper, each time they walk the room with a cranky small body spitting up on their shoulders, they are weaving the skein of the psychological and physical life of their child.

It is common for new mothers to experience some kind of sadness and anger in these first days after giving birth. The demands of the baby are constant and almost all mothers feel afraid that they may do something wrong. At the same time many mothers are angry at the loss of independence, freedom, and energy that taking care of the baby involves. They may be fascinated with and concerned for their infant, but profound love itself may build more slowly and this is perfectly natural. Mothers who cannot admit to their feelings of anger and irritation with the baby will find themselves more tense and unhappy than those who can see that while having a new baby is wonderful, it also has its drawbacks. It is entirely normal to feel angry and upset and exhausted in those first weeks, and it is better for the baby and better for the mother if these bad feelings are accepted as part of the whole new experience.

Infant psychiatrists have noticed some interesting patterns of behavior in both parents and babies. Girl babies are consistently talked to more, while boy children are touched and fondled to a greater degree. Is this culture or part of our biological program? The answer waits. The human baby appears to be genetically programmed to watch for the human face, and it has been shown that babies within the first days of life, when they are in their brief quiet alert periods without any distress of the body, can recognize the human voice and tell the difference between voices. The baby is ready and able to begin the profound connection to his mother.

Before they are three days old, infants will be able to recognize their own mother's voice. Amazingly enough, recent research has shown that babies do indeed hear and learn their mother's voice while they are still in the womb. Babies will clearly respond to a story their mother had read to them before birth: their sucking pattern will be completely different when hearing a familiar story compared to hearing one that they had not heard while in the uterus.

This startling discovery means that newborns are already prepared to be connected to their mothers. They obviously have a far more developed sense of connection and intellectual capacity for recognition and memory than we had previously thought. Your new baby is a more complicated person than we had dreamed.

It has even been demonstrated that six-day-old infants can discriminate reliably between the smell of their own mother's milk and another woman's. They will turn away from the stranger's milk pad and toward their own mother's. This is another example of how quickly and how profoundly our babies become ours. From the first moments on, we are known to them. Before the recent work on infant mentality we had only old wives' tales to tell us of babies frightened in the womb by a black cat and affected by the turnings of the moon. Scientists of course dismissed all that, but it now turns out that indeed the baby in the uterus will respond to a bright light focused on him by shifting his body and speeding up his heart rate.

The newborn is by no means the alienated, unknowing lump we had once assumed. By at least one month, babies can distinguish their mother's face from that of others and they can discriminate between different sound groups, such as *pa* and *ba*. The baby will rhythmically move his arms and legs back and forth, up and down, following the speed and patterns of the words that are spoken to him. A baby can distinguish the human being from a bright toy, a light, or a sound. Babies can tell the difference between flat pictures and three-dimensional objects.

The new baby is also biologically programmed to turn her cheek toward the touch on the face. This is called a rooting response, and helps the baby find the nipple. While the new baby cannot lift her head alone or turn over, she can follow her mother's face as it circles from left to right. The new baby is prepared to make the loving bond with her mother and has ways of eliciting care and attention. The baby's cry is perfectly designed to bring help and give clues as to what is wrong. The baby can grasp onto a finger, clinging and molding close to her mother to evoke the mother's care and protection.

In the first weeks, the baby's nervous system is adjusting to life outside the womb. The baby is learning how to breathe on his own and he is experiencing all kinds of internal distress as the digestive organs and the muscles and the heart begin unsteadily to perform their work. This is also a time of major adjustment for the parents. They feel the weight of the new responsibility, the curiousness of their change in relationship with each other now that they are at last parents. These adjustments—the baby's limbs twitching in her sleep, the stomach cramping with pain, the hands trembling—are really massive. The parent who expects nothing but a bundle of pink or blue sweetness is quickly disabused.

Of course the process of caring for a new infant has its glorious moments. The suckling at the breast, the times the baby full and content from a bottle falls asleep in one's arms, the inspection of the incredible toes and fingers, the feel of the amazing soft spot in the center of the skull, and the smell of clean powdered baby face to face or gently molding her body into yours as if you were both made of the same flesh and belonged permanently together—are unmatchable experiences. New parents are amazed at the sensation of small hands grasping at the adult finger. They are fascinated by the infant eyes focusing at just about two feet away, tracking the parent's face, receiving silently important information about the welcome it can expect in this new world.

Within hours of birth, babies seem to have gathered clues about the feelings of others toward them. It is a common enough sight to see a particularly fretful baby red and sweating in his mother's arms when the mother has turned her face away from the infant and holds him stiffly as if he were a particularly dangerous package. Babies can sense the emotional climate that greets them. Of course they do not have verbal conscious thoughts, but they do automatically understand certain gestures, feelings that appear in the unconscious duet that begins its first themes in those early days after birth.

Try to relax with your baby. Try to let your arms and shoulders mold toward the infant. Look the baby in the face even if he is not ready to look at you yet. Touch him gently. Give yourself time to get to know him, but try to let your baby feel your body close. Move slowly up and down. Don't worry about how strange it feels. Don't be ashamed of being frightened. So are all the other new mothers. Think how you would want to be held if you were the baby instead of the mother. Let your baby look into your face in his few quiet alert moments. Your eyes are now his umbilical cord, tying him to psychological life.

There are biological varieties in children's neurological patterns that make one infant more restless and harder to comfort than another. Some babies are more alert; some mold instantly into the shoulders offered them, and others stretch and tense their muscles when they are touched. Some seem more responsive to sound than others, and some struggle intensely with difficulties in setting the digestive system right. These differences affect parents, who also seem to have varying capacities for responding to their infants, for listening to what is causing the cry, for allowing their own bodies to become drained with exhaustion while caring for their infants. But there is no reason not to pick up a baby when he cries. The new baby cannot be spoilt. The cry is a signal of internal distress. As the baby becomes comforted and satisfied, he learns to depend on you, to connect to you. This will lead to his ultimate independence and strength. You cannot spoil an infant by doing what nature has programmed both you and your baby to do: respond to each other.

When the breasts fill up with milk on the second or third day after delivery, there is a certain kind of pain that nurses and doctors call engorgement. This pain comes as a surprise to most new mothers, and, like the pain of sore nipples, is perhaps symbolic of the entire beginning experience. It is a real pain and distracts us from the joy we are also feeling. It is very confusing to feel pain in a place we associate with sexual pleasure. On the other hand, the pain fades in a few days. Nipples treated with care will quickly toughen up and no longer feel irritated when the baby sucks. Many mothers experience a wonderful variant of sexual sensation in their breasts while nursing their children. This is perfectly normal and the pleasure should just be enjoyed for what it is, nature's way of encouraging mother and baby in this important, life-giving act.

Feeding the New Baby

Breast-feeding is the simplest and most natural way to feed the newborn, but some women do not have an adequate supply of milk and others may prefer the freedom of the bottle. Of course a baby can be psychologically nourished equally well on formula or on the breast. The essential matter is the closeness that the baby feels with the parent while he or she is sucking on breast or bottle. If the parent's arms are comforting; if the parent returns the intense look that the baby will cast into the adult's face for part of the feeding time; if the parent talks to the baby at the right time during the feeding—not too much so as to distract and disturb the baby's concentration, but enough so that the baby associates the voice with the face and body of the parent; and if the parent can find a way to gently touch the baby's hands and skin while holding him for a feeding, then it makes not a whit of difference whether the bottle or the breast is the actual container of milk.

We do feel that the breast-fed baby should have at least one relief bottle a day once the flow of milk has been established. This relief bottle serves many good purposes. It allows the mother to rest and perhaps sleep through a feeding or take a needed trip out of the house, and it allows the father or other caretakers a chance to participate in the care of the child. It allows the parents a small measure of time to themselves, a space to go out for a walk or a movie. It increases the father's sense of sharing in the work and the pleasure of the child. It will also make the eventual transition from breast to bottle or to cup far easier.

We strongly suggest that parents, even very busy parents with other children and responsibilities at home, not get into the habit of propping the bottle up with a pillow and having the child feed without the support of human arms and the comfort of the human face to gaze at while satisfying the hunger needs. The psychological task of the baby at this time of life is to build an attachment, a profound connection to the human world as represented by his mother or other primary caretakers. While the baby is feeding, these silent but crucial bonds are increasing. The combination of being held, being looked at, looking, and taking in nourishment is the ideal way for the baby to grow strong in both mind and body.

Sucking Needs in the New Infant

One of the signs of a vibrant, healthy baby is a good sucking response. Sucking is not only the infant's way of gaining nourishment. It is also a primary route the newborn will use to release the tensions of his body that plague him in the first months of his life. Some babies have stronger sucking needs than others. Some will happily comfort themselves with their own thumbs, and some if given a pacifier will use it well to satisfy these perfectly normal baby urges to pucker and pull. The baby will use his sucking capacity to relax his muscle and nerve tension. It would seem reasonable for parents to help their babies achieve this release. When it is not offered in place of the mother's face or arms, but as an adjunct to all the other methods of comforting, the pacifier can certainly be useful here.

Thumb-Sucking

Some newborn babies find their own thumbs almost immediately and begin happily to suck on them. Others may not develop this habit until some time in the first eight weeks of life. Breast-fed babies are less likely to become thumb-suckers than bottle-fed babies. Many parents react with horror when they see their small babies pulling away on tiny thumbs. They envision their child sitting in algebra class or marching down the wedding aisle sucking away noisily on that familiar thumb. In fact, there really is a kind of normal thumb-sucking that seems to come as naturally as breathing and eating to some babies. This is after all a form of comfort that a baby can offer himself. It is a most fortunate way for the helpless infant to achieve some kind of control, some way of satisfying himself.

Babies will use this sucking when easing themselves into sleep, when dealing with overexcitement and the stress of fatigue; or as the months pass, they will begin to use their thumbs to reassure themselves when their mothers or fathers leave the room or the house. It is a simple pleasure that helps the infant to balance the strains that come from inside the body and from the outside world. It is even common to see three-year-olds place a thumb into their mouths as their parents walk out the door. This normal thumb-sucking will be outgrown by the age of four or so, when the child will find even better ways to soothe the tensions that life must bring. The older child has many more resources, such as creative play, running, speech, daydreams, to ease uncomfortable internal feelings. Sucking will recede in time—an abandoned habit of babyhood.

Pacifiers

Many parents offer their babies the pacifier to soothe them between feedings. We feel this is perfectly reasonable and helps many babies ease their inner discomforts. It allows them more time to look around and enjoy the world. Babies will outgrow the pacifier as their intense sucking needs subside and they develop other interests, such as fondling objects, crawling, playing with their mother and father. The pacifier is a dangerous habit only if a parent uses it instead of his own arms and body and face. It should not be a substitute for human contact and it certainly is not a necessity for any baby. If mothers or fathers find it unpleasant for reasons of their own, their baby will learn alternative ways of soothing himself, such as using his own thumb or fingering his pajamas or his mother's arms.

The pacifier should be used *only* in addition to the rocking, holding, cooing, gazing, touching methods of comforting a baby, not as a substitute for these.

The Smile

In our society, we tend to cover over the more difficult aspects of childbirth and child care, and to paint idyllic pictures of smiling rosy-cheeked infants. Those ideal infants, however, are never under a month old. The social smile does not begin immediately, and parents must live through the first weeks or months when the baby mostly sleeps, seeming to respond primarily to inner physical cues. It isn't so easy for parents to reconcile the squirming, discontented infant with the perfect mental pictures we all have of mother/child bliss. But even during these first days when the baby does not seem to recognize or smile at her parents, there is a growing, emerging psychological human being within the tiny form. It is a mistake to think of your baby as only a crying, sleeping, eliminating machine. Each warming of the bottle, each rock of the arms, each change of the diaper, each tentative bath, brings the infant closer to personhood and that personhood emerges out of the attachment, the connection the baby makes to a loving parent. Without the capacity to form that attachment, there is no human being.

During this time, the infant works to make order out of both internal and external chaos. Objects appear before her eyes. She has no knowledge of use or purpose. She knows only a little about dimension and less about predictability. She can, as we've noted, immediately distinguish the human from the non-human, and can immediately identify her mother's voice and soon afterward her face. At the same time she is surrounded by noises, colors, and movements that have not yet been organized into patterns. The newborn is also bombarded by sensations from within: feelings of hunger, pain, wetness, exhaustion, cramps, bowel and bladder movements, skin sensations. The small body can be too cold, too warm, too empty, too full.

These inner events can make the baby cry. This cry is a most wonderful piece of adaptation because it contributes to the baby's survival. It summons the parent, offering comfort, easing the distress of the body, and bringing the baby back to a peaceful state. The periods of time that a very young baby can spend in alert calm wakefulness are brief indeed. The immature nervous system can cause the baby to shiver, to shake, to ache. Hunger is not just felt in the stomach but covers the entire body with pain. There is no sense of time for a newborn, no promise of future pleasure; there is only now. No wonder man, at some point in history, conceived of Hell, a place of constant unending pain.

Magically, as early as the first three to four weeks of life, the baby spontaneously smiles at the human face. This smile seems to be part of the genetic program of the human child. For the parent, it can be the first clear sign of the baby's connection to the world. It signals the baby's capacity to draw affection from the world, to return to it in some way the care that has been received. The appearance of this first smile directed right at the bending head of the delighted parent is the first sign that the baby and the mother are doing well together. Some time after the first month the baby will show a special smile for his parents.

This is the beginning of the parents' real love affair with their child. Now they know they have done it—a new person has been born. With this smile they feel more intensely needed, and these feelings nourish their capacity to give to the baby what is required. Along with this specific smile the baby increases his social babbling and will soon begin to imitate the sounds he hears. The smile is part of the baby's biological equipment. Blind babies will begin to smile but then without reinforcement their smile will fade. The smile is as clever an evolutionary device as the fin or the wing or the lung. Smile back at your baby. This will make him smile all the more.

The First Three Months

During the first three months, we watch the rapidly maturing baby learn to regulate the hours that he sleeps and gradually increase by minutes and then hours the amount of time spent in pleasant wakefulness and engagement with the world around him. If we remember that all of civilization is marked by calendars, by clocks, by seasons, and by our imposed order—a time to eat, a time to sleep—we realize that the infant struggling to gain control over the impulses that rack his small body is steadily working out the first important order of his life: sleep–wake–eat–digest–eliminate waste–sleep–wake. And the cycle repeats.

One of the most important things a parent discovers is that the baby responds to voice and motion, to being talked to, smiled at, lifted up, shifted from up to down. But there is a point for each newborn where the movement, the sound, the intensity of the human voice become too much. Each baby varies in his capacity to enjoy these experiences; what is too much for one child is just right for another. The mother picks up the baby and arches her eyebrows and smiles and chatters at him and the baby will lie comfortably in her arms, and coo or babble back at her for a few minutes. Then she may begin to tickle him under the chin and raise his arms playfully. Suddenly the baby closes his eyes, turns his face away, and begins to cry. His excitement barrier has been met—he has had enough. If your baby cries suddenly or turns his head away just as you are offering him your favorite rendition of "Old MacDonald Had a Farm," don't feel rejected or unwanted. All that has happened is that for the moment the baby has had as much excitement, pleasure, and fun as his small system can stand. Back away; give him a chance to collect himself, to restore his balance. Then you can begin the game again or wait for another time.

Each parent has to learn through experiment what sounds, what toys, what baby games, what kind of touch are right for their child. Some babies tense their bodies and show a kind of physical spasm when parents make noises that are abrupt or strange. The baby needs to be encouraged to respond to the outside world. He needs the human voice, the human smile, the touch of the human body against his just as much as he needs food and water and protection from extremes of cold and heat. Without human contact, the infant does not develop a psychological self. But he has limits of how much, when, and at what time. The parents must always exercise a kind of empathy.

Parents must learn the edges of their baby's attention to the caress and the voice. If a baby has had enough, he will only get tense and fall apart if the outside world continues to impose on his frazzled sensitivity. Babies begin to cough or to sneeze when they are over-loaded with excitement. The brightness of the sun or the sound of a symphony overture can make a baby's respiratory system react. Babies change color when they are over-stimulated; they may grow red or very pale. A baby playing a wonderful game of tickle and giggle with a parent may suddenly vomit up his last meal. This is a sign of too much pleasure.

The Father and the New Baby

Fortunately for today's parents, there is no need for men to pretend disinterest in their babies. Men can with ease and social approval share in the most routine care of their newborns. This is essential for many reasons. First, the father, by diapering, walking, burping the restless infant, binds himself to this new life. It becomes his work, too, and the child is doubly supported. The mother is not so alone in her task and the father is not an emotionally displaced, shadowy figure. As he bends over the crib, and shakes the mobile, and watches the face of his baby staring at him, he becomes a parent. Parenting is not really an abstract title conferred on the delivery of the sperm. Rather, it is made up of tiny moments, each one perhaps unimportant by itself, but together creating an act of major significance. All marriages are enriched by the sharing of the care of the baby, and each marriage is the soil in which the child's future has been planted.

Studies of the way babies are handled by mother and father show vast differences. The father tends to use bigger gestures, to speak in a louder voice, to move about the baby more abruptly. The mother is more soothing, her voice pattern is quieter, and she tends to try to calm the baby down; the father, on the other hand, is working to elicit responses. These differences remain consistent for the child up to the age of three, and both patterns of relating seem helpful to the child. The different manner of mother and father may be culturally determined, but the result for the baby is that both patterns are enriching and they complement each other in the best of ways. This does not mean that there will be something wrong with the baby who has no available father. It does mean that the single mother should try as best she can to have some male influence in even her very young child's life. A grandfather, an uncle, as much contact with the father as possible, will help fill in the gap.

Marriage: Baby Makes Three

A most important factor in the success of the baby's first months is the quality of the relationship between the parents. It is their mutual love, mutual support, and understanding of each other that create the emotional climate of the home. This sense of well-being, of caring between the parents, is the warp and the woof of the emotional blanket that warms the baby, inviting the infant into the world and carrying him through the inner storms his immature system produces from time to time.

It is also true that the most wonderful and stable of marriages are placed under special strains at the time a new child arrives. The addition of a new family member is considered one of the highest stress periods in the entire life cycle. It is absolutely natural for both parents to feel strange mood swings. They are elated, of course, but then they can experience sudden dark depressions, a kind of mourning for the freedom of mobility now lost, for the economic and social independence they once had, and for the exclusive relationship they previously enjoyed with each other.

It is a very rare parent that doesn't feel some jealousy on seeing the other, their sexual partner, their best friend, suddenly deeply involved with another human being. When the baby is resting sweetly in the arms of either parent, the other can feel an unexpected chill, a sense of terrible aloneness. These feelings, including the guilt they breed, settle down in time, just as the mother's hormonal system returns to normal and the infant adjusts his breathing, his eating, and his sleeping. Both parents during the first months are especially in need of admiration, reassurance, and physical intimacy. Babies do well when parents tolerate the strains and draw close to one another.

Colic

Most infants fuss and cry for periods of time in the first weeks of life. This crying cannot always be satisfied. This is not a cry for food, a cry to be held, a result of wetness or of thirst. It is a crying that comes from inner distress of the stomach or the nervous system. It helps new parents to know that some of this misery is a normal result of the inevitable adjustment problems the baby experiences in breathing, eating, eliminating, living in the world outside the womb. Most of the time we can soothe our babies by walking, holding, changing, feeding, rocking; but sometimes we just won't be able to calm them, and the crying and fussing will have to wear itself out.

For some babies this irritability and crying continues way past the first weeks. Often the crying is worse at night and will increase in intensity as a frantic parent tries everything to ease the child. The crying may build up to a crescendo in which the infant will draw his legs up against his stomach and pass gas, at which point he may feel relieved for a number of hours. We call this condition colic, and nobody really knows just what causes it or what to do about it.

Colic generally appears around two to three weeks after the baby's birth and may last up to ten to twelve weeks and then disappear, to the great relief of the family. The basic problem seems to be some kind of tense response on the part of the baby to all the excitements of sight and sound, taste and feel of the world around him. This excitement may set off a kind of swallowing of air that results in stomach troubles. That's one theory. The best thing a parent can do for a colicky baby is to stay calm and not increase the tension. This is of course like the kind of advice one gets from the Red Cross not to thrash around in the water if your boat has just overturned in raging seas. It is sensible advice but hard to follow. Mothers and fathers feel very anxious when they fail to comfort their babies rather quickly. If the situation persists, mothers not only are further physically exhausted but begin to question their own competence and mothering qualities. This anxiety, combined with the anger they cannot help but feel toward a baby who doesn't respond to their best and most constant efforts, makes the situation worse. The baby will begin to pick up the tension in the mother—and this can make it even harder for the settling process to take place.

Some few babies have prolonged colic, which can last until the fifth month. This kind of colic is most often seen in babies who are generally tense and jumpy. These babies will frequently stiffen when they are picked up. They find it hard to rest their bodies against their mothers and will appear to be in constant motion, with flailing limbs and jerky gestures. A baby whose colic lasts for the long pull is very difficult for mothers and fathers to enjoy. The baby makes them feel incompetent; in turn, they then feel depressed, irritable, and unsatisfied. This can start a long, dangerous, and destructive war inside the family.

It may help if parents can recognize the colicky baby as one with special problems that will go away in time. These problems are not caused by the parents' ineptness or angry feelings toward the infant but simply by the high-strung biological equipment of this particular child. If they haven't already tried it, parents can introduce the pacifier. They can try keeping lights dim and voices low around the baby, particularly in the evening. But it is most important that the parents of such a baby keep on encouraging each other, assuring each other that the difficulty will pass, and their child, while probably more electric than others, will be an interesting, wonderful baby, full of curiosity about the world around him. If parents can keep up their good spirits and keep feeding attention, care, and devotion to the child, some time between the third and fifth month, the colic, the crying, the sense of broken communication between parent and baby will end.

Parents of a colicky infant can sit down with each other and see if perhaps tensions between them, fights or unresolved bitterness, are reaching into the nursery. Sometimes parents focus on the troubles they are having with their child instead of recognizing the difficulties they have with each other. In that case, the baby's calm will often be restored when the parents face and deal with their dissatisfactions in marriage. Mothers who have sole care of a colicky baby should and really must have frequent relief. If it is not possible to hire household help, then relatives, neighbors, and friends must be found to give the mother a chance to recuperate—go out to a movie, buy a dress, or have lunch with a friend. All these activities will renew her strength to deal with the baby who won't or can't be comforted.

Sometimes a change of place away from an interfering grandmother who is making the mother nervous will help. Sometimes increased participation of the father will enable the mother to gain a second wind that will help relax the baby. But often nothing the parents do changes the situation at all. Time heals and the parents' job is to stay with the child, to recognize the problem, and above all not to feel guilty or turn against the baby.

Three to Twelve Months

After the first three months the infant makes a sudden developmental leap. The waking periods grow longer. The alert looking around, responding to sound and object, increases, and now the baby begins her most important task of slowly creating a self. By five or six months we will see her push up on her unsteady legs against the folds of a lap and strain to look around, behind, and away from her parent. Watch how she no longer lets her body go limp and mold against the arms that hold her. While in the first three months of life she may have felt as if she were a part of the mother, as if they belonged together like her own hand and foot, now she is gradually recognizing that her mother is another being. There is a new tension caused by all her muscles straining in the direction she would like to go.

From five months on, there is a greater purposefulness in the way she reaches for toys and the way she observes things around her. At about the age of seven or eight months, the first signs of trouble appear. The baby may turn her head away when being fed solid foods, preferring to feed herself and enjoy messing with the food. She may kick or cry when put down on the changing table, rejecting the new diaper and the hands that are trying to accomplish this previously simple job. The reason for this unreasonable behavior is that babies of this age just can't tolerate the helplessness of being held down.

At about eight months many babies will start to crawl. This increases their capacity to explore. At this age the baby will place all objects in her mouth, tasting and feeling shape and texture through sensations in the mouth. Parents are often at wits' end figuring how to keep things that might be dangerous out of the baby's reach and out of her mouth. The baby doesn't yet understand a verbal "No" and has no sense of the sharpness of a pin or the indigestibility of a mothball. It is very important for parents to baby-proof their home at this time. Take away the valuable objects and hide all the small things like buttons and matches that can be quickly swallowed. At this point the parents must learn to prevent accidents, to foresee and anticipate danger. Despite all our precautions, sometimes we will have to take something away from the baby. Sometimes we will have to disappoint her, putting the shining coffeepot on the back of the stove or removing from her hands the wonderful string of beads she has just found.

This is the beginning of a lifelong struggle with frustration. Some things just cannot be done. From this time on, the baby will no longer be passive. She will object to being changed, to being put to bed, and to losing her upright posture. In this five- to eleven-month period, the baby tells us clearly that she is no longer willing to be a mere appendage of the parent. She is no living doll but a spirit with a life force of her own. Daily her opinions on how and when and what should be done for her grow in number and in clarity. Daily our opinions on what she cannot have and cannot do multiply. However, the baby is still totally dependent on the care of the parents. Now she has a beginning awareness of how much her very life depends on them.

Stranger Anxiety

We know the baby experiences this tension between her desire to be independent and her need for her parents because we regularly see, at about eight months of age, a normal "stranger anxiety." Most children will suddenly look at the neighbor, or the butcher or the hairdresser or the babysitter, and grow solemn and quiet. They may hold still for a few moments as they somberly take in the new face. Many babies will stare at the new face, then turn their heads back to their mother's and then back to the stranger in obvious fascination. They look very sad and concerned. Some babies will resume smiling or playing, but others may burst into a short period of tears.

For some, the stranger anxiety is even more turbulent. A grandmother may come for her visit, and when she picks up the baby and showers him with kisses, he unexpectedly breaks into deep sobs that subside only when he is returned to his mother's arms. This can be an embarrassing moment, but there is no point in scolding the baby or insisting that Grandmother loves Johnny. The problem is beyond words. It helps to tell grandmother not to look directly at the baby and to stand a little way back. Very often if the baby is given a while to get used to the stranger, he will accept her calmly. If a mother quickly picks up the baby and turns his face away from the stranger, the crying will soon stop.

The baby's cry tells us that he knows that if his mother were suddenly to disappear, he would be helpless without her. This seems like a complicated thought for so small a brain, so new a mind, that doesn't yet know up from down, or red from green; and yet infant after infant shows us this separation response at approximately the same age. Indeed, when we do not see this development, brief and passing as it is, we know that something has gone wrong with the tie between mother and child. Something is not right with the infant's necessary growth of self. At the same time that stranger anxiety appears, many babies will also show fright and upset at sudden loud noises, such as the grinding of the garbage truck, vacuum cleaners, and jet planes. His fear of these strange sounds, like strange faces, tell us that the baby understands his fragility and his need for his mother and father.

Most of these responses to strangers are temporary. Within a few weeks after their initial appearance they subside and the baby can again look at the grocer, the mailman, his father's boss, and continue in good spirits. But the appearance of stranger anxiety tells us that just as the baby is pushing to sit, to stand, to gain mastery over his own body, he has become aware of his neediness and his dependence. The desire for independence and awareness of need is the great central psychological drama of childhood, and it has its beginnings right here, the first time the baby turns his head away from his loving aunt or friendly elevator man. There can be no question that although the baby cannot put it into words, he has conceived in some powerful primal way of his own possible abandonment and its terrible consequences. There is no stranger anxiety in the offspring of chimpanzees and little elephants do not trumpet to the skies when a relative appears unexpectedly at the edge of the watering hole. It is the human gift to recognize our own helplessness, to strive for independence, to fear a loss of love that might translate into loss of life itself.

This is why almost all babies can be delighted by a good game of peek-a-boo in the first year of life. Here is probably the first example of how a child's play can help control and work out the fears that seriously plague him. When the baby covers his face and then sees the mother or father again a second later, there is joy and laughter. This game can be repeated endlessly, never losing its power to amuse until the separation issues have gone on to a more complicated plane in later months. Peek-a-boo is a game about disappearance and reappearance, and the control is literally in the baby's hands. Now the child is not at the mercy of the comings and goings of the adult. Now the child is the master of the situation. In this simple, universal game we can see how serious is the work of child's play and how important its messages are to those of us who would understand the mind.

Most parents at this point are aware of a new anxiety of their own: What a disaster it would be if anything happened to me. What if I got sick or run over, or the airplane crashed when I go to visit my sister in another city? The realistic and unrealistic aspect of this parental anxiety is just a part of the baggage of parenthood, and lasts as long as children are dependent. Fortunately, this fear loses some of its intensity and high colors as babies work their way into genuine separation and independence. It is almost as if we catch the child's fear of loss and it echoes backwards into our own lives and our own real —and imagined—experiences with loss. As the baby turns into a child and becomes less afraid of losing us, we become less afraid of being lost. This new sense of the importance of one's own life for another is part of the overwhelming strangeness, the natural burden on the parent, during the first year of a baby's life.

The Second Year

The months that follow the baby's first birthday are rich in excitement for everyone. The baby's vocabulary begins and increases; the babbling and cooing are suddenly altered into identifiable, repeated sounds that are requests, demands, and signs of recognition of people and things. The baby's joy is obvious as he achieves the standing position and from there learns to walk. Everyone who watches infants at this stage remarks on the ebullience, the ecstasy that each lurch forward or backward seems to bring. Hardly minding a fall, easily comforted from even a bad bump, the baby is exhilarated with his capacity to move himself about.

Pain and caution both seem to be at a minimum during this glorious stage. At this time it is easy to satisfy the baby with a new toy, with the opportunity to move around, to learn to climb, to sit and stand again and again until mastery is perfected. Every parent is delighted with these signs of the physical and mental well-being of their child. The walking and the talking are the signals that all is well and normal, and that the long hard work of the early months is resulting in this wonderful harvest of baby activity, this fruit of new learning and achievement.

Competition

There is a possible dark cloud in the minds of parents at this point. With the child's new achievements comes an awareness of other parents and other children. We live in an extremely competitive society. We notice that as children pass their first birthday, mothers who previously chatted in easy companionship in the playground are now busy comparing their own child's progress with all the others'. Fathers who ought to know better are tabulating their child's vocabulary against the word count of their neighbor's child.

The temptation to compare can cause unnecessary grief. The range of time in which children learn to talk, to walk, to climb, to put together pieces of a puzzle varies greatly. Within normal limits these variations have no significance at all, tell us nothing about the child's future progress, her ability to get into law school or his capacity as a violinist. We burden our children with our ambitions and we misjudge the importance of the timing of these first accomplishments. They are wonderful and welcome, whether they appear early or late on the spectrum of normal development. Girls do tend to talk somewhat before boys and boys may master certain physical tasks sooner. But these are generalities only.

It is most important that parents do not get involved in pushing their children. Pointing out objects and naming them for the child is fine, but insisting that the child repeat your words will make the learning process less fun and the child will catch your anxiety about his success or failure. Learning to walk should be a triumph, a pleasure. It is not an accomplishment that requires a child to overcome terror and it should not be insisted on by anxious parents. The child must not feel that he is doing things to perform for you. Nor should he feel that he is failing you in some way. Relax, enjoy all the things that the baby does, and in good time, in his own time, on his own schedule all the skills will come. Above all, don't listen to the tales of the neighbor's brilliant precocious child. Most often the bragging parent is an insecure parent. The point is not to have the first baby to walk or talk but to have a baby happy, self-confident, and trusting of the world around him.

Most children will be sitting up unaided by six to seven months. They will begin to pull themselves up to a standing position around eight to ten months, and walking will begin some time between twelve and sixteen months. In middle-class families we expect a child to have a few words by at least eighteen months, although many children will begin earlier. In non-middle-class families, where speech is not valued as highly, we expect children to have some words by their second birthday. Within this time frame it does not make any difference if a child accomplishes these tasks a few months sooner or later. Speed may be a positive value on a factory assembly line but it is irrelevant in the development of the human being.

Separation After Twelve Months

It is an interesting fact that most children take their first steps away from their parents, not toward them. The capacity to move about on one's own not only creates a kind of euphoria in the young child but also brings an increased sense of his separateness. This is why we see so many babies of this age involved in games in which they bring a favorite toy, a crayon, a found piece of paper to the parent. They are bringing back discoveries made in the larger world. By accepting the proffered gift, the parent reassures the child that the basic connection is still there. The child is comforted to know that he is not alone exploring the Antarctic but rather in a familiar place with Mother or

33

Father right behind him, sharing the journey. At this age most children will interrupt their activities every five to ten minutes to go back to their parents or at least look back to reassure themselves that they are not alone. Even though this can be annoying for a parent engaged in a conversation with a friend, it is important to nod to the child, to say her name, to accept any gifts brought, and to hug or touch the child for a moment or two.

This helps ease the natural and common fear that soon follows the toddler's initial joy at being able to move away from his mother and into the wide beckoning world. The baby understands that he is still unable to survive without his parent. He fears that if he wanders too far, if he allows himself too much independence, too much separation, something terrible might happen to him. It is at this important point in development that children can use their fathers to help achieve comfortably the separation and independence that is essential for every growing child. As the baby walks away from the arms of his mother, it is comforting to see the welcoming hands of his equally protective father.

If both parents are active in the child's life at this time, they provide a kind of emotional space between them for the child to test his own strength and explore his own capacities without feeling that he is leaving the warmth of home for the indifferent world outside. In the single-parent home, grandparents, uncles, friends become very important now because the zigzag between adults makes possible a strong sense of distinct self—the "I," the "me"—that the child must have in order to survive. This concept, which we all take so for granted, is the great intellectual and emotional leap of the first three years of life. Where it has not been taken or has begun and failed, we see serious disturbance and the beginnings of profound mental illness.

The sense of being a separate person is gradually gained as the child tests his capacities to take over for himself without the ensuing loss of his parents. We hear the child saying, "Mary's ball," "Timmy's doll." We see the year-old girl baby smile with glee at a reflection of herself in the mirror. If we put a stripe of lipstick on a twelve-month-old baby boy's face and lift him to the mirror, we expect to see him poke at his own cheek and try to explore the red mark he has seen in the mirror. We see the baby weeping pitifully, pointing to his scraped knee and saying, "Harry's boo-boo." When the child pulls his head away as you offer the cereal, when he takes off the slippers you have just put on, when he says "No" to putting him in his crib, or "No" to your taking him out of the sandbox, then you can see that a sense of "I" has been created. Your child in saying "No" asserts himself as a separate person, an "I" as distinct from "you." No's are not easy to deal with, but without them there would be no real Harold, no Olivia, no Mary or Scott. The eventual mastery of the word "I" seems hardly remarkable, but we expect each child to have that word and concept by age two and a half. Without it, there is no further psychological growth. The knowledge of oneself as a separate person is the foundation, the archway, the buttresses, the nave, of the cathedral of personhood.

A New Insecurity

After walking has become secure, the child experiences a new, deeper sense of her own separateness and fragility, and we see in almost all children a change of mood. They lose that wonderful exhilaration of the first weeks of walking, suddenly appearing to be more subdued and uncertain of themselves. The toddler will then have an increased need to return to his mother and include her in his play. He may whine, demand things, stay close to his mother's side, and suddenly become far more cautious. The swing in the yard may become threatening; the slide so eagerly climbed just a few days ago may now be avoided and sleep itself becomes a complicated undertaking, requiring new reassurances, protests, and many extra visits. This mood change is caused by the fact that the baby is now being pulled in two opposite directions: one is the pull toward separation and independence; the other is the pull to remain where it is safe, where one can be sure of connection to the all-powerful, crucial parent.

At this time most children will develop a fierce attachment to some woolly bear, some dog-eared dirty stuffed animal, some worn-out old blanket or faded quilt. These dear and precious, odor-filled, soft-to-the-touch objects can become vital to the child's capacity to fall off to sleep, to comfort herself after a crisis. Every parent has at least one horror story of rushing about frantically at two in the morning trying to retrieve a lost Teddy or a shredded blanket that got mixed up in the laundry or forgotten on a visit to grandmother.

This is the child's first symbolic thought. The Teddy bear has become fused with the meaning of the mother's body and presence.

The child has endowed the bear with the magic powers to protect and comfort that have before belonged only to her mother. This turning to an object and giving it meaning, using it to find relief from fear, is the child's first sign of human creativity, of the unique human capacity to make designs, to create language, religion, art. The baby hugging his dear blanket, stroking it between his fingers as he once stroked his mother's arms or breasts, is making a great intellectual leap. The loved blanket or Teddy bear is the child's way to ease the fear of aloneness.

Sleep Anxieties

Sleep represents the most threatening of separations. In going into one's own crib, closing one's eyes, one must give up the world. When the child lets go of her parent, she is left with nothing but her frail self to face the darkness. No wonder so many children protest bedtime. No wonder it is so hard to stop asking for another drink, another story. The normal toddler will show every sign of this struggle but will eventually drift off, holding close the cotton threads of a toy lamb that smells familiar and promises a new day of togetherness tomorrow.

Crossing the barrier into sleep is a difficult hurdle for most children. A fever or a rash, a parent's trip away, a change in babysitter, a move to a new house, or the arrival of a new sibling will all make themselves felt in increased troubles around bedtime or in frequent night wakings. Moves and changes also make parents anxious, and a busy, fussy baby who refuses to fall asleep can drive parents to the edge of their patience and beyond. We all get angry and frustrated with our children at these times. It's absolutely normal to feel frayed, furious, and miserable when the baby won't give up and keeps demanding attention and care.

Hang in there. As the baby's fears about separation ease, the process of falling asleep becomes easier. While unusual events might make it harder for the child to sleep all through childhood, growing up will gradually diminish the problem. In the meanwhile perhaps it will help to remember how hard it is for your baby to give up the world, to give up your face and arms and voice, and to accept the threat, the loneliness, of sleep.

The Angry Baby

Some time after the first birthday, almost all children begin to show definite signs of anger. The baby increasingly does not want to be done to or done for, and this need to be a self, to control what's happening and when it happens, causes no small amount of conflict and rage. Melissa's mother wants to change her diaper and then go off to the park. Melissa runs away as she sees her mother coming, diaper in hand. Melissa cries and pushes her mother's hands away as her mother catches her and tries to lie her down on the couch. Oliver's mother wants to feed him dinner before his father comes home, so she tries to take him in from the front yard where he has been putting sticks into a pail. He shrieks and kicks and howls all the way into the house, and her promises of a delicious dessert, his favorite story, a chance to play with her jewelry box do not stop his protests.

At this stage a child may scream if interrupted while putting things into a can or taking them out. She may weep if prevented from spilling water on the floor or in the bathtub. She may bang her head on the floor and stamp her feet and turn red in the face if prevented from exploring the wires under the television set or from taking the shoes out of the closet. Melissa will refuse to put on a sweater whatever the temperature and Oliver fights each morning as his mother insists he wear his sneakers. Biting, hair-pulling, kicking, screaming, and pinching are all common in the baby's second year.

At this point on the developmental line, some parents who have been empathetic and gentle with their formerly conforming, molding, needy babies now show signs of strain and withdrawal of affection, and sometimes even open dislike of their child. It is easy to understand why the majority of child abuse incidents have their origins in this time of the baby's life. Some parents are so frustrated and upset by the baby's unwillingness to sit still, keep clothes on, stop putting dirty things in his mouth, stop crying, or eat what is offered, that they become sad and tense and feel as if their child does not love them any more. Now the burdens of child care seem heavy. The parent is staying home, getting up early, doing things all the time for a human being who seems ungrateful and angry with them. It is easy to love the baby who smiles sweetly at you and falls asleep snuggling in your arms. It is a lot harder to love the baby who turns over the container of juice, who screams at you when you try to put on his socks, who keeps taking the laundry out of the basket as you put it in.

It really is a shame that the first signs of independence in our children should be so provoking and irritating, but that is the way it is. Some mothers feel abandoned by the child who walks away from them and lets them know in clear terms that he will not be totally controlled by parental demand. Most parents of course manage to get through their children's anger and opposition by identifying with the child; after all, despite the difficulties in moment to moment care, they appreciate the fact that Melissa and Oliver are in fact showing minds of their own, souls of their own.

Most parents see the anger in their children and accept it with resigned good humor. They will sometimes feel beside themselves or infuriated. They will be angry that they are being pushed around or dominated by this tiny imperious spirit that so short a while ago could hardly lift its head. At the same time they will admire the spirit of their child and allow him to make more decisions and to control those events that will not result in harm if done the child's way. They will not feel that their parental role is threatened or that they are becoming spongecakes if they let the child call a shot or two now and then.

These signs of anger in the baby do not mean that the devil has put his mark on the child, although it is easy enough to understand how a harassed and tired parent could feel that way. The development in the child of aggression, rage, and destructiveness is a complicated matter. The exact origins of these clear feelings are still being debated by philosophers, theologians, and infant psychiatrists. The weight of current psychiatric opinion falls on the side of an almost inborn natural kind of destructive energy in the human animal. (This we identify as Freud's death instinct.) There is, as well, a developmental explanation for the appearance of anger in the baby's life. The infant, as he approaches and passes his first birthday, needs his parents desperately and understands his helplessness and his neediness. At the same time, because he is growing, he is pushing away from his mother's enclosing arms. He is looking away from her and walking away from her. This movement away frightens him and this fear evokes the anger that we see. He is torn between his need to be a part of the parent and to be separate. Anger is born out of this struggle.

There was a time when psychiatrists thought that if we just didn't say "No" to our children, they might be so content and comfortable in the world that they would not develop the anger that seems to cause so much unhappiness in our homes. That idea turned out to be pure hogwash. Children pulled their mother's hair, bit, scratched, and whined even when no obstacles appeared between them and their heart's desires. It seems quite clear now that anger is not simply a result of external frustration but rises almost spontaneously with the child's development of self. The power struggles, the urge to dominate, the sense of rage because the outside world can never fully conform to what is wanted at a precise moment—all place anger, like the heart and lungs, right within the human baby.

The early ways in which a child handles anger—does he have temper tantrums, does she grow very quiet and withdraw into herself; does he bite or pull at hair; does she hold her breath, grow rigid—develop into the patterns with which the adult will manage his or her anger. How much will be felt by the body as internal stress, a wear and tear on stomach tissue or immune systems or allergic responses? How quick and easy is it for an individual to express unpleasant feelings and thoughts? These are crucial matters for our mental health and we all have to deal with them throughout our lives. The beginning signs of our aggression and how they are met by our parents may direct the pathway our angers take.

It is of course important that parents prevent their babies from hurting themselves or anyone else. It is also important that parents communicate clearly the fact that the baby is not in charge of himself completely and that the adult is the guiding force, the power in the house. Children, even very little children, need to learn that there are limits to their domain, and that they are living with others and must sometimes suffer disappointment, frustration, and anger because they cannot have what they want all the time. However, it is equally important for the parents to understand that the child's assertion is a positive, wonderful sign of growth and that it be given room to flourish whenever possible. As the child passes into the second year

39

and toward the third, his increasing sense of mastery over the problem of separation and mastery over his own body needs will bring an easing of the bitter confrontations that have broken out so frequently before. It is very important that parents accept some expressions of anger in their children as part of the human package, just the way the skin comes with an apple, or the seeds circle the center of a cucumber, or the wind blows both hot and cold.

Discipline

Fiona wants to climb up on the window sill and pick the geraniums that are blooming in the box. She pulls a chair over to the window and starts her climb. Her mother calls out from across the room, "No, you can't do that. The window is a dangerous place to play. Little children can fall out the window. Don't touch the flowers, they are for everyone to see and they'll die if you pluck them." Meanwhile, as Fiona's mother is talking, Fiona has gotten up on the chair and taken a fistful of geraniums. Her mother is furious. Fiona is briefly triumphant but quickly becomes upset as her mother bursts into tears of frustration.

Martin has taken his good set of wooden blocks and crayoned on them all. Squiggles of red and blue now mar the fine set that Grandpa bought him on his first birthday. Martin's mother is beside herself. She's not the sort to find graffiti appealing. She does not think of Martin as a fledging artist; she looks at her son and sees, instead, a vandal. "We don't write on things," she tells Martin. "Crayoning on blocks is not nice. It ruins them," she tells him. He looks surprised. He doesn't think his handiwork has spoiled anything. "Don't write on wood," she tells him, trying to explain why it's all right to crayon on paper but not all right on toys. He looks confused, then cries and runs for his blanket. Martin's mother comforts him, feeling vaguely guilty herself.

To control your child—to discipline her without either wild anger or turning into a jellyfish—is no simple task. Advice is easy to give and very difficult to execute, and the parent who is always wise, calm, and firm the way the experts tell you to be is a parent who exists only between the covers of a book. The best way to survive is to recognize that you will not always be a perfect parent and that sometimes you will fail to maintain control of either your child or your temper. This failure is a double one because sometimes your child will fail to respond to your best efforts and sometimes your child will fail to control her rage, meanness, and destructiveness. Like spilled milk on the carpet, like the contents of the suitcase you just packed spread across the floor, like the magazines now covered with fruit juice, that is just normal family life.

If the baby attempts to do something dangerous to himself or others, we feel pretty confident in firmly saying "No," and if the baby persists, usually we will take him away from the source of danger. We all grab our toddlers' hands or motorbikes as we cross the street and we have no respect for their independence or opinions in the matter when it comes to choosing the exact moment to step off the curb. But most of us have some trouble in those gray areas where our wishes may be clear but the child's action presents no clear and present danger. Here we are in the supermarket and the baby asks for a cookie and you give it to her. It's close to lunchtime but you realize that you have some more shopping to do and a long line at the checkout counter and you need her patience. A few moments later she asks for another cookie and now you say, "No, it's too late. You've had enough." At this point the slightly tired toddler may feel that no one should be able to tell her when she may have another cookie. She may loudly demand her prize. She may begin to cry and beat her feet against the cart and the lady farther down the aisle will look at you—"Why not give your baby a cookie?" her arched eyebrows say. "Are you trying to starve your child?" What should you do?

Different mothers have different styles of handling the problem. Some of us are capitulators—"Give her the cookie; it's only a cookie, after all." Some of us get our backs up—"What I say goes and you have to listen to me because I have the power and I am in possession of the cookie box."

What does the ideal parent do? She might try distraction—would the baby like to get out and help push the cart? This might work because the pleasure of walking and the sense of power that pushing something gives might make up for the helplessness of not getting her way about having the cookie. But suppose it doesn't work; suppose the baby won't be sweet-talked out of this confrontation: a cookie or a major scene, that is your choice.

The chances are you're just going to be embarrassed and humiliated and that's all there is to it. You might even skip the rest of the shopping list and try to get out of the store as fast as possible. This was a rotten morning. After your child's nap, when she greets you with her usual grand smile and agreeably helps you dress her for the afternoon, you will recover your balance. These ghastly scenes happen to us all and they evoke deep anger in us. In fact, our own need to assert our authority is as great as the baby's need to claim her independence of us, her own control.

You can decide not to take her shopping when she is apt to be tired or hungry, and you can plan to avoid situations in which she is bored and her controls or temper are threatened; but you won't be able to make the world perfect for her. Sometimes you will say "No" when it might have been easier to say "Yes." Sometimes you will say "Yes" when it might have been wiser to say "No," and sometimes your child will fall apart in a loud and catastrophic way. This does not mean that she is spoiled or that you have no authority or control. This is merely the ordinary battle between parent and child, and the intensity and frequency of this kind of disaster will gradually lessen as she gains confidence in her own separateness and she gains in her real ability to have some control over her environment. When she tests the limits and finds herself not abandoned because of her anger and her need for independence, she will create fewer and fewer confrontations.

Here is James at eighteen months. He has gone after his mother's favorite Mozart recording again. He is attempting to pull it out of its case. His mother has seen him do this before and she has always stopped him with a firm, loud "No." This afternoon he is particularly tired because the dog woke him from his nap by jumping on the couch. The day has been rainy and he and his mother missed their morning outing and visits with friends. Now he is bored and cranky and his controls are at a low level. He once again goes for the record. His mother calls out, "No." But this time he doesn't stop. He pulls it out of the case and drops it on the floor. It takes his mother a moment to realize what has happened. As she rushes over to protect the record, he drops his metal truck on top of the disc, smashing it into little pieces. Now his mother is furious.

Maybe if they had gone out for the afternoon, or if it had been another record, her husband's Simon and Garfunkel, for instance, she would not have been so beside herself. Maybe if her best friend who isn't married yet hadn't called to tell her that she was going to Paris for six months, maybe she wouldn't have spanked her child. If she had been a perfect mother, the total saint we all wish to be, she might have taken her son and with a dark look placed him in his crib, telling him that he had been a bad boy and that she was disappointed. Then in ten minutes, after he had cried and kicked a while, she might have gone to let him out, explaining again about records and how they must be treated. Maybe she would just have picked up the broken shards and told him how sorry she was that he had broken something important to her. Maybe she would again have told him, "No," and then just gone herself into the bathroom for a few private moments to calm down. As it was, she spanked him hard. James's mother did not intend to spank her children. Then, as she heard James's surprised, angry, and betrayed wails, she felt instantly guilty, and this guilt only made her angrier and more upset.

Most parents have experienced times like these—bad afternoons in which temper erupts, a child is slapped hard, and the parent is left mortified and still angry. What can be done about this? Actually, nothing much . . . we just have to write the whole experience off as a series of calamitous events. By the time supper is over and the child is ready for a bedtime story, the chances are the whole episode will be gone from memory. Tomorrow will be another day in which to try again to handle the anger and teasing and guilt caused by the child's natural need to assert himself, and the frustrations of the adult that are sure to follow.

The child will wake in the morning requiring as always the love and protection of his parents. That enormous need is our great ally in teaching a sense of right and wrong; what is allowed and what is not. Sometimes things will go awry and we will not behave as saints or even as reasonable people. Although we will berate ourselves for this fall from grace, we will just go on and prepare to do better the next time we are tested. Parenthood is a series of skirmishes in which we are often not victorious over our own worst impulses. But if most of the time, if overall, we manage, our children will learn to develop a conscience of their own, controls over their behavior that come from within them and are not only imposed by us. If we offer the reward of our love and care, some time after four years we will have built into their characters a sense of good and bad.

We would not include spanking in our routine discipline. Hitting and hurting physically are dangerous teaching methods for several reasons. The first and perhaps most important is that spanking teaches the child that violence is acceptable human behavior. If Mommy and Daddy can hit me when they are angry, then I too can hit when I am the more powerful one. We want to teach our children to use words instead of fists. We want to teach them to respect the bodies and the feelings of other people. We cannot do this so well if we ourselves use our power to inflict pain. Secondly, spanking a child makes him feel totally helpless, overpowered, and enraged. His body has been attacked by the very people who are supposed to protect him and care for him. The overwhelming feelings of helplessness and fury that being hurt bring out in all of us are hard for small children to handle. Rather than teach them not to touch Mommy's jewelry or not to pull their sister's hair, a spanking generally evokes so much anger in the child that he or she will have increased difficulty in controlling behavior the next time, because the more rage that storms around inside a child, the harder it is for him to be reasonable.

It sometimes happens in small children that erotic feelings are experienced all over the body and that they get mixed up with pain, so that the spanking becomes a kind of pleasure. Sexual development can be badly damaged by such a confusion. If the parents he loves inflict pain, a child can confuse hurting with loving and with sexual arousal. This is avoided if we don't use our hands in disciplining our children. We are not concerned about the occasional spank on the bottom when a mother or father feels at wits' end and explodes. That will happen at some time or other to almost all parents. We strongly feel, however, that a systematic use of physical punishment is a dangerous way to impose authority.

There is, however, no single correct way to discipline a child. Different methods work for different parents and children. There are a few general guidelines we can use. The first is to make a decision about the importance of the issue as quickly as possible. If you are pushing your toddler in his stroller on a very cold day and he takes off his mittens and you tell him to put them back on and he says

"No," you then have to decide instantly whether or not it matters enough to you to make this a major confrontation. If you have decided that it isn't so important after all, you can suggest to him that his fingers will get cold, and that when he feels like it he can put his mittens back on. This gives him some sense that he is in charge and can make the decision himself. He might just put his mittens back on right then; but if he doesn't, you may have to watch his hands turn red and let the matter drop.

If you make the decision to insist that the mittens belong on the hands, than you must quickly state your position, firmly and definitely. Don't say, "I think you'll be cold if you don't," or, "Daddy would like you to wear mittens," or, "Mittens are so pretty, everybody wears mittens in twenty-degree weather." Just say, "Put them on now." A clear, firm, definite command will work better with a toddler than a lot of words and a lot of reasons that seem to leave room for wiggling around. If the child refuses to put the mittens back on, you should take him home as soon as possible. You should explain that he can't go out with you without mittens on. You should be clear that you mean it. You may have to give up your visit to your friends or your shopping or even a doctor or dentist appointment. But if you have made a decision that this question of warm hands is crucial, then you must follow through.

All of this is easier said than done. While it is best to be consistent, to be firm, to be decisive, and to be quick when the baby challenges, all of us sometimes make mistakes, vacillate, change our minds, and feel helpless in the face of a defiant eighteen-month-old. It may help to keep in mind the ideal of firmness. Ideals are meant to inspire us despite the fact that we so rarely reach them.

It is also important to judge the reasons for a child's stubbornness or bad behavior. Sometimes a baby is getting sick, or is hungry or just exhausted. In that case, rather than resolving the matter of mittens, one could go home and put the child to bed, buy a pretzel, comfort the child who is suffering from some inner distress which is expressing itself as naughtiness. We once had a child who had temper tantrums about every single thing for two straight days and we just couldn't understand what was going on. We finally discovered that the child had a tooth abscess that she hadn't been able to tell us about and was in constant pain.

One of the ways we know we should take firm action with a child is by checking our own anger level. When a mother feels herself coming to the boiling point, the best thing to do is to put a stop to whatever is going on. This is the time to take the reluctant bather, put him in his bed, and let him cry alone for five to ten minutes. This is a long time for a child and will certainly alter the situation when you return. Take some action that will bring the episode to completion. We get into the worst kind of trouble with our children when we allow ourselves to be angry and upset for too long. The child wants the whole matter ended too but very often doesn't know how to get out of what he started.

There are some areas of conflict between mother and child where we do better to let the child have her way. Eating is certainly best left up to the child. Children after a certain age may become very picky or insistent on messing or on eating things in a certain order. Some children really like one food better than another and they may find the taste of something disgusting or horrible. Children need to feel in control of what goes into their own bodies. The more choices we give them, the fewer issues we make about food, the more enjoyable mealtimes will be and the better they will eat in the long run. It is best not to be too concerned with nutrition, with manners, or with cleanliness. The table is a place where the child's "No" can be respected, making it less important for the child to say "No" at other times.

The child is curious about every object and wants to pull it, taste it, push it, and grab it. This means that parents will constantly be saying "No" to a child if they haven't child-proofed their house. You really don't want to discipline a child's curiosity away. You don't want to be in constant battles with her over baubles, dishes, treasures, and so on. It is far better to remove the things you don't want the baby to touch until she is old enough to lose interest in them or to handle them with care. Five-year-olds don't pick up Chinese vases and drop them on the floor. They know better, and besides they are completely uninterested in vases. They have better things to do.

Be careful of over-explaining yourself. Some parents give too many reasons why something should or should not be done. Sometimes a child can feel overburdened by the parent's words. When you want the child to do or not do something simple, clear, direct sentences work better. The reason that the light socket is dangerous can wait a few years. Don't feel that you always have to win. You can lose a few battles; every parent does, without losing all authority. You have authority because you are the parent—you don't have to win it or prove it each time you are challenged. If Harold jumps in the puddles with his new sneakers on or if Melissa puts her ice cream cone in the doll's hair, the world won't cave in. Oliver wanted to put the pink frilly doll bonnet on his own head; his mother removed it because it looked silly and embarrassed her. Oliver screamed and began to grow red in the face. Oliver's mother gave him back the bonnet and helped him tie it under his chin. She decided a little silliness would be good for both of them and off they went to grandmother's house for lunch.

On the other hand, don't feel that you must win your child's love and affection by giving in on issues. You don't have to do anything to gain children's affection except respond to them, love them, and protect them. You don't have to give them extra treats or allow them their way all the time. Being a parent is not a popularity contest. It is no kindness to children to allow them to think that the real world will bow to them, to prevent them from gaining experience in how to deal with frustration. The extremes of too much assertion of parental power and not enough are both equally disastrous. In the middle ground most of us muddle along, making mistakes from time to time, but using our own character styles, our own sense of what's important to educate our children to be careful, caring people.

Spoiling or Harshness

Most of us are worried about spoiling our children, letting them get away with more than they should and become horrors, unbearable to themselves and others. Spoiled children do exist, but spoiling doesn't happen because we sometimes say "Yes" when we should say "No." It doesn't come about because we are sometimes tired ourselves and do something just to avoid tears or screams. It happens only when parents are consistently unable to give their children a realistic view of what is possible for them. If a child is never disappointed, if frustration is looked upon with dread by the parents, if the child is assumed to be entitled to fulfill all his desires, and if his place in the parents' world is on top, then there will be problems.

Spoiling comes about when a child is not taught that the outside world will not, cannot allow every wish to be fulfilled. A child must learn that she is not the director of the play but only a member, an important valued member, but still only a member of the cast. Some parents feel very angry at the intrusion of the child into their lives. They feel guilty at these negative thoughts. Their guilt makes it hard for them to express any anger toward their child and to say "No" when necessary. It is usually the case that the little princes and princesses who rule their family kingdoms are not better loved than other children but rather live with parents who have many unexpressed but unhappy feelings about them.

The opposite error occurs when discipline is too rigid and strong. When a parent can permit no signs of opposition, of separate will, there is another kind of disaster brewing. A parent who never allows a child to touch anything he shouldn't, who insists on neatness and cleanliness, and who meets any display of aggression on the child's part with such profound and terrible anger that the child never dares to defy the parental will is weakening that child's potential for truly learning right and wrong.

This child will not abandon anger or the desire to assert his independence. The anger and the bad feelings will simply be driven underground into the back corners of the soul. The need to control something, the anger at being denied will reappear as eating problems, sleeping problems, and learning problems. The quiet, good child who never climbs too far or teases his baby sister or turns over the flowers in the vase is not really growing properly at all. Directly behind discipline problems lies the child's need to be a separate self with a growing will of his own. If we do not allow some expression of anger, and if we do not give the child as much room as possible to take over and experience mastery of himself, then we keep him shrunken, distorted, and limited.

On the other hand, if the child is allowed to feel all-powerful, if reality never presents him with the need to reduce and control his desires for power, for possession, then he will be a monster—and a frightened monster at that—because even the youngest child knows that he needs the additional support and control over his behavior that a firm parent gives. If a parent cannot control or assert final authority, it means that the parent may be too angry at that child or too indifferent. Either way the child feels something is badly wrong in his world. He feels unsafe and therefore unsure of himself. All children are afraid that their destructive thoughts and wishes will become reality; that the terrible momentary feelings they have toward a mother or father, brother or sister will, like magic wishes, come true. Children need to find out as time passes that bad feelings, destructive thoughts, even angry acts on their part do not destroy the world around them. As they realize this—and the process takes many years to be completed—they feel increasingly easy with themselves, able to tolerate their own anger without breaking down into panic or arousing fears of being abandoned.

Sharing

Children have trouble sharing their toys. This is not because the human animal is naturally selfish and greedy. It is rather that for the small child, those things that are his are part of his sense of self, his sense of being whole. If they vanish, perhaps his mother will vanish, or perhaps his own hand or eye will vanish. The little child is always struggling to sort out what is permanent, what is a part of himself, and what is removable at no risk to his integrity. Children at about two years of age will make a terrible fuss in the shoe store if the salesman tries to remove their old shoes and replace them with something new and shiny. They are not yet sure what is a part of their body and what is not. They believe in holding on to the familiar and will battle fiercely to do so. A haircut can also be a major threat. Small children are not only uncertain that it will not hurt; more important, they are frightened at losing anything that appears to be a part of themselves. Shoe stores often give little children presents and barbershops pass out lollypops because if the children get something, it is easier for them to give something up. This is not about greed. It is about issues of body safety and wholeness.

Temper Tantrums

Around the age of sixteen to eighteen months, along with an increase in hitting and biting and the loud "No" from the baby, we also see the first real temper tantrums. The child may want something forbidden, or attempt to go somewhere he may not, or take something away from someone that he cannot. The parental authority declares itself, and the child is faced suddenly with his own powerlessness. He is in the process of discovering that the world is not his to command and his wishes do not equal reality. This realization reminds the child of his dependence on us just as he is most anxious to be an independent voyager. Small children are easily overwhelmed by intense feelings. These initial rages directed at the frustrating parent are then followed by an acute sense of helplessness, which further infuriates the child. Mixed up in this bundle of passion comes fear—a fear that the parent who is needed so badly will no longer love and care for the child. The mixture of terror and fury that overcomes the weeping, red-faced, thrashing child is the storm we call a temper tantrum.

Usually you cannot distract a child at such a time. Once these feelings are unleashed, they seem to need to run their course like a cyclone sweeping through the personality. Often the child will lie on the floor, screaming and fighting off any attempt to pick him up and give comfort. With his body he is indicating that he is really helpless and in need of your care while with his voice and flailing arms he tells you he is alone and wants it that way. He is stuck in his own contradiction.

These temper tantrums are perfectly normal and will subside in frequency and intensity as the child gains control of his feelings. He will come to recognize and accept the fact that he is not the center of the world. As he learns that he can be angry and independent without being actually abandoned or harmed, as the child continues to be the explorer and the parent continues to be the protecting hand that watches over him, the temper tantrum will fade from the picture just like the other baby habits of thumb-sucking, messing food, and night wetting or soiling.

While they last, temper tantrums are very hard on parents, who often panic when they see their children reduced to such helpless rages. They tend to feel as if they have done something wrong, harmed their child in some way. At the same time they are feeling guilty, they also feel anger. There is nothing as contagious as anger, and a screaming, squirming toddler makes us feel helpless, out of control, and consequently furious. All this is the expected dark side of parenting. It is inevitable and natural that there is some measure of guilt, frustration, and fear of helplessness on both sides. But wait just ten to twenty minutes and the shrieking child will subside, perhaps in exhaustion or sleep. After a time play will be resumed and the incident that caused the temper tantrum itself will be forgotten.

Only an hour later, the horrible wailing, the banging and stamping will be ancient history. The child doesn't hold a grudge. The parent restored to normal status as a good parent will be content again. These little battles are not the last battles of childhood. They tell us nothing about the quality of love that is unfolding between parent and child, and they are so normal and common in the development of all children that they must be regarded like teething pains, like stomach aches, like winter colds and summer insect bites as nature's vengeance on us for being thinking creatures, able to feel so much of the human predicament.

A parent can try to cut down on temper tantrums by avoiding situations in which the child becomes overtired or hungry. Both these conditions create danger zones in which frustrations can turn to tantrums. Parents can try to offer the child an alternative to what he wishes: no candy but an apple; not another ride on the merry-go-round but he can push the stroller home himself. This will work sometimes and other times it won't. Bribes that involve something in the future are usually not effective, but an immediate gratification like a lift on Daddy's shoulders or a game of ball with Mommy might be.

Once the temper tantrum has begun, it is helpful to remain as calm as possible and to pay as little attention as possible. A simple statement such as, "When you feel better, we will go to the park or we will read a story." may shorten the duration of the tantrum. It may not. The best cure for tantrums is time. Don't be embarrassed. The passing strangers all threw temper tantrums themselves when they were small.

Vacation from the Young Baby

Many parents around the first birthday of their child or some months into the second year will take a vacation. They may leave their baby with a most beloved grandparent or a well-known baby-sitter. The baby will probably be perfectly behaved while the parents are gone. When they return, in almost every instance, whether the vacation has been for days or weeks, the baby will look away from the eager mother as if she were a total stranger. The child may greet the father with squeals of joy but have no smile at all for the mother. This is a very disappointing response for a mother who has probably felt torn all through her vacation about the decision to leave her child.

A surprisingly large number of children whose parents have just returned from a vacation develop an illness of one sort or another. Colds, stomach infections, earaches seem to follow the stress of separation almost routinely in young children. The frequency of these minor illnesses tells us how hard these periods of separation are for young babies. Many babies will show a severe sleep disturbance that may begin while the parents are away and will last for many weeks after their return. They will wake frequently during the night and require additional comforting before falling asleep. They express their fear of abandonment in these wakenings and they tell us how shredded are their important connections when they cannot trust themselves to the night.

On the other hand, after a few hours or at most a day or so the infant appears to forgive her mother for having gone off and again greets her with smiles of recognition and sounds of joy. After a few weeks the sleep disturbances will subside and the baby will return to the sleep pattern she held before her parents left on their trip. It has been noticed that most children make forward leaps in their speech development after a separation experience. If before the parents left they were babbling, the babbling suddenly becomes more elaborate. If they had single words, their vocabularies will double or triple in the week of the parents' return. The pain of separation seems to require intellectual symbolic work to contain the distress and keep the baby from being overcome with feelings of loss. This work of the mind to remember the parents, to hold on in their absence seems to spur the development of language.

Separation anxiety can appear in children around ten and eleven months. It will usually last in its noticeable form until eighteen or nineteen months of age. It does not appear or disappear overnight and traces of this problem influence behavior throughout childhood. If parents have a choice about vacation times, they can choose periods in which the baby is not showing undo alarm at minor separations —such as being left for a few hours with a babysitter or spending the afternoon with a relative. When a baby is already having severe sleep difficulties, we know that the separation will be more than routinely painful. If a baby is at a stage where she cries anxiously if her mother briefly moves into another room, it would be best to wait a few months until the baby is on surer footing. Parents should try not to go away at times when the household is in turmoil due to divorce or unemployment or in-law troubles. It would be wise for parents to postpone a trip if the baby has just been ill or has suffered an accident. If the baby feels insecure, the separation will be even harder and have longer and more painful effects for both baby and parent.

In our culture, children have to learn to cope with being separate. They cannot be carried forever on their mother's backs, and they will be expected to grow into richly textured individuals who can take responsibility for themselves. The response we see in infants to these early separations tells us something of the dramatic struggle we engage in to earn our individuality. While we expect parents to understand how painful their trips away are for the baby, it is important that parents remember that the quality and nature of their own lives also affect the baby. Parents may need some time to be together without their child to connect some worn threads of their marriage. They may simply need the time off for stimulation and pleasure that will help them renew their energy.

Because the baby reacts to the separation, it does not follow that parents must never leave home. It means, rather, that the numbers of separations should be kept to a minimum and the care of the baby while the parents are gone should preferably be done in the baby's own home to eliminate some of the changes. It means that mothers in particular should expect some anger when they return. Family life is made up of a thousand compromises; there are imperfections from the point of view of all members. It is, however, better for the baby to have parents who are contented with each other and their own lives than to have parents in constant attendance who are depressed or bitter or bored.

Toilet Training

Toilet training proceeds like other developmental milestones at different rates for different children. The normal range is very wide— from about fourteen months to three years. Bowel training is usually secured earlier than urine training. The daytime toileting is accomplished before nighttime dryness is achieved. Boys are on the average a little later in achieving total control than girls.

We ask the child to control his impulses, to delay his need to relieve himself of internal pressure just at the moment in his life when he is trying to assert his independence. We ask him to bow to our wish at a time when he is particularly anxious to prove to himself that he is in charge. What we are asking is not unreasonable. The capacity to delay an impulse is a crucial sign of growing up, of becoming an educable, contributing person. Everything in our modern world, all our accomplishments, depend on delaying, frustrating, slowing down some of our immediate desires. While we are teaching our children to use the potty, we are slowly, gradually giving them the psychological structure that will make them capable of all human work and play.

It is hard for an adult to recapture the fascination young children feel with the whole body waste system. We have been socialized to pay as little attention as possible or to feel shame and disgust at these repetitive natural functions; but the child is awed. Water sometimes comes out of him, a B.M. is made in him and comes out of him, and he can deposit it in his diaper or wherever he wishes. There is a certain amount of fear that accompanies this discovery. What else might come out of him? Could it be a necessary part of himself that has broken off?

An observer of infant play can see this fascination and these concerns acted out over and over. Sarah goes to the sink and pours water into a bottle, then pours the contents of the bottle down the drain. The hands of the clock move on and on while Sarah happily watches the water filling up and washing away. Jim puts all the logs in his truck, then pushes his truck along a path and dumps his logs out, and he repeats this game again and again. Things are put inside of other things, objects are spilled and gathered. This is the essence of nursery play. However many words we may teach in the process, children are thinking about the things that go into the body and the things that come out.

If allowed, most children will spend a good deal of time flushing things down the toilet and retrieving objects that have been thrown in. This interest in the toilet is not just because parents have made it a significant place by requesting a performance there. It is primarily because the toilet is an ideal laboratory to test out matters of comings and goings, separation and wholeness, and these are the infant's major concerns. It is against this background that we ask for control.

Most babies around fourteen or fifteen months will show clear signs that they are aware of their own bowel movements. They will stop whatever they are doing and stare into space, feeling the inner process. They will strain and squat and pause. This does not mean they are ready to put the B.M. in the toilet. Many children will begin to resist being changed right after they have had a bowel movement. They want to hold on to their own possession for a while. They are not concerned with cleanliness or comfort; they are interested in retaining what they consider to be theirs. They do not understand why we do not value this product. We admired the block tower they built, we admired the crayon smudge on paper; but we are ready to quickly whisk away the B.M., and the child does not want to be separated from a part of himself so soon. After a while the baby seems to lose interest in this B.M. and is willing to be changed. He has decided he doesn't need it after all.

Some frightening questions come up for the baby around this toileting process. If B.M.s come out and are thrown away, do noses come off, do arms come off, do mommies disappear? What happens to things you cannot see? Are they destroyed? If Mommy goes away, will she come back? The act of toilet-training a child evokes all these concerns, and that is why it takes most children a while to achieve. It is not that they couldn't do it almost immediately, and some few children do just that but for most there is a perfectly normal struggle before the toilet is mastered.

There does not seem to be any reason to toilet train the child much before eighteen months because the emotional maturity to deal with the inner workings of bowel and bladder are probably not yet there. It is most important that toileting not become a battleground between parent and child. The child needs to feel independent, and while eventual use of the toilet will enhance her sense of control over her life, the initial problem for her can be one of appearing to give in; so the child may need time to feel as if the toileting work is her own idea and her own accomplishment.

Children will quickly pick up our attitudes toward cleanliness and they also want to please very badly. They just need a little room and a little time to take over the ideas themselves. A child who has had an illness, or who has suffered some kind of separation from a parent, or whose home shows other kinds of disruption or tension will naturally go slower on the toileting process because issues of integrity and separation will be particularly sensitive for her. We do not want to terrify the child into obedience on this issue; we want the child to be able to see it our way gradually. We want the child to have a certain pride in her accomplishment.

Some months after you notice that your child is aware of her own bowel movement, get a potty. Don't introduce the potty at a time of minor illness or the weekend you are going away on a business trip, the day that grandmother has arrived or the painters have come to do over the dining room. Explain simply to the child that you want her to use the potty for her bowel and urinary needs in whatever words you use for these functions. Tell your child you want her to use the potty like Mommy and Daddy, like older boys and girls. You want her to be a big girl and big girls use the potty.

Many children will respond immediately and make a B.M.; but they will then be frightened that they have given up a part of themselves and refuse to go near the potty again for quite a while. This is normal. Casually, from time to time, make the suggestion that you want him to be grown-up and use the potty. It helps if the father is able to also make the suggestion and perhaps stay near while the child sits on the potty. If the child resists and seems not to hear or care about your desires, back off for a few months, then try again. There is no reason not to offer a reward of a particular toy that the child has been wanting that seems to belong to big children, perhaps a tricycle or a special doll or a truck. Bribery is just a form of the carrot–stick method of molding behavior, and it is effective sometimes in helping a child have a motive to overcome his natural reluctance to let his body products go. Tell your child that the special toy he will get is a big-boy toy.

Most children will within a matter of three or four months overcome their initial reluctance and use the potty during the day with some regularity. Children may then become very upset if they have an accident. They need to be reassured that accidents do happen to little children and that soon they will be able to use the potty all the time. They should not be scolded or made to feel terribly guilty. Sometimes a child will be too involved in play or too excited or an old conflict will have reared its unwelcome head and he or she will have occasional failures. Be calm. This is normal backsliding on the way to perfect control.

At a certain moment parents will have to make the decision to change the child from diapers to training pants. This decision need not wait until the child is sure of control because the very fact of pants that are big-girl or big-boy pants, pants that allow a greater awareness of accidents for both the child and the parent, often seem to speed the process along. The diaper tends to act as a baby identification, and baby behavior can follow. The training pants, if introduced calmly, can help the child to take this rather courageous leap forward.

Boys whose fathers help in the toileting process learn to urinate standing up sooner than those who don't have fathers showing them how to do it. For all children, the father can be a big help because the desire to please Daddy is less caught up in the battle of "I'll do just what I want" than it is with the mother.

Nighttime dryness comes slowly for most children. A flannel-lined rubber sheet is perhaps a good idea at first. It is important to take off the diapers at night after a while and let the child feel wet or soiled. Gradually, nighttime control will come and children should be reassured that accidents are normal.

There are always people who will tell you that they have some method of training a child instantly. It probably can be done sometimes, but why? The child needs time to absorb this rather frightening matter. If it is well understood and the mastery comes from the child's real victory over the fears involved, then the control will be better. The leap forward will be the signal that real growing up has occurred, not just a pressured conformity to parental command.

Aggression: The Bad Baby

Shortly after the child's first birthday, he becomes increasingly aware of the bowel movement and the anus itself. At the same time we always see an increased amount of aggression. Toddlers will bang a companion on the head with a shovel or take a good bite out of a neighbor's leg or yank at the cat's tail for no apparent reason. Often a kind of fleeting cruel smile accompanies these miniature acts of violence. There is no question that this mean smile reveals an almost universal pleasure in hurting someone else. As civilized parents, we tend to be shocked and angry at these signs of barbarism in our offspring. Yet these attacks on others are in fact not so unreasonable if we remember how difficult it is for the young baby both to need the parent desperately and to want to be a separate person. The child has to be angry at the parent because his feelings of helplessness and confusion are so painful.

The anger that we see emerging in the child at the same time that he is becoming aware of his bowel movements is both inborn in the child and a natural result of his struggle to discover what is a part of him and what is not. The difficulties, the frustrations that are met along the way join together at this time in a kind of mental cloud of anger that can, like any other weather condition, come along at a moment's notice and darken the sky. Pleasure in inflicting pain on others has its roots at this point in development. The child's body has a kind of erotic all-over sexual feeling to it, and at this age these sexual feelings get mixed up with anger. The result is the mean smile, the sudden bite, the hard slap. All of this is normal and does not mean that little Hitlers are being bred in the sandbox. It is true that sexual perversions have their beginnings in this stage of life. However, sexual perversions occur not because there was a blend of anger and pleasure in infancy but because some children were unable successfully to proceed to the next stage of development, in which erotic, good body feelings are separated out from anger and disappointment.

Many parents experience increasing discipline problems with their children throughout the second year of life. During this time we must be firm in our commands and in our continued love for the angry child. The child is experiencing real erotic feelings and these feelings also become enmeshed in the struggle over: What is mine—where are my edges—how will I manage if my mother leaves me—what is me and what is my father—what if I disappear all together—could I be flushed away? We will say "No" to our child for his protection, and for the protection and comfort of ourselves and others. At the same time we have to realize that his anger is as natural as a flowing river, as natural and necessary as his smile.

The child at this age can become a terrible tease. Teasing is another kind of meanness. We see him go to the lamp and start to push it over until the mother says "No." Then he starts cheerfully toward the bookcase to pull out the books and waits a beat for his mother to say "No." This is a kind of game, one that is clearly more pleasurable for the child than for the mother. The teasing tells us that the child can already anticipate the command and is making a sport out of what had been so unpleasant a frustration just a little while ago. It is in fact a great human triumph, a fine act of the imagination to turn so much unhappiness surrounding the major question of independence and sovereign will into a game.

All we can do about this is to allow ourselves to feel angry. If we pretend to ourselves that we just adore our little monster, we will express our anger in some hidden and dangerous way such as becoming over-controlling, or leaving the child too often, or suddenly exploding over some minor matter. It's best just to admit that sometimes our babies really make us mad. It helps to know that every other parent shares this experience.

Be firm with your child about not pulling the cat's tail and not poking at the eyes of the neighbor's baby, but don't be so angry or upset at this behavior that you make it impossible for your child occasionally to express his own meanness. If you do that, your child will turn his anger against himself, becoming docile but hurting himself in order to punish himself. If your child is hurting another child or biting you or teasing you, stop him before you are beside yourself. Don't let it build up. Change the situation. If the child is splashing you in the bath, take him out of the tub. If he is pulling his sister's hair, take him into another room.

Allow your child to destroy some toys. Let him bang his trucks till they fall apart—let him tear the eyes out of his dolls and stamp on his stuffed animals. This kind of behavior is a fine way for him to express his anger. While it may alarm us a little, we should accept the fact that even beloved objects may get beaten up at this stage of your child's life. Provide your child with objects that are all right to punch, to tear, to cut, to bang. Play diverts anger away from people and lets it out safely.

The Beginning of Sexual Identity

Shortly after the child has become aware of his own bowel function and shown interest in the act of urination, there comes about quite normally and naturally an increased feeling in the child's genitals. We see a naked little boy touching and rubbing his penis, smiling to himself. We see a little girl playing with her vagina while she is being

59

bathed or changed. This upsurge in genital feeling around sixteen to eighteen months, in both boys and girls, helps them to make themselves comfortable when they are not in the presence of their mothers. Children will also engage in a delighted masturbation while intensely gazing at their mother when she is touching their bodies. This natural sexual pleasure, while it may make some parents uncomfortable, is a clear sign of the child's normal progression on the path to physical and psychological maturity.

Because they are gaining such satisfaction from touching their own genitals, children of this age become suddenly curious about the genitals of others. This part of the body has become special to them because of all the good sensations they have associated with it. The little girl and boy will now try to follow both their mother and father into the bathroom to see what their genitals are like. Both boys and girls peer up skirts and rush over to watch when another baby is being diapered. This curiosity is soon rewarded by the discovery of the anatomical differences between the sexes.

No matter how casually the discovery is made and whatever reasonable explanations are given, it is of crucial importance to the child's forming sexual identity. This discovery presents to children a confusing and frightening intellectual concern, which they must resolve in order to get on with the task of becoming men and women. Explain to your child that boys and girls are made differently. Explain that girls will grow breasts and pubic hair and have a special space inside where they will one day grow babies, but remember that this fine reasonable explanation will be very hard for the child to really grasp. Even if you repeat it many times, the overwhelming sight of the body difference will trouble your child. Resolving this problem creates a normal intellectual and emotional challenge.

If we remember that the young boy or girl of eighteen months sees all problems in terms of separation and potential loss, of body safety and body fragility, of being cared for or being abandoned, then the importance of the discovery of the sexual difference begins to make sense in new terms.

At about eighteen months the little girl will see her father in the bathroom, or a male playmate in the tub, or an older brother naked on the staircase. She may immediately begin to touch her vagina frequently. Even if she is given an explanation of the different anatomy of male and female right at that moment, she may suffer through a few nights of sleeplessness. She may wake with nightmares and she may become fretful and anxious and refuse for just a brief while to leave her mother's side. She may become terrified and cry unconsolably when she scrapes herself on the sidewalk—an event that just a few days before she would have taken in stride. She may again become fascinated with the toilet, insisting on dropping things in it. She may for a few weeks lose the bladder and bowel control she had so proudly gained just a short while ago; or, if she had not yet achieved toileting, she may refuse to go near the potty and refuse to have her diapers changed without a major struggle. She can be seen for a brief while placing sticks, dolls, and other objects between her legs and holding them there. For several months after observing the difference between the genitals of boys and girls she may become very upset if a toy is broken, if a pencil cracks, or if eyes or noses fall off a stuffed animal or doll.

These reactions in the little girl are reported over and over again. They are almost universal although they quickly disappear. If we remember how hard it was for the child to conceive of the B.M. as an object that can rightfully and easily be separated from the body with no danger or harm to the child, then it is possible to understand how a young child who is so uncertain as to what is a part of her and what is not becomes unsettled at the discovery of the facts of anatomy.

Children are very concrete. The penis appears to be a part of the body that she is missing. She wonders if one may grow on her, if she has lost it in some bad accident. If the penis that she imagines was once there could be lost, then might she also lose her mother who is so important to her? If a part of the self can disappear, perhaps the entire self can disappear. The little girl values the genital region especially because she has had pleasant sensations from that place.

This interest in the penis does not signal male superiority. It should not in any way determine the female role in our culture. The little girl's feelings on seeing the penis for the first time are simply primitive, childish frights and confusions. The little girl sees that someone has something she does not and she will feel insulted and alarmed for a short while.

You can easily imagine a young child having a temper tantrum because another child has been given an extra cookie, or think of the child weeping because another has a birthday and the first has to turn over the present she brought. In reality, little girls handle this matter very well. Essentially, they are forced to start figuring out more about the real world, about what is going on. They develop speech faster than little boys and they will begin to play out their concerns about being intact, and having as much as the next person, in pretend and symbolic play.

Children have no sense of the future; promises of breasts and babies to come in other years do not really console them. The penis is a thing you can touch and hold. It is an object like a ball or a nose. Little girls must develop the capacity to imagine that what they have is inside and hidden, and wonderful. It takes a while for girls to understand that they are not boys lacking a penis; but, like their mothers, they are equal but different. Thinking all this through and truly accepting oneself as female takes many year of childhood. But the problem itself provokes an intellectual leap in little girls that gives them an edge over little boys of the same age.

Boys on seeing the naked little girl are equally shocked. They, however, confront the problem differently. They seem overnight to lose their curiosity in sexual matters. They stop peeping and following others into bathrooms; they stop the pleasurable masturbation that has given them so much comfort before. At the same time they suddenly increase their activity—climbing, jumping, knocking about, and running back and forth. They tend to be uninterested in pretend games, enjoying instead the exercise of the large muscles. They have some trouble sitting still and listening to stories or records. They tend to call all children "he."

It seems clear that the normally developing little boy from eighteen months to two years just doesn't let on to himself that someone else doesn't have this penis that he has just learned is such a source of comfort and joy. He doesn't choose to think about the problem at all. He denies its existence and is even willing for a short while to ignore his own penis. In little boys who can't ignore the anxiety caused by seeing the vagina, we see signs of upset like those seen fleetingly in the little girl. We know that for these few boys some kind of trouble is coming: their sexual identity is in danger and their growth is not proceeding well.

During this time the father plays a crucial role for both his son and daughter. For the little girl, he offers another person to love. This is important to her because she will be experiencing some anger and disappointment in her mother, who is also without this desired penis and whom she may blame for her female status. Little girls will show a kind of increased nastiness with their mothers and they may turn to their fathers in a flirtatious and joyous manner. Mothers, who in most cases do the primary care work, may well feel insulted at what appears to be the preference of their daughters for their husbands. They may feel excluded from the loving relationship.

In fact, this turn toward the father is completely natural. It is the little girl's way of saying that she is like the mother and will choose a male for the object of her affection. This is the pathway the little girl must take to find herself as a woman. And if the father returns her affection and admiration, he will ease her identification as a female; what at first appeared to be a less desirable category will become a simple matter of sexual identity, with its own pleasures and rewards. Single mothers can at this time help their daughters by encouraging relationships with the absent father, a grandfather, uncle, or male neighbor.

The father also has a major role for the little boy at this juncture. The little boy, too, will turn to his father and begin to walk like him, to hold his head at the same angle, to put his hands in his pockets the same way. If the father is available to the little boy, he makes this identification possible—I am a male like my father, and if my father is safe and loves me, then I am safe too. This is an important additional support for the little boy. He is different from his mother, which makes him feel separate and threatened; but he is like his father, and that makes him feel secure and attached.

Parents should not be disturbed if their children play with their own genitals at this time. Most children will not do this unless they are undressed and such occasions tend to be private. Parents should not call unnecessary attention to the child's play. If a parent is bothered, simple distraction will work. Children who are sexually curious may examine a playmate or attempt to see other adults without their clothes on. This is normal and should not be fussed about by parents.

The brief time during the second year of life when the sexual differences seem as alarming as the comings and goings of anal products will be replaced by the next stage of development. The little girl who had trouble sleeping the night she discovered that she did not have what someone else had will soon go to sleep happily, knowing that her body is exactly the way it should be and that her treasures are inside, not out. The boy who at eighteen months of age doesn't want to touch himself any more because it reminds him of the awesome discovery he would just as soon forget will, in a number of months, learn to appreciate his penis again; and gradually, through the next years of development, he will learn to accept its permanence and accept the biology of girls without any implications of loss or damage.

By the age of two and a half to three, most children will be clear about their sexual identity. They will understand that there are two human categories, male and female, and they will know to which of these they belong. Their language will reflect this knowledge. They will know which parent is like them and which is different, and they will be able to class other children as boys or girls. This simple piece of knowledge that we take so for granted is hard won for the little child and is a basic building block for the personality and sexual development to come. If the world we live in permits boys and girls to experience a full range of activities and behaviors, then the facts of biology can be accepted without creating a prison for either sex.

Nude Parents

Many parents with a child under three years will walk around nude in the privacy of their home. Some parents, because of their own more conservative upbringing, may feel more modest and will be uncomfortable without clothes in front of their children. These are differences of lifestyle and family attitude toward the naked body, and we don't know their exact effect on the child's developing sexuality.

However, all children around eighteen months of age will be curious about the genitals of both the opposite-sex and same-sex parent. This curiosity is perfectly natural and a sign of the baby's healthy maturing mind and body. Children will somehow find the opportunity to make these necessary discoveries in almost all families. Sexual curiosity needs to be satisfied just like all the other curiosities of the child.

Parental nudity can provide occasions for too much sexual excitement and sexual arousal for young children. It is important to remember that the child under three is easily awakened erotically and will respond to touch, play, too much fondling of bare skin, or too much tender genital attention with intense sexual feelings. In small children, this is not a happy sensation. It may cause them to feel as if they are falling apart or going to explode with sensations. It is very important that the nude parent avoid sexually arousing situations with the young child. If they notice the child responding by touching his own genitals or rubbing or rocking in an excited way, they should change the situation to a more neutral one. It is not that a parent should be angry with a child for sexual responsivity, but rather that parents should not deliberately or accidentally force sexually stimulating experiences on their children. The result is very frightening and creates trouble for the child in controlling his feelings of aggression and anxiety.

Children from around fifteen months on who frequently see their parents nude are continually confronted with the difference between the sexual anatomy of male and female. This constant sight, rather than helping the child to understand biology, makes it harder for some children gradually to incorporate this rather scary knowledge into their scheme of things. Many parents enjoy walking around without clothes on in their homes and they enjoy showing their bodies to other members of their family, including their children. If we remember how puzzling the matter of sexual difference is for small children and how easily excited they are, we can without too much bother cut down on the numbers of times our children see us naked.

Parental Sex and the Young Child

It is much better for the young child not to hear or see his parents having sexual relations with each other. The child will sense the enormous intimacy and involvement of one parent with another at that time and will feel left out, alone, and abandoned. The child will not understand the sounds or the sights; it is very easy for a youngster to misinterpret the act of love as one of violence. While there is no hard evidence that proves that the sight of sexual intercourse harms a child's development, we do have many reports of adults in various kinds of trouble who, during therapy, have uncovered disturbing memories of incidents in which they thought that their mothers were being hurt or their parents were harming each other.

Children are also equipped with sexual responses. Seeing the touching and rhythmic movements of their parents in the sex act, they can be overwhelmed themselves with sexual feelings that they do not know how to handle. In most families, however, it will happen some time that a child will wander into the bedroom at an unexpected moment. Parents should not assume that the child can wait for attention but should stop their activity and turn to the child. Don't for a moment feel that the child is scarred or harmed by this brief encounter. Children are made of sturdier stuff than that. While we try to keep our sexual life private, we must know that our children can manage the slight bruising involved in seeing things that would be better for them not to see.

If it is at all possible, we would recommend that children after three or four months of age sleep in their own rooms near but not in the parental bedroom. The noises of sexual contact are frightening. They wake children, who may not cry and let us know that they are awake but will become more fearful because they constantly overhear the nighttime drama.

Although it can often be convenient to take a child with you into the bathroom, it is really very hard for a young child to understand menstruation. Children become quite alarmed at the sight of blood coming from their mother's body or on their mother's underclothes. Most children at around eighteen months are already concerned about the vagina and they worry that perhaps a penis was once there and has been removed. Menstrual blood appears to them as confirmation of their worst fears. They cannot know that it is natural, monthly, and not the result of violence. They are really not old enough to absorb your explanation. Privacy for the mother at certain times is then essential.

Of course parents should feel free to kiss each other and express all kinds of physical affection toward one another in front of the child. It may be that the baby as he reaches the second year of his life and after will push himself right in between the kissing parents. He may call for attention, swing on legs, and if he is still ignored, may knock something over or fall down and cry. From his point of view the parental kiss is a way of leaving him out. Being aware of that should not prevent parents from showing affection openly in front of their children, because in the long run it is more important for a child to feel and experience the warmth that exists between man and woman

66

than to feel attention always turned on himself. However, we would suggest that the erotic kiss, the more intimate gestures of foreplay be kept to a minimum in front of the child. He can understand the special relationship and physical heat between Mommy and Daddy but should not be forced to watch it, a forlorn voyeur.

The Baby in the Parents' Bed

Pat and Joe Klemens are exhausted. He gets up at six in the morning to make the first commuter train; she takes care of the baby and the house and has gone back to school to complete her degree in social work. She has just typed the last words on a paper and joined her husband in bed when the baby cries. She comforts him, changes him, offers the bottle, and puts him back to bed. Fifteen minutes later, just as she is drifting off, he cries again. This time Joe gets up and repeats the comforting, puts the baby down, and returns to bed. He doesn't have a chance to turn off the light before the baby begins a mounting fussing that will soon lead to a loud cry. The parents lie in bed listening, numbed with fatigue, dreading the day ahead, knowing that this can go on for hours and hours.

Finally Pat gets up, snatches the baby from his crib, and places him in the bed beside her. They all fall asleep. It's a terrific short-term solution, but not so good for the long run.

Sleep problems appear in babies as they move into the second year of life. The waking hours are more exciting. The world is full of adventure and hard to part with each night. The child, alone in her crib, understands more profoundly than ever before her need for her parents. By now she can think of their faces and their bodies and their smell and feel. She can comfort herself with memories of daytime experiences. Babies will babble and sing themselves to sleep, repeating the parents' sounds as best they can. They will hold on to their precious blankets and Teddy bears, using them to stand for the mother's presence through the long night.

Nevertheless, the fear of abandonment will return from time to time, and the child will resist the bed as if it were an iron maiden left over from the days of the Inquisition instead of just an old familiar mattress. Sickness, teething, a change of place, a move to a new house, a new sibling, a fight between Mommy and Daddy, an injection by the pediatrician, a fall in the park—all may make the baby feel especially vulnerable at night and especially afraid something will happen to separate her from her parents.

Precisely because all modern children must learn to be alone at times, it is wiser not to allow the baby to sleep in one's own bed. It is easier of course to tuck a child between one's own covers and both of you return to sleep. Doing so avoids the child's pain of separation and saves the parent the effort of comforting and resettling the baby. In the long run, however, taking the baby into your bed makes things far more complicated. The child must find ways to be by himself, to fall asleep trusting that the parent will be there in the morning, that the morning will be there in the morning. Think how primitive cultures designed rituals to reassure themselves that the sun would rise each day, the seasons return as always.

It is important that our children learn to trust themselves to the night. When they learn to do so, they will be more at home in the world. They will use their minds to remember their parents. They will use their capacity for symbolic thought in cuddling their blankets and bears, and in the process they will strengthen themselves and their sense of mastery will grow. Extra drinks of water, a nightlight so that the child can see the familiar room, are effective supports on the way toward sleep. The baby who learns to use these instead of his mother's actual arms and body is taking a big step forward.

Feeding

A number of the most severe adult mental troubles are accompanied by and express themselves in eating problems. Many of us eat too much or misuse food for comfort instead of to appease hunger. Some develop food fads and in extreme cases diet or overeat to the edge of extinction and beyond. Our relationship with food begins with the bottle and breast at the time when our sucking and mouth needs are the means of survival, the major content of our lives. Receiving food is certainly experienced by the baby as being loved. While all cultures make a great to-do about the giving and the preparing of food, and the pleasure and companionship of eating, it is vital for our physical and mental health that food not become caught up in the struggle for self and independence or used to bring about the release of tensions and anxieties not caused by simple physical hunger.

Where there are gross distortions of eating patterns, and a sauce of primitive emotions has been poured over every dish, people are expressing their anger, not their hunger. These paths are often taken in the early years of childhood and they are very difficult to alter in the adult. Parents who have food problems themselves often pass them on to their children. This is why the healthy feeding of the baby is so crucial for normal development.

Newborn babies should be fed with as much opportunity for molding as possible. Molding means that the baby seems almost to melt her body into the mother's. This folding of bodies into each other eases the baby's way into the outside world and keeps the new infant's experience of separation down to a minimum. While being fed, a baby should be able to gaze into her mother's face, absorbing the particulars of mother, and not only drinking in the nourishment of the breast or bottle but, for a few moments, experiencing the connection of comfort with mother. Some time around five to six months, with the baby's need for independence growing every day, it is a good idea to let the baby hold her own bottle and, when she is able to sit by herself, to do some of her own feeding with finger foods. This is the mother's way of supporting the baby's push toward independence, fostering the baby's individuality.

By eight to ten months there are a number of children who will resist being fed even their favorite foods like chocolate ice cream or mashed potatoes. They may start to fuss when put in the high chair and will push their mother's hands away as she tries to bring the spoon to the baby's mouth. While annoying, this is not at all abnormal. It reveals a good healthy urge on the baby's part to have some control over what goes into her mouth. Mothers can try switching to more self-feeding at this time. Some drop in intake will naturally occur because of the baby's lack of skill with fingers and implements, but the baby and the mother are both better off when the dinner table is not used as the focus of a struggle for independence. The necessary means for self-feeding will quickly develop as the baby has the opportunity for practice.

There is a temptation for parents to use a bottle filled with juice or milk as a comforter or a calmer-down in times of stress or disappointment. The bottle is offered to the baby not because hunger is suspected but because of crying and irritability from some other cause such as teething, diaper rash, or just bad-day crankiness. The bottle when regularly used this way can help the child make the dangerous connection between food and a lowering of anxiety. The baby can begin to experience taking nourishment as a kind of tranquilizer. This can lead to trouble later on. Most of the time it is best to offer the pacifier or one's own arms and body to soothe an irritable but not hungry baby.

Toward ten or eleven months many babies show a temporarily decreased interest in their bottle. This is a good time to switch from the breast or bottle to the cup. It seems that this age is in many children a kind of plateau (a psychological balance), where they are very interested in doing things for themselves. They are not yet so deep in the struggles over separation that they feel anxious with each step toward independence. After the baby has learned to use the bottle as a kind of additional precious blanket or Teddy bear, the bottle itself stands for the mother's presence. Sucking on the nipple then becomes a way to hold on to the memories of that special closeness with the mother. Once the child is using the bottle to maintain images of the mother, it can be most painful and disturbing to take the bottle away and substitute the cup. The loss of the bottle, even though it promises to make the baby more grown-up, will also be understood by the baby as a threat of further separation.

If you sense that the baby is using the bottle to keep his mother close in his mind, then it is best to wait until the end of the second year or some months later before asking the baby to use a cup. Some time after two years of age the baby will probably have solved the worst of the separation anxieties and again express a steady forward interest in achieving independence, and the cup can be offered again.

Almost all children will want the bottle returned in times of stress, such as an illness, a parent going off on a trip, the birth of a brother or sister, the loss of a parent, or even a move to a new house. These perfectly natural backward steps are as much a part of the picture as are the forward ones.

If a baby can be switched to a cup around one year of age, there is less of a chance of sucking and mouth pleasures getting caught in the tension-relieving activities of the next few years. The baby who has weaned early will have to turn to symbolic play and symbolic objects to resolve some of the tension that would otherwise be drained off in the sucking of the bottle. This turn toward symbolic thought gives the baby a boost toward the next stage of his life, in which mastery comes about through pretend play. However, different babies have different intensities of sucking needs and will be able to give up the bottle at widely different times. Babies who use pacifiers may be able to give up the bottle earlier, but some may not. It really makes no difference whether the baby turns to a cup at about a year or at about two and a half.

The way to go about it is to take the cue from your baby, who may want the mastery of the cup and the grownup status it confers earlier or later. The giving up of the bottle should never be sudden or insisted on by the grownup. It is best to let the child lead you in making this decision. We cannot measure sucking needs exactly, the way we can the baby's height or weight, and we have to let the baby let us know when he is ready to move on. We have to be ready to let him move on and not keep him a baby beyond his time. Some mothers feel sad when their children turn to the cup. This is natural enough; nevertheless, we must be alert to our responsibility to nudge our child forward while providing the amount of babying he needs but no more.

Between one year and three many children develop food fads. They will only eat peanut butter sandwiches or they go for months refusing all meat but broiled chicken. They may only eat raspberry Jello for dessert and refuse any other tastes. For these children, the familiar is best. They feel more secure and happy eating only a few items that remain the same day after day. This habit, frustrating for the cook of the family, signals the child's independent push—I am the boss of myself—expressed in refusing broccoli or coconut cake. The child is also reducing the number of sensations and textures in her life to the familiar. By imposing these food restrictions, she is taking control where once as a very little baby she had no choice but to open her mouth for her mother and docilely receive whatever was put there. Also, for some children, change, even change of taste, awakens a fear of being too separate, of being lost.

These food fads are harmless and don't usually affect the child's nutrition at all. If they are seen as temporary nuisances, it is certain they will recede in time. We know of a child who ate only rice and hamburger for two solid years and is now a connoisseur of Indian restaurants. Recent research by nutritionists has shown that children will over a period of time balance their own meals well enough if they are given choices, and allowed to make them. Vegetables and fruits, while important in the diet, can be suspended for a bit with no harm done. We should assume that our children will like food, good food, in time. A lot of parental anxiety about whether or not the baby is getting enough of this or that is unnecessary. Sometimes these food worries stem from a parent's guilt about his or her own angry feelings toward the baby, feelings which are disguised as over-concern.

The most important aspect of feeding a child under three is not to let the dinner table become a battlefield. Food should not become the means for resistance. The child should experience her preferences as valued. She should feel that her mother and father are pleased that she can do things for herself. This means tolerating a certain amount of messing as well as some food refusal and some excesses. If the mess is too disturbing to any member of the family, the baby's dinnertime can be kept separate. The important factor is that the baby's meal not be clouded with fights over table manners or any other kinds of coercion.

Breath-Holding

Philip owns a shiny new Big Wheel bike, but his father didn't take it along to the park because of a scheduled stop at the barber. On the street Philip sees another child with just such a fine set of wheels; he runs over to the child and tries to take it from him. The other child screams and pulls away, escaping as the adults put out restraining hands and make soothing noises. Philip stamps his feet, gets red in the face, and howls. Then all of a sudden he goes absolutely silent. He stands there rigid, holding his breath, his face drained of color. His father picks him up, hugs him, shakes him, begs him to stop, but Philip goes right on holding his breath.

Some children hold their breath in a most alarming way. However, this very disturbing habit is really harmless. While it may begin as early as six months of age, it is always outgrown by the age of four or so. A child will, while crying or when very angry and frustrated, in the midst of what might be a temper tantrum or just a strong emotional outburst, begin to hold his breath. Some children will do this until they turn blue around the lips and a rare child will hold his breath to the point of unconsciousness. This does not cause any permanent damage to the child. It mostly frightens the wits out of a parent.

With such children, special efforts can be made to break the frustrated angry crying before the breath-holding begins. This does not mean a parent should give in to a child's every whim and want. It means that distraction, change of place, a favorite toy can be quickly offered as the situation starts to build up. These breath-holding spells are particularly apt to occur when the child is overtired or hungry and has stretched his controls as far as they will go. If care is taken not to keep the baby out in the park the extra half hour, not to stay at his cousin's house past dinner, the number of breath-holding episodes can be cut down.

However, no child can avoid frustration, even extreme frustration once in a while, and all children get very angry and upset when the world does not do just as they wish at the moment they wish it. Although breath-holding is a frightening symptom, it is only a passing expression of normal rage, no more than another example of how our bodies and minds can work against each other. Parents should not be intimidated by the threat that their child will hold his breath. Let him. Stay calm; remember that at worst he will faint and with that resume breathing. The child cannot harm his brain or his heart. Reassure yourself that this habit will disappear forever before he enters kindergarten.

Speech

Around seven months to a year most children will begin to identify Mama and then Dada with the right words. Long before this, they have been babbling and cooing and imitating the vowel sounds around them, adding consonants as their babbling grows more and more elaborate, bringing them to the edge of speech. The first words are a great joy for parents and always seem somewhat miraculous. We are overwhelmed with their first verbs: *Look, sit, eat, touch, give,* make our hearts leap. Speech is expected of course in children, and yet each time with each child, it seems magical and beautiful beyond belief. The oldest hands among us feel proud, even thrilled, as the sentences grow longer, the grammar more complex, the negatives, the imperatives, the conjunctions, the adverbs fall into place. We all fall deeper in love with our children as we hear them say, "The ball is pretty," or, "The dog is behind the couch." Language, like the human smile, like the baby's attachment to his parents, seems to be an inborn capacity, the mark of distinction that places us above all other creatures of the earth.

As with other landmarks of growth, speech comes at different months with different children, and the normal range is very wide. There is no reason to be concerned if the first words do not appear until thirteen or fourteen months. Anxious parents should keep in mind that Albert Einstein did not speak until he was close to four. Parents can get competitive about the number of words their children employ, but we have no evidence at all that early speech promises high intelligence or accomplishment, or that, within normal range, slower development of speech indicates anything at all about the gifts of the child. Professors of English and presidents have been among the last on their blocks to begin naming objects and stringing words into sentences. However, we would under normal circumstances begin to be concerned about a child in whom there was no speech development at all by eighteen months.

Speech was Adam's first act in the Garden of Eden, and each child seems to be creating the universe again as he or she recognizes and gives names to cookie, bottle, light, water, and so on. There would have been no point in being in Eden if Adam could not make order out of his chaotic world by giving each thing a name. The development of speech helps children to control impulses and delay and fulfill wishes. They don't have to scream and turn red in the face if they want the blue truck or a story told to them or a bottle of juice. With words they can direct the parent to satisfy their needs. This gives them more control and helps them feel less overwhelmed by others, less vulnerable to desertion.

Children learn early to comfort themselves by repeating the sounds of other people. This repetition eases the separation when they are alone in their cribs in the morning and at night. As they gain in speech, they gain in memory and in ways of storing memories, and so they can further comfort themselves with descriptions of going to the park, of taking a bath, of playing with Mommy or throwing a ball to Daddy. Language is the sign of thought and thought is the country of the civilized self. The more complicated the child's language skills become, the less he will be prey to being undone by body states, by fears, by gross primitive needs. If the word "light" turns on the lamp because someone has understood the child's wish, then there is less to fear in the dark. Speech is a great pleasure of the mouth; it follows the sucking and eating satisfactions as a primary need for human life.

Children develop speech in the same way they acquire other skills —forward a bit and than backward some—and the use of speech is always subject to upset. A child with a fever will lose vocabulary or stop using verbs. A child whose parents have gone off on a trip may temporarily appear to have forgotten adjectives or connectives. A two-and-a-half-year-old whose newborn sister has just come home from the hospital may appear to lose speech entirely and revert to the earliest baby sounds. This is normal and no cause for concern.

Some children stutter as they learn speech, which is disturbing to parents who worry that it will develop into a permanent handicap. The early stuttering that we frequently see is due merely to the immaturity of the child's brain, and the settling down of speech patterns will occur before five or six years of age. No one knows yet why some children have early stuttering but in most instances it is outgrown and signifies nothing. It is not a sign of a tense or nervous child. It is just that the mechanisms of speech within the brain seem to mature irregularly in some children. Naturally if parents become unduly alarmed, fussing with the child about his speech, forcing him to repeat sentences, then difficulties with speech patterns can settle in. It is best for parents to ignore this early stuttering in the same way they would ignore the stumbling of the feet as walking begins.

Boys gain speech more slowly than girls, but the difference is usually evened out by about three years of age. A taciturn mother or father will have a child less interested in acquiring speech. Parents who talk a lot to their children and use speech as a way of drawing their children close to them have more verbal babies, who connect speech with pleasure and closeness and therefore increase their vocabularies at greater rates. Speech is a gift that encourages the return of itself to the giver.

Speech is so natural that we can make nuisances of ourselves if we constantly try to teach our children words. We can become overbearing if we don't just rely on natural conversation. Yes, we can look at picture books with them and give objects names. But in general it is better to speak to one's child for the pleasure of it, for the necessity of it, rather than to be his teacher.

The Incessant Why

Many children who have recently passed their second birthday begin to drive even the most patient parent crazy with strings of questions that threaten to go on forever, each answer, careful or careless, leading to a new why. This is a form of teasing on the child's part. Our offspring catch on very quickly that we are eager to explain the world to them. They recognize that we not only derive pleasure from their questions but consider it our sacred obligation to answer them as best we can. Children's real curiosity is a beautiful thing, but it can be satisfied fairly easily and never leads to the sense of irritation and frustration we all feel with that most normal but infuriating continual "Why?"

The child who responds to your answer with an automatic new why is expressing a kind of indirect anger at you, the same sort that can provoke a loud "No" about so simple a matter as putting on slippers or using a washcloth. The child who pesters you endlessly with pointless why's is also forcing you to respond to him. Perhaps this particular afternoon you have been preoccupied with other matters and he senses your attention wandering from him. He may barrage you with why after why, knowing that you can't resist answering him. Your answer reconnects you to him. A little extra attention, a storybook read on your lap, a special time together sharing juice and cookies may just end these unpleasant why's for the time being.

The why may be used to stall you from leaving the room at night or from leaving the house during the day. Don't listen to the question, which may be meaningless and requires no answer; but do listen to your child's bid for attention. Usually the child who is expressing his complaint with an irritating series of questions has a real why hidden behind the others—"Why aren't you paying more attention to me? I feel lonely."

Learning

Between birth and three years, learning is as natural as breathing. It never stops. The child of one placing spoons in a container is learning the difference between large and small, round and long. The baby who puts his rubber duck in his mouth is learning the difference between edible and inedible. He is learning the texture of rubber and the shape of his toy. He is learning the textures smooth and soft, and soon he will learn the words for "duck" and "water" and "float." As he watches the different objects in his life, and as he handles them (first by putting them in his mouth), he is learning the basic elements of things. As he goes on into the second and third year, he will learn their meaning in our world. The fire truck puts out fires, the farmer grows food, and the box is for his mother's tools.

Our role in this learning process is very simple. We must provide enough excitement for the child's mind to thrive and yet must not provide so much activity that the small developing brain loses interest in our attempts to educate and turns away toward the reassuring quiet of its own thoughts. How can one judge what is the right amount and the right kind of learning environment for a child? What is too much or too demanding? The answers lie in the parent's careful observation and empathetic bond with the child. The parent must be a follower. The child will indicate exhaustion or excess excitement by turning his head away, by crying, by changing color, by wriggling around, by moving away, by coughing or sneezing or jumping up and down.

There is no sense in giving a baby an electric train and there is no sense in expecting him to pay attention to a story until he is ready. Babies need peek-a-boo games. They need to play pat-a-cake with adults. They need to be encouraged to look at colors, at animals, and at pictures of things and people. They don't need to be taught to add or read before three years of age. Those are the proper projects of five- and six-year-olds. It may be possible to teach a particular two- or three-year-old to read, but there is a price to be paid for such advanced learning. The child will have to focus his attention on those things that seem important to you instead of exploring and understanding his world in his own terms. It is not helpful for a child to feel your anxiety for him to achieve quickly. Some children will then let the whole learning process get caught up in their negative "I won't do what you want me to" feelings. Some children begin to feel as if they are loved or wanted only because of their responses to parental coaching. This will cloud the learning process, which normally unfolds so easily and naturally, with worry and uncertainty.

Children do not need to learn how to swim as babies. They do not need to learn how to hold a tennis racket that stands as tall as they do. They don't need to be pressured to catch a ball before their coordination has matured. They will learn everything in good time if they are permitted to direct the pace, if it is offered and not forced.

Children have to play at games of hide-and-seek, games of giving and getting, going and coming. That is an important part of their psychological work and provides them with a healthy eager capacity to learn. Reading and numbers will come easily to the comfortable child who has mastered the task of separation and feels secure in his world. Children whose parents are so ambitious for their offspring that they begin training programs for them to succeed academically while they are still in diapers are apt to be missing the emotional and mental content of their children's lives. Even if they achieve the goals that they have set, they cannot measure what energies have been lost from the exploring and imagining tasks of those early years.

We live in a society that clearly rewards competition and there is a great push for many of us to excel over friends and relations. Some few children will actually learn to read without much prompting from their parents. But despite the fact that these are certainly bright children, there is no evidence that they are any more remarkable in their subsequent academic lives than their age mates who learn to read at a more conventional age. A mother reported teaching her eighteen-month-old twin girls letters each night in their crib. She was proud of how well they were doing until she noticed that as she and her husband held up the printed cards, the babies stood holding the bars of their cribs with white knuckles and trembling legs as they gave the answers. This mother wisely abandoned the tutoring program.

The important factor in a child's capacity to learn, aside from native endowment, appears to be a free space in his mind, a place where he is not dealing with other fears or conflicts so that he can use his intelligence without anxiety. Creating this kind of internal climate for the child is the parent's best path toward assuring future mental skills.

Children who have been left in bare rooms with no toys and with not enough adult talk and communication—without enough opportunity to explore, taste, and feel objects and places—are apt to show a slower intellectual development than their peers. It is very hard to make up for this early lack of learning. The mind that lacks nourishment seems to become crippled and bent. Deprivation is surely as destructive as too much pressure. Finding just the right balance of new words, new sights, and new challenges, while at the same time encouraging the child to find things out for himself, is the work of the caring parent.

Day Care

Thomas resists getting dressed in the morning. As his mother puts on his sneakers, he kicks his feet; as she reaches for a sweater, he turns his head away. Later, as she pushes the stroller to the day care center where he will spend the next seven hours, he says it very clearly: "Mommy, don't go bye-bye. Mommy stay with Thomas." This is in the first weeks of Thomas's mother's return to work. She feels sick to her stomach when she hears his complaint. He feels sick as they approach the center. Altogether, this is not an easy business. It is painful for the child, painful for the parent.

It is true that the small child needs the steady and loving care of a particular parent and it is true that all children under three have great difficulties with separation from the mother and father they have depended on so profoundly. Nevertheless, day care is a reality in the lives of many babies and toddlers, and this reality, like most other realities, is a necessary and tolerable compromise with the ideal.

Today, over 60 percent of women are working outside the home, either out of financial necessity or because of their own needs for personal fulfillment. We absolutely do not have any long-term studies that tell us that children brought up for the first three years of their lives by a nurse or by a surrogate provided in a day care center are any worse off, any more troubled or compromised, than other children. We do not yet know if there will or will not be any observable difference at all between the young child who has had his mother available for twenty-four hours a day and the one who has learned to be dependent on several other people as well as his parents.

Because the main thrust of growth for the child in the first years of life is toward attachment to a parent, and then toward development of a self that remains connected to the parent but at a gradually increasing distance, it is only common sense that the experience of parent substitutes, either within the home or without, must create some special strains. This does not mean that these strains may not be overcome and the tensions they create used to further growth, as mastery over the painful separations is achieved.

Important variables in the day care question are obviously the quality of the caretakers, the number of children each is responsible for, and the stability of the place and the personnel. If you are going to enroll your child in a day care center, it is of crucial importance that you visit first and spend some time watching. Fancy toys and fine equipment mean very little. Watch how the staff talk to children. Watch how they handle the child who is sad and withdrawn—do they leave her alone because she is causing no trouble, or do they quietly help her begin to play? Watch how they handle the child who is feeling angry that day. One child will snatch a toy from another and the first will begin to scream. What does the staff do? Are they aware of both children's need for comfort and reassurance? Do they look at each child when talking to him or changing his diaper? Do they prop bottles up and leave children to eat without human company and the warmth of human arms? Do the very young babies in their charge mold their bodies against the caretakers, or do they hold themselves stiffly apart? Does the staff hug and kiss and touch children? How do they handle the child's resistance to being changed or fed? Do the children seem too good and too quiet, or is there a reasonable amount of noise and activity going on? Is there a place for a child to be quiet and calm if he needs to sleep or just be by himself for a while? Do they allow children to feed themselves and do they tolerate some level of food messing? Do they feed the young babies with smiles and games and allow them some finger foods?

If your infant is in day care, expect some difficulties over separation in the morning and again some kind of whining and crying, aggression and withdrawal, at the evening parting from his day care environment. It is very hard for young children to go from one routine to another—to change the persons they love and need from hour to hour. When a child starts day care, you will surely see some disturbance at home. The child will perhaps not sleep well and wake you frequently during the night. She may become sick with colds or stomach problems or she may lose some of the achievements she had previously made in bladder and bowel control, or in speech or walking. Children usually need to take something from home to keep with them all day, and they may need to bring something back from the day care center to their homes in the evening to keep with them at night. The precious blanket, the beloved Teddy bear are great assets in these difficult transitions.

If the people at the day care center change too often, if they do not do things in consistent ways, and if your child does not receive enough kind adult attention, he will suffer and fail to develop vocabulary and age-appropriate skills. Day care nurseries are not all good or all bad, any more than parents are all good or all bad. But there are differences of quality, and these have fateful implications for the well-being of your child.

Some parents are well enough off financially to be able to choose a baby nurse or a housekeeper over the day care nursery for their young babies. We have no evidence at this time that this choice is better than the day care center, or on the other hand that it has a negative effect on either the child's growth or the child's relationship with his parents.

Mothers who return to work shortly after the birth of their child or within the first year are often concerned that the baby will think the housekeeper is the real mother and that they themselves are unnecessary outsiders. That just doesn't appear to be true. The working parent who is truly concerned with the child, who learns how to take care of her if she is sick, who can do the feeding at times when she is there, will clearly be known to the baby as the mother, as the most important person in her life.

It is hard for a mother not to feel guilty about a housekeeper arrangement. Many mothers feel upset that they are missing their baby's infancy if they spend too many hours of the work week away from their child. But sometimes compromise with the ideal is necessary. Some mothers have to work for economic reasons, and others cannot, without psychological harm to themselves, interrupt their own careers or rewarding work lives. If the housekeeper is a good one and stays for a long period of time, the infant will flourish. As the parents see the baby progressing, their own anxiety and guilt over this arrangement will subside.

It is hard for the mother who goes off to her job early in the morning and returns after her baby is bathed and ready for bed not to experience severe pangs of jealousy when she sees how attached to the housekeeper the child has become. She will feel replaced and displaced in her child's affections, and these envious stirrings can lead to trouble between the parent and the housekeeper. This is a danger that can be avoided if the mother recognizes that babies do become attached to the person they see most, and that this attachment is a sign of health and absolutely necessary for the baby's growth.

To permit this attachment to another is the mother's gift to the baby—the first and perhaps most important of many. In time, the baby will turn to the parents as well as to teachers and friends, and the housekeeper will fade in importance. However, for the infant and the toddler, the permanence and the quality of the substitute mother care are so important that it is clearly best to allow this relationship to flourish. Working mothers will just have to suffer the natural jealousy that arises and comfort themselves with the knowledge that this sharing is best for the child. In the long run, what is best for the child is best for the parent. While these jealous feelings do make parents feel guilty and ashamed, they are very natural even when they are most irrational.

There are certain significant matters to be watched in the matter of employing housekeepers and nurses. It is very important that there not be frequent changes of personnel. The baby will become attached, connected to the caretaker, and if that person leaves the baby will experience profound loss. If these losses are repeated, the baby will show signs of depression and distress. She will wake often, be cranky, and become prone to minor illnesses. If changes keep occurring, the baby will learn not to become attached and will distrust all adults. The importance for the baby of holding on to the housekeeper means that care must be taken in the initial choice and serious attempts must be made to work out any difficulties that arise. Changing caretakers is destructive to the baby.

Not only should the housekeeper be loving and tender, but she must also speak to the child. It is helpful if her language is the same as the family's. Housekeepers with an impoverished vocabulary will not be able to help your child in learning the words and concepts he needs in the first years of life. Parents must remember to supply for the child visits to the zoo, books, records, games, sports, and the words that they feel are part of their own lives.

Because we still have the idyllic, if unrealistic, image of the old-fashioned family of Mother, Father, Dick and Jane and their dog Spot, in which Father went off to work and Mother stayed home and made cookies, we tend to feel some kind of guilt when we turn to day care or housekeepers to resolve our real conflicts of interest. A certain amount of guilt is unavoidable in this situation, but it is something parents have to learn to live with—especially since staying with the child could produce equal pain, deprivation, and emotional strain for all family members. In the end, the fact that the mother is not a martyr can only benefit the child in creating a home free of the atmosphere of self-sacrifice and anger that poisoned the childhoods of so many in the past. If the mother is earning money, she may feel better about herself. These good feelings and her self-esteem may balance out the hard times of leavings and separations, giving the entire family a happier and healthier mood.

Remember that for centuries the upper classes handed over their children entirely to nannies and wet-nurses, and civilization certainly did not decline into generations of feeble-minded or psychotic children. No one knows just how much time a parent should spend with a child under three, but we do know that increasingly society will have to adjust to the reality of the working mother and the infant who needs some form of day care.

In this country we are at a turbulent point of change: during the years to come we will have to make a more serious effort as a society to provide fine day care, available to everyone. That a society can accomplish this if it is determined has been proved in Israel and in Sweden. If we cared as much about the mental health of our children as we do about the viability and number of warheads on our missiles, we would spend more of our resources on building and maintaining day care centers. These would give each small child an equal opportunity to develop the necessary attachments to caring adults and the necessary intellectual and emotional foundations of maturity.

Dreams

We do not know exactly how early dreaming begins in children. Certainly, in order to be able to dream, they must have memory of daytime events and they must be able to anticipate and retain images in their minds. When the child becomes frightened of a strange face and cries or turns her head away at about eight or nine months, we know that she must have an image in her mind of her mother in order to be scared or startled by the stranger. This reaction to the stranger is then a sure sign that her memory has begun to work.

Some children with advanced verbal development have reported dreams as early as eighteen months. They will speak of being frightened at night by an animal, a giant, or a loud noise. Children do not know that they have only had a dream, and may waken frightened but unable to tell a parent what they have seen that caused them to cry out. Since many dreams are wishes in disguise, we assume that infants may also dream of being in their mother's arms, recalling sensations of comfort and pleasure they have received there. But this is all speculation. We do not know when the baby begins to dream or what those early dreams are about.

We do know that from about two years on, children will have dreams that are both good and bad, and they will begin to tell us about them. At this time we can begin to talk with them about the difference between the dream that is a picture in the mind and the real world they experience while awake. After two years, their dreams will become increasingly complicated, containing their angers and frustrations, their wishes to be all-powerful, enabling them to undo separations they do not want or create those that they do. By three years of age most children will have experienced some nightmares and will understand the difference between the dream and reality. We will continue this discussion of childhood dreams in the following sections, where they play an increasingly important role in the child's emotional life.

The New Baby

Many parents bring their second baby home some time before their first child's third birthday. This joyous event for the parents and grandparents is not, of course, equally appreciated by the older sibling, who has been rudely displaced in his position as baby in the home—the one entitled to the breast, the lap, or the arms of the parent. It really doesn't matter how well you prepare the small child for the wonderful addition to the family. Even if he is capable of speech and understanding, he will still not grasp the why of the new birth. From his point of view this stranger is a rival, an intruder, and a major threat to his life. Remember that children see the attachment to their parents as crucial for their survival. The birth of a new baby, with his own demands on their time and full array of clever attention-getting devices, places the first child in apparent jeopardy.

Some children do not react badly to the infant's first appearance in the home, but when the baby begins to crawl about and talk, the older child may then show all the signs of major upset and anger. He may wake at night, have bad dreams, start to soil or wet again, hit out at other children, cling to his mother, fuss when she leaves the room, refuse food, ask for a bottle, and generally demand more attention.

Children under three shouldn't be told about the arrival of the new baby too early. Even though they may grasp the coming event intellectually they will still perceive the new baby as a threat to themselves. This is true no matter how happily and calmly you present the coming birth. Little children do not benefit from having a long time in which to dread the change in family life. At about eighteen or nineteen months, they may notice the alteration in their mother's shape. They can be told that a new baby is growing inside the mother in a special place and will come out soon and be a part of the family. It is better never to lie to a child about anything important, and at the same time it isn't helpful to the child to give her more information than she can absorb. The amazing facts of sexual reproduction and the details of birth will only be distorted and become frightening to the young child if they are presented before she has the intellectual capacity to deal with them. For the child under three, we do not invent or tell stories about storks or such which will mark us as untrustworthy later. At the same time we answer questions directly but without all the knowledge and detail that we have. (This holds true for all issues, not just the extremely sensitive ones.)

All women during pregnancy turn their attention at least in part toward the growth and movement of the fetus within. They think a great deal about the baby to come: its sex, its face, its character. How will the family change? There is some natural apprehension of the birth itself and concern for the new baby's health. Even a young child of fourteen or fifteen months may sense that her mother's attention is directed toward and involved with the pregnancy, and can feel somewhat abandoned. The older toddler may give her mother a harder time and begin tiring her just when she is most in need of rest and relaxation. The toddler will sense the mother's turning inward while not understanding the causes, and she may feel frightened. We often see toddlers with pregnant mothers showing some signs of this additional stress. They may whine or become quieter and more with-drawn, or they may dash about aimlessly. The fact is that once the pregnancy is established, the relationship between the mother and the child is no longer exclusive, and that is a reality of the child's life.

Children should be prepared for the separation from the mother when she enters the hospital to give birth. It is best if the child can be taken care of during the mother's absence by familiar people. We would hope that the father would be available to give the child atten-tion at this critical time. It is certainly best if the child can be taken care of in her own home so that the changes seem less drastic or catastrophic. The child should speak with the mother on the phone and if the maternity center permits be taken to visit as soon as possi-ble.

The arrival of a sibling will provoke a backward sliding in most of the young child's accomplishments. She may wake at night. She may demand a bottle given up months ago. She may refuse solid foods or develop bowel disorders and soil and wet again. These are all expres-sions of anxiety and ways of saying to the parent that she, too, is still a baby and in need of care. Speech may be lost or revert to mis-pronunciations and lisps that had disappeared months ago. To be forced to share family appears so threatening to the very life of the child that for a while forward growth is slowed or stopped as the child, day by day, learns that the new baby is here to stay but that she herself is not being thrown out, exchanged, or abandoned by the parents. Words are not very reassuring. Only time and the continued care by the parents can convince the child, eventually restoring balance and forward development. The rivalry that begins the day the new baby is brought home never goes away entirely, and anxiety over who is best loved and who is more wanted may in some form or another last a lifetime. But the immediate symptoms of severe disturbance will fade and normal progress resume.

The child's anxiety about the new baby provokes aggression not only against the new infant but also against the parents who have brought the unwanted rival into the family. Many children are afraid of this anger against the very parents they now need more than ever, and will become especially compliant and good while hiding their anger and their fear. Children of two or nearing three may suddenly express great fear of the noises from the vacuum cleaner or the fire engine or thunder. They may become terrified of the neighbor's dog, or of the dark, or of the woman who wears a strange hat and sells fruit at the corner store. An angry child who is afraid to express any of that anger may instead become frightened of what others may do to him. He takes his own anger, places it outside of himself, and becomes afraid of being hurt.

For the child of fifteen or sixteen months, the threat of the new baby may result in a direct attempt to hit or harm the infant. He will also increase his demands to be babied himself. Aggression must be firmly stopped, but not in such a way that the child fears he will lose his parents' love and support because he is angry at the new baby. This is a fine line for a tired parent to have to walk and none of us succeed all the time.

Parents often become guilty and grieved when they witness this disturbance in their first children. Mothers and fathers on experiencing their child's distress remember their own childhood jealousy of brothers and sisters and often feel as if they had violated a bond with their older child. These are hard feelings to struggle with, particularly when they are added to the other fatigues, hormonal imbalances, and life-rhythm disruptions that accompany a new baby. Some parents will lean over backward to deny any interest in the newborn. They hope this pretended indifference will help to ease the pain of the invasion. Such a false drama fools no one and gives the older sibling an erroneous picture of his place in the family. It simply feeds his fear of abandonment. If the parents can ignore one baby, they can choose to ignore the other.

The new baby is entitled to an equal share of the affection and care of the parents, and the older child will grow more quickly accustomed to being a member of a larger family if the parents can keep a clear hold of the new reality. It is important for parents to suffer along with their first children, to understand their pain; at the same time it is not valid to disguise reality and give to the older child time and attention that is immediately needed by the new baby. Dealing with the rivalry between one's children is a lifelong problem. It is one of the major obstacle courses that parents must run and we all bring to it some leftover emotions that boiled during our own childhoods. We have to fend off certain attitudes toward the older or younger child that stem from our own position in our families of origin. We must remember that each of our children is entitled to a balanced share of whatever we have to offer.

If the older child tries to hurt the younger, you must intervene immediately. The older child must be told firmly, "No." It is a good idea not to leave the baby alone even for a few minutes with a two-year-old until you can be certain that the toddler can control himself. Very often affectionate pats on the head suddenly turn into slaps and stroking can be transformed into pinching in a split second. Don't be overly harsh about this but don't allow it to continue either.

As much as possible permit your child to act like a baby himself sometimes. He may need to pretend to nurse, to make baby sounds, to curl up in your lap. You can allow this while telling him that you love him as a big boy. Admire the things he can do that the baby can't, like building with blocks, jumping, or brushing his teeth. Perhaps he can have a special outing with his father or go one afternoon with you to the zoo or the store. Don't try to bribe him with expensive toys. A small present now and then is fine, but the parent who loads his child with gifts when a new baby has arrived increases rather than decreases worries. You should not feel guilty that your family has grown, and your child should not be compensated as if he has really lost something. In fact, he has gained.

The birth of a sister or a brother has many beneficial effects on the life of the young child. These benefits are not immediately clear but they gradually unfold. The companionship of children close in age is a great pleasure to both of them. They will learn to share, to play fairly, and to accommodate the other's deficits and abilities. They will learn to lose games and to fight for what they want. They will create things together. They will have an ally against the sometimes unpleasant authority of the parents. They will each have a special claim on another child who will be their support and buttress against the outside world of playground and school. They will have the possibility of a lifelong connection of deep meaning and shared memories.

The birth of a third child is always easier for the other children to accept. The oldest knows that he won't be abandoned. The youngest, while upset at having his baby place taken, is already accustomed to sharing time and space with another. But there will still be temporary regressions, and probably a greater degree of fighting and jealous behavior between the two older children. The clamor can be distressing for parents; however, it will subside in time as each child adjusts to the place he now occupies and finds ways to distinguish himself, to win your attention, and to live with the competition.

The birth of a second or third child in a family is not, despite immediate appearances to the contrary, a calamity for the older child. It is, rather, an opportunity to learn how to share, how to be a part of a larger group. It is a moment in which parents, by remaining steady and loyal while insisting on the reality of the changed family, can eventually increase their child's security in the larger world, his sense of belonging, being worthwhile and cared for. Having more than one child in a family gives parents a chance to see the differences between children, to enjoy the gifts, the style, the experiences of different people who are part of their own life in this deepest and most special of ways.

The Growing Conscience

The child from fifteen months on clearly knows that that some actions bring the disapproval of the all-important parents. We see a two-year-old walking toward a fellow playmate in the sandbox saying "No, no," and at the same moment grabbing the shovel and running away. We can see a two-and-a-half-year-old in a cranky mood holding a cup of milk up and saying "Bad baby, bad baby," then spilling the milk all over the kitchen floor. Gradually, as the child approaches three years of age, he may be able to stop himself, most of the time, from grabbing the shovel, spilling the milk, or doing any number of things he has learned that his mother and father forbid. This increasing control is certainly a welcome sign for parents but it does not mark a real conscience because the child does not himself think that it would be a bad thing to take another's toy or to make a mess on the floor.

At the beginning these are ideas that come from the outside. The child remembers how mad Mommy got last time he poked another child in the eye and so he stops his hand halfway there. He remembers that Daddy shouted at him when he touched his fishing pole last time and so he turns away from it now. He himself does not believe in right or wrong, good or bad, independently of how his parents will react. This is the emerging of conscience but it is hardly the whole story. If he were to grow no more the child would remain a savage, dependent on the force of society to control all his bad impulses. Fortunately, however, in the years after three his conscience will gradually become a part of himself, a voice of his own that directs him from within. As he nears his third birthday that big leap lies just ahead.

In the Hospital

For the child under three, the hospital can be a terrifying and damaging experience. Illness and pain are often accompanied by strange faces, and these strange faces and strange places can be more distressing to the baby than the illness itself. Needles, examinations, and medical procedures must seem like an attack to the child, and the loss of familiar walls and familiar smells will be equally threatening. The young child placed in the hospital for any reason is suddenly out of her mother's control, out of the orbit of her protection. Fear of being abandoned is greater than ever. It is crucial that the parents, mother or father, stay with the child at all times. Most hospitals today permit parents to spend the night with their child.

No matter how inconvenient, how disruptive to the home or the office, this is an essential protection for your child. If the child can see your face, can be held in your arms while something is happening to him, then the experience will be far less disruptive to his further growth. If the only hospital in your community does not permit parents to stay, visit as often as possible, but be prepared for the child's anger at you when you come. To be in a hospital without the constant presence of one parent or another is a very difficult emotional experience for a child. He may behave well with the nurses but then cry and fuss with you. This is normal. You can also expect your child to show intense reactions to the hospital experience when he comes home.

Remember that hospital life tends to the impersonal—efficiency, not empathy, is emphasized. Remember how many doctors, interns, and medical students may want to examine your child, crowding around his bed over and over again. With a child in the hospital you may have to stand up to doctors or nursing staff, but your child should not be wheeled away from you for tests of any sort. You should be with the child up until the moment he enters the operating room and you should be in the recovery room so that he can see you immediately upon awakening. During tests and procedures, try to stay where your child can see you. Don't let nurses or doctors push you out of the room. You cannot prepare a baby very well for what is about to happen, but you can stay with him, reassuring him by your very presence that his world, his universe, is still there.

Parents are only human beings; they get tired and frightened and worn out by being in a hospital. It is important to spell each other, to support each other, to use available grandparents, brothers, sisters, anyone close to the child, and to remember that the baby should not be left alone in the hospital for anything more than very short periods, and then only after the baby has formed some relationship with one of the nurses that would make your departure tolerable.

Of course bring him a present; of course have grandparents or aunts come to visit. But remember that the baby wants *your* attention. Gifts will be only momentary distractions, and too much company can mean that the adults talk and ignore the baby. Keep visits from friends and other family short. Try to be near when your baby wakes from a nap. Don't allow nurses to do things for your child that you can easily do yourself.

For children who have to be in the hospital frequently, the upset of the experience will make them particularly cranky and difficult to deal with when they are home. They don't understand what is happening or why. They feel as if their parents have let them down by permitting the needles and the other procedures they must endure. Like adults, they feel helpless in the hospital, and this helplessness will make it even more necessary for them to express their bad feelings and their independence when they come home.

While you cannot let a child who has been through a difficult experience do whatever he wants, you can help by understanding why he is being so difficult and try to reassure him that you are angry at his bad behavior but you love him just the same. If he starts refusing to eat what you offer or take a bath, when you wish, you can hold him a while, read a story, tell him how happy you are that he is home, and then try again. You can allow him to drink from the bottle although he knows how to use the cup, and you can be patient with soiling accidents. As he feels safer and steadier and the memories of the hospital experience become less threatening and immediate, his behavior will return to normal. He may need to act babyish for a little longer than another child who did not have his experience. You can permit this while reminding him of his big-boy pleasures and privileges.

Divorce

Divorce for the child under three can be particularly difficult. It may seem that because the child does not yet have expectations of a particular family life, an early divorce will have no major impact on his life. It is true that a child under one year may not immediately notice the departure of the parent and so will in all likelihood not show any signs of immediate upset. Sleeping and eating and growing may, if the departing parent has been peripheral in the child's life, continue without interruption. However, the very young baby as well as his slightly older brother or sister will certainly feel the effects of the depression and concern of the parent who remains in the home. Babies are dependent on their parents not only for basic physical care but for creating an alive, warm, emotionally satisfying, happy environment. This is very hard for a parent who has been recently separated or divorced to do. Young babies need their parents to be confident, to feel good about themselves and good about life and the future. The divorced parent of the young infant may have a hard time seeing her own future clearly, and will be prone to all the natural sadness, emotional and physical fatigue, and loss of hope that divorced people initially experience. This mood can easily affect the baby.

It is important for the divorced parent to find help from family and friends, and to allow others to grow close to the baby so that a climate of depression and fear need not be the child's only experience.

Remember that the baby will cling especially tightly to a parent if there is only one available. This clinging is dangerous in that it can make the mother angry at the insistent demands of the child; her anger will further frighten the baby and make separations even more difficult. Some mothers try to gain from their young children the kind of absolute love and commitment that had expected from their marriage. They will use their babies to feel attached, connected, and wanted. If this aspect of the relationship carries too heavy a load, it can be hard for the baby to take the first steps away from his mother, and the two can become enmeshed in a bond that will cripple them both.

Even very young babies need the individual styles of two parents. They use each parent differently and learn to feel secure moving back and forth from one to another. Babies in single-parent homes will take longer to feel confident away from their mothers, and the single relationship will have to carry all the feelings of love and anger that are more easily divided up between two parents.

This is a complication in the child's life but it need not have tragic implications. Single mothers of young babies need to find friends and family to surround the baby and increase her comfort with others. Single mothers owe it to their babies to reorganize themselves as quickly as possible and regain their sense of well-being. They should go out with other people. They should take jobs or go back to school or do whatever will speed them toward their goals. Babies will do best if their mothers are not overwhelmed with economic and emotional problems. Babies can tolerate good day care, they can tolerate being left with relatives or housekeepers for long periods of time, far better than they can endure breathing the air of a depressed and hopeless home.

Girls living exclusively with their mothers, even under the age of three, may be very flirtatious with casual male acquaintances and will sometimes embarrassingly exhibit their need for male attention. This is normal, and while it indicates how important fathers are to little girls, it bodes no evil for their future. Boys in the same circumstances may be especially protective of their mothers and resentful of men who come to call or spend time with the family. It helps children of both sexes if single parents do not invite into the home everyone they may spend a little time with. Of course a real relationship that promises to last a while must be included in family life, but it is very confusing for babies to have adults come and go. This increases their fear of losing their mothers and will aggravate clinging, anxious behavior.

Although it is hard for visiting fathers to spend long periods of time with toddlers, it is important that the child be permitted to maintain a relationship with the divorced parent. Visits with young children need not be long but should be as consistent and frequent as possible. It helps if mothers can encourage the relationship of the baby to the divorced father by talking about him, by allowing him free access to his child, and by supporting the child's evolving love for the parent who is not living in the house. This of course is equally true if the father has the prime custody of the child and the mother does the visiting.

Some divorced parents just drop out and disappear. Under the age of three, the child feels the loss only indirectly. Eventually he will wonder why he was deserted, what he did or what the parent did to drive the other away, and he will feel wounded and diminished by the desertion. The remaining parent can help by explaining to the child when he is old enough to understand that the other parent left for reasons that had nothing to do with the child or the child's behavior.

Grandfathers, grandmothers, uncles, and aunts can partially fill in for a child the missing place of the departed parent. It is necessary for single parents to work at maintaining these other relationships that will bring enrichment into the child's life. Being the divorced parent of a baby under three is very difficult. The hard work and the constant attention and alertness it requires does not leave over a lot of energy for reaching out into the world and rebuilding one's own emotional life. But precisely because one has a child whose total existence is dependent on yours, the single parent must restore the balance, use resources in the family and the community to help, and find a middle path between emotionally abandoning the child and emotionally binding him too tightly into a mother–child relationship. None of this is easy, yet it is possible. Many people have raised successful and beautiful children whose early years were clouded by divorce and its sad aftermath.

Conclusions

The normal development of the child during the first three years of life is a story of a long and sometimes painful labor to achieve psychological birth. First, a connection to the human caretaker must be formed; and then, with gradual maturation, a sense of the separateness of the self, of the helplessness of the self, must come. After that, a slow kind of balance between need and independence must be reached. Increasingly the child must be able to be alone without his parents for a brief while. He must be able to maintain an image of his mother in his head, and he must trust the world around him to remain predictable and steady so that he can safely continue to explore and learn, knowing that his vital needs will be protected.

The change from the weak newborn who cannot even hold up his own head to the climbing, running, pushing, pulling, speaking toddler is not simply a physical miracle; it contains a psychological flowering that includes awareness of sexual identity, "I am a boy—I am a girl," and the dawnings of conscience. The normal three-year-old will understand very well the difference between the signals that come from within his body and those that come from without. Most of the time he will be able to control his impulses to soil or wet or hit or bite or take something away from someone else. He will have acquired the beginnings of speech and the basic noun–verb–adjective grammatical structures. He will have absorbed the rhythms of human life, the times for sleeping, for eating, the difference between dark and light, night and day. He will know that there is a place to be messy and a place to be clean, and sometimes he will begin to insist on being clean himself. He will have begun to enjoy the company of other children, first by playing alongside them, and then, as his third birthday approaches, he may begin to build with a friend, or run with a friend, or pretend something together with another child. He will have begun to create imaginary events, and he will use his play to help him endure his worries about loss and separation and control of his anger. He will have a pretty clear idea of what behavior pleases his parents and what disappoints them.

95

All children from the second year on experience some kind of erotic genital pleasure. At three, many of them will touch themselves for comfort at night and perhaps at other times of fatigue or stress during the day. They will again be curious about the bodies of the opposite sex.

The normal three-year-old is still a barbarian. He would ravage the landscape and dominate everyone if permitted. But the process of becoming civilized has made a firm beginning, and he will feel guilt and shame when he fails to please others. The normal three-year-old has still not developed the capacity to feel what others feel and he can be tactless or cruel, selfish or destructive, as the moment dictates. The normal three-year-old, getting ready to go off to nursery school and able now to tolerate longer periods of separation from his mother, is rather like a bird that has pecked its way out of its shell and is now waiting for the strength to fly. The difference between the bird and the baby is that for the baby the breaking of the shell could not have occurred without the parents' attentive care and continual support.

The baby's relationship to her mother is the major organizing force in her development. At first she must make the crucial attachment to another human being. She must learn to depend on this other human being and she must recognize that without her mother she may perish. In the first weeks of life she must connect herself absolutely and completely to her mother in order to survive. Maternal neglect, or the mother's illness, will lead to real problems in mental growth for the child. She will be behind in speech, in motion, in learning. But a baby who remains totally connected to her mother does not survive well, either. The baby must gradually tolerate separation. She must live through her fears of being abandoned, her fears that her body may come apart, her sense that she is nothing but a reflection of her mother's wish.

The drama of attachment and separation, and the angers and fears that accompany it, tell the story of the first three years of life. Through her nurturing care, the mother brings the world to the baby. The baby must learn to move away—not so far away that she dies of loneliness but not so near that she smothers in the close air of the nursery. What happens to the child during toileting, bedtime, eating, playing, talking is enormously affected by this underlying drama.

The three-year-old is a wonder of ingenuity, affection, and enthusiasm. We begin to see in our three-year-old the development of particular qualities of humor, of style, of a way with others. We begin to see in our three-year-old the outlines of the person she will one day be. We have come to know her at her worst and at her best. We no longer consider ourselves new parents. Now we are in the thick of it, amazed at what we have done so far, and in love, in ways we had never before experienced, with our child.

Section II

The Hard Road

The first section of this book described the ideal normal development of the child from birth to three. All ideals are of course simplifications and abstractions; very rarely does messy, erratic real life follow the perfect designs we have outlined. Rare but profound troubles in the child's mind can be identified by pediatricians and psychiatrists as early as two or three months of age. The all-important relationship between parent and child that is woven by acts of reaching out on both sides can begin to show major and minor irregularities, even serious distortions, by the end of the first six months of life.

We have to remember that parents are not all alike. We come to our reproductive time burdened by our own pasts, affected by the culture in which we live, and struggling with the angers, frustrations, and anxieties of our own existence. We all in our own way do our best, within the limits of our control, to create a happy child.

Sometimes psychological obstacles encountered along the way are the fault of biology and its tragic margin of error. Sometimes the brain is damaged and the genetic codes have betrayed the baby, condemning him or her to a life of emotional isolation and anguish. Sometimes the baby is born with normal potential, but the vast range of pressures on the parents, tensions that can stem from their own relationships in childhood or present economic and marital problems, lead them to do the very thing they would have most liked to avoid—contaminate the new life entrusted to them with the unsolved conflicts that haunt their own souls.

Children most at risk of developing severe mental illness are those from homes where one or more of the close relatives have themselves had deep problems. Boys are more vulnerable to almost every kind of mental disturbance than girls; children from homes in which alcoholism, death of a parent, illness, or extreme poverty have forced many changes of people and places in their lives are also at high risk. In middle-class families, children of anxious, compulsive, excessively competitive parents, or absent or indifferent parents, are walking high wires under which there are no safety nets. Like so many invisible bacteria, the causes of mental pain breed in the intimacy of our homes. Some children, however, seem to have a kind of natural immunity and others a natural or inborn frailty.

Some external events bring intolerable pressures to bear on the infant and so stall or derail her continued developmental push. One such event might be the death of a parent, causing not only the absence of a crucial person but also depression and the potential emotional withdrawal of the remaining parent. A long and difficult illness in the first three years of life, requiring surgery or other painful procedures and prolonged separation from parents, is another condition that places the child at risk. Some small percentage of children are born with physical handicaps. Whether these are as severe as blindness or deafness or as mild as a clubfoot or webbed fingers, they too present special psychological problems and place their young victims in danger of developmental difficulties. Nature can be cruel, but we have developed the knowledge and the skills to fight back, and can often bring to a fulfilled life many of those children who were unfairly burdened.

If one thinks of the mental growth of the child as a series of tasks, each of which must be accomplished before the next can be successfully undertaken, then it is clear that the first three years present the essential foundation for the human mind. Often the fact that one or another of these basic structures is inadequately secured, or that the wood itself is rotten, is not apparent until a later stage of growth. The first three years present fewer and less varied signs of mental disturbance than will reveal themselves in later stages. But many of the instabilities that may affect older children are rooted in these early years. The mental troubles we will be describing in this section are necessarily most severe because the milder and less damaging irregularities of development that really affect many more of us are not apparent in the child under three years.

We must not forget that there is a powerful forward rush of positive emotional and intellectual development in all normally endowed children. This force seems to carry most children through and ahead into the next stages of mental life. There are wonderful strengths within each child that can correct and balance temporary distortions of feeling and thought, and create new and better solutions to old problems as the child grows. Many children are able to take the difficult tensions of their inner problems and shift them, actually using them to fuel their creativity and their intellectual growth. Some children seem to be able to squeeze adequate nourishment from the most dry and dead of parental circumstances, while others will suffer knots of crippling tension and bouts of fierce anxiety with very little provocation. We do not yet understand this or know how to predict the mental strength of one baby as against another. We are like the first discoverers of germs, peering through their primitive microscopes, amazed at what they knew and all too aware of what they didn't.

Because of the child's resilience and because each stage of development offers the child a chance to solve problems that occurred earlier, to find new and better solutions to old conflicts, parents should not feel that each mistake of their parenting life is going to cause misery. We all make many mistakes, and children have a way of bouncing back, jumping over and overcoming all kinds of difficulties. They are not so fragile as they look. They will surprise us over and over again with their strength and ingenuity, and their capacity to draw for themselves the necessary nourishment while discarding the nonsense we sometimes provide.

In this section we will describe the visible problems that affect the baby. Some are unfortunately beyond our capacity to cure; others are minor detours on the route to normal growth. Sometimes parents worry needlessly about problems that are only temporary and will undoubtedly be outgrown in time. For a very few children, however, these same symptoms will become unrelenting and they may couple themselves with other problems, creating a variety of disturbances. These clusters of problems tell us that the child is in more than passing difficulty. One symptom such as eating problems or shyness probably means nothing at all but shows how this particular child is handling the very normal tension of growing up. But when the shy child also stops talking, has trouble sleeping, and starts rocking back and forth in a peculiar way, then we become alarmed.

The important questions that professionals will ask about any given child are how long the problem has been there, what else is going on with the child, what might have started the difficulty, such as the parents going off on a trip or a dog bite. Problems that have come about because of a specific fright or difficulty tend to disappear by themselves in time. Problems whose origins are harder to trace, that are part of an entire troubled picture, are of more concern. The child who is truly starting off his young life with difficulties he may not be able to overcome shows not just one but many signs of distress.

We will try to indicate where we think problems may just pass away in the course of time, and where they need attention from concerned parents and when it might be best to seek professional advice and help.

It's hard to find a perfect parent. Most of us lose jobs, fight with our spouses; sometimes we are selfish or angry or misunderstand the needs of those we most love. Fortunately our children will not be scarred by our small daily errors and they can often be helped to strengthen themselves as they grow.

Postnatal Depression: The After-Birth Blues

Many women are surprised to find that after giving birth they feel down and irritable, despite the fact that they expected to be extremely happy. In the days following delivery they suffer from a bleak emotional exhaustion, a lack of appetite for their usual pleasures. This attack of the blues is quite normal and will usually lift in a matter of weeks. It may be caused by the hormonal upheaval involved in the birth process, or it may be a result of the new responsibilities and burdens of the demanding infant, representing a kind of grieving over the loss of freedoms that accompanies the birth of the baby. The care of the newborn is also extremely physically wearing and many women stagger emotionally in response to the lack of sufficient sleep. This blue streak in the emotional landscape ordinarily clears up quickly as the mother gains in confidence and competence with her baby, as the household routines are established, and as the adjustments to her new status, both physical and emotional, are made.

For some small fraction of women, however, the first sadness does not lift. On the contrary, it may begin a serious process of decline into apathy, listlessness, weepiness, and an increasing inability to organize, an inability to accomplish the tasks of the day. A new mother may find that she does not have the capacity to dress herself, to take care of chores, to resume outside work if that had been the plan, to meet friends, to organize a dinner party, to go to the ball game. It is as if the first bad feelings that followed immediately after the delivery awoke a host of others that now rise to plague her. This depression is a process that feeds on itself. It awakens guilt and brings about self-dislike, which can further stoke the furnace of bad feelings. The depression can now last many months, pushing some women into a dangerous loss of control where they may have terrifying thoughts of harming the baby and harming themselves.

In the milder instances, the openly expressed love of the husband for both mother and baby can considerably shorten the duration of the dark mood. Of course this is a strain on him, too. Just as he must get used to the new person in his life and the major changes in the family it brings about, he feels his wife turning away from him and sliding down a black tunnel to a place he cannot reach. He, too, needs comfort and reassurance at this time, and if his wife is caught up in her own sadness, she cannot give it to him. Fathers who can remain steady through this trying situation and who can continually assure their wives that they are pleased with the baby and pleased with their new family will be of invaluable support. This is surely an example of the "worse," in the "for better or worse," and the father who does not withdraw from his wife and baby has kept his vow.

In the more severe instances of maternal sadness, there is not much a husband can do to stay the malignant process. Some of these depressions that bring women right to the edge of a profound loss of reality will spontaneously lift, and the woman will be able to turn again toward her child, her family, her work with a new energy. But many depressions will not go away without professional help. Psychiatrists have at their service an armory of helpful medicines and they also have the effective tools of psychotherapy to bring to the aid of the troubled mother. We would feel that the blue mood has lasted too long if it is still there after three months. If it appears to be getting bleaker each day, and if the mother continues to pull away from her baby or to express thoughts that she might hurt the baby either by accident or intentionally, we would be concerned. If a few months after the birth the mother is still uninterested in sex and is paying no attention to her personal appearance, and if she is withdrawing from friends and other family members, we would suggest that the moment has come to bring her the help she really needs. If there is any question at all as to the possible advantage of professional help, we would suggest that a consultation be held with a psychiatrist who can best evaluate the seriousness of the situation. It is better in this serious matter to be overly cautious than to wait too long.

Depression after having given birth is an illness that affects both mother and baby. In the throes of such a sadness it can be impossible for a woman to give the emotional warmth, the eye contact, and the tenderness of care that we know are essential for the baby in the first weeks after delivery. A mother's prolonged and deep depression can place the new baby at grave risk of losing his chance to develop well. He is preprogrammed by his genes to search out the smiling face, to make certain appealing gestures that call forth the warmth of adults. If the world greets his first approaches with indifference, he cannot draw the necessary emotional nourishment from his environment. He will wither as surely as if he had not been fed.

This is an important reason to get help for the mother when it is needed. She will feel even more guilty and distraught if she begins to realize that her child is not growing normally. If the baby is not holding his head up unsupported by one month of age, if by three weeks he is not following the human face and seeking to make eye contact, if within six weeks to three months we don't see the baby's smile when an adult approaches, we know that baby has already been damaged by maternal grief. We would suggest whenever possible that if the mother slides into a severe depression a substitute caretaker for the baby be found immediately. It would certainly be best if that substitute could remain a steady and reliable figure in the baby's life throughout this period, until the mother is ready to take over.

If at the age of eight months or so the baby starts to cry when he sees a stranger, if his face clouds and becomes subdued or he looks away from a new person who approaches him too quickly, we know that he is progressing normally and has made the necessary attachments to another human being. If the mother is still not ready to take over his care, at least she will not be further wounded by the knowledge that she has harmed her child.

The causes of these postdelivery depressions are not known. It is not clear why one woman will be felled and another not. Chemical changes take place in both mind and body during pregnancy and these must make some particular women more vulnerable to emotional collapse. Pregnancy and delivery are times of stress in which a great deal is at stake: every women feels to some degree as if she is being tested and must perform well. Sometimes a disappointment in the sex of the baby can trigger a depression. Sometimes the birth of the baby awakens long-buried memories of the arrival of an unwanted brother or sister and anger felt long ago toward the sibling is splashed onto the new baby. Sometimes a woman faced with the biological confrontation with her own body that the birth brings wishes she could reject her femaleness and not be a woman at all.

Some women are shocked by the degree of pain they may have felt during delivery, and others can be humiliated by the loss of control and the degree of helplessness they felt while they were in labor. Some women feel that their husbands no longer find them as attractive or desirable as before, or they sense the father's disappointment for one reason or another with the baby. All women feel some degree of anger at their babies simply for being so demanding, so present, for changing their lives so dramatically. This anger toward the child can make some women feel so guilty that they begin to dislike themselves and fall into a quicksand of blacker and blacker moods.

It is a terrible irony that the birth of a baby, even a long-awaited, planned-for baby, can bring such trouble to the mother. The happiest, most wonderful events of our lives can turn themselves inside out and present their monstrous sides. We cannot always be happy when we are supposed to be happy any more than we can always be sad when we are supposed to be sad. Things can be so much more complicated than the greeting card industry would have us believe. But serious postnatal depressions are not all that common, and the milder variety is usually chased away by the real joy the new baby can bring and the support of other members of the family.

Premature Babies

Modern technology has brought us an incredible miracle: we can now save the lives of premature babies weighing as little as two pounds and on some occasions even less. These advances have been made only within the last ten years, and improvements in the care of the premature baby are still advancing rapidly. This is good news. Many parents now have babies that just half a generation ago would surely have died.

There is unfortunately a darker side to this scientific development. New technologies always create their own problems. Some of these tiny babies will show signs of serious emotional, psychological trouble, as well as being at risk for a wide range of physical problems. Many of them appear to be hyperactive and to have serious learning problems. Some have a degree of retardation; others have an unusually high degree of anger and a very low tolerance for being frustrated in any way.

Infant psychiatrists seem to feel that the excessive handling that is required to save the lives of these babies—the needles, tubes, touching, examining, sucking mucus from immature lungs, etc.—does not allow the nervous system to adapt as it normally would. These babies also endure a prolonged period in the hospital without the necessary attachment to their mothers evolving in a normal way. Certainly the beginnings of the mother–child connection are interfered with by all the medical procedures and the extreme fragility of the child, which frighten most mothers. Even when they are permitted a role in the premature baby's care, it is hard for them not to be anxious and overwhelmed. We do not have the results of long-term studies on the well-being of these babies because the medical advances are still too new. But we do know that the premature infant is at risk of developing emotional problems as well as physical problems, and needs special efforts on the part of the mother to stay involved in the care of her infant.

There is, of course, a range of psychological risk to the baby that varies with the birth weight. A four-pound infant will spend a very short time in the premature unit. She will be large enough so that her mother will not feel especially anxious about handling, feeding, and allowing herself to get close to the baby. Within weeks she will be brought home. But for the mother of the tiny premature infant, there are other problems. Often she may feel irrationally guilty about the small size of her child. Her husband too, even knowing better, may blame her, citing some activity she undertook, some food she didn't eat, some imagined action she might have taken to prevent the early delivery.

Such marital tension can cloud the baby's first months at home. While her baby is in the hospital the mother is scared by all the equipment, the monitors, the lights, the professional air of the nurses around her baby, and feels shut out and incompetent. She spends several months not knowing for sure whether or not the baby will make it. This fear for the baby's life makes it harder for her to begin to love the child, to commit herself to a being she can hardly touch and perhaps only watch at a distance. She protects herself against the possible loss of the baby by not allowing herself to make a connection to him.

Premature babies even when at last they are allowed to leave the hospital are immature physically for their age. They may respond oddly when the mother leans over and coos at them. Some tiny babies will react to such a sign of interest and love by shaking all over and turning pale and blue around the lips—the excitement has just been too much for them. Other babies may for some months ignore the mother's voice and not fix their gaze on her face at all. They may need to shut out the extra stimulation for a time. This is very hard on the mother, who will feel frightened and unsure of herself.

Mothers and fathers of premature babies need to be in contact with their children as often and as much as the nursing staff of the hospital can manage. It is vital for parents not to give up, even when it appears as if they are the least necessary mortals in their newborn's universe. In time, if they just keep at it, most babies will respond normally. Parents must prepare themselves for the hard work of settling a baby whose breathing and eating and digestive systems will have more trouble than most. With determination, many parents have survived this initial difficult period and gone on to enjoy a normal parenting experience.

Don't let the hospital's efficiency and amazing life-saving machinery impress you so much that you forget that what every baby really needs is a strong attachment to a parent. In fact, there are some good indications from follow-up studies that the difference between the babies who can quickly order themselves, whose digestive and breathing problems clear up, and those who remain in trouble for longer periods of time is the degree of constant care and connection with the mother each receives.

Sleep Problems

The baby's sleep is a most important part of his growth. During sleep the nerve endings of his brain are taking on their final form; while sleeping he uses the food and the emotional care he has received in his waking hours to knit his mind and body into a healthy whole.

Sleep problems in the baby range from the most minor of temporary annoyances to the most jarring and ongoing symptoms of early childhood mental illness. All our lives our sleep patterns will be turned upside down by stress, by increased tension within or around us. Most all of us will have trouble falling asleep or will wake at inconvenient hours when we move from place to place or job to job, when we start a new term at school, or when an important relationship begins or ends. The events that frequently cause insomnia in adults all have to do in one way or another with problems of loss. This is even more true for the tiny baby.

Several things can go wrong with our sleep. We can sleep too much or we can wake too often or we can not fall asleep at the appropriate times. We can have night terrors, which are profound night frights that occur in our deepest sleep and cause us to wake screaming. These night terrors take place so far down in our levels of consciousness that we cannot even remember what was so frightening and why we screamed. We can have nightmares, which are anxiety dreams in which death or disaster approaches us from the many crevices of our hidden imaginary worlds. We can (although this is very rare) walk in our sleep. An infant under three shows only some of these sleep disturbances. How serious they are and what they signal can be interpreted only if we know how long the sleep problems have lasted and what other signs of difficulty exist in the child. Waking often or sleeping too much become symptoms of alarming mental trouble only when they continue over a period of several months, and when they are accompanied by other problems concerning feeding, talking, walking, avoiding eye contact with adults, or little or no smiling.

During the first month of life most children will wake needing to be fed around every three or four hours and sometimes even more frequently. As their biological systems adjust to life outside the womb, they begin to be able to sleep five or six hours during the night. This usually happens around three to five months. By three months, 70 percent of all infants will sleep from midnight to dawn. By six months, 83 percent of all children will have a solid night's sleep. At about three months the brain waves of a sleeping infant become similar to those of an adult. The settling down into longer periods of sleep and longer periods of awake alertness is a sign of good biological and psychological development. But for a small group of children the three- to four-hour waking periods may last throughout the entire first year. This more erratic pattern seems to be normal for them and does not impede their development at all.

During the entire first year sleep is often interrupted by teething pains, and by the occasional baby illness, such as stomach cramps or fevers. After the first six months of life, if the parents have taken a vacation of a week or so or even a weekend, leaving the baby with a known babysitter or a beloved relative, the baby may well wake in the middle of the night several times after their return. All of these wakings and interruptions of the routine, although they can be exhausting or infuriating for parents, are a perfectly normal part of the expected up and down, better and worse rhythm of any normal infant's experience.

Some infants, however, show a continued and consistent inability to sleep more than a few hours at a time well into the second year of life. We understand that after the six-month birthday the baby is struggling with a need to be separate and a fear of abandonment— Am I alone in this world? What is a part of me and what is not? Will I be swallowed up or left to fall apart alone?

We can appreciate that the child will wake at night to reassure herself that her all-important other people are still there. If the child is having an especially hard time in trusting the continued good care of the mother and father, she will be apt to wake even more often. If there is marital discord in the house and loud angry voices or even bitter dark looks find their way into the nursery, babies may react with constant waking. Babies seem to have an extra-fine sense of this threat to their most needed objects. In homes where parents are having battles, silent or otherwise, or are just in the process of disappointing each other, babies are apt to wake again and again throughout the night to check on their presence.

If the mother has had a depression or a hard time herself during the first year of the baby's life, it is quite possible that the infant will take a long time to fall asleep. When he becomes a toddler, he will call out for repeated reassurances that she is still there. He may wake often for reunions with her. The child who has not had sufficient care and attention from his mother, or mother substitute, will become especially frightened when he begins to feel the natural push to become independent and separate. He may be enraged at his mother and overwhelmed with angry feelings that he then fears may destroy her. This child may easily wake throughout the night to make sure that his worst fears have not come true and that he is not cut off from those he needs so much.

If a child has had a serious illness, one that might require hospitalization or induces severe pain, he too will be apt to show a short sleeping span during the first two years. Threatened by the outside world, he has discovered his own vulnerability and is less apt to trust the darkness and the waves of sleep to safely carry him across the night. If a parent has died, or if there has been a divorce after the first year, then the child may wake again and again to make sure that someone is still there for him.

Some infants have trouble sleeping because their entire activity level is too high. They may, for organic reasons, have a more excitable nervous system than most and they may be unable to regulate themselves into patterns of waking and sleeping. These children may grow into the toddlers who can't stop running and climbing and spinning, and have trouble focusing their attention, organizing their thoughts and movements. With these children, parents can try to cut down on any excitement the child experiences before bedtime, keeping as calm as possible around the child in the evening.

But for some children this continual interruption of restful sleep is simply a biological given. Rather than aggravate themselves over the child's erratic sleeping pattern, parents should just accept that this particular child will wake often and need extra care. The parents of such exhausting children need a great deal of support. They should take vacation time and use as much outside help as possible.

Bedtime rituals—the cuddling with the worn and ragged blanket, the extra glass of water, the final bedtime story, the nightlight, the extra kisses and final visits—are all part of the small child's normal difficulty in letting go of the people he needs so much. Children who have been too controlled, whose mothers have not let them gradually take over their own feeding, their own dressing when possible, who don't let their children make any decisions for themselves, may not be able to go to sleep at night. These children have not had a chance to master a sense of themselves as separate people; as a result, they become even more frightened of the loneliness of the night. They have a great deal of anger that they have not been allowed to express during the day, anger which frightens them at night.

If a child is taken into the parents' bedroom and rewarded for his waking with an extended period of time in bed with his mother and father, then it is only natural that he will wake the next night and the one after that. It is important to help children to tolerate the separation that the night brings and to guide them toward the capacity to fall asleep alone and wake alone without panic. This marks a growth of the child's mind, allowing him more room to be a person himself —a person with the mental capacity to remember the comfort of his parents and to trust that it will come again.

If children sleep in their parents' bedroom, they tend to be awoken by the noises of sexual activity. While they cannot understand just what is going on, they will feel either alarmed by the noises or left out of the activity and isolated in a painful way. Even a baby of a year or so looking out of the bars of her crib at the tangle of arms and legs and the closeness of two adults can feel that she has been forgotton and therefore is in mortal danger.

Sometimes a child's nighttime waking will become a habit, a way of gaining a little extra attention and comfort. A child may have discovered the pleasure of a nighttime visit when she awoke from a bad dream or a stomach ache. She then continued the night waking because she enjoyed the reunion it brought. Exhausted and frustrated parents can try letting such a baby cry it out for a night or two; most often the baby will give up and return to a better sleeping pattern. If the waking was not due to some real deep disturbance in the attachment of parent and child, and all else is going well in the baby's development, there is no need for parents to suffer through the erratic waking patterns of the child—hard as it may be for the concerned mother and father to ignore the pathetic calls of their baby.

When toilet training has begun, children may start to wake up in the middle of the night again not because they want to use the potty but because the stress this new experience puts on them makes them fear any long separation from their parents. They may be afraid they are not approved of. The child's stubbornness in giving up the B.M. in the morning may frighten him at night with fear that he will be abandoned. He is struggling at this time with understanding what is a part of him and what is not, and how to safely let go of the B.M. Children are quite normally afraid of being flushed away or of coming apart themselves, and these fears make them need reassurance during the night more than ever. Some children at the early stages of toilet training or in the midst of a tug-of-war with their parents over their body products will wake frequently. If the toilet training is not too harsh and does not evoke too much fear and anger in the child, and if he is allowed to proceed at his own pace, than the sleep will soon return to normal.

It is primarily in the retarded or the severely mentally damaged child that we see excessive sleeping. In the depressed baby, who has not received enough touching or smiling and care, we may also see a terrible lethargy where the sleeping and the waking hours are barely distinguishable from each other.

When a child is not sleeping well and has not been for a long time, there are several approaches to the problem. First, many parents focus on the child's sleep and forget that the child responds to the tension in the home. Instead of worrying about getting the child to sleep better, it is worth while for parents to sit down and talk with each other and see if they can clear up troubles between themselves. If there have been too many moves in a child's young life, it is best to try to settle down, keep the child in one place for as long as possible. If there have been many changes of caretaker, try to alter the situation by sticking to one person who will steady the child. If parents have begun toilet training and then see sleep problems that last for weeks on end, they should postpone the toileting.

Encourage the child when he is successful but stop pushing him to perform well. Parents can check themselves to see if their form of discipline is too harsh or frightening for the child. Perhaps a "No" in a quieter voice might do. If you are putting your child into his crib alone when he misbehaves, perhaps the child is being separated from the family for too long a time for such a small criminal to bear. Encourage the child to like himself; reassure him that you think he is a good boy, even if he soils his pants, knocks over the milk, or covers his baby sister's face with a blanket. All these seemingly irrelevant actions may help him sleep better.

If a child is having trouble sleeping through the night, it is a good idea to offer the nightlight. A child who wakes and sees a familiar room may be able to get himself back to sleep. Doors can be kept open so that the child feels less isolated from the rest of the family. Bedtime stories, second glasses of water, and a fourth kiss are all perfectly all right up to the point of the parent's impatience and exhaustion. Don't let your child push you in these activities to the edge of fury. Your own anger, openly expressed or not, will frighten the child and undo the calming effect of your good deeds. Stop, firmly, when you have had enough, when you are feeling exploited. If a child wakes and calls, come to him briefly. Don't play with him or wake him further. Don't change his diaper or turn on the light unless necessary. Make it clear to him that you expect him to sleep.

Feeding Problems

A few feeding problems in the child from six months to three are worrisome. Sometimes the feeding situation has become an unpleasant experience for both mother and baby. Some children suck poorly; they will be slow to feed and will drink only a little from a cup. Some children will eat very few foods and will dawdle endlessly; they will often gain weight slowly. Sometimes they will habitually vomit up a meal, particularly if they have been coaxed and forced into eating.

Marsha and her mother have been at it for weeks. Marsha turns her head away, refuses even to look at her plate, won't pick up the french fries with her fingers, won't use a spoon on the tapioca pudding, and won't do more than take a sip or two from her cup of milk. Marsha will eat a cookie in the middle of the afternoon. She will nibble on a bite of chicken and sometimes she'll put a few grains of rice in her mouth. Her mother is going mad, is feeling mad. She makes everything she can think of, but things that pleased a few months ago are now considered dog food, and things that other children love, like Jello and bananas, this one thinks are for the birds.

Marsha's father and mother are beside themselves. They get anxious before mealtimes. They watch tensely as their daughter watches them prepare the food and place it in front of her. They feel helpless as she stares off indifferently into the distance. They feel guilty— What have we done wrong?—as she once again refuses a little piece of bread and butter. Marsha pretend-feeds her dolls. It's her favorite kind of play. "Nice dolly," she says; "you have to eat, or else you won't grow."

While these eating problems are not as serious as those we see in the babies who do not grow or thrive at all, they can nevertheless be quite serious. They usually appear in children of parents who themselves had severe feeding disturbances as young children. They also appear in those infants and toddlers whose mothers or fathers bear an unusual degree of anger and resentment toward their babies. This anger can be hidden from the parents themselves, who feel that they are honestly trying hard to feed their children. But unconscious anger directed at a child can prompt him to resist the life-giving act of eating.

This is a problem that will not go away in time and will not be resolved by parents altering their methods of offering food. It is a reflection of some serious break in the caring connection of parent and child. A consultation with a child psychiatrist may help the parents to sort out some of their painful feelings and enable them to reach out to their babies in a happier way.

A few infants under one year of age will spit up their food and keep the regurgitated matter in their mouths a long time. We call this rumination, and it is a sign of serious disturbance in the child. We see it only in babies whose connection to their mothers has been dangerously weakened, either because of a hostile home or because the babies themselves are severely retarded or have some other significant genetic brain damage. If the parents notice that their child is holding vomited matter in the mouth, a pediatrician should be immediately consulted.

Failure to Thrive: The Baby Who Won't Grow

Lack of physical growth in childhood shows us again the intimate connection between mind and body, and gives us an example of the still mysterious messages that permit the psychological life to have such a profound and dramatic effect on the well-being of the muscles and the bones, the tissues, and the vital organs. This disease appears in infants who were normal in weight and length at birth. But by the end of the first year their pediatricians are expressing concern because these children remain way below the average in growth and weight gain.

The pediatrician will do a variety of tests to see if there is something wrong with the child's digestion, enzymes, or metabolism. The infant will have no particular sickness, although she will be especially prone to the full range of minor infections that children easily weather in the first year of life. The tests will all be normal; the infants will go home again to their mothers. The strange thing is that as this medical drama is played out over and over again during the first three years of the child's life, a peculiar pattern emerges. When the child is away from her mother (even in the hospital), she will begin to gain weight rapidly; but as soon as she is once again in her familiar home, all progress will come to a sudden halt.

While at home, these children appear to be finicky eaters. They crumble cookies into their carriage corners. They take an eternity to finish a bottle of milk and often leave the last third. In other areas they will move forward in a fairly normal way. They show no immediate signs of retardation. They accomplish the tasks of small babies on schedule, such as using their index fingers, rolling over, and sitting up. But this failure to thrive is potentially a very serious matter because the human brain needs to grow in the first years of life. If it does not receive adequate nourishment and it stays small, there is a high chance of permanent mental slowness.

In an adult, we can separate mental functioning from physical well-being; wounds in one area do not necessarily scar the other. But in an infant, the nutriments of the body must be absorbed in order for the capacity for speech, abstract thought, and creative play to emerge. Pediatricians will identify this problem and distinguish it from ordinary feeding difficulties. Mothers must listen to the pediatrician's advice on this since so much is at stake.

These failure-to-thrive children have puzzled doctors for a long time. Every month in a major city hospital, such as Mt. Sinai in New York, there will be at least three or four such children in the cribs on the pediatric floors. Many of them are now referred to the child psychiatrists on the hospital staff. When the psychiatrists work with the mothers of these tiny children, who appear to be shrinking instead of growing, they find that very often the mothers are themselves depressed, neglected, and immature. These mothers are frequently overburdened and angry at their babies. They experience such confusions and unhappiness in their own lives that they cannot feel or express any real tenderness or delight in their children. The mother's mood can be caught by the young baby and translated into a kind of stubborn resistance to life that expresses itself in the refusal to eat.

In some instances, psychiatrists will recommend that the baby be taken out of the home and placed in a foster home. But frequently it is possible to offer the mother enough support and encouragement so that she begins to pay more positive attention to her baby. Psychiatrists and their staff try to help these women overcome the effects of neglect and abuse that so often clouded their own childhood. They will try to help the mother recognize her own anger at her baby and understand its results. Very often the simple fact that other people care and become concerned about the feelings and experiences of these mothers enables them to turn with the necessary love and affection to their babies.

It is hard to believe that a child will recognize his mother's anger at him for coming at an inconvenient time in her life, or her anger at him because she must take care of him when she herself is so in need of care. But it is clear that some little babies will agree with mothers who do not value them. If psychiatrists help these mothers to feel better about their own lives, the angers and sadness lift, and the child begins to eat and to flourish. In the same way that we say that animals hear and smell things at ranges that human beings cannot, we must acknowledge that babies respond to feelings and moods not always known even to the mother herself. These responses in the infant can, in certain children, cause them to stop growing.

Though relatively rare a complication compared to such common childhood difficulties as earaches and chest colds, this disease is awesome in its implications. It tells us how much we still don't understand about how the baby interprets his emotional environment. Why do some children fail to thrive while others in a similar situation do not? How extraordinary are the workings between the mind of the mother and the mind of the child if they can have such profound consequences.

Infant Depression: The Grief That Brings Death

During the 1930s, the German psychoanalyst Rene Spitz observed infants in orphanages and discovered that 80 to 90 percent of them were dying before the end of their second year of life. These babies seemed to manage fairly well for the first six months, despite the fact that they might have lost their mothers soon after birth. But the nurses or nuns who were their caretakers did not have sufficient time to spend with any one infant. They frequently propped bottles up and they changed babies without talking or looking at them; generally, they seemed to believe that assuring cleanliness and providing food was all that was required of them. After six months these children showed a remarkable pause in their growth. They looked away from human beings, avoiding all eye contact. They looked sad, but cried very little. They did not babble and the older babies could not be engaged in a game of peek-a-boo or pat-a-cake. They were especially susceptible to all the childhood epidemics like measles and mumps, and many of them died from illnesses that in family-raised children were very rarely killers. These babies did not smile or respond to being smiled at.

Many of the infants would spit up their food and then keep part of it in their mouths for hours. This is similar to the way the cow digests, but serves no purpose in the human child. Babies may develop this curious habit because they are holding on in their minds to some slight remembered closeness with another that had come about through the feeding situation. In these babies, the intake of food was quite minimal.

During the first six months of life, many of these doomed babies showed tremors in their large muscles and a strange kind of tightness in their trunks and legs. Some on the other hand seemed oddly floppy, as if they had no muscle tension at all. Most did not walk or stand at the expected time.

Since the first observations of Dr. Spitz this miserable picture has been observed again and again, until we have finally learned that it is dangerous if not murderous to take care of babies in a sterile institutional setting. Since the discovery of antibiotics, many more of these children are surviving physically; but it is still estimated that in such wards some 30 to 40 percent of the babies will surely die. Almost all of those who live into the third year have suffered mental retardation and are unable to catch up with their peers whose first years were spent in homes with constant maternal care.

These babies most dramatically show us how crucial for intelligence, for growth, for life itself is the attachment of the baby to the human world. Unlike alligators and turtles, unlike monkeys, who suffer but do not die, the human baby must have a loving connection in order to survive. Without this attachment the baby is too often unwilling, incapable of going on. These hospitalized infants show us an extreme of deprivation. Their fate illustrates how a mother who is distracted by the other tensions and responsibilities of her life can endanger this all-important connection.

There is an exception to this grim picture. Dr. Spitz and others have discovered that consistently in each batch of children there are one or two who manage to be so engaging that every nurse stops to talk to them. They manage to eke necessary nourishment out of the most sterile of environments. This makes them still stronger and more appealing than their peers. They may have special attributes of physical beauty; they may just stand up early and look at the door, their faces lighting up when they see an adult passing by. They are rewarded for their responsiveness by being responded to.

These especially vibrant children are less damaged by their sterile environment, and when they are placed in family homes, they quickly make up for lost time. They are not the ones who are carried off by illness or who show the strange eating and spitting-up habits. The fact that such children exist reminds us that the factor of genetics, of the biologically strong as well as the biologically weak, is of enormous consequence. These survivor children tell us that infants have various capabilities to elicit the necessary response from the world at large, and that the baby is by no means simply a blank page on which we write whatever we will.

Infantile Autism: The Baby Who Can't Find a Mother

Autism—severe withdrawal of the infant from the human world—is the most compromising trouble of the mind that we see in any baby before the third year. It occurs in about four out of every ten thousand births and dooms the vast majority of its victims to institutions. It leaves them without the possibility of ever knowing human love and comfort, the pleasure of conversation, the joy of a new idea shared with a friend. No matter how long they may live, many never have a sexual identity; even control of bowel and bladder is rarely achieved. They do not deal with events that take place outside their minds and they do not test and explore or gain in knowledge. They are always prey to inner storms of violent feelings that can sweep over them at any time. The only positive thing to say about this cruel plague is that researchers have learned many important facts about normal development as they studied the bizarre and distraught ways of the autistic. This is, of course, no comfort for the parents of the afflicted child. But in every area where medicine has advanced, there had to be knowledge before there could be a cure. Perhaps in our lifetimes the work of understanding this illness will lead us to a long-awaited method of prevention.

Psychiatrists are still arguing among themselves about the cause of autism. Since it first reveals itself as an inability to notice or respond to the care of the mother, some experts have felt that mothers are at fault, that only an unfeeling or icy mother could have so severely discouraged her child from smiling at her, from reaching for her hands, from crying out to her in pain or hunger. For many years professionals eyed the mothers of these children as if they were among the walking dead. They assumed that it was the mother's failing that she did not bring her child to psychological life. But careful examination of the parents of these children has shown that they are not zombies at all. Often they had first, second, or third babies who not only had no symptoms of disease but became especially fine and capable children. And it was noticed that if a baby is continually unresponsive to its mother, the mother becomes discouraged and then appears to the observer as cold and unfeeling. If the baby shuts out the mother, she will begin to behave in a mechanical way. The fragile web of relationship, the all-important life-nourishing weave of mother and baby, is interrupted in the autistic child, beginning an inexorable process of disease.

Many psychiatrists now take the position, which seems most reasonable to us, that a definite vulnerability, a kind of brain damage must exist in these children at birth. Perhaps in some rare cases this weakness is overcome by expert care and in other cases it is pushed over the edge by a certain coldness or confusion on the part of the mother. Certainly some children under three who suffer from autism have been badly abused or neglected by their mothers. Yet other equally abused infants, while they suffer from many other problems, do not show autism. It would appear then that in the vast majority of sick children the causes of this disease are akin to those that create mental retardation or a missing limb. It was certainly part of our attitude toward women in the first half of this century that we were so willing to blame them for one of the worst catastrophes that could befall a parent.

Infantile autism can be definitely diagnosed after the first twelve months of life. The baby has probably smiled infrequently up to that point and not necessarily at the mother or at any human beings. The baby will not have shown the normal stranger anxiety and will most likely not have developed an attachment to a blanket or a Teddy bear at the usual age of eight or nine months. He will have formed no bond with his mother and will not strive for separateness. He will not have experienced the normal fear of abandonment nor longing for closeness. He will not experience the frustration of wanting to be his own person while wanting to remain attached to his mother. Indeed, all signs of normal struggle are missing in the autistic child.

Physically, he will develop perfectly well, but he will not have passed through the psychological landmarks of the first year of life in a normal way. This baby will rarely if ever cry when hungry or wet. Some parents have discovered that their autistic babies have serious ear infections or other sources of fever only by picking them up and feeling how hot they are. These children do not become irritable with teething and they may not babble at all, or they may babble for a short while, then stop completely. They show very little response to being picked up and held; often they will push away with their arms and feet and pull their heads back or turn away from their mother's voice. They won't play peek-a-boo or pat-a-cake and their expressions remain remote and distant. Parents usually know that something is wrong but they don't know what. Pediatricians may test for deafness and other physical troubles, find nothing, and may prematurely reassure the parent.

In the second year, or toward the end of the first, the baby may start head-banging on the wall or on the end board of his crib. Many of these children develop a nervous and incessant kind of rocking back and forth as if they were going to start crawling, but the rocking becomes a self-soothing device that can go on for hours at a time. When these children walk, they may begin twirling in place, repeatedly making bizarre shaking gestures with their hands. Nobody knows exactly why autistic children rock and twirl and bang their heads. Perhaps it is part of their method of shutting out the real world and controlling their inner chaos.

In the second year of life they may become fiercely attached to certain objects—a toy train, a bottle, a set of beads, a jar of jam— carrying these around with them wherever they go. These things are not used like the familiar blanket or Teddy bear to symbolize the mother's presence. Instead, they come to substitute for the world of people. They further connect the child to the universe of dead things.

It is very difficult to toilet-train autistic children at any age because they are not connected to the parent through a desire to please. They, even more intensely than normal children, view the idea of something going out of their bodies and disappearing down the toilet as a frightening process. They will try to hold on as long as possible and may develop massive constipations, or they will simply blot out the disturbing issues by ignoring their own body signals. Unlike normal children, they cannot gradually correct their fears and misperceptions because they are not involved in the parents' world. They may have very bad insomnia or sleep long hours at strange times. They will not easily be brought into the rhythms of households, of seasons, of human time.

The autistic child usually does not learn to talk. He has no need for language since his communications are not directed toward other people. Isolated, mute, he will scream if overcome with panic because someone has come too close to him, tried to touch him, or brought her face close. These can be terrible, strange screams, reminding us of a trapped and terrified animal.

Some autistic children do briefly develop words at about fifteen months, but usually these rudiments of language are quickly lost, never to reappear again. Language is such a strong biological force that perhaps it erupts in these children naturally only to slide away because it is the servant of communication, the very thing this child wants to avoid. Some children will develop a form of language called echolalia. This means that they will repeat the last few words of your sentence after you. They may say words that they hear other people saying, but not in proper context or with the normal rhythms or inflection, but rather flattened out, senseless, as if language were no more than the sound of a phonograph needle scratching on the turntable.

Very often these extremely damaged children will show an interest in music, and some mothers and therapists have found that the child can be better managed and brought through the necessary routines of the day when music is used as the major means of reaching him or her. Some few later develop an amazing capacity to deal with numbers. They may be able to tell you the exact day of the week a certain event fell on forty-eight years ago, or the number of hours it would take to reach an asteroid moving at a particular rate through the cosmos. This fantastic mathematical skill is unfortunately not used for creative or communicative purposes; rather, it ends up in walls of numbers that are used to protect the child from the universe of feelings.

As the autistic child grows older and larger, he becomes less and less manageable. His strangeness increasingly embarrasses and disturbs the rest of the family. Therapists have been able to reach through the remoteness of the child and there are now special nursery schools that work with such children. They know many techniques that can improve their behavior and draw some of them back toward the human community. Unfortunately, those in whom the forward progress remains steady are few. Most slip back into their own minds at the signs of the simplest frustration or the mildest of illnesses or fevers. These children can on occasion become aggressive and rageful, blindly striking out at whatever human or inhuman objects are in the way. They may chew their own lips till they require stitches; indeed, they may harm themselves in a thousand ways.

There are special schools in most large communities where these children can be treated. Most experts in the field believe that if the diagnosis is made early, in the first year and one half of life, there is a better chance of at least a partial recovery. At present there are no grand breakthroughs. Although there are claims from time to time that vitamin therapy or discipline therapy will work wonders, we are at this moment mostly defeated by the illness. The major advances in our knowledge of brain chemistry that have been made during the last twenty years may one day lead us to a way of curing or preventing this disease.

For now we must recognize the havoc and severe pain the existence of such a child causes the family. Parents will tend to blame themselves, even if the professionals have backed off. Each parent will suspect his own genes and those of the spouse. There will always linger a suspicion that somehow this baby was failed by his mother in the first few weeks of life. This guilt and blame can cause trouble in a marriage, and have a dismal effect on how other children in the family view themselves and their parents. The birth of an autistic child wrecks the family dream, making parents feel weak and helpless and unworthy. They find themselves in mourning for a child who is still alive. They experience great anger and disappointment in the child and that anger causes them even more guilt.

Some families are faced with the absolute necessity of institutionalizing their child because he or she has become so self-destructive— head-banging until the bone on the skull is exposed, or apt to crash through windows or harm other children. In these cases the decision to put the child in an institution is painful, but the guilt of abandonment is eased by the clear lack of choice.

For other families there is a gray kind of choice. The child will improve some, then slip back. He may not harm himself but may be so passive and withdrawn that it seems as if he notices nothing, receives no pleasure from anything. Yet he may permit only his mother or father to change his diapers or lead him to the table. This bare touch of dependence further aggravates the parents' guilt and terror if they should choose to institutionalize their child. But if he stays, the sick child may begin to absorb so much of the family's attention and resources that the other children start to show symptoms of deprivation.

No one can or should tell a parent when to give up, or whether or not to give up. These are private decisions that are forged in the marital furnace and are not made overnight. There is no doubt that the birth of an autistic child scars everyone in the family, and that all our greatest strengths are needed to regain our basic trust and faith in the goodness of the world. This is not the only one of nature's cruelties, but because it affects the mind and not the body it frightens us particularly. No matter how sane we are, thoughts of demons haunt us.

Although these tragic children underline for us the importance of the first attachments in infancy and show us what we would be without them, it is important to remember that 99.9 percent of parents have non-autistic children. The odds are overwhelming that any particular set of parents will never have such a baby or even hear of or know anyone who does. The horror of this illness is fortunately matched by its rarity.

Mental Retardation: The Child with a Limited Mind

Mental retardation is a wide category ranging from mild to severe. Somewhere on that line is a division between those who will be able to achieve an independent life, working and taking care of their personal needs, and those who must be watched over all their lives. Those with moderate to mild retardation will test out with I.Q.s from 52 to 85. The most severely damaged will have I.Q.s that slip down below 50 and sink under 20, where no testing is possible. These cold figures are not so exact as we would like to think, yet they do draw certain broad pictures that are reasonably reliable.

Almost all of the most severely brain-diseased children will show some kind of physical deformity as well; the mental damage will be only a part of the miserable distortion of mind and body that genetic defects have caused. Many of the milder forms of retardation are not picked up until the child starts school, and this group of children will appear physically average in every respect. However, the tasks of learning to read, to add and subtract, to remember the contents of a storybook or a lesson are next to impossible for children with I.Q.s of 50 to 70, and very difficult for those whose I.Q.s range from 70 to 85. Some children with normal or superior intelligence levels also have trouble learning to use numbers and letters; they have special problems that are not related to mental retardation. Therefore mental retardation cannot be assumed on the basis of learning problems alone. We have excellent testing methods to distinguish the child who suffers from retardation from the one whose difficulties are confined to the learning areas.

Severely retarded children may have cerebral palsy and they may also be blind or deaf. They may have been born with an opening in the spine as well as an imperfect heart, esophagus, or bone structure. They may have chromosomal defects and other damage. They may have hydrocephalus, which means fluid pressing on the brain, causing a marked loss of rational thought and mental activity. They may suffer from microcephalus, which means having a tiny brain that has not grown in the womb and does not have the capacity for normal growth. Small brain size is an indication that mental equipment is limited. Such severe birth defects are very rare, fewer than one in ten thousand births, and any given parent has only an infinitesimal chance of having such a child. However, these organically savaged children are born to parents of every social class and appear in all populations of the world with about the same frequency. Nature makes no patriotic or class distinctions in its gross errors.

Roughly 37 out of every 100,000 babies are born with Down's syndrome. Down's syndrome children are identified at birth because they are born with particular faces. Their eyes appear slanted and their noses may be flat and close to their lips. They have a particular kind of stubby fingers. Intelligence in these children can range from the most severely impaired to those that hover in the low 80's. Such children are known to be especially friendly and good-natured, but the innocence that they retain costs them everything in achievement and independence. Because of their distinctive looks they may always remain outside the boundaries of normal society.

Babies pass the significant milestones at varied times and some completely healthy children move more slowly in one area or another than their age mates. Only the mentally retarded child moves at a slower pace in *all* areas of maturation. He can be identified only by looking at his entire history. The normal baby will smile some time between three weeks and three months. He will be sitting up by six or seven months. He will start to crawl anywhere from four months to ten months. He will stand and walk somewhere between eleven to sixteen months. He will begin babbling around five to six months and will begin using single words some time between twelve or eighteen months.

The retarded child will be consistently behind in all endeavors. He will achieve these landmarks but at an older age than others. The pediatrician will have noticed by a year that this baby is lagging in all aspects of his growth. Sometimes neglect or illness can slow a child down. The effect of this on the baby can often be reversed and such a child, given good care, can catch up. But organic mental retardation cannot be cured or erased by excellent or special care. Its presence becomes increasingly clear as the baby reaches a year and a half and his development still is delayed in all areas.

It is now estimated that about 3 percent of the entire population of the United States has an I.Q. under 70. One percent of the population (about two million) has been officially labeled retarded. Among them are many more males than females, probably because the male is biologically the weaker sex. While we spend vast sums of money in research looking for causes and prevention, and though we know a great deal about genes and how they transmit their messages, we are not yet at the point where the mystery of why or how appears solvable.

However, scientists have within the last decade been able to identify a fetus with Down's syndrome in the womb by testing the mother's amniotic fluid. Since mothers over the age of thirty-five are at an increased statistical risk of having a Down's syndrome child, many of them are now routinely tested. If a damaged child is identified while still in the womb, the mother must face the choice of whether to bring the child to birth or not. These are private and sometimes religious decisions. But this test does provide the opportunity for many woman to prevent the birth of a damaged baby and to conceive a normal child at a later time. We expect that the incidence of Down's syndrome births will decrease in the years to come.

Seventy-five percent of the group of people labeled retarded fall into the category of sociocultural deprivation. This is a fancy way of saying that there is nothing apparently wrong with their brains. But the chaos and disorder of their homes, the silence of overworked or depressed parents, or the level of potential violence in their homes has produced children who, when they appear at school looking physically perfectly normal, have serious trouble in the kind of thinking required in a classroom. Their I.Q.s may range from 52 to 85 and they may be placed in classes for slow learners. It appears that they cannot make up developmental deficits that occurred during the first three years, when other children were exercising their minds in talking to their parents and absorbing fact after fact about the goings-on in the world.

These children may not have been given toys that helped them understand *big* and *little, in* and *out, up* and *down.* Often they have spent hours in front of the television set instead of playing outside or with other children. These are the mentally deprived who have often been permanently locked into poverty by the time they are three years old. With the school failure and the stigma of being labeled a "dummy," many of these children develop social problems and become difficult to control and eventually delinquent. Risk of mild retardation is fifteen times greater for poor and minority children than for those coming from middle-class suburbs. Some of this is due to the poor nutrition and inadequate prenatal care in our inner cities, causing low birth weight and other problems. Some of it is due to the effects of drug and alcohol abuse by the mother. Some of it is caused by chaotic and unloving homes where loss and change of place and person are frequent.

However, some of our statistics on school-age children who are labeled slow learners or mildly retarded might be mistakes caused by language problems, or by the difference between the kind of knowledge a child from the inner city may have garnered and the expectations of a middle-class school system. It is certainly likely that some of those labeled retarded are the victims of cultural confusions. Their potential would be normal if we could learn to identify these children and help them.

For all kinds of mild social retardation we are not as helpless as we are in combating the kind that has arisen through organic causes. We can reach into the families of those at risk for mild retardation. We can increase our prenatal counseling for pregnant teenagers, who are particularly apt to be undernourished or abusing drugs or alcohol.

We can work to correct our cultural, social, and economic inequalities. There is, however, no social remedy for the biologically retarded. Many communities now have infant centers where specialists provide extra stimulation and education for the retarded baby. These early interventions are valuable and often make it possible for an organically damaged baby to live comfortably at home and achieve a level of functioning beyond what might otherwise have been expected.

All of those whose I.Q.s fall below 50 will need intensive care throughout their lives. In the days before antibiotics, most of them died before they were five years old since they were far more prone to serious illness than the normal child. Now they can continue to live an almost normal life span. Most all of these children will be cared for throughout their days in an institution. This need not raise pictures of horror in parents' minds. Parent groups are fighting to improve the care where it still rests in the muddy backwaters of the nineteenth century. Many locations around the country now have decent, humane care for the severely and moderately retarded. Of course, some of these are children who experience life almost as if they were vegetables, with sensations of wet, cold, hunger dominating their mental life. Others will have desires for love, sex, and freedom that cannot be met in an institution, and others, again, rock themselves constantly, withdrawing to places in their minds where they cannot be hurt or disappointed. Some will struggle for years to learn to tie a shoe, to do a simple puzzle, to make a friend; these accomplishments achieved, they will feel proud and happy. If we don't think being like everyone else is the only hallmark of happiness, we can see that for at least some of these children life can be well worth living. Those of us who gain pleasure from the execution of a complicated recipe or the workings of a micro-chip know all too well that happiness is not guaranteed by intelligence.

To say that is not to cover up or deny the intense pain and the depth of the wound experienced by parents whose children are born with severe retardation or those whose children appear at school age to be unequal to their peers. We view our children as extensions of ourselves, as part of our own sense of worth. The parents of a mentally retarded child, given the information just hours after the delivery, will have been dealt a crippling blow to their self-love and to their expectations of success in this world. Frequently, the mother will be blamed and will blame herself for something she may have done or not done during pregnancy. Parents will blame their physician, the hospital, or the in-laws.

The knowledge that a child cannot take his expected place in the human community, cannot reproduce, cannot learn to love Mozart or Emily Dickinson, or the Rangers or the Yankees, or fly-casting or mountain climbing, is a reasonable cause for deep and long sadness.

Parents tend to deny the diagnosis. They go from doctor to doctor trying to get a more optimistic view of their child. They suffer from social shame, wanting to hide the bad news they are unable to digest themselves. They may withdraw from family and friends just at a time when they need them most. The parents of infants labeled mentally retarded appear at their pediatrician's office repeatedly with minor and hypochondriacal complaints about the child's physical condition. What they really want is for the doctor to cure the baby's mind—and that he cannot do.

Parents of retarded children carry the secondary burden of guilt that arises as they begin to wish the child had never been born, would die or magically disappear. This is a perfectly normal wish under the circumstances, arising out of the anger, frustration, and disappointment they are experiencing. These awful feelings grow as the months turn into years. The burden of this kind of child, who will have trouble in toilet training or in self-feeding and who will present so many obstacles to the freedom of the mother and father, mounts and mounts. Many parents resist the advice of pediatricians and psychiatrists to place their baby in an institution. They become protective and convinced that only their own vigilance saves the life of the child. This is in part the effect of their guilt. Guilt, or their own anger at the child, can turn into its opposite and appear as total devotion, even irrational devotion.

Parents will arrive at the decision to institutionalize a child only slowly and at the right moment for them. In order for the mother to be able to release her child, she must have begun to come to terms with the guilt she feels at wishing to be free of him or her. She will have to have at least begun to mourn for her child in her own way, without the help of ritual, religion, neighbors, or family. More and more families are now beginning to live with their moderately retarded children. This of course does not solve their problem of what to do with the child when they themselves die; but many parents have found it possible to absorb the disappointment, to survive the guilt their own angers provoke, and to love and care for their damaged child, finding pride and pleasure in the human connection they have made.

This is a less selfish, perhaps purer kind of parenting than any other, and while it would be nobody's choice it marks an incredible achievement in human love and caring. Many families find themselves strengthened through the struggle they have made to accept and care for their child. They find a value in the life of their child that offers them rich reward. Although intelligence itself does not substantially improve with time, we are awed by the good quality of life in a moderately retarded child who is supported with loving care. In a bad institution where no personal attention is offered, the small sparks of mind the child has are quickly extinguished.

Mild retardation has different effects on different families. In high-achieving college-educated parents, it can be a severe disappointment and cause for major worry and grief. In a family where expectations of academic success are less and the environment offers warmth and reward for other activities, the diagnosis can mean very little. If the child is not humiliated in school and can manage reasonably well with peers, the distinction of the retardation may pass the minute the child leaves school at age sixteen.

For middle-class families with a mildly retarded child, the task is to overcome the initial disappointment and to find in this child the special and distinct qualities of self that are valuable and precious, to abandon plans to achieve glory through the accomplishments of this child and help him to find a place in the world where he can be content and function well. None of this is easy. Anger and guilt come along to make the process harder. This child is vulnerable to all the other emotional ills that his difference from others may provoke. It may be hard to deal with the child's own awareness of his incapacity as compared to his parents and siblings. He may need a great deal of help to respect and like himself. The parents can accomplish this by providing their child with the right school, where he will be with others like himself and where he will learn the social skills to get along with his age mates. Parents can also make it clear that their respect for the child is real and that they feel proud of what he has learned and overcome.

Parents have to be careful not to overprotect their mildly retarded child, thus not allowing him the opportunity to stretch and grow where it is possible. They have to make a special effort to help him find ways to like himself. This one will love animals, that one will love to paint, a third will be content fishing, and another will find happiness in learning to sew or decorate a cake. The important thing is that the parents accept their own child, come to terms with the deficit. This will help the child accept himself and it will determine the attitude of brothers and sisters toward their less biologically favored sibling.

The birth of a retarded child presents parents with a challenge to love a possibly unlovable or unrewarding human being, one who needs care way beyond the time when most children will be seeking independence. How parents meet this challenge, how they overcome their own sadness, and what they make of their lives and their children's lives is the forge in which their courage and humanity are fired.

The Clinging Child

All small children cling to their mothers, sometimes crying when they try to leave the room or the house. When children are ill, or over-tired, or have just had a new experience, they may become particularly clinging for a few days. A move to a new house or a new city or even a summer vacation may provoke some hanging on, some whining, some following of mother about from room to room. A new play group, a barbershop, a doctor's office, all strange places with unfamiliar faces are very apt to make a child grasp his mother's hand or climb insistently into her lap. This is quite normal, part of the ups and downs of the child's ongoing battle to be simultaneously cared for and independent.

However, some children show a severe disturbance around the separation issue. They are children who will after a year of age protest violently if their mothers try to leave them with babysitters or relatives. If they feel their mother preparing to go out of the house, they may begin to wail, to hold on to her knees. They express such pain that the mother becomes so disturbed and upset herself, she may decide not to go on her errand or meet her friend for lunch after all.

Many of these children will be seen holding onto their mother's hands long after they have the physical capacity to stand and walk alone. While other babies at eighteen months or so will begin to explore the far corners of a room, checking back only from time to time on the whereabouts of their parent, these babies will tend to stay by their mother's side. They will smile for her; they will play all sorts of games with her, but they will not show any interest in other adults, in other children, or in toys that are at some distance from the mother's place. They may not even be relaxed or easy with their fathers. They will develop perfectly normal speech and they will enjoy communicating with words, but only to their mothers. They may be totally mute with strangers, and if they have been left with a babysitter, even a familiar one, sometimes even the father, they may not move or speak at all but will whimper or cry or lie still staring at the door at which they last saw their mother standing. Even if they are toilet-trained, they will wet and soil themselves, reverting to all the baby ways they may have given up. These toddlers may not have learned to use the Teddy bear or the favorite blanket to tide them through the mother's absences. They simply must have the real mother in their sight in order to be reassured that all is well in their world and that they are not being abandoned.

Nighttime is always especially hard for such children: the struggle over going to bed can become extremely unpleasant for both mother and baby. The usual bedtime rituals of cookie and story and bottle and extra attention may not relieve these children from the anxiety they feel over the threat of being alone. These are children who have trouble in starting the work of being a separate person. They have trouble holding on to the image of their mothers in their minds. When she is gone from their sight, they feel a great rage which further frightens them. They are angry at that very mother they need so desperately and they are afraid that somehow their own anger will destroy or harm her.

No wonder these children have anxious expressions and hold their bodies in a tense way. Other toddlers at a year and a half to three are learning to spend increasingly long periods of time without their mother's direct attention. They will of course return to her to show her what they are doing; they will come to lean on her when tired or hungry or in a struggle with another child over a toy; but they are pushing to do things on their own and to take over more and more of their body care for themselves. They will try to wash their faces and brush their hair and will often push away a hovering mother. For children who are suffering from an extreme fear of separation, however, these learning tasks represent threats to the closeness they have achieved with their mother, and so they will resist them as long as they possibly can.

Eventually, these children will stop screaming when mother leaves and begin to accept the fact that they cannot have their parent with them all the time; but the work of becoming a separate person will not have properly begun. When they enter nursery school, they may be especially shy and unable to play with other children on an appropriate level. They will not have a strong sense of themselves without the reinforcement of their mother's approval, and so they will be less adventurous, both physically and intellectually, than the child who has negotiated the separation from his mother with greater ease. Psychiatrists are concerned about these children and their parents. They feel that this disturbance when it is extreme marks a weakness in the psychological structure of the child that may reappear in adolescence as a serious mental illness, causing the young person to lose a sense of reality and his place in it.

The clinging and dependent child was not born that way. It seems these children are created by mothers who were too attached to their own mothers, or for other reasons are extremely overprotective and anxious about the well-being of their babies. Sometimes a physical illness can start this process, creating a situation in which the time for the child to begin his independent journey passed and was never picked up again. Sometimes these mothers feel two ways about their children. They love them, of course, but they also resent them and carry more than the usual anger toward them for their demandingness and helplessness. This mixture of anger and love sometimes comes out as an overprotectiveness, an over-closeness that blocks the baby from being a separate person in his own right. The baby, sensing the mother's hidden anger, will become all the more frightened of being abandoned and will increase his clinging and his babyishness in order to hold on to what he fears will slip away from him.

The kind of child caught in this struggle is apt to have either constipation or loose bowels. He may have very frequent nightmares as he approaches three and he will wake many times during the night because of his fear of being left alone forever. If a psychiatrist should see this child, work would be done to help the mother encourage separateness and help her to explore what her feelings are toward herself and her baby that have made it so hard for him to exist independently. The sticky glue of their relationship must dissolve before the child will be able to proceed.

If a mother notices that her child seems unusually unwilling to let her go out, or if clinging behavior persists over a long period of time and doesn't subside when the child is used to the place and people around him, it would be a good idea for both parents to sit down with each other and think of ways that the father can become more involved with the child. Father's care promotes independence and growth. The mother can encourage the child's independence, perhaps by pushing him to do more things such as washing or dressing himself. Parents can check their methods of discipline to see if they are being too harsh and provoking excessive anger and fear in the child. They can see if they are expecting too much from their toddler by way of learning or physical expertise. Perhaps the child is afraid of losing parental love by not learning fast enough or performing well enough. Parents can also check to see if their own fears of the world are out of control.

Sometimes a mother is anxious and timid herself and communicates her fears to her child. While there are no courses given in bravery, it is important that mothers fight against their own irrational fears. The first step in doing that is recognizing them. Some mothers of clinging children should increase their activities outside of the home. It is important for the child that the mother not make the child her only source of pleasure. This, too, can lead to a child's fear of leaving the mother. It may be that this child has been rushed in toilet training and hurried through the earlier stages of life. If this has produced a clinging two-and-a-half-year-old, parents can try to relax a little and let the child resume some baby ways—the pacifier, the bottle, messing with food—in order to give him strength to leave his mother's side after a while.

Parents should also talk with each other about possible hidden or open marital discord. Children are very apt to sense the tension in the household and react by holding onto their mother even more tightly. The parents can also evaluate their way of living. Perhaps they have moved around four or five times since the baby's birth, or perhaps they have left her too often with a grandparent or changing housekeepers. If they then stay in one place with their child for a while, the clinging behavior will in all likelihood subside after some months. Children have great recuperative powers, and if parents pay attention to the causes of the clinging, most children will be able to gather their strength together and begin their journey forward again.

Male and Female: Early Confusions

There is no doubt that we treat boy babies differently from girl babies from the very first moment that we learn the sex of our children. Cultural expectations of what a boy should be and what a girl should be explain our different ways of handling the infant in blue and the infant in pink. Even so, there may well be biological explanations for the separating developmental paths that we begin to see emerging after the first year and a half of life. For the moment, we will have to assume that both culture and nature play a role in creating a sexual identity for the young child. We are not talking about girls learning passivity and maternal roles and boys learning action, aggression, and dominance. Those seem clearly to be limitations created by focusing the cultural lens in just one way. We are concerned with the biological facts of life and the obvious need for each child to claim a sexual identity, to come to enjoy and appreciate his or her sexual parts and sexuality.

The child must develop a capacity for receiving and giving sexual pleasure and feeling comfortable with the male and female role in biological functioning. That really means for children, even very young children, that they must negotiate the sometimes complicated and sometimes alarming sexual feelings within themselves. They must grow to understand what male and female mean, and to take their rightful place in these most basic and crucial of human categories. Sexual identity and sexual capacity for adult genital love have their roots in the first three years of life, and the good quality of this development depends on how the child manages the separation issues of the early years. It is in this period that we can see the initial signs of sexual disruption and sexual identity problems.

As we've seen, at about sixteen to eighteen months most children will discover the genitals of the opposite sex. Because they have already learned through touching and rubbing that the area of the penis or the vagina offers special sensations and the promise of comfort, all children respond to the observation of sexual difference with some signs of confusion and concern. For the little girl, the observation may prompt a short period of feeling frightened and angry. She may feel that she is missing something, that she is more vulnerable to further loss, and that her body may not be dependable, firm and strong as another's. Little girls under two have been seen to stuff their diapers with cotton, to place sticks between their legs, and to become for a brief time afraid of going to sleep alone, of using the toilet, or leaving their mothers. For most children this is a short passing disturbance that comes about as the child struggles initially to understand the sexual difference. They will emerge from this cloud knowing that they are girls. Little girls will know that they are like their mothers, not like their fathers, and that this is a fact of life. They will turn to their fathers in a new way, and they will begin to play at being mothers and women. This does not mean that they must play at being secretaries rather than bosses or that they must be nurses rather than doctors—that is just the mischief of a rigid culture. But by two and a half, most little girls will have secured a sexual identity based not only on other people calling them girls, but more profoundly on their own understanding of biological reality.

For the little boy, the observation of the girl's vagina causes a kind of fright. What happened? Where did the penis go? Could I lose this penis that I am just becoming so fond of—that feels good to touch and that tells me I am in one piece? Intellectual explanations for the little boy don't quite answer his concerns, and he is apt to just pretend he never saw a vagina and doesn't want to hear anything more about it. He may show an increased interest in his father and he may begin to imitate him. By two and a half, he also will have a strong sense of himself as a boy. His climbing, running, dashing-about activities will increase as he assures himself that he is whole, intact, that nothing has happened to change his status as a boy, and that he still has his wonderful-feeling penis. This is the way it normally goes. But for children who, for example, have experienced a severe illness that threatens their good feelings about their bodies, the path may be more difficult. Some children have been given enemas or had many needles placed in their arms or suffered other painful medical procedures. These interferences with a child's sense of control over his own body and his own ability to defend himself from pain or assault leave him vulnerable to sexual confusions when he first realizes that boys and girls are different. For those children whose mothers have not been able to give them a strong enough sense of being a separate person, the discovery of the sexual difference at about sixteen to eighteen months can provoke a severe reaction that signals a major problem in forming a positive, unshakable sexual identity.

Tommy is a little boy of seventeen months whose parents fought bitterly after his birth. Soon, his father left the home and has since lost contact with the family. His mother was understandably under a great deal of pressure during this time to overcome her own sense of failure and fear for her future. She took as good care of Tommy as possible but did have to leave him frequently with different baby-sitters and relatives as she looked for work and a place to live. Tommy was an alert but unsmiling baby, who stayed close to his mother when she was there and he looked for her constantly, interrupting whatever other things he might be doing to reassure himself that he was still in her company.

One afternoon, he was left with a friend of hers who was the mother of a little girl just a few months older than Tommy. This mother bathed the children together before giving them supper. That night Tommy woke several times crying out for his mother. The next day, when he found a broken crayon in his box, he burst into tears and was inconsolable until his mother replaced the crayon with a new one. In the months that followed, Tommy became excessively fearful of any small cut or scrape, and he would scream for long periods of time if he were bumped against or if he accidentally fell. His sleep continued to be fitful; he began to eat poorly and to refuse foods that were cut up into little pieces. When the eye of his stuffed elephant fell off, he went into a panic that was resolved only when his mother sewed a new eye on the toy. He touched his penis constantly and insisted on holding himself when in public places. His mother's attempts to discourage him from rubbing himself were of no avail. He was afraid of trucks backfiring, airplanes passing overhead. He spent hours in the bathroom flushing the toilet although he himself now refused to use the potty at all.

Tommy was showing a set of symptoms that we see only in those children who have extraordinary difficulty in accepting the fact that women are made differently from men. They see the absence of the penis as a threat: "If it could be gone from anyone, then I could lose it too." They are so concerned with the fear of losing something or someone important to them that the penis gets caught up in this drama of being a separate self that may be lost or abandoned. The divorce, which meant the loss of his father, and his mother's subsequent difficulties, which made it hard for her to respond to him when she was needed, made Tommy vulnerable to all those peculiar and inaccurate responses to seeing the difference between the sexes. It was hard for him to be a secure male. Further difficulties can occur as he grows older and his sexual feelings naturally increase.

If these signs of severe reaction to the sight of the vagina appear in a little boy, the best approach a mother can take is to reassure her child frequently that boys and girls were meant to be different, and that girls have not lost a penis but are simply formed in another way. It would help if the father or grandfather, brother or male friend can be brought in to spend some time with the child. The mother can say over and over again while bathing the child or while looking with him at a doll, "Parts of the body don't come off." Mothers can try to keep their sons' exposure to their own nude bodies or those of little girls to the absolute minimum for a while. If the mother has made the child feel guilty about touching his penis, she can reassure him that this is fine in private and that she knows it feels good to him and that is perfectly all right with her. If her discipline has been harsh, she can try to give her son more approval and not frighten him with his "badness."

Some little girls also have trouble understanding the difference between the sexes. Girls whose first year and a half has been tumultuous may have particular difficulty. Their capacity to move away from their mother may have been limited by illness or some unhappiness in the home. When a troubled girl observes that the little boy has something she does not, she feels deeply insulted. She often reacts by denying what she has seen. If she is talking, she may in fact say, "I am a boy. I am not a girl." She will show the same fear of broken objects that Tommy did. She may also lose control of bowel or bladder training. She may show severe sleep disturbance and will not begin the kind of creative play that we normally expect in little girls at this time. She may not pretend to be a mother, dress up, or in other ways imitate the adult world. These little girls, who can't accept that women are endowed with treasures that are not apparent to the naked eye, will also masturbate frequently and in public. They may show further sexual difficulty when they pass on to the next stage of development since their female identity has not been firmly planted.

It is easy to understand that a child who has been hospitalized and separated from her mother may have a specially hard time over this question of the anatomical difference between the sexes. Children must have a sense of safety as they move away from their mothers. They must have a sense of being physically intact and admired in order to negotiate over the puzzling and understandably confusing fact that little girls appear to be missing something that is of importance. Children think in terms of things that you can see and touch. They see that pieces of the stuffed dog come off. They see that crayons break in two. They see that clothes come off their backs, hair is cut, nails are cut, B.M.s come out and disappear. They are just not certain what is attached to them and what is not.

This is all part of the normal discoveries of the first two to three years. The difference between male and female can be caught up in the drama of striving to be whole, or fearing that one might come apart. Sexual identity is a complicated matter: if the early stages do not go well, they promise trouble for the next years. However, children do have a capacity to correct and undo, and the erotic force within children and the life developments that greet them as they move out of babyhood can alter directions taken. Their sexual identity can become secure at a later time. If a mother sees signs of such a sharp reaction to the discovery of the difference between the sexes, she can help by reassuring her daughter over and over again that she is made just the right way. Daily life should be made as secure as possible, with minimal changes and separations. Her father can help by admiring her for being a little girl, like his wife. If he spends more time with his girl child, this will drain away some of her anger at her mother, who has disappointed her by not giving her the body she would have wanted. She should be reassured over and over again that her parents wanted a little girl and all little girls have vaginas, not penises. This is perhaps the time to buy her a special doll that she can mother. Be certain that she is not greeted with too much harshness or disapproval as she expresses her anger and her bad feelings.

For some very small group of children, sexual identity seems to be firm and innate and yet biologically wrong. That is to say, these children will be convinced that they are girls or boys even though they are in the body of the other sex. They simply don't accept the physical evidence of their bodies. For some, this may be the result of a strong wish by a parent to have a child of a different sex. For other children, we have no explanation for their absolute and unshakable conviction that they are boys in girls' bodies or girls in boys' bodies. This is a puzzling psychological condition known as transsexuality: we will discuss it further in the chapters that concern older children.

Before Freud, society believed that children were innocent of sexual thoughts and experiences. We now know that the mysteries of sexual problems have their origins in the first years of life. The beginning steps we take to claim our selves as people include sexual definition. The toddler who cannot yet tie her shoes or make his bed struggles with the ideas of male and female—what are they and what am I. By three the vast majority of children will be moving forward toward a comfortable sexual identity.

Bowel Problems

We first see disturbances in the bowels in the early months of life. Some babies will be constipated without any physical cause. Babies can show considerable straining with their bowel movements; they may go several days without a movement. These difficulties will continue despite change in diet. Obviously this is a matter of concern because the baby is acutely uncomfortable. In some few cases the pediatrician will find anatomical problems that cause the difficulty, and these require specific medical intervention. Many babies will outgrow this tendency toward constipation and stool softeners often help. Some few babies continue to have trouble for long periods of time.

We have found that when mothers and babies are having trouble connecting well with each other, sometimes the very young baby will resist releasing her stool. At about nine months to a year and a half, when all children express anger toward their mothers, some babies who have experienced extraordinary pain or neglect will feel a great rage toward their parent. This anger is unacceptable to both the parent and the child. Often we see such infants hiding their anger inside their bodies by developing constipations that are long standing and resistant to most medications.

Some time around eighteen months we again see a new group of constipations or diarrheas. These appear in children who have reacted strongly to the sight of the opposite sex. They are children who are suddenly concerned about losing a part of their own bodies. This is more common in girls than in boys. Such children may shift attention away from the genital area by developing bowel disturbances. They may hold on to their stool fiercely as it becomes a symbolic body part. These bowel disturbances will pass as the child adjusts to the biological differences between the sexes and begins between two and three to accept the facts of anatomy. For children whose sexual identity is in question, and who continue to be alarmed at the male and female difference, bowel problems may persist or flare up again intermittently.

We also see bowel disturbances in children at the time that parents have begun toilet training. The child who is fighting to hold on to his stool may easily become constipated. Diarrheas also occur as children allow their bowels to express their reluctance or their fear of the whole toileting process. These disturbances will pass as the child accepts the separation of the bowel movement from his body with increasing calm and as his fight for independence moves on to other arenas. Parents whose toddlers are experiencing repeated bouts of constipation may want to see if perhaps they have been too harsh and forceful in their insistence on cleanliness. Perhaps it would be a good idea for a parent to back off for a while and let the child soil as he wishes. In time the child can be led again, perhaps more gently, to the toilet.

Constipation and diarrhea can become a part of a child's daily life from stress and conflict caused by the birth of a sibling, the loss of a parent through divorce or death, or other sources of unhappiness. The bowels in young children easily reflect tension and anger. Sometimes a child will become constipated when entering nursery school or if some problem with other children arises there. Sometimes children will develop diarrhea if they have been punished or scolded severely and have felt helpless and betrayed. All these bowel disturbances are usually temporary. However, if bowel problems continue over a long period of time and do not respond either to medical treatment or to a change in toileting demands, we would suggest that a psychiatric consultation may be helpful. The bowels are a sensitive area that can express troubles in the whole developmental picture. A psychiatrist may find a way to bring the mother and child closer together to end these difficulties, as well as the others that will likely follow.

Many children will begin soiling again temporarily after the birth of a sibling or with a separation or an illness. This is of no concern. Some few children seem to lose control completely and are unable to regain it. If three or four months have passed and a parent cannot restore a child's control, it would be a good idea to seek help from a pediatrician or a child psychiatrist. It is possible that the loss of achieved control signals some serious trouble.

The Hyperactive Child

The child who can't sit still, who moves frantically from one activity to another, is, unless helped, headed for severe difficulties in school and is certain to have problems with friends, with parents, and with teachers. Despite punishment and scoldings such children seem unable to control their sudden angers, their impulsive movements. At home and at school they always seem to be in a fight with someone. They are forever tipping over the milk or scattering the pieces of a game into the four corners of the room. If you refuse them a second candy bar, they are apt to scream. If you try to read them a story, they squirm and jiggle and bang their feet together. Other children are always mad at them because they knock over the blocks and grab for toys they want, and they cry and yell if they don't get their way.

Even under the age of three, we can see the hyperactive child having trouble learning numbers or letters or sequences in a puzzle that other children of his age may do quite easily. It is as if inside their minds there is a restless ocean always crashing on the shore. These children, long after the appropriate baby stage, will finger objects and put everything from nails to toy cars in their mouths; they will be dirty and unkempt even by the standards of the sandbox. They seem to be distracted by every small sound or movement in the room. They may have great difficulty sleeping and will have nightmares and fears of catastrophe occurring in their family. These children are hard to like and they dislike themselves. They have heard so often, "Billy is a bad boy," that they have probably come to believe it. Such bad feelings lead to further despair and further bad behavior. The child feels helpless to control himself, and angry at all those who have made him feel guilty and worthless.

We used to think that these were just the rotten apples in our barrel, but now we have learned that these children are easily distracted and cannot control themselves. We do not know the causes, but we do know that stimulants, medicines that are meant in adults to awaken and increase activity, do seem to have the opposite effect on these children. These medicines have been used on children as young as three. They are most commonly used in school-age children who may be calmed down so dramatically that many of them can learn and listen and settle into normal life. If a child at three is irritable, distractable, and in constant motion, parents should contact their family physician.

Hyperactivity subsides naturally to some degree as children reach their adolescence, but by then they will often have been classified as non-learners. They will have developed so few controls over their angers and their moods that they will have patterns of relating to people and expectations of themselves that can be extremely destructive. They will not have practiced concentrating and their skills will be way below those that our society expects.

Many of these children are now identified and brought to therapists as they fail in the task of adjusting to the initial school years. The medicines available and the advice and help to families struggling with these different stormy children have proved effective. These children, whose intelligence and potential range from normal to superior, can then find their way back into a harmonious relationship with teachers, friends, and parents.

Hyperactivity is an illness that appears six times more often in males than in females. Estimates of teachers around the country would place the incidence of hyperactivity at about 4 to 5 percent of the school-age population. It is twice as likely to appear in a minority male child than in one from the middle-class, but the more affluent child is more likely to appear troubled to his parents and teachers and will be far more likely to receive the necessary medical help.

The child with hyperactivity is usually recognized only at around age six, as the increasing difference between him and his peers becomes obvious to parents and teachers. But this illness is identifiable as early as age two, and there are many advantages to discovering it then. This child will learn to walk at the usual age but will almost immediately begin to run about. At two years he will have many more accidents than his age mates and will seem to be unable to avoid bumping into other children or inanimate objects. He will constantly be putting things into his mouth long after the other toddlers have abandoned this method of exploring. He will have a hard time sleeping, and his mood will be fretful, irritable, and anxious more often than not. He will have trouble settling down into a lap for a story or to listen to a record. He will not be interested in puzzles or in sustained play such as putting things into containers and taking them out. He will begin these activities but then will quickly be distracted by something else.

It is not that he will always be into everything as all toddlers are; it is rather that his activities will continue until he drops from exhaustion. He will not be able to use the bath or the nap to refuel himself but may continue to dash about all day. He will have trouble remembering the "No," and will repeatedly pull on the lamp cord or knock over his brother's blocks. The difference between this child and a normally active one is in the unfocused activity and the distractibility.

Mothers of hyperactive children often report that as babies they were difficult, tense, hard to comfort, and always moving about. They kicked more in the womb, they turned over early, they moved their arms and legs while being breast- or bottle-fed. They stiffened up when being held and squirmed around in the mother's lap. If we can identify such toddlers before they get into school, parents can through understanding prevent some of the sad effects of this illness on the child's sense of self-esteem. Such children need especially strong structures around them. That means they need predictability. Routines should be the same each day. What they are required to do at mealtimes should be the same at each meal. Outings and adventures should be kept short and to the minimum. The hyperactive child does not tolerate change or excitement very well. Parents who understand the special problems their child is experiencing within his own stormy mind are better able to create the calm, stable, uneventful environment in which the learning process can begin.

Asthma

Occasionally, children are born with particular vulnerabilities. This means that there may be one or another part of their bodies that is especially worn by stress or anxiety. For some, this may be their stomachs, all sadness and anger will have a reflection in stomach pains or digestive troubles. For others, their skin may erupt when they are frightened or angry or in despair; and for still others, the pathway for emotions to express themselves is through the respiratory system. For the most part these physical illnesses are not caused by emotional troubles. They are caused by the child's own biological frailties. However, tension, anger, and special stress can aggravate the natural vulnerability in some children and make these real physical illnesses more difficult to control and get rid of. There are many puzzles about the exact way the mind affects the body. All we know at the moment is that there are some sicknesses that have demonstrated a close connection to the emotional state of the child and can be helped not only by medicines and physical care but in addition by alterations in the emotional climate in which the child lives.

Asthma is one such illness. We assume that some babies are born prone to breathing difficulties, and have allergic responses, either to something outside themselves or to an infection within their own system. We do know that asthma can be made more complicated and its instances increased as the breathing and lung functions mingle with emotional distress. Even in babies as young as eight or nine months, we see the beginnings of asthmatic conditions. Many children will simply outgrow early asthma but others will be hindered all through childhood by episodes of mild to severe wheezing.

Experiencing the fright and the discomfort of asthma has a distinct effect on both the mother and the child. Parents can easily and understandably become overprotective and overanxious, communicating to their children that they will not be able to survive if they don't stay close. It is possible that the asthmatic child feels more keenly his need for his mother to help him breathe and therefore is less able to openly express his angry independent feelings. Because of his vulnerability he may fear her anger and possible desertion more than another child. It may be that this creates additional stress for the child, which expresses itself in still more asthmatic episodes. Parents don't create asthma in their children. Possibly asthmatic children express through their lungs a level of tensions that in other children would produce no symptoms at all. On the other hand, if the parenting is less than good, the asthmatic situation can get worse. Life problems such as divorce, moves from place to place, tensions within the family can all show themselves in the asthmatic child's struggle to catch his breath.

The anxiety experienced during an asthmatic attack, in which a child will surely feel he is suffocating and might die, leads to his having a more anxious and uncertain feeling about the world. In addition he becomes angry at the parent who could not protect him against sickness. This anger and sense of helplessness may make the asthmatic child even more likely to have another asthma attack. The sickness does bring the attention and concern of the mother to direct focus on the child, and for some children this attention becomes a welcome side effect, one that is hard to give up for health. The triggering causes of asthma begin to go round and round in overlapping circles.

Mothers can watch their asthmatic children and see if they can pick up the points at which asthma attacks begin. If they notice that the breathing difficulty comes on at moments of emotional stress, of new separations, of frustration, they can seek a consultation with a psychiatrist. He or she may be able to offer ways that this particular family can cut down on the family stress and offer methods for the child to handle his feelings, to express them clearly, without developing asthma. The villain of this piece is nature or biology; however, there can be emotional fallout that accompanies this disease. A psychiatrist may help the pediatrician and the family to keep the child in better health.

Skin Problems

Some babies show skin problems as early as the first week while others develop eczema or other itchy rashes toward the end of the first year. The baby's skin is an all-important part of her well-being. Touching, holding, rubbing are sensations that give the baby a sense of being loved and protected, and the comfort of the skin is a major part of a new baby's needs. The skin troubles that we see in little babies are probably signs that their skin is especially vulnerable to internal stress, both physical and psychological. In the child up to three we can easily understand how the eruptions of skin rashes and the discomfort that follows would disrupt the harmony of the mother–child relationship, and when severe cause disturbances in the child's own sense of her body and her ability to like herself.

Where we have seen other signs of mother–child disturbance, the skin eruptions seem to be a part of the symptomatic picture of a baby who is not being touched and held and valued sufficiently. There have been studies done which show that some mothers of children with eczema do not touch their babies' skin directly but always use a cloth or a towel. This is not necessarily true of every mother of every baby with eczema; we are still studying the very complicated relationship between skin symptoms and maternal care.

When babies have constant, recurring skin difficulties it would be a good idea for the mother and father to spend some time thinking about their feelings about the baby. Sometimes if parents can recognize their own angers at the new and burdensome demands being made on them, they can devise solutions that would lead them to feel more contented. Perhaps the mother needs some household help. Perhaps a grandparent or a sister can be called in to provide relief. Perhaps a mother should resume her work or a father should step in more often when the mother is tired and needs some time to herself. Perhaps the baby's skin problems stem from a mother who just can't be physically tender with her baby although she may love her very much. In that case it would be helpful to have a mother-substitute bathe and tend the baby a good part of the time so the infant can get the kind of physical mothering she requires. Later the mother can take charge again, and will perhaps be happier with a child whose needs are more verbal and less directly physical.

If a child is suffering from the discomfort of skin eruptions, it is very important to continue to provide the baby with as many alternative means of contact as possible. The baby can be looked at longer, sung to, stroked on an area where there is no rash, rocked in a blanket, nuzzled face to face. Parents have to provide these babies with a lot of touching in imaginative, inventive ways since the simple usual kinds of touch may be too painful. Don't waste a moment feeling guilty. The baby has a vulnerability in the skin area that will be outgrown in time. What the parent can do is to prevent any damage to the bond between mother and child from occurring. The pimples and the pus can be well used by parents as a signal that they must contact and love this baby even more closely than before.

Pica, or Eating the Inedible

There are some children who, beginning around a year of age, will begin to eat all sorts of things that are not mean to be food, such as plaster, paint, toys, or paperclips. This illness has been named pica, the Latin word for the magpie, a bird that is supposed to be a scavenger of all odds and ends. The child who cannot or will not distinguish between what is food and should be swallowed and what is not has a very serious and possibly life-threatening illness. Pica appears more often in economically marginal families but is seen everywhere. Frequently it is a symptom of iron-deficiency anemia and pediatricians should check out this possibility. However, if the anemia is absent, the pica will be a sign of something wrong with the child's relationship with his mother through which the earliest messages about eating came. It is as if these children were constantly trying to recreate feeding situations that might satisfy them better than those they had received. This symptom is not always outgrown and signals a real disturbance in the attachment of mother to child.

If parents find their child constantly swallowing odd small objects and the pediatrician has ruled out anemia, they should try to evaluate how best to reach the child and redo some of the earlier missed connections. Mothers might take over the feeding of the child as if they were again infants. Certainly they should spend time with them over the meal, and make it a happy occasion. Mothers might try feeding the child special treats while they are having some kind of quiet time together. Mothers should check themselves to see if they have become overburdened with work, money, or marital tensions, and have been too harried or tired to give the child the kind of loving attention he needs.

It would be a good idea, *after organic causes have been ruled out,* to consult a physician or psychiatrist to help sort out the family strains that are showing up so clearly in this child's behavior. In some few children pica is the beginning symptom of a severe mental collapse that is completely beyond the parents' control. This is most likely caused by chemical imbalance and was destined by the genes.

Part Two

THREE
to
SIX

Section I

The Years from Three to Six: An Overview

The three-year-old, unlike the newborn infant, has a memory. During the first year of his life he developed the capacity to remember his mother, and even when he is briefly separated from her, he will be overjoyed to see her again. Now that he is no longer a baby, the anger he feels at being abandoned will not cause him to turn away from her when she returns. He can be mad at her and still keep in his mind the image of his good mother. He has a capacity to test reality. He has language and the means to talk to other people about what he wants and what he feels. He will have mostly achieved bowel control and he will certainly have the beginnings of a conscience. He will frequently tell himself "No," even as he grabs the truck away from another child or pulls his baby sister's hair.

He will not have very good control over his powerful angry and destructive feelings. They will rage inside him in a way that can cause him to be overwhelmed with fear and helplessness. He will very likely still be afraid of the darkness, loneliness, new places, perhaps thunder and wind. You can try to reassure him that the vacuum cleaner is not a beast and the thunder is only the sound of clouds clapping, but his capacity for logic is still limited, and his reasoning powers are quickly overcome by the powerful irrational fears that will dominate him from time to time.

The three-year-old will not be able to distinguish between the thing he wishes and reality itself. He will always confuse his own bad thoughts toward people with terrible events which he anticipates will happen in the real world. He assumes that others are as angry at him and would destroy him as quickly as he would destroy them. In many ways he is a wild savage, who believes in magic and may use primitive rituals to ward off evil and destroy his enemies.

At three, the child is still dependent and has a haunting memory of how it was to be helpless and to need his mother and father to ensure his survival, his pleasure, his freedom from fear and want. He is reluctant to give up that total kind of care and at the same time he is terrified that events will throw him back into a state of babyishness, of chaotic and confused unknowing, when he wasn't even a self, a person who knew his own name. This pull in opposite directions causes him to have temper tantrums sometimes, to act babyish and whine and whimper, or to demand independence and try to cross the street himself, or to run downhill at a heart-stopping speed.

In the next years of his life he must grow into a social animal, a person comfortable with his age mates. He will develop real friendships and do things together with another child, not just beside him as he had in the earlier years. He will learn to cooperate and to share. He will learn to gain pleasure from things the group can do together. This is a major shift of perspective and comes to no child without some degree of heartbreak. But the pleasure of giggling with a friend, of building a block city, of playing tag or tumbling one on top of the other in the fall leaves is so great that it is worth the sacrifice of self-centeredness it requires.

The tricycle is the expression of the three-year-old's pride in her body and the amazing things it can do at her command. The tricycle is the symbol of her power and her newfound freedoms. But the six-year-old is more apt to be seen involved in a group game. The pleasure in her bike will then be augmented by the friends one rides with. This is the journey toward being a social person that the child must take between the third birthday and the sixth.

Babies are usually in contact with a mother or a father alternately. But when a child is three years old he begins to be a part of what he conceives as a love triangle, a family romance in which he is the weakest but the most fervent competitor. He will desire the exclusive love of one parent and become frightened by the bad thoughts he has about the other. He will, at the same time that he desires one parent for himself alone, continue to love both parents and want them both to love and protect him. His sexuality will increase in intensity, bringing him all kinds of pleasure as well as potential anxiety and disturbance. As he nears his sixth birthday his sexual feelings will dampen down, to be put aside for a while as he enters the next and last stage of his childhood.

In the years from three to six, sexual identity must be confirmed and enjoyed. A girl will gradually identify herself with her mother's body, anticipating the growth of breasts and the eventual possibility of giving birth. The boy will learn over time to feel safe and comfortable as a male, a male like his father and the other males in the culture around him. This is a complicated process in which the penis and the vagina, the story of human anatomy, must be fully understood and accepted.

The child from three to six develops a conscience, a morality that brings her into the civilized world. At first the conscience is harsh and, like the early systems of justice in the remotest of African tribes, deals only in absolutes. It is cruel and unbending. By six years old the child will have a clear sense of right and wrong, and a somewhat more realistic conception of how severe a punishment should be and how critical a sin has been committed. By six, reality will have begun to modulate the savage mind and permit a larger human view to supersede the impulsive storms of destruction that so frequently crossed the landscape of the three-year-old.

A three-year-old under stress of fever or exclusion from a play activity will retreat to thumb or blanket or the lap of a nearby adult. But babyish ways such as bedwetting, thumb-sucking, and hair-twirling should be gradually given up over the next three years. They should essentially disappear by the age of six. The persistence of some babyish habits in a child of three is not of major consequence; but if we see constant thumb-sucking, bedwetting, or hair-twirling in a child of four or five, we may become concerned that something is making it hard for this child to turn his attention to his playmates and to continue growing up. A four-, five-, or six-year-old will ordinarily not need to retreat to thumb-sucking or wetting his bed. He will be able to talk more about what's bothering him. He will look for another solution and will turn to creative play to master more and more of his tension.

Three-year-olds are full of curiosity. The why's that had been irritating and repetitive in the two-year-old have suddenly become real questions that should be answered. Three-year-olds are beginning to understand other people's feelings and say wonderful things like "Mommy is tired," or "Poor Jimmy hurt his hand." Some time between three and six, children will begin to make their mothers happy with real expressions of appreciation and pleasure: "What a beautiful cake," "What a pretty flower." Three-year-olds can concentrate for what seems an amazingly long time on a puzzle or a building activity. They are flushed with victory and pleasure when you admire their work. Three-year-olds can pretend to be cars or witches or grownups, and in their play you catch glimpses of yourself, funny and sweet.

The three-year-old soaks up language, learning dozens of new expressions, new words, each day. It is a great joy for parents to hear their little children adding clauses to their speech, using modifying adjectives and a wide variety of adverbs. These forward leaps in language help the children to play better and more elaborate games. They now do more than just play beside each other. They begin to have friends—"Billy is nicer than Joel," and "I want to go the park with Mary." The three-year-old whispers in his friend's ear and they play a trick together on you by hiding behind the closet door and making you call their names. The three-year-old loves things that move, like trains and trucks and cranes. He marvels at construction sites and garbage trucks. The three-year-old loves to play with dolls and stuffed animals and pretends to be a mommy or a daddy or a doctor, nurse, or teacher. Whatever appears in the adult world reappears in the child's play life, and you stand amused and amazed at the incredible powers of imitation. Your child noticed how you wobble in your new high heels, she caught the hoarse whisper of the butcher, and she clearly saw the teacher purse her lips again and again. Children are mimics and students of human behavior. At the same time they will play alone for a long while stringing beads, racing toy cars. You can begin to play board games with a three-year-old, but beware: they have no tolerance for losing and the fun of the game can quickly disappear in a flurry of tears. The rules are frequently forgotten or abandoned in the desire to win.

The three-year-old is a warm, affectionate person, needing to be hugged and held and cuddled but also capable of actively kissing, hugging, and molding his body against his parents. He is independent sometimes but at other times he is still a little child in need of the reassurance of your body as well as your words. He enjoys giving affection as much as receiving it. This is all a great pleasure for parents, who feel appreciated as the child reaches for a hand while walking down the street, or climbs into a lap for a story, or warm and sleepy comes into the parents' bed in the morning for a few special moments of being held.

Now children have recognizable personalities. You are beginning to know them, not just as your baby or your child but as the particular individual they are on the way to becoming. The journey between the third birthday and the sixth is as long as Marco Polo's to China and just as exciting, as arduous, and as full of unexpected wonders.

Nursery School

Many children begin nursery school at the age of three or a little after. This entry into the larger world is a landmark experience for both parent and child, signaling the change from babyhood to childhood. The meaning of the first days—when name tags are given out, cubbies are assigned, and new expectations of when to be quiet, and where to sit, and what is allowable and what is not are made clear— is as significant in the life of mother, father, and child as the birthdays, graduations, and weddings that are more commonly celebrated in our society.

Children do not all take to nursery school like the proverbial ducks to water. Considering their intense dependency on their mothers and their fears of abandonment, which make many of them leery and quiet in new places, with new people, it is no wonder that the first weeks of nursery school come as a shock—a partially pleasant shock, but a shock nevertheless to most small children.

By three years most children will be able to tolerate the separation from their mothers for a number of hours and they will accept her reassurance that she will pick them up later. Most will be willing to become interested in new adults who offer them friendship and care. They are also tempted and excited by the toys and equipment of the nursery school, and can be distracted from their initial concerns about the strangeness of the place and the people by interest in a new task, such as a puzzle or a jungle gym. At first they notice other children only as fellow travelers on the same road. They will do something at a table beside another child but not really with him; they do not at first exchange and do things together. During the initial months of nursery school they will build towers next to each other and only later when they are very comfortable in their new environment will they take that enormous civilizing step to sharing, cooperating, gaining pleasure from doing something with someone else.

The first weeks of nursery school can arouse many signs of regression in normal children, who will want to be babies again when they come home. They may wet in the afternoon, suck their thumbs, or cry irritably over the slightest frustration. While the world of the nursery school room looks wonderful to the parent, the child still experiences it as a kind of rocket ship in which he is being asked to strap himself into a seat for a takeoff into a future away from his home, to a universe in a distant galaxy. Of course he has doubts and uncertainties, wakes often, wants toys he has discarded months ago, and feels exhausted at the wrong times.

A slow entry into the school situation is best. It is helpful if the child can go back to his mother from time to time for the first week or so. Some children take longer than others to trust that the school world is a kind one and that they will truly return to their own family as promised. The first days of nursery school are also a very peculiar experience for parents. Even if they have smaller babies at home, they are confronted for the first time with the fact that their child is now a part of the public world, the community at large, and that other people, parents, children, teachers will now be looking at their child and finding him acceptable, well brought up, as amazingly intelligent and gifted as they believed—or not. The "or not" in that sentence is the hard part for parents. They, too, feel tested. They look at all the other children and compare their own. It is a odd moment of judgment, not the first nor the last, but unavoidable. For many parents it serves as a welcome break in the hothouse isolation that can be the American nuclear family.

It is a good thing to see one's child as just one among others, special to you of course, but an equal in a group, a peer among peers, not the center of the world but one among the several. Strangely enough, this emphasizes the child's individuality and uniqueness. He is no longer the "baby," but Charlie or Oliver, a citizen in the human community.

Many mothers will miss the closeness that they had with their pre–nursery school child and feel a certain sadness and regret. Some will get pregnant again; others will just struggle with the separation. Growing up forces the mother to move in gradual steps away from the child just as it requires the child to make tracks in the opposite direction.

Among parents of nursery school children, certain types appear in each class year after year. There is always the mother who finds a way to make other mothers feel there is something wrong with their own child. She uses every available opportunity to tell you about her child's remarkable cleverness, amazing physical prowess, and outstanding beauty. Avoid this mother. She is using her child in some competitive game in which her child has become the bat and yours has become the ball. Forgive her. She can't help herself.

There is also the mother who feels that the nursery school staff is not doing enough to educate and teach academic skills to her child. She wants to see solid accomplishments on worksheets. Her definition of learning is narrow, confined to the fundamentals of reading and arithmetic. Her discontent stems from an inability to see her child as a human being in need of those social experiences that teach the child to take turns, to serve, and to give as well as to get, and to solve problems of game-playing and building and making things of clay and glue. This kind of a mother will think all that fooling around is all right for other people's children but not for her especially gifted baby. Ignore her. She isn't seeing her child, she is seeing her ambitions piled up in the shape of a three-year-old. Some mothers are especially vulnerable to the cruelties of more aggressive mothers and will feel that their children are less strong, less bright, less mature than someone else's child. These negative feelings are very dangerous and can wash right onto the child, who will catch them as easily as the more common viruses that run around nursery schools. When you bring a child to the door of his first classroom, fight against your own insecurities and fears of being inadequate. Most mothers have these fears, admitted or not, and there are always some who will terrorize the others.

Selecting a Nursery School

In many of our cities the entrance to private nursery schools has become selective—there are more candidates for some schools than there are places. The schools interview the parents and the child, choosing which little three-year-old will enter their doors. Rejections can hurt parents deeply. The school administrators imply that they have some means of selecting the most intelligent, promising, wonderful of children for their classes, so no wonder parents feel profoundly upset if they are not among the elect.

Actually, the schools know nothing at all about most children. Their screening methods can only eliminate those who are in obvious psychological trouble. They cannot distinguish among the mass of normal kids they see. They don't know who will be a scholar, who will be an artist, who will be a troublemaker in class, and who will be valedictorian fifteen years down the line. The schools make their choices on the basis of contacts, social position, professions of parents, wealth, and a host of other irrelevant factors that have nothing whatever to do with the potential of any given child. Some children are shy in strange places and with new adults and will make a less vivid impression on the testers than others. This shyness will disappear within a few years, and what it covers will be revealed. Some children act wild and out of control in strange situations and this behavior, too, while not endearing to school personnel, will also vanish with the advancing months. In places where nursery school admission is tight, remember that anyone who tells you that they can look at a three-year-old and predict his academic pattern is whistling in the dark. Remaining steady as a parent requires that you sometimes recognize the humbug, the charlatan who dresses himself in professional roles and walks around with the authority of an official position.

When the choice of nursery school is yours, look around carefully and avoid those schools where the puzzles are still in cellophane, the tables spotless, and the children sit too still. Look at the paintings that are hung on the wall. Avoid a school in which the paintings all look alike; avoid one in which the paintings are all centered in the middle of the paper and the subjects are identical to each other. On the other hand, avoid those schools where the teachers talk endlessly about the individuality of each young mind and there is chaos, noise, and disorder everywhere. If you spend some time in a nursery school classroom and you feel like you're in a zoo because the screaming and fighting, the tears and constant movement have become unbearable, you know that the adults, well meaning as they may be, have lost control and this is not a healthy place for your child. Don't pay too much attention to the philosophy of any given school. They can all sound reasonable. Look for teachers who can create in their classrooms a balance of freedom and order, a structure to the day that is flexible enough to support the stormy emotional life of the three-year-old while encouraging all the curiosity and desire to learn that each child will bring to the school along with his passions and peculiarities.

There are many families who cannot provide nursery school education for their children for either economic or geographic reasons. While we feel that a three-year-old will benefit enormously from the social experience and the intellectual offerings of the school, it is certainly true that parents can inventively and creatively find substitutes for school settings. The important thing to remember is that your child will be ready to play cooperatively and imaginatively with other children. Playgrounds, parks, church and neighborhood groups make ideal settings for the child to observe other children and to begin to enjoy the companionship of friends. It is also important for the parents of a non–nursery school child at this age to invite the child to recognize letters, to begin to count, to distinguish triangles, circles, and squares, and to draw and make things on his own. These experiences, while they do not guarantee academic excellence, are important intellectual foundations. The child of three is ready and eager to make them his own.

Parents who do not send their children to nursery school have to take particular steps to avoid letting the television set take up too much of the child's time. Programs such as *Sesame Street* and *Mr. Rogers* are fine and helpful, but an endless morning of cartoons can stun the young mind and begin the bad habit of limply receiving images instead of creating them. Remember that your child at this age needs physical activity. Climbing and running, throwing and rolling about are all expressions of pride and pleasure in the body, and they should be encouraged. Hard as it is to provide space for such activity, as parents we have to make sure that three-year-olds do indeed have a world to explore, and that they have someone to talk to about their journey. Language development is not nourished by television. Only in the human exchange of thought and confidence is speech enriched.

Nursery School Play

At two and a half, most children will play happily beside another child. In the months following the third birthday, children will gradually, with the help of a nursery school teacher, begin cooperative play. If you watch this play closely, a lot of it has to do with two or three children getting together and excluding another. The fun seems to be in making someone feel left out. At this age the object of the exclusion usually changes from day to day; clearly the children are playing out their own feelings of being left out of the wonderful union of mother and father. At the same time children will play vigorous physical games with each other that involve a lot of touching and exploring. It is amazing how much sexual activity can be sneaked into a game of astronauts in a capsule, fireman on the way to a fire, and cowboys and Indians. Boys and girls play together although they are aware of sexual differences, and they develop tiny love affairs with each other. They carry on flirtations and in each nursery school class some of the children may pretend to be married to others. They play marriage, house, children. They play out their concerns of being bad and they mete out punishments that make most military juntas look like angels of mercy.

At the age of three we clearly see that boys are more openly aggressive than girls. This may be the effect of testosterone, a hormone that is found only in males, or it may stem from the cultural repercussions of the way we expect girls and boys to behave. At this point we have no culture-free children, so we can only say that girls are more controlled and easier to involve in quiet games that require following some rules. They are willing to sit longer and they are more interested in doing things that require fine muscle control, like drawing or stringing beads, than boys. Girls will spend more time in doll play and dress-up activities than will boys; but given these natural differences (at least in this culture at this time), a good nursery school will avoid the sex stereotyping of work and play. Sometimes boys enjoy dressing in girls' clothes and putting on lipstick; sometimes girls will build rockets and race around the room like Indians. The different sexual identities of the children should not be confused with active and passive. Both sexes should be encouraged to play at everything, to imagine themselves any way at all, and to build and fantasize any kind of future for themselves that they wish.

Teasing at this age is passing and obvious. Children will be teased if something about them appears very different from other children, such as being very fat, or having a limp or a facial birthmark. Children are direct and without much feeling for others' sensitivity. They will point out quickly that someone has an ugly nose or that their dress is torn. This is not the elaborate form of teasing that will develop later, but some small children do need to be protected by their parents from cruel remarks. Let the fat child understand that other children will make him feel unhappy about his weight but that if he can ignore their remarks, in a little while they will all be playing together happily.

Small children will be hurt by the openness and rudeness of their peers, but for most children the differences they have noticed immediately will diminish in importance as they get to know the marked child. We should encourage sensitivity in our children about how the other child feels when someone says something cruel to him. We must reassure our child who may have been wounded that tomorrow is another day and that he will soon have real friends who will love him just as he is. The important thing is not to let the teased child feel he is a hopeless outcast since this will lead to behavior that further isolates him. Young children can find friends in other groups if things have gone badly in one place. It may be worth a parent's effort to change schools or playgrounds, providing a new social arena.

Cry Babies

All children under the age of five or six sometimes cry when they are frustrated, frightened, or hurt. For the most part these tears are a natural expression of feeling. Boys should not be embarrassed by their tears. It is not unmanly to be open about one's pain and it does not make anyone stronger to be forced to hide, to put on a brave face, to cover genuine feelings all of the time. Little children have a low threshold for frustration and for physical pain. They will immediately weep if denied a popsicle or if they scrape their knee on the sidewalk. We can comfort them without making them ashamed of their tears. Gradually between the ages of three and six most children learn to express their frustration or disappointment in words and not with tears. By five most children will not cry if they can't have a toy or a present or if they are told that they have to wear a hat or have to put away their blocks. Gradually children learn to tolerate the more common kinds of irritations without resorting to weeping.

Some children, however, will use tears to get their way long after their age mates have given up on this method of manipulation. Some other children will simply not have good enough controls and will be overwhelmed with grief at the slightest upset and burst into tears when they can't be first in line, when their cookie looks smaller than a playmate's. Such a child tends to be called a cry baby by other children. The name is apt because all children know that crying, not talking, crying, not waiting, crying, not adapting, is the baby's right, the baby's way. As children enter kindergarten they struggle with their own babyish impulses and they get very angry at a child who fails to measure up to what is considered proper behavior. A child in a first-grade class who cries when she is pushed, who cries when she doesn't get the book with the red cover she wanted, who cries when someone knocks over her juice is sure to be unpopular and a likely target for teasing. Teasing of course only makes the child who cries too easily, cry some more.

Parents can try to explain to such a child that other children don't like it when she cries and that she must stop if she wants friends. The child must not be allowed to get what she wants if she cries. This can be an indulgence fostered by parents who capitulate whenever tears are produced.

Some cry babies are just immature and in a some months their controls will catch up and they will make friends and join the group in time. Some cry babies learn that they are harming themselves by not controlling their tears and change their behavior. Other children simply cannot stop. If this goes on well into the seventh year we would become concerned that this child is having too a hard time and must be suffering from a lot of inner pressure that has interfered with her development of controls. Probably such a child will show some other signs of difficulties—learning problems, bowel and bladder control problems, sleep or eating difficulties—or may be overly active or too quiet.

The cry baby who cannot stop by herself, who continues to have trouble making friends and is teased for her easy tears, may need some help. This can be one of set of symptoms that would concern a therapist. However, frequent crying, by itself, in an otherwise sturdy child under the age of six, is a passing problem. Time alone will bring about a wonderful cure. Most children learn quickly what does and what does not work in a group and if they are out of step they change their own pace.

Becoming Male: The First Jealousy

Some time after the age of three, the little boy feels an increasing pleasure in his penis. He will have erections and he will discover that touching and rubbing himself causes his penis to grow. (He will, however, experience some anxiety each time the penis returns to its smaller and more usual size.) The boy will quite normally begin to connect these good feelings with the tender care of his mother. He will begin to have fantasies of marrying his mother, of being near her always and of being her favorite and exclusive loved one. Before, he loved his mother because she had given him food and comfort and stood between him and the vast unknown of the large strange world. Now his love changes its form, becoming connected in his mind with the pleasures of the penis and the erotic feelings that the presence of his mother near him in the bath, reading to him on the couch, helping him take off his snow-pants, smiling at him across a room can bring. In other words, he has fallen in love with his mother in very much the same romantic way that any male can desire and long for the possession of a particular woman.

At the same time he places an increased value on his penis. He will enjoy all the jumping, thrusting, climbing activities that give his whole body a feeling of power and mastery. He will especially love his bike, and all things with wheels that thrust forward, go fast. He will be fascinated with trains and cranes and cement mixers and every

163

kind of machinery that moves powerfully, quickly forward and backward, up and down.

The erotic feelings that the little boy has for his mother are extremely pleasant, causing him to want to please her, do things for her, and learn whatever it is she wants him to learn. At nursery school he will make drawings for her. In the park he will climb to the top of the gym or speed his bike past her hoping for her approval and admiration. If the world consisted only of himself and his mother, all would be very easy and happiness his assured fate. However, most of these Edens contain a snake, and the snake in the three- and four-year-old's Eden is the continuing presence of his dad.

There are two sides to the boy's problem. The first is that his new love for his mother makes him angry and jealous of his father. He sees that his father has a much larger penis than he has and is in every way more powerful. His father could hurt him. He perceives that he could not protect himself against the anger of his father, whom he assumes must know all the thoughts that run through a child's head —thoughts of getting rid of the father, thoughts of moving into the mother's bed himself and replacing the father, thoughts of violence being done to the old man. These thoughts appear only fleetingly in the conscious mind but they are there.

In the three- and four-year-old child, the borders between the countries of the conscious and unconscious still remain fairly open. Many thoughts travel back and forth each way all the time. The love the little boy feels for his mother may sound like a wild tale invented by Sophocles or Freud, but proof comes again and again from the mouths of children themselves. There is no secret in this erotic love. The little boy tells you about it openly. He announces he wants to marry Mommy. He may tell you that he wishes Daddy would go away. He will play games of being Mommy's husband, and in his pretend play Daddy will be killed off in a variety of ways: giant ants consuming him, Martians lifting him into the stratosphere, or collisions of cars and trucks that will demolish him, conveniently leaving the little boy and his mommy to go on together.

The jealousy the child feels and the fantasies that follow it are particularly confusing and painful for the little boy because he is still so young that he cannot yet clearly tell the difference between fantasy and act. He fears that his father might do to him some of the things he has invented for his father.

The little boy really loves and needs his father, and this is the other side of his problem. It would be a lot simpler if his father were just a nasty snake one could bash over the head and dispose of in the garbage can; but the little boy wants his father, too. The confusion that follows the new wonderful feelings in his penis creates for him vast muddles of emotions that must be sorted out over the next three years of his life if he is one day to be a male who will choose a mate and have his own children.

He will almost certainly experience new fears at this time, fears that can be understood if we know what he is daring to think and feel about his mother. Most little boys will show some exaggerated response to the slightest cut or fall and for a while will be alarmed at the sight of their own blood. This is in response to their fear that something will happen to their penis because of the angry wishes and destructive fantasies they have had about their father. Many little boys will become afraid of giants in the closet, robbers who will attack the house, dogs that might bite them, tigers that might have broken out of their cages in the zoo. This temporary fearfulness on the part of most all boys is because of their fear that their own wishes will be punished and something terrible will happen to them. With whatever images they have available to them, from television and books, things they have heard and seen, they will construct dangerous persecutors. Their own feelings are so violent toward their fathers that they expect violence is everywhere and may be turned against them.

Little boys may have trouble sleeping at this time, in part because they do not like to leave the father and mother alone together and feel especially excluded at night; in part because they may have bad dreams in which they are damaged, mutilated, or threatened by dangers that in fact represent their fear of their father's anger. Some children will develop passing fears of hoses that spurt water or umbrellas with sharp points or of loud noises that sound to them like the roaring voices of angry fathers gathering their might to crush them.

Imaginary dangers offer a way for little boys to protect and preserve the love they feel toward their fathers. Very often boys will stop themselves from thinking destructive thoughts, but the anger is still there, and so they take those bad feelings that were originally meant for the father and attribute them to the neighbor's dog, the lion in the zoo, the evil magician who dwells behind the bureau in the bedroom. Fear then is a major ingredient in the normal three- and four-year-old mind. He is afraid of his own bad wishes; he is afraid of retribution from his father. He acts all this out in an imaginative way with the giant in the closet and the neighbor's barking poodle.

It used to be that we thought of children as innocent of sexual feelings, guilt, and jealousy. That was because no one listened to the words and thoughts of children and no one tried to explain their games, their nightmares, their daily fears. Now we know that the years that follow on babyhood and lead to the first grade in school are filled with loud, large, raw, primitive feelings of sexual love, hate, and guilt. The small child has no way of judging reality and separating out his fantasies from actual events that may or may not occur.

As we watch little boys, we see them smash towers that they have built. We see them play with toy weapons in which they slice, slash, and destroy imaginary enemies over and over again. We see them arranging a violent bloody crash of their toy cars, and they decapitate toy soldiers and grind stray ants into the dust. They will tear off butterfly wings and stamp on the walls of sandcastles. These are all expressions of anger and frustration. They are jealous.

This universal drama, while it seems somewhat lurid and violent, is part of the human condition, part of the making of the sexuality of male and female. As we've said, it calms down around the sixth birthday. All that jealousy, all that sexual excitement, all that fear of retaliation, all that anger is as normal as learning to place the adjective before the noun, learning to take turns with a desired toy, learning to listen to a friend's story, learning to ask for something before grabbing, learning that crossing a street may be dangerous but noises from airplanes overhead are not. The outside world—the world of friendships, of logic, of reason, of time and geography and history—is slowly opening to the child at the same time as he struggles with his inner passions.

At times the little boy will quite normally feel an erotic love for his father, wish to have his father all to himself, and wish that his mother would go away. There will be days when he wants his father's love exclusively for himself, and on those days his mother will be seen as the intruder. The problem for the little boy is that his erotic sensual feelings can be turned toward the mother or the father but that either way he wants sole rights. Sharing, being part of a threesome, or of a family with siblings who also make claims, is very difficult for a child of this age. For most little boys the love for the father and the wish for the mother to go away is a weaker and less frequent factor in life. Most little boys focus mainly on their desire for their mothers. This will be the major theme that affects their play, their dreams, and their anxieties.

We will see them in nursery school wrestling with or attacking little girls: they throw them to the floor, jump on them. The play will be exciting, with great squeals of laughter and wild joy. They will play doctor with little girls, exploring them and touching them as much as is permitted by the teachers and parents. They will play at being married to little girls and they will play at being fathers in games of house. But the real pleasure for them lies in the games of physical contact, of touching and pulling and tickling that are so common a part of all free play between children at this age.

From the years when this jealousy and love of the mother first appear until around the sixth birthday, the child gradually reconciles himself to the fact that he is a child and cannot compete with his father for his mother. He slowly accepts his defeat and pushes out of his mind his former erotic feelings for his mother and his angry feelings for his father. At about five or six years old, the borders between the conscious and unconscious become closed on this matter and the boy no longer has troubling thoughts. He now will totally accept the fact that he is only a little boy and his father is a man who is entitled to the the sexual possession of his mother. He gives up and pushes out of conscious memory his erotic quest for his mother, partially out of fear of what his father might do to him, partially out of increased love for his father. He does not want to lose that love by becoming a rival instead of a beloved child. He gives up out of an increasing sense of reality. His cause is lost because of his size, his age, his place in the world. He gives up because his mother, while loving him dearly, has clearly not chosen him for the single exclusive object of her affections. He gives up because he gains in a real knowledge of the world, and in the world women and men share beds and other intimacies that are forbidden all sons. In giving up this first competition, in relinquishing his first erotic love, the little boy begins to win his manhood.

He discovers that his mother admires him when he is like his father, so more and more he begins to pattern himself after his father. He enjoys increasingly the things that he and his father do together. He walks like his father. He imagines himself a grown man like his father. If his father is an avid reader, he too will turn toward books, and if his father also likes golf, he will practice his own swing in the backyard. Slowly over the fourth and fifth year he becomes clearer about his role in the family and decides that he will be a male like his father instead of engaging in a struggle to replace him. This solution will ease many of his earlier fears. He will no longer worry that his father might harm him for his jealous thoughts. He will no longer have tigers in the closet and robbers climbing through every window because he will be less afraid of something happening to him. He will, in other words, no longer feel so guilty or deserving of punishment.

As he reaches his sixth year, the little boy will not be as regularly aroused erotically. His sexual energy will just slow down, not really disappear entirely, but simmer down so that he can concentrate more freely on the tasks of learning that lie ahead of him in the years preceding puberty. His identification as a male will be increasingly important to him and he will for a while appear to lose interest in little girls, scorning them and their activities. His maleness is now the center of his identity—he feels safe and secure in his body, and takes great pleasure in the physical accomplishments, the throwing, the running, the catching, the things his body can do.

This is the path of normal sexual development for the male child. It depends on several events happening in his world in an ordinary way. First, his mother must not be too seductive; she must not encourage his fantasy of being her lover instead of her child. It is important for the little boy that the father be active in his life at this time, offering care and support. If the father is absent, the child will have fantasies about the father's anger toward him and they will not be checked by the real father's real love. If the father is not available, it is very important that the little boy have some males to identify with and that he not be allowed to believe he is the most important male in his mother's life. A loving father is the best counterbalance to the terrible angers and guilts that plague every child at this time.

In single-parent homes, the boy of three or four will have a longer period of time before reality brakes his desires for his mother. He will be more anxious about the visits of his father or the dates his mother may bring home. Each represents a threat to his desired position. He may fantasize about what his father might do to him if he returned home; these fantasies can make the child fearful at this time. Mothers should try their best not to encourage their sons' romantic aspirations. They should remind them often that they will marry a girl their own age one day. They should not overly fondle or encourage sexual expression on the child's part. They should make it clear that the little boy is not the man in the house, that the little boy is just a child. In time—perhaps a little more slowly and with more fears along the way—the son in a single-parent home also gives up, forgets his sexual feelings for his mother, and turns his attention to his friends, his school, his own life.

If the separation from the mother in the early years has gone well, then the little boy in any family will most certainly weather the sexual storms of the next years. If he has a good sense of himself as separate from his mother, not needing her to make him complete, then he will be less vulnerable to the developmental problems that can accompany the upsurge in sexual feeling after three years of age. But if the little boy is angry at his mother because she has been unable to protect him from the physical pain of illness or emotional pain of abandonment, then the sexual feelings become fused with angry feelings and the competitive aspects of the drama with the father become even more important, the fears of retaliation even greater. A child who has mastered the separation in a loving way will be better able to use the affection of his mother and father to adjust to the reality of his place in the world.

Becoming Female: The First Jealousy

The three-year-old girl makes her own complicated journey through sexual awakenings, love, jealousy, and anxiety to secure her female sexual identity. After she has negotiated her way to a separate individual self and conquered her fears of being abandoned by her mother, she begins to feel strong and powerful sensations in her genital area. She does not, like the little boy, locate these pleasurable feelings in one spot, but she finds that if she squeezes her thighs and if she touches her vaginal area she can become vastly excited. She has already turned some of her attention toward her father because he has helped her in the first steps away from total dependency on her mother. She may be feeling some disappointment in her mother, who after all did not, as she sees it, give her either a penis or large breasts or pubic hair. But she knows by three years of age that she is a girl, a female like her mother, and in imitating her mother, spurred on by her own biological urges, she turns her romantic erotic attention to her father.

Now she begins to feel a bitter jealousy. She wants her father all to herself. She wants his attention and some kind of erotic satisfaction from him. As she learns that the father has an important role in the creation of the baby, she will begin to want her father to give her a baby too, just as he has given one to her mother. We know this because little girls have said it aloud over and over again: "I want to marry Daddy," "I want to go away with Daddy on a boat and not come home," "I want to be Daddy's wife." Little girls will begin to please their fathers in any way possible to elicit the desired attention from them. They become coy, flirtatious, adoring, worshipping—and they rarely show their fathers their tempers, their grouchy moments. There is in the household a new kind of tension as the little girl vies with her mother for the love of her father.

This turn toward the father is a complicated step for the little girl. In order to start the process she must separate herself from her mother, who was after all her original love in this world. Then she will be able to turn her erotic and romantic feelings toward her father. This happens gradually; as the little girl feels the increased sexual tension and pleasure in the father's company, she pulls further away from her mother, viewing her as a rival for the man.

Naturally this does not mean that the average three-year-old girl has stopped loving, needing, or caring about her mother. It does mean that in addition to the love that has flourished out of the baby's need and dependency now comes a new complication—jealousy and rivalry. These bad feelings can make the little girl behave quite monstrously. She can become excessively stubborn, dawdling or delaying or deliberately refusing food or turning away from a favorite game the mother offers. She may appear adorable when she is with her father and turn into a veritable demon with her mother. Hard as that is on mothers who have given so much in love and care to their daughters, it is a kind of hidden compliment to them that their girl children can for a brief while play out this natural and necessary drama of rivalry. Of course the feelings and passions involved also scare the little girl. What if Mommy wished me far away? What if Mommy stopped feeding me, caring for me? What would happen to me? The mother is clearly bigger and stronger. It is a hopeless competition. Each little girl eventually has to reconcile herself to the fact that for the romantic sexual love of her father, she has been bested—her mother has won.

The little girl is given a promise to sweeten her defeat. One day when she grows up she will have breasts and the capacity to have babies and she will have a man of her own whom she will marry and who will belong to her exclusively. The future of course seems remote and the present defeat is harsh; but out of the dust of these dashed hopes the little girl creates her sexual interest in men and her female identity.

For the little girl living alone with her mother the sexual urges exist but are directed outside the household, to an idealized absent father, a father who visits regularly, or, occasionally, an uncle, a grandfather. In many little girls around three and four we see a dramatic flirtation that gets carried on with the plumber, the mailman, the construction worker down the street. The little girl who has no father to turn to must continue to depend totally on her mother, and this makes it harder for her openly to express the anger that she feels. The little girl, despite clear explanations about the real facts of the matter, will believe that her mother has driven out her father by being mean or unfit. The little girl living alone with her mother will have many fears and worries that are disguised forms of her anger at her mother. Time will bring a greater sense of reality to the child. She will be able to see the mother as less of a villain as she also grows less dependent on her and more involved in her real world of friends and school.

It is important for single mothers of girls to help their daughters have as much contact with their fathers as possible, or to provide other relationships with brothers or friends in which they can test out their femaleness and express their age-appropriate loving feelings for a man. Single mothers of little girls must be patient with the irrational anger the child will often show and calm the several fears that are likely to appear. Mothers should not bring too many different men into the house because this over-excites the little girl, arousing both her jealousy of the mother and her fear of losing the closeness she has with her. Although any serious relationship of the mother's must be shared with the child, casual encounters need not be. A mother should be extremely careful not to build up a daughter's closeness to a man, only to have him leave, bringing another disappointment and creating a second void. The girl child of a divorced or widowed mother learns to identify with her, too. While it is easier and faster to straighten out the sexual muddle of these years if a father is present, if he is not, many opportunities with friends and relatives exist in which a daughter can experience good feelings about her sexual identity. By six years old she will have pushed away all thoughts about her mother having deprived her of a father. In her fantasy and her play, she will begin to think ahead to the time when she will have her own mate.

Masturbation

Masturbation is a habit of sorts that begins as early as fifteen or sixteen months. Today we know that fondling one's own genitals, experiencing some kind of sexual pleasure through one's own hands, is a perfectly normal and even necessary part of growth. It will not lead to madness or blindness or sin. Children at age three or four will fondle themselves or rub their legs together usually when they are quiet, at naptime, before falling asleep at night, and perhaps while resting between activities in front of the television. The pleasure is not so much exciting as it is comforting or soothing, and may be accompanied by fantasies of being near one's parent or being touched or held by that parent. We all will explain to our children that people don't touch themselves in public or in front of friends or neighbors. Gently and without creating guilt, we can tell children that some things are just best done when one is alone. Children will quickly accept this.

Some few children may become overly anxious about the well-being of their genitals and they may touch them often to be sure that they are intact. Some children will retreat from playing with others and turn away from the outside world to fantasies of their own that accompany touching of the genitals. This is when we become concerned about the habit of masturbation.

A very fearful or anxious child with many other symptoms of disturbance may misuse masturbation. We would worry about a child who repeatedly will retreat from a play group and masturbate or who cannot stop masturbating in front of others despite having been asked to do so frequently. We would be concerned about a child who will consistently hold on to his penis when he hears a loud noise, when he sees a large dog or encounters a new person or place. For the majority of children, we welcome the signs of their ability to enjoy their genitals and we recognize that if by "innocent" we mean without sexual feelings, then no child is ever, or has ever been, innocent. Children who are prevented from touching their genitals will find other ways of comforting themselves; they may substitute picking their noses, rubbing their hair, or scratching themselves for the original impulse. Boys and girls both masturbate and for the same reasons. Moderate masturbation appears to be a necessary prelude to successful mature sexuality.

Nudity

Parents have different attitudes toward walking around in front of their children without clothes on. Some families find it natural and easy, while others from more religious or traditional backgrounds may prefer modesty and rarely if ever permit their children to see them undressed. We do not know how this choice affects mental health. It is important only that parents do whatever they feel most comfortable doing.

In the years between three to six, however, we know that children are easily sexually aroused by the parent of the opposite sex. Little boys while playing tickling games, or just cuddling close to their mother, may show erections. Little girls being bounced up and down by Daddy may begin to rub themselves in ways that clearly show they are experiencing sexual excitement. This is normal and expected, but as parents we don't want to flood our children with strong sensations that they cannot control. We don't want to encourage their sexual arousal. It is perhaps better not to play exciting physical games with little children when you are naked. It is probably a reasonable act of caution not to bathe with children of this age or to take them into your bed at night. Of course, we don't want to make them feel guilty or bad about sexual pleasure, but at the same time we don't want to encourage their fantasies of having one parent all to themselves and we want to allow the sexual competition with the other parent to fade away as easily as possible.

It is the child's task to gradually give up the sexual competition, and instead to concentrate on becoming an adult like Mommy or Daddy. A child who is constantly in a state of sexual excitement will have a harder time controlling all his impulses and will grow increasingly anxious and fearful of the parent of the same sex. Nude or clothed, the important issue is to remain a parent to one's child, and not to provoke his or her sexual desires so that they erupt into the open.

Sexual Curiosity

Along with the increased good feelings in the penis or the vagina during the third and fourth year comes a renewed curiosity about the opposite sex and about the sexual organs of parents and other adults. This is a healthy, normal curiosity; we welcome it as a sign of an inquiring mind and good emotional development. Rational explanations about the difference between the sexes and the difference between the child's body and the adult body have to be repeated over and over. Here is the time for Jacob and Shirley to play doctor in the closet, for Mary to hover around the bathroom door whenever her father is taking a shower, and for Fritz to peek under the toilet doors when his mother takes him into the ladies' room while shopping. Little boys will once more experience a kind of shock on seeing and believing in the little girl's absence of a penis. Boys may touch themselves more frequently for a short while and become temporarily concerned about cuts and bruises, since this occurs just at the time when they may be angry at their fathers while struggling to have the mother all to themselves. They may become afraid that the father will harm them, or specifically will harm their penis (which is particularly valuable to them because of all its pleasurable feelings). Little girls, on hearing the difference between the sexes explained and seeing the penis again, may for a while express a desire to be boys. They may even declare that they really are boys. They may insist on wearing boy's clothes. They may become difficult and angry with their mother, who not only is their rival in love but also has somehow denied them the desired penis.

Both girls and boys soon adapt to the reality of the sexual difference. If the earlier separation from their mother has gone well, and if they have in the first three years accepted themselves as male or female, then the facts of sexual life will be absorbed without much difficulty. If the little boy is not terrified that his father will harm him, and if the little girl is reassured that she will have breasts and pubic hair and grow up to be like her mother, then the signs of anxiety about sexual differences will soon fade away.

Children at three and four, even if their mothers have not given birth to a baby brother or sister, are extremely curious about how the baby is born and where it is before birth. They have their own theories, which are based on eating and eliminating. A four-year-old will ask many questions, and it is best to answer just those questions as simply, precisely, and truthfully as possible—The baby grows in a special place in Mommy's body called the womb and after nine months gently comes out through a special place in Mommy's vagina. Breasts then have milk in them to feed the baby. Children will ask the same questions over and over, as if you had not given them the answers. The facts of birth seem fantastic to a small child; and they stimulate strange and inaccurate fantasies no matter what we say.

Too much information only confuses children. If your son does not ask how the baby got inside of the mother, you know he is not really ready to hear the complicated and somewhat scary answer. He will most likely ask you when he really wants to know. At about five or six years of age, as his knowledge of reality is increasing and his sexual feelings naturally subsiding, he may ask questions that need to be answered directly about the connection between male and female, sexual intercourse and birth. Even then he may forget your explanation and need to be told the answers week after week. Be patient. We do not want to lie or deceive children. Stork myths and the like only cast shadows of distrust and suspicion over all aspects of parent–child talk.

On the other hand, remember how concrete a child's mind is and how hard it is to visualize and understand the process of sexual intercourse and conception. Remember that the idea of sexual activity is frightening and awesome, and gets mixed up in the child's mind with angry and jealous wishes. Lead your child gently and slowly toward a complete understanding of human biology. Listen carefully to your child and let him tell you what knowledge is needed at any particular moment.

If your child doesn't ask by around five, it might be a good idea to introduce the subject yourself. Your child is thinking about it even if he or she hasn't summoned up the courage to wonder aloud. By five or six almost all children will have ideas about sexual intercourse and birth. They will have seen Mommy and Daddy together and they may have heard accurate or inaccurate definitions of "fucking" from other children. They will be curious and frightened. It is very important for your child's own sexual development that you be frank and open with him or her at this time. It is important to emphasize that sexual intercourse is part of adult life. It is an adult privilege that lies far, far ahead in the child's grownup future.

The New Addition to the Family

It is simply devastating to the child when the new baby is brought home from the hospital. The three- to six-year-old will feel displaced. She will be afraid that her mother and father will prefer the dependent infant to the independent person she is on her way to becoming. She will see no point or advantage in the new baby. She will feel betrayed. She will feel angry and then afraid that her anger will make her unlovable or unacceptable to the parents she needs so much and is so afraid of losing. She will feel that in some way she must have failed to be a good girl or her parents would not have wanted or needed another child. Because she is in the midst of a struggle for Daddy's exclusive love, she will feel further angered and upset that her father has given the baby to her mother and not to her. She will be jealous of attention to the baby and jealous that she herself doesn't have a real baby to care for.

The little boy will feel all those things, too, but because he is trying to win his mother away from his father, the new baby is an additional threat to his hopes of attaining his mother's total affection. The little boy feels squeezed between the father's greater powers and the baby's enormous dependence.

Boys and girls will probably show some signs of wishing to still be babies themselves. They may revert to baby talk, or begin again for a short while to wet or soil themselves. They may wake frequently with bad dreams, needing special reassurance. They may return to thumb-sucking or hair-twirling or seek out a precious blanket that had rested in the closet ignored for many months. They may express open aggression against the baby. A pat on the head can quickly turn into a knock, a kiss on the cheek swiftly become a sharp bite. Some children become quiet and good but repeatedly fall down and hurt themselves.

Many children do not show severe reactions to the newborn but will then experience dark jealousy when the baby begins to crawl and to talk. The baby appears to be a real rival at this time and the older child can be overwhelmed with anger and jealousy. This, too, will settle down. The relationship between the children depends somewhat on the marital relationship. In those families where the parents are doing well with each other, the children seem to be better friends and playmates. Tension between the mother and father is sometimes reflected by the children in their constant quarrels.

As parents it hurts us deeply to feel we have so threatened and wounded our own child, whom we would do anything in the world to protect from all pain and unhappiness. But remember that the acute reaction to the new baby will pass in a matter of months. The truth is that we have enough love for all our children and that learning to share, to be a part of a family, to give up the hope of an exclusive love affair with one of the parents is exactly the proper task for children at this age. It is a painful process but in the end it is essential.

It is true that the new child will profoundly affect the first child, and that the first will have great influence over the life and character of the second. Brothers and sisters carry a lifelong rivalry that can run like a stream through a shared landscape of many pleasures and comforts. If one is musical, the other may become athletic; if one is mathematically inclined, the other in search for a separate place may become artistic. The peculiar balances and detours of personality are often worked out in games, friendly and unfriendly, with siblings. One child might resemble the mother more and the other fulfill the father's expectations. One child may be a disappointment while the other brings home all the prizes. One may become the goat of the family who is always scolded and blamed while the other appears to be sailing through life on angel wings. One child, because of sex or physical appearance, can remind a parent either of a hated relative or of a particularly loved one, and memories of the past can affect the way we portion out our love and good feelings between our children. These are the exciting, slightly dangerous gambles of family life.

Parents need not be concerned at a fair degree of teasing and hostility expressed towards a sibling by a child in the years between three and six. The older child will take things away from the younger. He will push her when his mother isn't looking. He will complain when she is being bathed or sung to and he may act obnoxious just to attract attention away from the baby. This is all normal. You can tell your child that you understand his being angry with the baby but he must not hurt her. He must share some of his things. He cannot destroy her building or tear her picture.

You set the rules and place the limits on how his anger can be expressed. Encourage him to use words. Be calm if he tells you he wants you to leave his sister in the park. Let him know that you accept his feelings but not his actions. He needs to be protected sometimes from the incursions of the smaller child. He needs to know that you will favor him once in a while and that you won't let the baby harm him or his precious things. Fighting between children gets out of hand only when something is badly bothering one child. If at any time you feel the jealousy is unmanageable, creating constant disturbances throughout the day, then you must look at all aspects of your child's life and your marriage to find the source of the trouble. Different families have different levels of tolerance for expression of jealousy and anger. However, we would be concerned if a family permitted no quarrels, no tears, no complaints. We would also worry about those brothers and sisters who never have good moments that they share together, who never stop juggling for the advantageous position.

Parents can get caught in a trap of reliving the struggles they experienced with their own brothers and sisters when they themselves were children. Some parents rush in too fast to protect the little one and express too much anger at the older child. Some parents allow the older too much leeway so that the little one gets hurt more often than is necessary. Parents must check themselves for fairness, for hasty judgments, for intolerance of the behavior of one child. To some extent parents will see their own style with each other and with their children reflected in the child's own acts. Harsh parents will have harsh children, who treat each other cruelly.

Conscience: The Inner Voice of Right and Wrong

At the age of two and a half or three, most children will sometimes say "No, no," in imitation of a parent's voice. They will try to stop themselves from doing something that they know displeases their beloved mother or father. On the other side they are pushed by strong urges and impulses impelling them to do the very thing they have been told not to do. They can't resist taking a handful of the mints that have been put out on the coffeetable for company. They can't resist jumping in the leaves that have just been carefully raked. They may be overcome with a desire to pull the hair of the visiting child who has picked up their own stuffed elephant. They may take a block and drop it almost accidentally on the new baby's head. The problem is control of wish and desire, and the only help they have is the memory of the parent's voice saying "No." Sometimes this is enough to make them change direction, drop the block on the floor, only put a foot into the pile of leaves, pat the visiting child's head instead of pulling her hair. Sometimes it is not. At the beginning, at this young age, the force that controls or attempts to control the impulses comes from the outside. It is still a parent's voice. Children behave, if they can, in order to please the parent. This is the foreshadowing of conscience, but it is not the real thing at all.

Conscience is an inner voice that is a real part of the self. It doesn't rely on outside controls, threats, or opinions but has its own standards of right and wrong and its own methods of enforcing its views. If we think of conscience as a kind of moral thermostat that sets itself, runs itself, and is as important to the well-being of the inner soul as the outside climate is to the body, then we can see that the growth of a conscience is a crucial regulator of the human mind.

If a conscience is too harsh, it will punish the rest of the self and create havoc and pain in all areas of life. If it is too weak, it will not serve its function of containing those impulses that must be controlled if a person is to have a rewarding life in a world of civilized people. A conscience, like Goldilocks's porridge, must be just right. From ages three to six, conscience is growing and becoming set in its manner of operation. It changes from a primitive tool wielded by the parent to a sophisticated, complicated inner mechanism, like a pilot's radar instrument or the computer's micro-chip.

The child learns what is right and what is not from the parent; but by three and half and toward the fourth year most children can, within themselves, anticipate the parent's response. They know it is wrong to take another child's pail and shovel. They know it is wrong to hurt another human being in any way at all. But they do not yet have empathy with the feelings of the other person. They cannot imagine what it would be like to have their favorite doll torn apart or to have their building knocked over by careless feet. They don't yet feel what another child feels although they do know what is considered good and what is considered bad. Most children will try to be good and will feel guilty when they have been bad. As they begin to conceive a picture of good and bad in their own heads, as they begin to strive to be good, they take the voice of the parent and place it inside themselves, making it their own. This is the real germ of conscience.

The process of building an internal conscience is spurred on by the drama of the child's angry wishes and feelings toward the parent of the opposite sex. The little girl has fantasies of getting rid of her mother, whom she sees as standing between herself and her loved father. The little boy will have similar daydreams, with the sexes reversed, about his parents. These fantasies can be violent. Children's fear of parental retribution becomes the force within that causes them to pull back from other unacceptable thoughts and actions. In other words, the fear of retaliation is taken as a voice inside the child's mind that begins to demand good behavior.

At first this voice is harsh and cruel. But as the child progresses into the fifth year of life and the process of identification with the mother or the father increases, the conscience becomes kinder and more realistic, closer to the parents' actual feelings of right and wrong and their punishments and rewards. The identification with the mother or the father makes it possible for the child to recreate inside himself the voice that determines goodness and badness, that passes judgment on acts that have been done or might be done.

As the child grows, she can begin to understand the feelings of other children and grownups. This is a slow process, only at its beginning stages in the five-year-old, but the capacity to feel what others feel is the outgrowth of the identification process. A three-year-old will squash a bug without thinking. A five-year-old might avoid the bug, imagining the pain it would experience. This leap begins with the child's imagining what the mother or father would feel or would want.

When conscience has become a balanced inner voice that can take in realistic demands and mete out guilt in moderation, we know that the drama of anger at the parent of the opposite sex and the sexual passions of the three- and four-year-old have matured into the steady sense of identity and social behavior we expect of the normal six-year-old.

Fears of Things That Go Bump in the Night

Dawn's parents have settled down in the living room. Dawn's mother is curled up on the sofa, with her head in her husband's lap; they are about to talk when Dawn calls out again for another glass of water. It seems she's thirstier than the dust bowl and more annoying than a horde of gnats. Her father gets the water and reseats himself near his wife. Then Dawn calls out once again. She doesn't feel well: her stomach hurts. Her parents check this out, reassure her, and leave. They haven't gotten down the hall before Dawn calls again. Her favorite Teddy has fallen out of bed. When her irate father returns to her room, he finds her hidden under her covers. A small frightened voice tells him that there may be a robber in the closet. All along, Dawn had been frightened.

It is absolutely normal for three- to four-year-olds to suddenly develop a whole range of amazing, irrational fears. These can be alarming to parents and can become large nuisances in the daily routines of children, but they are as common as the cold, as ordinary as the scraped knee, and as lasting as a summer storm.

Fears of wild animals, ghosts, noises, witches, darkness, robbers, kidnappers, and things of no name that go bump in the night tell us of the child's struggle to preserve his love for his parents, even as he is most angry with them and troubled by jealous sexual feelings. The child will not want to think of his father as killing him, or tearing him apart. That is a very painful idea. Instead, he manages to invent a tiger that lives in the closet and might come out at night and chew him up. He is still afraid, but he is not afraid of the father whom he also loves and needs and enjoys, so this solution of inventing the tiger in the closet is actually not a bad one.

If the little boy feels very angry at his father one particular evening, when perhaps his parents have gone off together to dinner, leaving him home with a babysitter, he might have a terrible dream in which he is being chased by soldiers with bayonets. He is dreaming about his own anger, which he has turned into soldiers and turned against himself. In this dream he is punishing himself for his own anger against his father. Sometimes he may dream that the soldiers are killing his father and this too will frighten him a great deal. It may take the child a few moments after waking to calm down and realize that he simply had a dream and everybody is safe. Parents can help by taking the child out of his bed and turning on the lights. This helps restore reality quickly. The child should be reassured that he only had a bad dream and that all children have bad dreams. He can be talked to about other things until the scary images have gone away. Don't take him into your bed even though that might seem like the quickest way for everyone to return to sleep. That will only provoke more jealousies and fears later. Sit with him, cuddle him, then put him back to bed firmly.

Both boys and girls will have fears of dogs that might bite them or ghosts that might carry them off to a horrid foreign kingdom. These fears are caused by the intense swelling of anger at the parent of the same sex—anger that is too painful to be kept inside, and must be recast as outside dangers.

There are two reasons why these fears die down at about five or six. The first is that the anger against the parent also subsides and the child, abandoning hope of replacing the parent in the love triangle, now identifies with that parent. The second reason is that a greater reality sense has taught the child that the closet is only a closet, the ghost is only the shadow of a curtain moving in the wind, and the neighbor's dog is really friendly if you pat him on the head. In other words, experience and a greater capacity to distinguish between the real and the unreal, the imaginary and the actual, weaken these fears as time goes on. The increasing identification with the parent also helps. Mommy is not afraid of witches and Daddy has no concern that robbers are sneaking into the house each night. The child takes on the parents' view of reality.

For children of three and four who have actually been bitten by a dog, or lived through a fire or a robbery, or have been in the hospital and experienced real pain and sickness, the exaggerated fears of ghosts, witches, kidnappers, etc., take longer to melt away. Their real-life experiences have set off their imaginations, feeding what was already there. They will tend to imagine situations that repeat the actual unhappy events over and over. They will play them out with blocks, dolls, and stuffed animals. In their play they may sometimes be the robber or the dog that bites, but in some form they will include these terrible memories in their games until their power to terrify them has been exhausted.

Time will work for the child who has been hurt. It will take him longer to overcome his fears and they may be more intense and frequent than those of his playmates, but eventually reality will take over. Every day he is not robbed, every night there is no fire, every moment of physical health and well-being brings him closer to losing his fears and seeing the dangers in the world for what they are and where they actually are. The parents can help by letting him talk about what has happened, by letting him play-act the events over and over again even when it makes parents nervous or uncomfortable. Parents can talk with a child about what is real and what is not. They should be patient and accepting of a child who has been hurt in any way, as he may return to bedwetting, night-waking, thumb-sucking, or lisping. He will abandon these activities in a while, as soon as he feels again it is safe to grow up.

Frightening dreams and strange terrors are part of the passage through jealousy, rage, and fear of retaliation that each child experiences as part of normal development. It is important that children become capable of being angry and accept their anger as their own. When this happens, the anger does not need to be pictured in the form of tiger or ghost. Children must develop a realistic picture of their parents. How angry will they get at them? Will they really harm them or not? The three-year-old must resort to imaginary characters to act out his internal struggle. The six-year-old should be able to tolerate his own anger and claim it for himself, and to judge realistically how his parents will respond to his feelings.

Rituals and Habits

Along with common fears and bad dreams many children invent a kind of magical safety belt, a series of behaviors or actions they expect will protect them from the danger they sense in the world around them. They will take the same five stuffed animals to bed every night and then arrange them in the same positions around the covers. They may become distressed if one of these creatures is missing or has met with some unfortunate accident. They may insist on turning down the covers the same way each night and on saying the same three words on getting into bed. Many children will insist on wearing only certain familiar clothes. Some will need the same story read to them night after night.

These rituals are not the signals of some awful character trouble. They are perfectly normal magical practices of a young mind trying to control intense anger. The rituals will disappear as sexual jealousy subsides and the rivalry with the parent of the same sex is given up. It is best to be patient with these harmless magical rites. They don't protect against tigers in the closet but they don't cause any harm either.

Discipline: Being the Boss

Parents frequently find themselves using the word "naughty." They might tell the child, "You are a naughty girl," or "a naughty boy," and they may become angered by the provocative tactics of a young rebel who has a new dictatorship in mind. How we handle these situations is important for the child's balanced growth. We can't abdicate authority. We can't let the child think that no one is in control and his imperious command is the last word. Remember how violent his inner thoughts are; remember how scared he is of his own anger and how afraid he is that you will do something terrible to him. He can't be allowed to decide when he will come to dinner and what he will wear on a snowy day. He can't be permitted to throw his toys all over his father's desk and he can't be allowed to put a pillow over the face of the baby. He doesn't have a sense yet of how far to go, when to stop. Sometimes just because he has such angry thoughts he feels he should be punished, and he will behave in a particularly annoying way until he gets some response.

Pushover parents, parents who are afraid of inhibiting the wonders of their child's mind by a firm "No," are not helping their child to control his worst impulses. They are frightening their child by giving him the sense that he is out in orbit riding without a compass, without contact with earth, without a guiding manual; he is afraid the ship will explode. He needs to learn from his parents what is and what is not acceptable.

But the parent who does an imitation of Count Dracula at the drop of a sneaker in the wrong place, and who feels that each little misstep must be attacked with the full force of his might and power, also cripples his child, even though he may appear to be successful in getting his child to behave properly. Remember, the child is already afraid of his parent, he is already angry at that parent for having the love of the other one, and he is already afraid of being excluded from love in the family. A parent who screams too much, who punishes too hard, who threatens and glowers like a lion or a tiger, and who withholds affection and love for long periods after minor transgressions only frightens the child more and makes him anxious and angry. That state of increased fear and anger may cause him to rebel and behave badly again and again.

The trick is moderation. If a child is feeling aggressive one morning and takes away another's toy, perhaps that child should be removed from the park or the play area until he is ready to play without disturbing others. If a little girl has decided she won't wear her overcoat and is ready to make a major scene over the matter, perhaps she should stay home or go into her room, or perhaps she should be told how disappointed her mother feels that they cannot do what was planned for the day. If a child makes noise after he has been told to be quiet, perhaps he should be sent out of the room. Perhaps he can be distracted with another activity.

The parent of a three- to six-year-old must remember that it is all right to be openly angry with a child but that the anger should be in proportion to the event that caused it. We don't have to hide our anger from our children, but we don't have to release every frustration we have felt all week on their heads, either. Increasingly, the child will anticipate the parent's response and will learn to control himself. This comes about best when the parent is a firm, kind, reliable teacher and not a fury released from the netherworld.

The process of developing inner controls is a slow one, moving in step with the other signs of growth in this age period. Children often are better behaved with strangers, teachers, neighbors than with their own parents. After all, it is in the company of the mother and father that the child struggles with feelings of anger and jealousy, and these bad feelings can lead to bad behavior. What you don't want at this age is a child who is good all the time. A child who never takes a poke at another one and who acts like an angel under all circumstances is a child who is holding in and pushing back his natural anger and aggression. This will cause him a great deal of anxiety and inner pain, and will stunt his development as surely as if you bound his feet.

It is easy to speak of moderation and the middle road, and not so easy to find it. We all have our own problems with anger. Some of us have tempers that we can't control; others are too restrained, fearful of our own feelings. We each have our own breaking points and many pressures on us that have nothing to do with the children themselves. We can be frustrated or angry at our mates, at our bosses, at our economic troubles. We may then use our children's misbehavior as an excuse to release tension that belongs elsewhere or to demonstrate our authority when we are feeling helpless. We are only human parents and as a result we will not be able to find the gentle, moderate road all the time. In the two-parent family, one of the parents can take over when the other is exhausted or feeling out of control. Sometimes we have to step back and view the child and his behavior to see why we are having so much trouble. Sometimes we have to check our souls and make sure that we are really disturbed about the child's behavior and not just angry at our sister or our husband, or our unpaid bills.

Spanking

Spanking is one of those subjects in American life that can get a rousing argument going any place, any time. The little boy who has just stolen all the home-baked cookies deserves a good swat, says one mother. "Horrors!" says the next. "You must never, never hit a child.

You will teach him to be violent if you do." Parents who spank their children may feel defensive and parents who don't can be irritatingly self-righteous.

It seems to us that, in principle, we do not want to teach our children that using physical strength is the right solution to any problem. If we feel that way ourselves, then we must find alternative forms of expressing our power and our disapproval. But that is an ideal guideline. Almost all parents at some point feel a kind of frustration with a four-year-old who has hurt his sister or has stepped into the street without waiting for his mother, or has for the fifteenth time thrown his ball on the dinner table. We reach out and smack him. This is not the same as a systematic discipline method of spanking a child. It is a clear indication to the child of how angry we feel and it may be better to have that communication out in the open. We can have a storm, tears, screams; then we have a reconciliation so that the day can continue. It is hard to believe in a home in which such saints reside that this doesn't occasionally happen.

Spanking, however, not in the heat of sudden anger but when used as a method of discipline has its dangers. The child may begin to enjoy the feel of pain on his body. This enjoyment is erotic. The child who at this age has many sexual feelings all over his body can confuse pain and pleasure—and that sad confusion can hinder his adult sexual connections. Spanking also makes the child feel most vulnerable and helpless before the all-powerful, all-needed adult. The feeling of being overwhelmed, out of control, makes a child so angry and frightened that these feelings can remain with him for a long time and threaten his sense of well-being. His anger and his anxiety will be so great that he may have even more trouble behaving himself. His violent feelings will weaken his sense of being a grownup good boy. A child of three or four feels humiliated by the power of the adult. This humiliation will stir up fantasies of revenge, which in turn will only make the child more anxious and less capable of self-control.

We further feel that in this world, force is not the means to teach civilized behavior. Words should be used even with very young children so that they can learn that words and not violence bring them the rewards they seek. Having said all that, we must add that there are some families in which spanking is used sometimes, coolly and without excess anger, and that no special harm seems to come of this method of discipline if the parents manage in other areas to maintain loving and caring ways. Spanking may be an inherited and hallowed family tradition, but it is nevertheless dangerous. We think the use of physical force can be a mere repetition, a wreaking on the next generation of a revenge that was really directed at one's own parents. Unfortunately, for some parents, what starts out as a spanking to teach the child right from wrong ends up as outright child abuse. In the act of hitting, these parents lose control of their own rages and vent them on small and vulnerable bodies.

Boys get hit a great deal more than girls in most families. Perhaps we believe that boys are supposed to be able to take it, that they are tough and that aggression is natural for them, to receive and to give. This seems like a bad message for our children. The child of either sex who is hit is liable to hit out at other people as soon as he is strong enough to do so. Boys are no less upset and humiliated by a spanking than girls. The ways we want to make them tough do not really include the ability to withstand or to give physical punishment.

The Spoiled Child

Arnold and his mother have gone to the toy store to buy a birthday present for Arnold's friend. The moment they enter the store, Arnold begins to rush around from counter to counter—I want a plane, I want a new space gun. I need a big Lego set, I need a tank, I want a pirate hat. Everything his eye hits he desires. His mother reminds him that they have come to get a friend a present. Arnold gets louder in his demands; he is beginning to embarrass his mother, who catches the looks the other people in the store are exchanging. Arnold refuses to leave until his mother buys him something he wants. On the one hand, she is furious—he already has so many things. On the other hand, she is sympathetic—poor Arnold, it's hard to buy a toy for someone else, and she experiences his demands as if he were in pain and she must soothe him.

Poor Arnold walks out of the store with a far more fantastic toy than the one he has purchased for his friend. Yet poor Arnold really does not feel as pleased with himself as one would think. A few minutes later, when his mother stops to look in the window of a bookstore, he pulls at her hand, makes loud noises, and stamps his feet.

* * *

Many parents are worried about spoiling their child by giving in to too many demands and permitting him to indulge in nasty behavior. Children can become overly demanding of attention and things. They can become used to getting their way more often than they should. More than spoiling children, excess makes them anxious and uncertain. The mark of a really spoiled child is that nothing ever satisfies; whatever is given, more is asked. These are children who have a hard time playing by themselves and need an enormous amount of adult approval at each step of the way.

All parents have occasional feelings of anger at their children and all parents have moments when they miss the freedom and the activities open to them before they had any children. All parents sometimes wish their children would just disappear for a bit and leave them alone. These perfectly normal passing feelings can evoke great guilt in some parents, who then cover up angry feelings with an inability to say "No" to request after request. Guilt, not love, is the cause of the really spoiled child. Since the spoiled child becomes an increasing nuisance, this evokes mounting anger and guilt in the parent: the situation feeds itself like a snake biting its own tail.

If the parent can recognize the problem, a solution is available. Feel, admit, and allow the anger toward the child to enter the mind, and then go past it to all the positive feelings that are also there. Children need the limits set by a firm parent. They must not be able to disturb the parents' private time together. They must not always get the present they wish or the extra sweet they request. They must learn that their greed may be as wide as the ocean and their neediness as vast as a continent, but still they will be taken care of, will be supported and loved with less. Since what the child of three and four really wants is the exclusive and erotic love of the parent of the opposite sex, and since that is the one thing he or she cannot receive, there is bound to be some disappointment and anger on the child's part. The parents must accept the fact that for all of us paradise has been lost long ago.

The Whining Child

Whining is one of the child's most effective methods of driving parents wild. Whining when continued over a period of hours begins to sound like the dentist's drill. Children whine repeatedly because they are truly feeling discontented. They also whine because they have learned it gets a response, even a negative one, from adults. Whining is normal but awful. A great deal of normal behavior is awful. Children whine when tired and they whine because they are feeling dissatisfied with their position in the family. They are suffering jealousy they cannot express or anxiety they can't find a name for.

You can try to change the situation the child is in. Leave the park, change the activity, try a bath, offer some food, play a game, read a story. You can also insist that the whining stop. You can pull a child out of a whining frame of mind by a determined refusal to accept that kind of communication. Tell your child directly that anything he whines for, he'll never get. Be careful! Whining is catching—frequently a parent will begin to whine back at the child. The whine is also a warning system. Your child is just at the edge of losing control of her anger, of her fear, and a storm may be coming. Children must learn from parents that the whine is a disgraceful unpleasant sound and we really want them to find a better way to let us know that something is wrong.

Learning

Learning is a healthy and happy matter for the three- to six-year-old. All the heavy textbooks that tell professionals exactly when a child should know what seem like pedantic comments on a process as complicated as a spider spinning a web and just as natural. However, there are some things most three-year-olds should know. They should be able to identify colors and to form simple sequences. If an adult shows a child a picture of a dog, one of a cat, then one of a rat, and then returns to the picture of the dog and then the cat, a child of three should be able to tell you that the next picture will be of a rat. Most three-year-olds, thanks to *Sesame Street,* can count up to 10 or more without prompting and they will use the basic grammatical structures of our language correctly. They will be able to identify a circle, a triangle, a square. Many, again thanks to *Sesame Street,* will recognize all of the letters of the alphabet, will be able to read their own names, will be able to build towers of four cubes, and a bridge of blocks. Some children will approach new tasks by trial and error;

others will not attempt to do anything new until they are fairly certain they can master the job. These are different styles in learning. Both seem to work. For children who have not been taught these things before the age of three, the nursery school years provide an important opportunity to catch up and absorb the basic ingredients of academic learning.

Some time around her fourth birthday the child will show a capacity for abstraction. She will easily do analogies like "Brother is a boy, sister is a ——." The years between three and six will bring increasing capacities for logical reasoned thought. A four-year-old can trace a diamond on a piece of paper or draw a line between two parallel lines. Many four-year-olds can hold a pencil in an adult fashion and can remember four or five objects that were placed in view and then removed. Children do not develop in lock-step fashion; for some normal children these intellectual accomplishments will come a little later and for some earlier.

The major learning of these years lies in the social arena, where the child will have changed from a being capable of only one relationship at a time into a social animal, a group member who can get and give pleasure from shared activities with others. The learning of these years is about control of anger, control of greed, control of neediness of self, and a focus newly directed outward toward others. A child who feels sad when another is hurt and who feels happy when she has finished a puzzle together with a friend is a child who has learned her lessons superbly well. A child of four and five who can play with others in an imaginary planet or can help put out an imaginary fire or can prepare imaginary meals for an imaginary family is a child who has learned well.

There is absolutely no advantage to teaching a child to read, add, or subtract at this age. It can be done for some special children easily; for others it can be accomplished with only a little effort. But the end result is to deprive children of these special years of learning, in their own way, the things that are important and meaningful for them. There is a risk that a child will begin to fear failure and grow anxious over disappointing a pushing parent. There is also the risk that a child will grow stubborn or rebellious, and make learning or not learning his particular barricade. Parents can become involved in teaching their children academic skills out of vanity and out of a desire to prove themselves, to win some imaginary competition. This is not really done out of love for the child and it can easily backfire. The child does not need to learn academic subjects earlier than his friend. He will not be smarter or better at school because of this early coaching; he will not move more quickly toward the prizes our society awards. He may only be worn out from racing so long.

Offer your child all kinds of knowledge about the world and the people who live in it. Take him to museums for short periods of time and show him one or two interesting things each visit. Let him look at picture books with you of all kinds of places and objects, but don't push him to perform for you, to read, to spell, to do long division. These are important activities in a school-age child but irrelevant to the needs and the soul of even the most remarkable of three-year-olds. No one has demonstrated any higher S.A.T. scores as a result of being drilled in basics before the age of five. Building a bird house, baking cookies, making a model ship, doing a puzzle, pasting and cutting are all activities that teach children important things about space, measurement, color, size. Doing things with your child, engaging in activities together, teaches your child far more than any formal program could. Do not push for early achievement. You could end up robbing your child of his natural joy and pleasure in learning.

Guns

Over the sofa peers a small head; slowly, cautiously, a body follows. Hanging close to the wall he turns swiftly. "Bang, bang, you're dead!" He replaces his gun in his holster and fairly swaggers into the kitchen for a glass of apple juice.

Jonah is practicing for later in the afternoon, when his friend from across the street is coming over and they intend to take on the Russian army in an all-out battle involving toy soldiers, his friend's space gun, and a plastic sword his uncle gave him for his birthday. *Varoom, boom,* and *bang* may be the most frequent sounds he utters. In his play, bombs are always falling and guns at the ready fire at moving targets under the bed, over the ceiling, behind the bathroom door. Watching little boys play, one could wonder at the fact that mankind has managed even a few years of peace between major battles.

* * *

There are some families who do not want their children to play with guns. They feel that the world is violent enough without letting little children imitate that violence in imaginary battles. The goals of world peace and human gentleness are certainly valid. The problem is that, deprived of the actual toy gun, the child will find a stick and turn it into a gun and "Bang, bang, you're dead" will become a familiar household refrain anyway. It is not the toy gun that promotes the violence in the game but the anger and the natural aggressiveness of each child, which finds its outlet and its form in these "bang, bang" games. While we might wish that human nature were spared its desire to dominate and to destroy, our wishes alter the world very little.

The truth is that the boys and girls with the guns are not necessarily the soldiers or outlaws of the future. They are, however, overcoming a sense of helplessness so often experienced in this large and frightening world. They are harmlessly expressing some of the angry feelings that color the day with or without the actual toy gun in hand. After a while these soldier games are outgrown. And after a while, as the primitive angers of these years subside, aggression can find other more indirect and socially pleasing outlets. But for the little child, a toy gun is a symbol of power in the same way that the doll is a symbol of nurturing. Some girls will want guns and enjoy battle play. Why not? This is not a sign of sexual confusion. It is a welcome sign of freedom from culturally stereotyped roles.

Television

The television set is a tired parent's best friend. It is also a potential viper in one's nest. Television is not suddenly going to become enlightened and present only wonderful educational children's programs, nor are parents going to be able to monitor everything their children see on the screen. Television works in the lives of our children in the same way that myths of primitive tribes united their members in ceremonies that took place around the fires at night. Spider Man, Superman, and Smurfs fight out battles of good and evil over and over again—and our children are mesmerized. The violence that they see, the illogical jumps from sequence to sequence bother them not at all. They wait for the hero to triumph and the bad to be beaten. In small doses, television, even bad television, feeds the imagination of the child, teaches about objects and places of all kinds and all sorts. In small doses, television echoes the violent and strange dreams and fantasies of the three-, four-, and five-year-old, and these echoes do no real harm.

In large doses, if used to keep children quiet, out of the way, from underfoot, if used by parents who don't want to be bothered, television becomes a mind-stealer. It encourages passivity and dullness. It provides images instead of letting the child create his own. It portrays the world as dangerous and unpredictable. If the young child is dazed by too much television watching, he is not doing the work of childhood—exploring, making, and, most crucial of all, connecting to other real people. The television set is like the iron. It has its uses but it can burn if used carelessly.

We feel an hour a day of television is more than enough. A half hour a day is best of all. Only on the bleakest, bleakest of mornings when both parents are in bed with stomach viruses and all friends and neighbors have left town should the television be kept on and on. Parents can use television viewing as a simple punishment or reward. A child who has misbehaved all afternoon can be forbidden his favorite program that evening; and a child who has allowed his sister to play with his new spaceship can be granted an extra half hour. Many parents find this an easy and effective form of discipline and inducement, both the carrot and the stick. We have to be careful that it doesn't turn the television set into a kind of deity, an altar within the home. If parents themselves do things other than watch television, if they offer their children activities, sports, excursions, and opportunities to play with other children, then the viewing will not become addictive. If parents sometimes sit down and watch with a child, holding and talking to him during the program, the set can become a kind of hearth that encourages family warmth instead of extinguishing it.

The Imaginary Friend

Missie appeared at the dinner table one night obviously engaged in conversation with Sara. Of course no one else at the table could see or hear Missie; nevertheless, she was definitely there. Sara made sure she had a share of food and used her napkin and didn't spill her milk. After that Missie took a bath with Sara, brushed her teeth when Sara did, and was scolded for leaving the top off the toothpaste. Missie was there when Sara woke up the next morning and stayed for about six months.

From the age of two and a half to five, it is not uncommon for a child to have an imaginary friend. This friend, usually of the same sex, will have a name and a place to sleep, and may occupy your child in games and conversation at the dinner table, in the park, on bus rides. This creature of the imagination is a wonderful invention, a sign of creativity and human ingenuity. It is not, as some parents may fear, a symptom of early madness, an incapacity to tell the real from the unreal.

The imaginary friend serves two purposes. The most important is to help the child separate from the mother and become a self that can tolerate being alone. If one invents a playmate who never goes home, who always does what you tell him, who eats and sleeps and stays with you always, then loneliness is blunted. If the imaginary friend is in bed with you at night, then the darkness is less frightening. If one thinks of the imaginary friend as the blanket or the Teddy bear taken on to a more complicated stage, it all becomes clear. Even for a four- or five-year-old, it is still sometimes hard to feel his body and his mind cut off from his mother, existing alone in space.

The child knows the friend is not real like the boy down the block or the little girl who lives upstairs. But children get very involved and happily lost in their pretend play, and while they are playing, they are capable of true belief—similar to what happens to adults in the movies or the theater. The difference is that children are fortunate enough to be able to call up this pleasure from within themselves. They don't want to have you ruin their illusion, so if you play along and give Harold or Mary, who is invisible to all at the table, a spoon or a cup, it won't hurt. It didn't hurt to keep retrieving your child's threadbare blanket from behind the couch, and this won't hurt either.

The imaginary friend can serve another useful purpose for the young child. He can contain all the nasty evil thoughts that are within the child himself. Pretend Mary can take the blame for actual acts of naughtiness done by the real child. Invented Harold can be the one who thinks about Daddy crashing his car and never coming home again. The real child can protect himself from the bad thoughts and occasional misdeeds that fill his days by foisting them all off on his invisible playmate. This is a device that is used for just a short while, until the child is strong enough to tolerate the bad feelings within himself. The imaginary friend drops out of the picture and is forgotten as soon as the child is able to endure separateness from the parent and tolerate the inner angers that accompany that aloneness. Reality, the fact that the child is not punished unduly for bad thoughts, the fact that bad wishes do not come true, the fact that real people are more interesting than imaginary ones, all cause the imaginary friend to pale gradually until he or she fades away to nothing. Like the pacifier and the diaper, he becomes an abandoned relic of early childhood.

Swearing, Obscenities, and Bathroom Talk

What great fun it is for the four-year-old to say a "bad" word! How he relishes the shocked look on your face the first time he comes home from the playground and loudly announces to the family his newly discovered sophistication, his knowledge of the forbidden. More often than not this happens just as Great Aunt Mary arrives for a visit or the elevator is filled with a convention of ministers. Two generations ago parents reacted with anger to all bad words. They washed children's mouths out with soap: They severely punished the offending tongue and the small criminal to whom the tongue was attached. These were days in which the use of swear words had the power not only to shatter one of the Ten Commandments but to shock and offend. The extreme adult reaction to bad language only made it more interesting, more exciting and tempting. It made the sexual, bathroom content seem enticing in its power to arouse and frighten the adult. Even in these more liberal days it is still upsetting for parents to hear small children swear. Most of us don't like it, and that's exactly why it's fun and exciting for children to do it once in a while.

We have to let a child know very firmly that this swearing like a sailor may be all right on the high seas but is unacceptable in the playground or the dining room. Explain to your child that some words that refer to body parts or to things men and women do privately together are considered impolite and not to be used by children. Yes, adults use these words, but there are many things that adults can do that children cannot. Be sure not to make the child feel that it is the sexual activity or the sexual interest that is itself wrong. Be clear with your child that the words themselves are not nice words and that we have others to describe the same function, activity, or object that are perfectly all right to use. Children, after an initial period of teasing you, usually stop using bad words except to show off to their friends.

We wouldn't make too big a fuss about swearing even if sexual matter is brutally included. Most little children don't know exactly what these words mean. Almost all children will go through a period of cracking up over bathroom jokes. Anybody who refers to "kaka" or "poopoo" will be rewarded with gales of laughter. Children will fall to the floor at the mention of the word "breasts." They may giggle with pleasure if someone around takes the Lord's name in vain. Parents should just ignore the bathroom silliness, the giggles, and the rather broad jokes. This will pass as the child becomes more attuned to what is socially all right and what is not. By eight or nine most children would be deeply embarrassed if by some accident they used a "nasty" word in front of a teacher or a parent.

Among themselves, bad language may be in common use. These words serve to release tension, to express anger, and to create a veneer of toughness among peers. Different groups of children will to one extent or another use bad words if others in their group do so. It seems to us that the way children speak to each other is their own business. The words themselves are only words. If we try to interfere we only make those words seem more appealing, more powerful than in fact they are.

Remember that we are models for our children. If we use the language we forbid them in our own casual conversations with each other, then they will sooner or later do what we do, not what we say. We can push the idea that what is sauce for the goose is not sauce for the goslings only so far.

Stuttering and Lisping

Some children will begin to stutter or lisp as they develop more and more complicated speech patterns. Some of these irregularities will disappear before the age of six; others may become definite handicaps that will require the attention of speech therapists. Lisps can interfere with a child's capacity to learn the sound of letters and hinder reading. Stuttering is a painful symptom that has profound emotional implications, although it may be caused by brain and nerve patterns. Children who stutter or lisp will do so even more under pressure. They become anxious about speaking and lose interest in communicating if parents constantly call attention to the problem. Since the majority of speech problems are only reflections of an immaturity of the physiological system that will be outgrown before the sixth birthday, it is best to ignore them as much as possible.

Certainly if stuttering or lisping persists into the middle of the fifth year, it would be a good idea to consult a speech therapist. Psychological problems can accompany or even cause some speech difficulties, but in that case the speech problem would most likely be only one among several disturbances the child is showing. In a three- or four-year-old child who is otherwise demonstrating no special troubles, one can wait and watch the speech development carefully.

Some children hold on to baby talk longer than would seem necessary. We often see this in nursery school children who have a baby brother or sister. They use the baby speech as a way of reminding the world that they too are in need of care and are still very small and helpless. Sometimes they are simply competing with the baby for baby care. This kind of babyish speech will disappear as they are reassured of their important place in the family and rewarded with admiration and affection for all the more grownup things that they can do and say.

We have found that some children who are unable to express their anger clearly and directly may develop disrupted speech. It might be a good idea to be sure that a stuttering, lisping, or baby-talking child has parental permission to occasionally be bad or angry and is not too conforming or "good."

Habits

There are a set of habits that disturb parents and are very common among children of this age. Nail-biting, hair-pulling and -twisting, thumb-sucking, and masturbation are all common in children from three to six. We look at these habits in terms of length of persistence and intensity. Then we judge whether they are harmless, passing expressions of the normal wear and tear of life or are symptoms of severe or troubling concern. This judgment is made by looking at the whole child, weighing how she is doing in all the important matters of her age. We look to see if these habits are interfering with the general development of the child, or if they are simply outlets for the normal tensions of this age, used not in excess and not in place of real relationships and experiences with the outside world. For the vast majority of thumb-suckers, nail-biters, hair-twirlers, the habit is harmless. It will pass as the child learns other means of reducing tension.

Thumb-Sucking

Thumb-sucking is actually a very good way for a baby to comfort himself. It used to be thought that children damaged their permanent teeth by pushing against the roof of their mouths. This has been totally and finally debunked; there is no harm in this habit at all. Some children will suck their thumbs when confronted with a new situation, or overwhelmed with fatigue. Some children well into the fifth or sixth year may use their thumbs as a kind of reunion with their babyhood, a reminder of the comforting they received from their mothers. If the child has friends and can play happily with other children, and if he forgets about his thumb while enjoying the many activities of his age, then the occasional retreat to a more babyish kind of self-comforting means nothing at all. If parents let the thumb-sucking fade of its own accord as the child enters school, all will be fine.

Habits such as thumb-sucking are, however, flammable areas

where the struggle between the parent and the child can easily flare up. The child will not want to be told what to do with his own thumb and will consider interference with his comforting as an attempt to destroy his independence and his autonomy. Once that has happened, it becomes harder still for him to give up the habit. As parents we do best not to make our children feel that they are giving in to us, but rather to let them grow up gradually on their own. Children will revert to thumb-sucking when sick or faced with a parent's trip or a move to a new house or the arrival of a new baby. These slides backward on the road to maturity are to be both expected and respected. By itself, thumb-sucking is not a danger signal. Until well after the age of six we would not be concerned with this habit in a child who is otherwise flourishing.

Nail-Biting

Melissa, intent on her TV program, is biting furiously at her nails. She may not even know she is doing it, but later she may notice that in her concern over the heroine's plight she drew blood around her own cuticles. Melissa probably doesn't care what her nails look like. She bites them in the bathtub, while waiting her turn to jump rope, while watching the cookies rise in the oven, while listening to a story or riding the bus. Her fingertips may look red and raw, but reminding her to stop will have no effect at all except to uselessly annoy her.

Nail-biting is one of those habits that seem to appear suddenly in three-year-olds and may last through adolescence and sometimes throughout a lifetime. Some studies have found that almost 40 percent of all three- to six-year-olds bite their nails. Nail-biting is used to discharge tension, as a means of releasing a certain energy connected with anger. Children who are expected to be quiet in school and who have to control many of their angry impulses may quite routinely attack their own nails. Considering the fact that all normal children experience anger and tension and are under great pressure to behave themselves—to make nice when they might want to bite—it is no wonder that so many nails fall victim to so many teeth.

This habit by itself signifies no particular disturbance of the child and is best ignored. Nail-biting does occur along with many other symptoms in especially anxious or distressed children. But as we watch our children bite at their fingertips, we do best simply to acknowledge that there are strains and hardships in growing up; there is no path to adulthood that is not overgrown with bushes of tension and brambles of conflict.

Neatness and Messiness

When children have achieved bowel control, they have absorbed our attitude toward fecal products and they have learned to ignore, discard, and push away their previous natural desire to play with their own body products. By three, they have gone through a long stage of playing with water and messing about with clay and paint. Now they will show reactions to dirt and mess and strange textures that at first may seem exaggerated. Some children will dislike the feeling of sand on their feet. Some will become concerned if the smallest spot appears on a shirt; and some for a brief while will be unable to tolerate putting their hands in anything gooey, sticky, or unfamiliar. If they don't last for years, these reactions are reasonable responses to the disgust we have taught them about the bowel function.

As reality becomes clearer and clearer to the child, she will be able to separate out the dirt in the yard that has gotten on her shoes from the bathroom matter that we don't want touched. Then she will be able to be dirty without undue concern. As a result of their parents' attitudes and the methods used to toilet-train them, some children will become excessively neat and clean, constantly concerned about dirt. Other children will become messy; their hair, face, hands, clothes seeming to attract filth in some magnetic way. We would be concerned only if this extreme reaction continued for years. (It will be discussed further in our next section.)

Washing

After the age of three, many children prefer to take over the responsibility for washing themselves in the bath. While they are naked in the tub they can feel overpowered by the larger adult. The strangeness of the water itself and the fact that something is being done to their bodies can make them anxious. It is best as much as possible to allow them to take over.

Some children are frightened of and resist the process of shampooing into the fifth year. The suffocating sense of water over the face and the need to close one's eyes to protect against soap alarms these children, waking their fears of their body coming apart, of being washed away from those they need. This fear too will pass shortly after the child is able to pour the water and do the soaping himself.

Keep your child company in the bath but offer him the washcloth and begin to tell him what to do with it. He will know from all the times you have done it before. Your child wants to take care of himself, and with a little encouragement will feel very proud of his accomplishments. It is more important to have him do it himself than to clean every speck of dirt off from behind his neck. His skills will improve with practice. If your three-year-old son asks that you clean his genitals or rub them dry, tell him quite calmly that big boys do these things themselves and you expect the same of him. If he vehemently protests, allow a few weeks to go by, then tell him again that this is what you expect. Most children enjoy their bath far more after they themselves take over the soap and cloth.

The Shy Child

Waking from a nap, Harry walks into his own living room and finds a friend of his mother's and her child have come to visit. Harry stands stiff and still. He is introduced but he turns his head away. "Come and show Michael your new train," says his mother, but Harry doesn't move. He acts as if his feet were embedded in cement. The other little boy runs over and pushes Harry. "Where's the train?" he says. Harry doesn't answer. Harry doesn't look up or down. He is pale and still. Finally he slips behind his mother and stays there, peering out when he thinks no one is looking to see what the other child is up to. Michael finds a puzzle, chatters away to both adults in the room, and cheerfully climbs on the furniture exploring the unknown space. Harry's mother feels embarrassed by her frozen zombie child. He does talk, she wants to say; he smiles and laughs and is very clever, but never in front of strangers, not in strange places. A mother's self-confidence can be affected by the shyness of her child.

* * *

Shyness is a leftover side effect of the early separation anxiety and tells us that the child is still struggling with the fear of being too separate, too alone in the world. Shyness is an expression of discomfort in new places and with new people. The shy child will not look a stranger in the face and will look down as if to blot out this unhappy reality. Like the ostrich, the shy child hopes the unfamiliar will not notice her and just go away.

If the early separations have been hard to handle because there were too many of them, or because of early illness, or because the child has experienced some painful kind of aloneness, or if there has been marital tension, divorce, or a mother who was not steadily available to the child in the first years, shyness is a possible result.

Many, many children at age three and four will be quiet and sober in new places and with new people. Some children are shy for many months in a new nursery school setting. This early shyness is usually overcome around the age of six or so. If all other developmental areas are progressing, and if the child is able after a while in a play setting to make friends with other children, then the shyness can be considered only a transitory sign of some special sensitivity to separation and is of no concern to either parents or teachers. If a shy child warms up after a while to a teacher or neighbor, and if she eventually enters into play with other children, the shyness itself will dissolve as she becomes more certain of her capacity to be a self, unsupported by the constant arms of her mother or father.

The Angry Child

Liza wants a Fudgsicle but her mother has bought her an ice cream cup instead. Liza throws the cup on the ground. She kicks her mother and screams. Her mother tries to reason with her, explaining how Fudgsicles drip and how delicious ice cream tastes in a cup. Liza, no longer crying, runs off to the sandbox, where she steps on the fingers of another child. Then, picking up a pail that doesn't belong to her, she runs away so that her mother has to chase her and return the pail to its rightful owner. Next, Liza goes over to the slide but has to wait for the child ahead of her to reach the top. She pushes this child in the back, and, taking a fistful of hair in her hand, yanks.

* * *

Liza may just be having a bad day or she may behave like this frequently. She may be coming down with a virus, or her dad may have just left for a business trip, or she may act this way sometimes for no reason at all. Anger in the three-year-old is released in waves from time to time.

Some children arrive at the age of three with more anger in them than others. The new competitiveness and jealousy that a three-year-old begins to experience awaken new anxiety, producing new anger. That is only normal and natural.

One child will hit another child if she tries to take something from him. Sometimes a child will want something another has so badly that he will push, shove, and grab. Little girls particularly will pull hair when angered, and pinch. Anyone who has been pinched by a three-year-old knows that is a considerable weapon. Little boys will punch and kick at their fathers when they are in bad moods and little girls have been known deliberately to break Mommy's necklace or smash her favorite vase. Some children when they feel particularly helpless and particularly furious will bite. This horrifies other parents and other children. We are afraid of each other's teeth; we are uneasy when the human being behaves like a wild animal. But in fact, the child is just using an available handy weapon.

Parents and teachers of course stop open aggression. We disapprove of hitting or knocking down, banging against, or biting. We may separate the angry child from others. As parents we may get really angry when the aggression is directed at us, and in so doing we help the child learn to control his behavior. Where we have to be careful is not to be so powerful and quick in our response that our children become afraid to express their anger in any way at all. A child who is too good, who never hits or strikes out at another, may also be a child who cannot hit back. His anger will not disappear—anger never just evaporates. It goes underground and works to feed on guilt. It can punish the child in ways we would not wish. Children need aggression in order to move eagerly and energetically around the world. Aggression turned in the right direction makes us vivid and capable people, even if we are not always nice. We have to stop antisocial behavior without intimidating or terrorizing our child into abandoning all open angers. We are talking about moderation of response. You shouldn't be too angry at your angry child, but you can't let your angry child run wild, either. He is depending on you to help create his controls.

The parent should try to encourage a change from a physical angry response to a verbal one. We want the child to be able to tell us what is causing him to be so upset. Sometimes we can solve the problem; sometimes we can only offer sympathy. But three-year-olds should begin to use words to express their feelings. By five or six we expect most children to be able to be angry and talk about it without resorting to physical action.

Divorce

At this writing at least one out of every five children lives in a home with only one parent. With more than one-third of all marriages ending in divorce, we cannot call this situation unusual. Divorce causes real grief for all involved children. Divorces in which parents continue to fight over the children or in which one parent or another discontinues contact with the child are especially grueling for young developing minds and hearts. Remarriages and step-families provoke other problems for everyone and our country is brimful of divided and relinked mothers, fathers, and children.

Divorce is an ordeal for a child. So is illness. Divorce is a fact of American life, and after an initial period of inevitable upset, if the divorce is managed with some grace by both parents, children, like adults, will recover their equilibrium and continue the forward path of their lives. We cannot ignore the special and complicated hurdles that the child of divorced parents faces, yet at the same time we cannot fall into a bog of despair assuming that our children's lives have been permanently ruined. Affected, yes. Ruined, not necessarily. We have seen too many vital, contributing, interesting, contented grown up children from divorced families to believe that the divorce automatically cripples or maims.

Divorce is a result of an unhappy marriage and unhappiness in the household has its own devastating effects on children. Depressed or angry parents have difficulty in standing strong and steady for their children day in and day out. Distrust and dislike have a way of polluting the home. Yet divorce comes as a shock to all children. It awakens every shred of terror that the child ever had of being abandoned.

The child between the ages of three and six has special difficulties with divorce. The child is engaged in a competitive jealous battle with the parent of the same sex for the erotic love of the other. She feels angry at the parent and afraid of some kind of angry response, a punitive retaliation. She has wild fantasies in which she gets rid of the other parent or is punished horridly for the thought. If in the midst of this internal drama the child is confronted with divorce, the guilt and fear become greater. Most children at this age need continued reassurance that nothing that they thought or did caused the divorce. But remember that the guilt is deep, and even with the parent's frequent realistic explanations most children will retain some sense that they were responsible. This is natural. Children see the situation and their role in it more realistically in time.

There are other fears. If one parent can leave the home, perhaps the other one will also. If a mother can stop loving a father, perhaps she can also stop loving a child. If a crucial member of the house leaves, perhaps a crucial part of the body can also disappear. In order to defend herself against the pain of all these fears, the child may believe that through some magic the parents will be reunited and the family be whole once more.

In struggling with these thoughts, most young children will show regressions to earlier stages of development. If they had just acquired bowel and bladder control at night, they may lose it again. If they had stopped stuttering or sleeping with their favorite blanket, they may need the blanket again and the stutter will reappear. If they were playing well with friends in nursery school, they may be suddenly unable to pay any attention to others. If they were easily able to go to school in the morning, they may suddenly cling and cry at the time of separation. They may wake frequently at night needing to know that the remaining parent is still there. They may have an upsurge of nightmares. If they had stopped sucking their thumbs or pulling on a lock of hair, this behavior may reappear. These are all signs of stress and anxiety and they are particularly hard for parents to deal with at a time when they themselves feel so confused and frightened about their own futures.

Some children will use denial. They will insist that Daddy is really coming home soon or that Mommy is just away on a vacation. Some will become very, very good, hiding all signs of anger and upset, hoping that this goodness will undo the divorce. Others can no longer control the angry feelings that swell within them, and will take to hitting, biting, and pushing other children around.

These symptoms of disturbance do not subside overnight. But they will gradually fade away if both parents can manage to keep seeing the child in some regular fashion, and if the parents themselves in the following two-year period begin to stabilize their own lives and their relationship with each other. Money is almost always an issue between people, and if parents can make the financial arrangements without lasting hostility that seeps over onto the child, this also speeds the healing process.

Reality is on the side of health and happiness. If the child's worst fears of being abandoned, of losing a loved parent are not fulfilled, slowly the child absorbs the new reality of his now split family and sees that although it is split, he is still taken care of and loved. As the child gets older, the competitive and erotic feelings subside. Now the child—if not pushed to become the man in the family for his mother or the woman for her father—can settle the age-appropriate issues of identification with the same-sexed parent and defer romantic love until a later time.

If a parent does move far away or actually deserts the child, then that child must live through a period of mourning. This is a time in which she will be both angry at the remaining parent and angry at the parent who has left. She will feel that she is worthless, or else the parent would have stayed. At the same moment she will blame the parent who is at home for having driven the other away. These feelings and the signs of upset that accompany them are almost inevitable, and the best a parent can do is to weather the storm, support the child, and repair his or her own life so that the child can eventually adjust to the reality of a home in which she is truly loved and protected. Desertion by a parent leaves a scar wide and deep. But it need not leave an open wound if the remaining parent can be supportive through the child's grief and can restore steadiness and an optimistic atmosphere to the home.

Most divorced parents will begin to have relationships with other men or women. These initial voyages out into the single world are difficult enough for parents to endure, without the extra burden of the child's anxieties. But the anxieties are there. Even the most casual date who comes to the house to pick you up and leaves you at the front door is seen by the child as proof of your betrayal of the other parent. The intruder is an unwelcome reminder of the divorce, a sign of its irreversibility. The date also represents a threat to the closeness of parent and child. Children don't like to share either parent. When there has been a divorce, they are feeling particularly vulnerable and afraid you will leave them for someone else.

Of course, this doesn't mean you shouldn't date, make good friends of the opposite sex, entertain them in your home as you wish. What it does mean is that you have to be prepared for some bad behavior on the part of your child. She may have a temper tantrum in front of a perfect stranger. She may act overly cute and sweet, then wet her bed and wake up with nightmares at three in the morning. If you have a date spend the night with you, the child will become particularly anxious that a stranger is taking the place of the original parent. It seems like a good idea to avoid this until you are deep in a relationship with someone who has begun to know your child. Too many faces and bodies coming and going only keep the child in a state of constant agitation. She will feel as if she has been traveling, living in strange hotel rooms for months on end.

When a parent is serious about someone as a long-term partner, it is a good idea to introduce the new person to the child in a neutral place and at a time of day that doesn't force the child to think of two adults in bed together. Don't expect instant love or affection—or even moderate politeness. The child may interrupt all conversation, allow the adults no time alone, and demand everything from toys to food. This will simmer down in time as the child gets used to the new person. It helps if neither parent is resentful; if each parent can accept the new mate in the former partner's life, naturally this makes it easier for the child to do so.

We are talking about parents behaving in an ideal, giving way at a time when they are under the greatest of strains and are experiencing grief, failure, and depression themselves. It would be absurd to expect parents at this dreadful juncture in their own lives to be perfect nurturers, joyful caretakers, and patient and loving companions. Parenting requires a good deal of self-discipline. The situation of divorce is one of the times when this discipline, this ability to see the child's needs and fulfill them over, above, and even against one's own, is called on. It is exhausting to stay up night after night with a sick child in the hospital. It is hard to hurry home from a job and listen to a five-year-old's puppet play when you really need some quiet and a hot bath. It is harder still to support a child through the pain of divorce when you yourself are hurting so much. But here is where discipline is needed, and where, if you can find it, the rewards will be great. Children do recover from the initial shock and grief of divorce, and if they are not abandoned emotionally they will regain their footing. Even if the vows of marriage are broken, the even more important unspoken vows to one's child need not be.

Custody

Different forms of custody may be right for one family or another. A switch in custody arrangements may even be desirable as the child grows or as the parents' lives change and new partners enter. The important matter is not which one is the custodial parent but how to make the divorce work for the child.

Though difficult, the goal is to create the least amount of disruption in the child's life. It is probably better to allow the child to have a home in which one set of messages is dominant rather than a constant shuffling about. We do not recommend two nights in one place and two nights in the next, because the child needs some kind of permanence and real home base. Children should be excluded from all arguments about money or visitation rights. These are the issues that call upon the child's loyalty. The ideal divorce does not ask the child to reject or become angry at one parent or another; it does not force the child into loyalty decisions. Parents in pain are apt to require the complete love and devotion of their children and tend to use them against the other parent or to demand some kind of rejection of the ex-partner. The child from three to six has so many of his own competitive loyalty struggles that this places an intolerable strain on the youngster, provoking guilt and fear.

The best kind of custody arrangement would be, in spirit, a joint custody in which both parents feel equally involved and responsible but in which the child makes a weekday home in one household and a weekend home in another, or one parent has as many long visits as they wish. This should be accomplished without disrupting the child's school or social life more than necessary. One summer the child could be with the mother while the father went to Europe;

the next she could be with the father and his friend because they were going to the beach. If both parents, instead of insisting on rigid schedules (which rarely work anyway) or on limitations of the other's rights, would just try to do what seems best for the child on all occasions, then joint custody would after some rough spots be the best arrangement of all. We have by now been to enough weddings where four sets of parents stood beaming beside the bride and groom to know that eventually the bitterness fades and everyone can feel comfortable being a part of the child's happiness and well-being.

Visiting a Parent

Whether they occur weekly or biweekly, visits to a divorced parent are apt to be strained at first. The young child is away from his known home and feels himself a stranger in the parent's new place. Don't fall into the trap of feeling that you have to entertain your child every minute or offer extraordinary presents or activities. What the child really wants is natural time with you. Set your place up so the child can play alone or join you. Plan some activity but keep things quiet and unpressured. Remember, the child will be missing the other parent and is angry and upset about the divorce. Expect either bad behavior or withdrawn and shy behavior. Be patient; eventually, the child can experience your place as a second home, but this takes time. It may take several years.

It is best not to introduce your child to every passing person you may be dating. The child will feel competitive and upset at your new involvement and will feel disloyal to his own mother or father by involving himself at all with the new person. These are strong and important feelings and there is no sense in stirring them up constantly.

When you are seriously involved with someone, then of course your child must meet this person and you must all spend time together. But the child will not be as happy as you are over this turn of events and will take a long time to adjust to the idea. A three- or four-year-old has secretly been expecting you to return one day to his home, and the new person will puncture that illusion. There is no sense in doing this casually.

Death

Some people believe that children do not understand death at all. This is probably an adult wish rather than a fact. The child playing peek-a-boo is laughing at death. The child playing hide-and-seek is surely playing at death and resurrection. Children see balloons burst. They see water disappear down the drain. They see plants wither and die, and they see snow melt and puddles dry up and disappear. They feel their own vulnerability and helplessness. They cry when they are left because they do believe in death, not because they don't.

If a pet dog or hamster dies, children will mourn. They will be upset. They will quickly make the analogy, If Blackie or Fuzzy died, then so can I. They will have already suspected that. Talk honestly about the death of a pet, a grandparent—or anyone. Children must learn that life has an end and that some things disappear forever. It is no kindness to try to hide the truth from a three- or four-year-old. They sense death, they see it around them. They hear about it from friends. They play games of death and life. They must come to terms with mortality. They may have bad dreams the week or so after a pet dies. They may cling to the mother or father in a more babyish way. This will pass. If it is part of your religion to speak of heaven and reunion, then of course you will do so. Children seem to accept the idea of death and to deny it just as adults do. They may make up their own stories or borrow yours. Either way children surely understand the concept of separation and that is really all death is.

The Death of a Parent

Children must be told honestly and quickly if a parent has died. They will be stunned and shocked by the information, even if the death was expected and some preparation given. Unlike grownups, children show their sadness only briefly. They will perhaps cry for a bit or look pale and still, but after a short while they again begin to play. They may cheerfully greet relatives as they come to the house and they will appear not to understand what is going on. Adults assume that the child is not mourning and has not understood. This is not true. It is just that children cannot tolerate sadness for long periods. They push it out of their minds and deny its cause.

They may ask, When is Daddy coming home? When can I go see Mommy in the hospital? They have not really forgotten. They are testing out the reality. They are playing with their denial. It is important that they be included as much as possible in the mourning process of the other parent. They must be allowed to express their feelings about the death when they are ready. This does not mean that grownups can invade their privacy or try to attack their denial of what has happened. Each child defends against great pain in his own way. We must respect his decisions while making it clear that we are ready to talk about the dead parent with him whenever he wants. We must wait until he is ready to expose and share his feelings.

Rather than cry or be sad, children will instead show various kinds of regression. They will wake at night. They may have bowel and bladder accidents, or become afraid again of the vacuum cleaner. They may become very aggressive in nursery school or attempt to harm a baby sister or brother. They may have a temper tantrum if the kind of dessert they want is not available. Children under stress lose controls they had previously gained. This is normal and should be expected.

The young child between three and six is also bound to experience some guilt and some sense that the death was his own fault for not being good enough, for having bad, angry, or jealous thoughts about the parent. A child of this age is not yet aware that thoughts do not influence events. The child will need reassurance that he is a good child and had nothing to do with the death.

The child will have many fantasies of reunion with the lost parent. This is perfectly normal and may continue throughout childhood. A four-, five-, or six-year-old may be unable to tell his friends or teachers about the death—little children do not want to talk about death. They may feel ashamed and painfully different. They may begin to be afraid of ghosts. This is a reflection of the fact that children feel angry at the parent who has died and left them. On one level they may understand clearly that the sickness or the accident was not the fault of the dead parent; but on another they will feel as if they have been deliberately deserted. The parent appears to have broken the unspoken vow between parent and child: I will always be there for you when you need me.

Many children will fantasize about joining their parents in heaven after their own death. These thoughts are often coupled with the feeling that the dead parent is really watching over them and is aware of how well they ride a bike or paint a picture. Some may even state that they wish to die themselves. Don't be alarmed. These are normal feelings for a bereaved child and will pass as the child makes new and deep connections to other important adults in his life.

We can help the child by not withdrawing from her at this time. Caught in our own grief we can assume we should hide our true feelings from the child and try to aid in her general denial. This doesn't help very much. The child needs to experience real emotional closeness with the remaining parent, even if that means sharing sadness. Sometimes the child is so angry at the loss and so guilty that she cannot help but behave badly with the remaining parent. This is hard for a bereaved parent to deal with but will pass in time.

Naturally a child who has experienced a major loss will be more anxious about the other parent and more anxious about his own physical integrity and safety. Time will restore a child's confidence in the stability of his world. But a child who has experienced such a major catastrophe will always be more vulnerable to separations and will take longer to resolve the jealous and competitive feelings natural to this age. Children after a while begin to remember the dead parent as a perfect being. They sometimes feel bad because they are not so perfect themselves. They feel as if they should be as good as they imagine the parent to have been. They cannot correct their misconceptions by testing reality and so may become harsh judges of themselves. We can help by talking honestly about the dead parent with the child from time to time, by presenting again and again the reality of what happened, and by our continued support, love, and care even through our own depression and chaotic mourning.

Small children should be included in the funeral plans and permitted to share the rituals to whatever degree they wish. It is a good idea to have a babysitter available to take the child away from the relatives when he shows signs of fatigue or strain. The child may not appear to take in the significance of the funeral and the family gathering. But it is better for him to be included in the family experience than shunted off, where he will surely feel further abandoned.

The Hospital

For the child over three, the experience of going to the hospital is terrifying not only because of the fear of separation from his parents but because he understands that something dangerous and threatening is happening to him. He has some glimmer of the connection of illness with death. He understands the parents' natural worry and concern.

The little child is also struggling to maintain a sense of his body as belonging to him, being under his control. He feels afraid that his sexual thoughts will be known and that the parent of the opposite sex might be prepared to harm him. Painful needles and examinations in which he is forced to lie still or be vulnerable to strange hands and strange eyes are particularly upsetting and frightening.

The child of four or five does not want to be a baby who lies limply in the crib and is picked up and fed by others. Yet the hospital asks him to stay in bed, to be done to instead of doing. Pain and upset stomachs, the taking of medicine, and the flowing of strange fluids into the body are routine parts of most hospital experiences. It is easy to understand how overwhelming and difficult this is for the young child.

Sometimes surgery or a prolonged stay in the hospital is necessary. In this event it is crucial that parents stay with their children, as close to them all the time as possible. The reassurance of the familiar face is not just an assurance that the mother and father have not abandoned their child to the ministrations of strangers; it is a confirmation of who that child is. Identity and self-respect are returned to the child by the constant care of the parents throughout this difficult time.

Children of three, four, and five will not necessarily be lovingly grateful for the parents' vigil by the bedside. They may very well behave rudely, turn away from a parent, reject a carefully picked out gift. refuse to have their pajamas changed, or insist on staying outside the covers. They may knock things over or crayon on tables instead of paper. They may have temper tantrums if frustrated in any way by the parents, yet behave like angels for the nurses. The fright of the strange situation and the helplessness and vulnerability they feel make them angry, and they have no safe place to vent that anger except on the heads of already exhausted parents. This is a natural by-product of the hospital experience. However, when the child comes home and the threat is gone, she can better recover not only from the illness but from the attack on her dignity, integrity, and safety, if the parent has stayed by the bedside.

Children at this age should be prepared as best as possible for all the things that will happen to them. Leave nothing out. Having the cold sensation of an antiseptic on the stomach can be as important to a child as a stitch. Tell him about everything he will see and hear and feel. Sometimes it is hard for parents to do this. Hospitals frighten us, too. But the lasting effects of this hard time are reduced emormously if the child is not overwhelmed by the unexpected. Children are far less frightened by events that do not come as surprises.

If the reason for the hospitalization is not serious (tonsils or the removal of a small growth), parents tend to forget that the child is frightened by the strange environment anyway and needs constant reassurance that all will be well. When children are really sick and life-threatening conditions have brought them to the hospital, parents must try as best they can to remain calm and confident in the presence of the child. Children should not be lied to and told all will be fine tomorrow when that is not true. On the other hand, we tell children only what they absolutely need to know, what they ask about directly. We do not want to burden them with our fears of what-ifs and what-mights. We must tell children as simply and as accurately as possible what is wrong with them and what the doctors will do to help them. Think in terms of day by day, not month by month. The parents of a really sick child need to spell each other and to use the other members of the family. Time out of the hospital is essential to refuel or gain the energy needed to carry the weight of worry.

Children are particularly afraid of needles. They may focus almost entirely on the dreaded changing of an I.V. or an expected blood test. The needle is horrifying to the child not only because of the pain but because it makes him feel so helpless and out of control. If he doesn't like to have someone wash his face, think how he feels about being punctured against his will. Expect your child to be angry about this, allow him to be rude to the nurses, to throw his toys, to protest. His dignity needs that.

Surgery can intensify a child's fear that something will happen to his body parts and increase his fear of genital harm. A child after surgery, even very minor surgery, may be anxious about his body wholeness. He may be cautious and fearful for a while. Parents can help by reassuring the child that his body is made just right and will stay that way. Children after surgery may frequently touch their genitals to make sure everything is all right. They may express fears of broken objects or loud noises. In time, these disturbances will die down.

The Adopted Child

The adopted child is always a wanted child, and this is the important message to be conveyed to her with the very first explanations of the adoption. Children after the age of three will begin to ask questions about where babies come from. Even if they don't, they are wondering about the facts of birth. Whether you hear direct questions or not, you should introduce the subject of adoption. Tell your child about birth in simple terms and let her know that her parents were not able to have a child grow inside and so instead they were lucky enough to be able to adopt her. Three-year-old children accept adoption easily, and will want to hear the story over and over again about the excitement when you all first met each other and how happy you were when you found out you would have a baby of your own.

The explanation can be given in such a way that the child does not feel rejected or angry at her biological parents, at least not at this age. Tell the child that the parents who gave birth to her loved her very much but were unable to take care of her, and so they gave her to her mommy and daddy, who were overjoyed and who love her very much and will take care of her forever and ever. Parents should feel comfortable about talking to the child about the adoption. They should no longer be feeling the acute pain of disappointment that they could not have a biological child. If they have tended the baby and watched over her with work and affection, that requires they should feel proud of the adoption. The child will not feel less "theirs." She will not be less "theirs." She will belong to them because they, by taking care of her, have made themselves the true parents. Make sure you believe this fully and understand it completely before you talk to your child, because even a three-year-old will pick up your anxiety if you are in any way ashamed or uncertain.

Children who find out that they are adopted after the age of five or so are shocked. They feel betrayed that their parents had not told them earlier. If they hear about it from a neighbor or a relative, they will be furious. They will feel as if the adoption was a family disgrace in that it was kept secret. They will not have good feelings about themselves or about their adoptive parents. It is very important that the child and the parents both easily and openly appreciate the special chosenness of their relationship, and that this is accepted and taken for granted from the earliest years on.

Parents who adopt must know that as the child grows older there may be questions and concern about the facts of the biological birth, as well as the faces, places, and names of the biological parents. All children must struggle to create their identities. For the adopted child, there is always the added complication of the biological unknowns and the faint sense of something haunting, something not quite right in their past. Children are anxious to be like everyone else and the fact of adoption can make a child feel different, set apart. Sometimes other children, on learning that a child is adopted, may taunt or tease or make her feel self-conscious or weird. Support your child by telling her that you are proud you could adopt her and you are proud to have her for your daughter. Almost all human beings feel themselves to be different from the pack in one way or another, and living with this can make a child stronger and more sure of her own identity in the long run.

Make sure your child does not feel it disloyal to you to wonder aloud about his natural parents. This may not happen until the child is over ten, and in some families it never comes up. But we would feel it a good idea for children after the age of ten to be given whatever information you may have. "Your biological mother was a young student who needed to complete her education," or, "There was a terrible war in the country you were born in and your mother was afraid for your safety." Children will spin all kinds of fantasies from little information, so tell them those things that will help them to be proud of their genes as well as their adopted place.

Parents who have adopted a child often feel threatened by the child's curiosity about the natural parents. Older children can use the fact of the adoption to hurt their parents, but in all families at some time or other the child will become angry and use whatever weapons are at hand to hurt. The fact of the adoption does give the child a weapon. Other children have other weapons. Just remember that the phrase, "You're not my real mommy, I don't have to do what you say," takes other forms in other households, where children also deny parental authority and claim to prefer aunts, uncles, or rich cousins to their own parents. If you are comfortable with the fact of the adoption, the child may tease but she too will accept the reality of her place and love you just the way any other child loves her parents—that is to say, imperfectly and not all the time, and yet absolutely and without condition; a paradox, but nevertheless a truth.

Adoptive parents may themselves feel particularly guilty when, on a bad day, when everything has gone wrong, they wish they had never adopted a child. All parents at some time or other grow so angry at their children that they wish they had never conceived them, never gotten married, stayed in the Army, entered a convent, and so on. These passing thoughts are the normal, common dark side of the parenting experience. They are no more significant for the adopted parent than for the biological one. We all sometimes wish our children on another planet. The parent who adopts is not special in this. The parents of the adopted child will also feel the full flush of pride in their child's accomplishments and share her enjoyments in sport, in music, in whatever direction her inner talents lead. At the school play when your daughter plays the Princess, you will be as proud as the parents of the Frog. She will be just as anxious to please you, to know you admired her performance, as the child who has the same nose as her father and the same squint as her mother.

The parent who has adopted should be prepared for the older child's possible desire to search out the biological parents. Some children may never show that interest and keep their fantasies buried; others may be quite outspoken and demand answers. Different states have different laws on the opening of adoption papers that have been sealed. We are now at a stage where some children will be able to trace their natural parents while others will not. For the parent of the adopted child, the desire for this search must be understood as part of the older teenager's normal and healthy need to solidify her identity, to find her own place separate from her parents in this world. This desire to know the biological parent is not a rejection, although it may be couched in those terms; it is rather part of the child's necessary and sometimes violent pulling away. An adoptive parent is very much the true parent. But the other, the ghost, the shadow, is also rightfully there, and an adoptive parent must be able to allow the child to put together the pieces as she needs to and in the way she wants. The parent who has been there through the nights and days of the growing up is always the "real" parent—the one the child has taken into herself.

Adopted children are no more unhealthy physically or mentally than any other children. They are lucky children because they have come into homes that wanted them. It is true that their sense of identity and self is complicated by the fact of adoption, but patience, skill, and love will take them through the mild detours to maturity. It helps the child if the parents can openly accept and talk about his adoption. It should not be a dark secret buried in a desk drawer. It may initially hurt a parent to admit to the world that they could not have their own children. But the more open the parent is, the more easily the child will be able to accept his special status.

Because of the number of would-be parents and the shortage of infants, many people must wait on lists a long time before a baby is available to them. Others are turning to private sources. Whatever the origin of adoption, we think it crucial that parents receive a baby as soon after the birth as possible, preferably within a day or two. The first moments of a baby's life are very important; days, weeks, or months of cold, custodial care can handicap a child in many ways. It is important to assure yourself that your baby's natural mother has not been addicted to drugs or alcohol and has received adequate prenatal care.

When children of different races or nationalities are adopted into families whose color, features, sizes they don't share, there are special problems. But these problems can be easily overcome by sensitive and concerned parents. The dark child in a light home does best if the parents can seek out friends for themselves and school mates who share the nationality or race of the child. If this is not possible it is important to give the child pictures, history, and an identity that acknowledges his biological background. As soon as he is old enough, he can be taught about Africa or Asia and shown the art and the religious work created by his birth people. He will be a child of two cultures. If you recognize this, and help him to have the best of both your world and the one he was born to, then the adoption will make him strong and doubly fortunate. You cannot take a black or Asian child and turn him into a white American. He can share your culture with you completely but will be stronger if you also share what might have been his.

Children whose adoption creates an interracial family will get used to the odd looks the family may on occasion receive. As they grow older, they will feel a real pride in their family for breaking through the boundaries that separate so many of us on the globe. They will as they grow older probably be somewhat outside of their own race and somewhat outside of yours. Be prepared—there will be some pain in this for both of you. But this is a small price to pay for the rewards of living within a loving family. In this country there are many millions of people who do not live exactly within one slot or another, and your child will find many places where she can belong, not because of her race or religion, but because of who she is and what she can do.

The adopted child who comes into a family in which there will be or are already natural children will feel some jealousy toward the other children. This will feed into the natural, constant jealousy that exists between children in all families. It provides a weapon for the natural child to use against the adopted one, and makes it hard for the adopted child not to wonder, when he is punished, scolded, or given something he considers less in value than his sibling, if his parents truly love him as much as they do their natural child. This complication can be dealt with if parents are truly even-handed in their love and commitment. Experience dispels fears: the adopted child will be as sure of himself and of your love and affection as reality dictates. It is your job to make the reality a good one.

Intelligence and the I.Q. Test

Many private schools around the country will use a form of the I.Q. test to determine admissions for children entering kindergarten. The test is also used in many public school systems to identify children who are mildly retarded or are having learning troubles. The tests and the figures that they supply carry a certain awesome authority and appear to have a mysterious power of judgment over the life of a child. In truth, the numbers achieved on an intelligence test tell us very little about the quality and future achievements of any given child. At the extreme ends of the testing scale we can identify those children who will never be able to live independently, and those few whose capacity for abstract thinking, for memory, place them in a position where they might be able to make creative contributions to the world we share. But we all know brilliant people who have fallen far short of their potential because the necessary emotional strengths were missing. Either they could not tolerate failure or disappointment, or they collapsed on some personal level. We all know people who did not shine in math classes and bumbled through English course after English course, who have because of warmth and dignity, energy, and style achieved all kinds of high-level accomplishments.

In the case of retarded children, we know that affection, warmth, and a caring environment will alter the actual numbers on the I.Q. test, and that many children thought originally incapable of self-care turn out when supplied with emotional nourishment to be capable of a fair degree of accomplishment. We also know that the numbers of the I.Q. test refer only to certain aspects of mental functioning. They do not measure character; they do not measure determination; they do not measure kindness or gracefulness, humor or charm. In short, the I.Q. test should not be used as a scale on which to weigh one's child's future. It is a limited tool; more often than not in telling its partial story it distorts the truth.

A normal I.Q. is about 100. A bright normal I.Q. is about 120, and a superior I.Q. is over 130. In theory, a person's I.Q. measurements should not change over a lifetime, but in fact emotional strain has a huge effect on the numbers. These tests are ideally set up to be culturally free, but there is no doubt that middle-class white children have an advantage over other groups. This does not mean that one group is superior in intelligence to another; only that the test is slanted toward the kinds of knowledge and experience more commonly available in one particular set of homes.

Creativity, musical ability, curiosity, athletic ability, capacity to make and keep friends, capacity to love and be loved, capacity to see danger and avoid it, capacity for courage and adventurousness, etc., all remain unmeasured by I.Q. tests. Parents should keep in mind just how defective and limited they are. Professionals may take them seriously; they have to take their tools seriously. No doubt there was a time when doctors treated each of their tiny leeches with respect. As parents, we should be skeptical of all partial measurements of the human mind.

Section II

The Harder Road

The first years of a baby's life are filled with constant work for both parents. The marriage has been tested. The parents have learned a great deal about each other and themselves. They have given to another human being immeasurable amounts of energy, dedication, and concern. All this makes it especially painful when a child shows signs of trouble, when the development of the emotional life is not smooth. Both parents feel accused and experience torturous guilt when their children stumble and fall, get stuck, or go backward on the path to maturity. When children of three or more are in trouble, parents tend to blame each other, to become sad, mourning the ideal child they intended to raise. We all assume our children are the mirrors of our souls. Eventually, we have to learn to accept our own imperfections. Real life causes scars and blemishes. We change what we can and we get help from others when we need to. We learn to live with the rest.

The children who are in the most trouble are those for whom the first three years did not pass uneventfully. Oliver will be clinging and afraid to leave his mother. Shirley will be so angry at her mother that she hits and bites at the least provocation. Harold, who hardly talks, will have spent months in the hospital because of needed surgery. Marina's parents have divorced, her father has deserted the family,

223

and now Marina refuses to admit that she is a girl. Tim, who flaps his hands up and down and bangs his head against the wall, is suffering from an incurable disease most likely carried in his genes or contracted while he was still in the womb. The disturbances of children this age are revealed as they deal with the new stress of sexual feelings for their mothers or fathers, and with the constraints and enticements of the larger social world they are now entering.

If the separation of baby from mother has not occurred gracefully, if rage and fear have grown too large and the child is still afraid of being abandoned or of claiming his place as a separate person, then the new emotional work of the third through sixth years of life will put additional pressure on him and we will begin to see the development of symptoms. Some are minor and will go away in time. Some, particularly when they are grouped with several others, are the red flags of mental illness.

The emotional well-being of the child depends on successfully mastering each of the stages of development. Cracks in the foundation, broken beams, bad designs will cause trouble as the structure becomes more and more complicated with each year of life. Even so, the child from three to six has an amazing capacity to change, to strengthen and resupport some of the older weak spots. Children are incredibly resilient and can bend and weave around most emotional difficulties. Symptoms that look serious can appear and disappear within months. Single symptoms are most often of little concern.

Children cope with their impulsive sexual feelings, with their primitive angers and fears of retaliation, by setting up defenses. Some of these defenses are fine and work like levees against the floodtides. Others are defective or ineffective, and themselves cause symptoms that are destructive to the child. To see how any particular child is doing, we look for clusters of symptoms. We check to see if the child has accomplished the tasks we consider important for his age group. It is amazing how at such a young age we can see the child struggling valiently in his own way to construct strong defenses, to preserve good feelings about himself and his parents, to maintain the connection to his parents without being harmed or swallowed up. It is wondrous how many specific fantasies a little child can have—how rich the internal life can be, how different one from another, even in pain, each child will be. We are, of course, awed before the miracle of human personality—even, or perhaps especially, the damaged human personality.

Psychotic Children

Psychosis is the professional catch-all phrase for something we all recognize as insanity or madness. When the disease appears in children, parents and professionals are usually defeated. Fortunately, the disease is very rare and any particular parents' chances of having a psychotic child are so small that one could better anticipate being hit by a brick from a falling building or getting caught in a tornado's path.

The severity of the illness varies, and there may be a variety of possible causes, but the outcome, at best, is a brittle human being, one who may achieve some small capacity to take care of himself, to keep a simple job, but who lives always with the shadow of an institution behind him, in a kind of twilight zone or imitation world. This is the best one can expect. The vast majority of young children who are diagnosed as psychotic will live out their lives in the protective monotony of mental hospitals.

Childhood psychosis appears in only four or five out of every ten thousand children. Five times more boys than girls are clearly psychotic, another example of the greater vulnerability of males. The symptoms can suddenly appear with absolute clarity any time between two and a half and nine years of age. Certainly, severe emotional neglect or cruelty to the baby may result in insanity, although many babies have suffered from incredible levels of abuse without developing this illness. In some cases several other relatives in the family have been hospitalized for severe mental problems, indicating genetic error. It is also possible that these children may have been afflicted in the womb by some hormonal imbalance in the pregnant mother or by a virus that crossed the placenta at a crucial moment in the development of the fetus.

In some instances, perhaps a biological vulnerability has matched with some failure in the family, causing the child's mind to crumble irretrievably into madness. Many parents of psychotic children have other perfectly normal children. There is no clear villain on whom to pin the blame. All societies, from those of the darkest Amazon to those producing micro-chips, seem to have the same number of psychotic children.

Many psychotic children have histories of a special kind of infant behavior. All infants with this kind of picture, however, do not go on to become psychotic. A baby may have been particularly irritable and hard to comfort throughout the first two years of life. He may have cried a great deal or he may have been excessively quiet and withdrawn. Many will have shown no interest in peek-a-boo games, pat-a-cake, or bye-bye; others will have been demanding of attention and very excitable. Such babies will show extremes of sadness and joy at a very early age. They will have made strong connections to their parents, and will scream or cry inconsolably or have fierce temper tantrums if they are faced with a separation. Their speech, if it develops at all, will be slow. They will be somewhat behind in starting walking and running; they will also be slow in holding a pencil, picking things up with thumb and forefinger. Many of these children will have shown growth spurts followed by long periods during which nothing changes. (This erratic growth pattern is unusual, since most children proceed in a fairly steady fashion.) Long before the outbreak of major symptoms, many psychotic children have withdrawn from contact with other children and other adults. Their play will seem babyish for their age—they will not throw a ball with another child, nor enter a pretend game of "house."

While some psychotic children do not ever develop speech, for others the first major symptom of the illness may occur when a child suddenly turns mute. Some 20 to 40 percent of all psychotic children remain mute for the rest of their lives. Other children may develop a kind of unintelligible jargon that they mix up with normal words and syntax. The child may simply imitate words without paying any attention to meaning or communication. Some children have a very strange pitch to their voices—they may always shout or whisper, or may inflect odd words or use only invented sounds and incomplete sentences. Almost all of the psychotic children who do speak will show pronoun reversal, using the word "You" when referring to themselves and "I" when meaning the other person. These speech disturbances are often seen along with a severe clinging behavior in which the child may grab anybody who comes by and hold on for dear life; or, at another time of the day, they may ignore all other people and refuse to look at or touch anyone.

226

The psychotic child does some very unusual things with his body. He constantly flaps his hands or his arms in an agitated, excited way as if he were a small bird in flight, or twiddles his fingers constantly for hours on end. He may turn his whole body around and around in endless circles, whirling as if he were a top, pausing only to catch his breath from time to time. He may walk on his toes until puberty, when this particular symptom seems to disappear. He may stand in a corner rocking his whole body back and forth as if he were a chair or a pendulum on a grandfather clock. He may bang his head against the wall as a means of defining his own body edges and of using pain to mark the outside limits of a self that feels as if it were disintegrating or disappearing. Or he may sway from side to side as if he were a small rowboat out on the high seas.

If presented with a large selection of toys, he will become interested in only one function of all of them. For example, he may spin the wheels on toy cars, cranes, loading trucks, army tanks, and toy ambulances. He will not go on to use the toys to stage an imaginative accident, wage a war, or pretend to build or fly an airplane. He will only be interested in spinning wheels. At another time he may simply line up the objects in some order that has great meaning to him and become wildly upset if anyone tries to disturb his arrangement. He will be prone to panic attacks. If something in his routine is changed, if his mother leaves the room, if someone takes something from him, he may become wild with fear. He will scream and weep and have a tantrum for reasons that adults often cannot fathom. These panic states and dreadful tantrums may be followed by long periods of disinterest in all people and all things, as the child rocks and sways, his attention now turned entirely inward.

It is very hard for anyone to get a clear picture of such a child's intelligence potential. Such serious and constant emotional disintegration prevents a young child from observing and learning all sorts of things in his world. The intelligence test is nevertheless important for the psychotic child because if at any time he tests at an I.Q. of 70 or above, then the chance of some improvement through psychiatric treatment increases. Those children whose I.Q.s fall below 70 seem to be unreachable by any means we now have available. The destruction of the integrating, knowing, learning parts of their minds has just been too massive for any intervention to alter the child's fate. However, a child with an I.Q. of 70 or more may be reached enough eventually to lead some kind of independent non-institutional life. Such a child will not become a normal adult but can manage to gain some intermittent satisfaction from his days on this earth. Since it is so difficult to get a clear testing of a psychotic child, the I.Q. indicator allows us only an educated guess into the future.

Some psychotic children develop into adolescents who hallucinate. They might assume that they are being poisoned or are the subject of supervision by some mysterious force in their malevolent universe. Some might just stand still and not budge at all for days at a time. If you move their arms to one position or another, as if they were wax statues, they will stay posed as you have placed them. They may be mute or their words may flow continuously in reams of disconnected irrational associations, like a well-tossed word salad. The majority of the psychotic children will remain just as they were at four or five, never changing. The symptoms and the behavior will stay the same until they die.

Some small percentage of psychotic children have a few neurological signs of actual brain disease, yet many do not. We cannot see anything wrong on physical tests. It is no wonder that in other ages man believed in demons and possession by evil spirits. In our own rational, scientific era, where no witches are handy to blame and burn, we are simply left with our frustration and anger at what appears to be random cruelty. The parents of such children need an enormous amount of support to cope with daily difficulties. We feel that it would be a good idea for all parents of these damaged children to receive some counseling. Guilt arises to haunt us no matter what anyone says. Professionals may well ask questions in a way that evokes parental guilt. The personnel in any residential or non-residential treatment center can easily make parents feel responsible. The tensions of the situation immediately spill over onto the marriage itself and onto any other children. It is so easy for such an extraordinarily sick child to demand and command all the emotional and financial resources of a family that the other children become scarred and marked by inadvertent neglect simply through their mere closeness to this real tragedy. Parents of psychotic children deserve extra support just as if their house had been hit by a flood, avalanche, or earthquake.

There is no need for parents to worry about whether or not their child is psychotic. The illness is rare and the symptoms when they come are unmistakable. The situation is as black and white as anything can be.

Children at the Edge

These are a group of children whom psychiatrists call borderline because all their lives they uneasily straddle the fences that divide the territories of sane and insane, rational and irrational. These children do not hallucinate. They do not have bizarre mannerisms, like flapping their hands or twirling in place. Their speech develops normally and remains normal. They do not lose contact with reality. At the same time they have an inability to contain and control the feelings and impulses that sweep through their minds, gathering hurricane strength. These impulses knock over the defenses that are more than strong enough to keep most other children from panic, despair, and great fear. If they have an angry feeling, or a sexual urge, they cannot easily calm themselves, distract themselves, or reduce the intensity of their feelings to a manageable level. Often they are overcome by the violence of their own desires and scream in anger and fear, thrashing about in the most horrendous of temper tantrums. Along with anxiety dreams they have bloody, unholy, disastrous nightmares that can frequently plague them all their lives.

Of course we cannot examine the physical brain of such a child and find the synapses or nerve connections that have frayed or worn away. We cannot point to a change in a cell or identify a virus in the bloodstream. But picture a landscape with a large lake in one corner and houses arranged in a neat circle around the lake. There is a church on a hill, with its white steeple confidently pointing to the heavens, and nearby is a schoolhouse and a railroad station. Along the hillside, there are farms, with acres of fertile soil carefully blocked out and planted with corn, lettuce, carrots, and beans. You can hear some distant thunder from the other side of the hill. There are fierce dogs barking in the yard of one of the houses by the lake. There is a wolf that periodically steals the farmers' chickens; a child playing in a rubber boat drifts too far out in the lake and has to be rescued by some boys in a canoe. This landscape is the mind of the normal child.

Now take the same scene, but for reasons hardly known to local geologists the lake swells with a heavy rainstorm and floods the little houses by its side. The wind blows furiously, ruining the stalks of corn and ripping the lettuce from the soil. The railroad train crashes off the tracks and slams into the side of the schoolhouse. The child in the rubber boat is always about to drown and the rescuers are nowhere to be seen. An avalanche of rocks from the hill rains down on the church, breaking the stained-glass windows. In this scene the wolf has changed to a maurauding tiger escaped from a passing circus. The dogs have turned rabid and have broken out of the yard that contained them. The lake keeps growing bigger and bigger, swallowing up houses and people in its path. This is the landscape of the child at the edge.

These children at age three or so will still be clinging tightly to their mothers. They will have acute tantrums when she tries to leave for the store or an evening out. They will cling to other adults but they experience a real and severe panic when their mother leaves. At the same time they will feel a fierce rage at her for leaving. They wish horrible things would happen to her because they're so angry at her. Then they become frightened that their wishes might come true. They may get themselves into such a panic that they will feel as if their bodies are coming apart or they are dissolving into nothing.

These children will fight back against the high level of anxiety they feel, and like other children they will build a defense system; but their defenses are not strong enough to hold back the tidal wave of anxiety that attacks them. They will have many fears, of dogs, of the dark, of witches, of giants in the closet. For other children these fears, while not pleasant, allow them to separate out their bad feelings toward their parents. The normal child places his angry feelings outside of himself and dresses them up as witches, mad dogs, giants. This helps him control the anger that he feels toward his sometimes frustrating or disappointing parents, and allows him to maintain a trusting, loving relationship with his real mother and father.

For the child at the edge, however, these common fears don't work as defenses, and such children are intensely frightened that they will be punished because of their bad wishes toward their parents. Like other children they may develop at around three or four rituals of lining things up a certain way, of dressing and undressing in a certain order. But, for them, these rituals will not help to make them less afraid, less angry. Soon they will abandon their ceremonials because they don't work.

Naturally these children don't like themselves very much: they feel as if they are bad all the time. Along with the feeling of being no good, unlovable, ugly, and stupid, they develop a fantasy life in which they can play for hours. In these wishful pretend games, they are the superheroes, generals of mighty armies, kings of jungle and plain, rulers of distant galaxies. Because they feel such strong angers, their fantasies are filled with cruel and harsh happenings. Sometimes they will be the victim in these dramas and other times they will be the dominant power, taking the role of torturer. Many normal children have a rich fantasy life and can also play within the boundaries of pretend games for hours, but for the child at the edge these inventions become particularly all-absorbing and have an intense violence about them that marks them as special.

Children at the edge are exhausting for mothers, fathers, and teachers. The child will complain loudly if his mother talks for a moment on the phone to a friend. He will impatiently stamp his feet and fuss if his mother pauses to chat with a storekeeper. He will be slow to learn how to control his angry impulses. He will hit, bite, or strike out at another child long after his brothers and sisters have learned to replace actions with words. He will break down into screams of anger and fear if frustrated in the smallest of ways. If he can't have the toy he wants, if he has to wait for someone else to order at a lunch counter, if he must share a bike with a neighbor's child, he may be overcome with rage.

This low tolerance for frustration and the large amount of anxiety these children feel at all times makes it hard for them to follow even the simplest of nursery school rules. They will have trouble waiting for the cookies to be passed; they will not be able to be quiet while the teacher or another child is talking. They seem to be deliberately bad or disobedient, and as they grow they are in constant trouble with puzzled and distressed parents and teachers who feel they could learn if only they would listen; they could be good if only they would try. Mothers find themselves distraught. They can't reason with this child. They know they can't give in to every whim, but in order to avoid scenes they often find themselves dominated or controlled by the child, who threatens a terrible screaming panic if she doesn't get immediate satisfaction. Parents become angered and very frustrated by this kind of child. As they express their anger, they only further confirm the child's feeling of being bad and increase her already out-sized fear of being abandoned.

All of these children develop harsh consciences. One little boy begged to have his hands cut off because he had tried to scratch his baby sister. The strength of their violent feelings is often turned against themselves and they will frequently cut or bruise their bodies or repeatedly fall and break bones. These children need to arrange situations in which they will be punished.

At around age three and four, when other children are beginning to find enormous pleasure in the company of their age mates, these children tend to withdraw because they cannot control their anger and their impulses. They have learned that other children will reject and exclude them; often they isolate themselves. They can indeed play alone for hours, involved in their increasingly elaborate fantasies. Their intelligences are normal or above normal. But because of their flowing anxiety they have trouble paying attention to the details of the outside world, and they may not know some of the things that are quite routine for children of their age. They remain dependent on their mothers and will insist on babyish kinds of attachments, such as having their mother dress and undress them or tie their shoes.

We do not know exactly what causes a child to have this particular kind of mind. As babies they may have been like Mark, who had trouble sucking, who cried constantly and was impossible to comfort, and who would scream sometimes for no apparent reason. He refused to chew foods for a long time. Then at four years, when his mother was beside herself because he had such terrible temper tantrums and so many nightmares, he was brought to a psychotherapist who identified him as a child balancing on the edge. Another possible history might be similar to Helga's. She had severe stomach pains as an infant and vomited frequently. She had cramps after each meal until about nine months of age. She rarely smiled as a baby. She bit toys instead of playing with them, and she pulled away from her mother's arms, arching her back when her mother tried to hold her close. She began to rock back and forth and hit her head on the end of the crib. At five her kindergarten teacher recommended therapy because she was so excitable and uncontrollable, given to rages that disturbed the entire class.

We assume that in some instances the mother's neglect, abuse, or dislike of the child can produce this kind of acute difficulty, but in many other children the disease appears to have been brought with the child into the world. Some children are born with mental damage that prevents the development of proper drains and controls for anger and anxiety. Perhaps the child was attacked by a virus in the womb or something in the mother's hormonal system harmed the embryo in ways that we cannot yet observe under our microscopes. At any rate, these children need psychotherapy to help them gain ways to live with their handicap, to help them maintain some sense of themselves as worthwhile and good, and to support them through a childhood that is bound to be stormy and difficult.

These children are particularly prone to drug and alcohol addiction in their teen-age years. They may have chronic learning and behavioral problems, and they will always struggle with intolerable amounts of feeling that frighten them and disorganize their thinking. They are at a marked disadvantage in a world where control and delay of satisfaction lead to real social rewards. Some few find artistic strength in music, painting, or poetry; for them the intensity of emotion can fortunately be bent to serve artistic ends. For most who stand at the edge, however, the risks are great; whatever obstacles the normal child must overcome are a thousand times larger for children at the edge.

This is an illness that cannot be identified by a single symptom. Temper tantrums or nightmares or social problems do not in themselves define such a child. Only a combination of intense and long-lasting problems leads us to make this fortunately uncommon diagnosis. If a parent is concerned by this cluster of symptoms in his or her child we would suggest consultation with a child psychiatrist. In some instances a qualified therapist can make a difference in the child's capacity to work around his handicap and may make a substantial difference in the child's capacity to get along with others and to calm his inner storms.

Mental Retardation

The severely retarded child will have been identified long before his third birthday. The Down's syndrome child was recognized at birth. The moderate or mildly retarded child may not be recognized until slowness of speech joins with slowness in toilet training. Pediatrician and parent will notice that the child is not alert and fails to remember words and stories, to learn new physical skills like tying shoes or using buttons. It is most important that such children receive special education as soon as possible. Most communities will have centers of education where they can be taught by experienced teachers and trained in the necessary skills for self-care and dignity.

It is very painful for parents to admit that their normal-appearing child is retarded, and that the variety and scope of his human existence will necessarily be limited in many ways. Yet recognizing and facing the truth is the only way to protect and help the child. Parents tend to ignore the first doubts they have. Pediatricians tend to be reassuring and speak of growth lags, and sometimes they are right; but some children are retarded. For them, the words of the nursery rhymes are too many to remember and the names of the colors just don't stick and the recognition of letters and numbers doesn't come no matter how often they are welcomed to *Sesame Street*.

Retarded children who are identified before they enter school will have been slow or impossible to toilet-train. They will be slow in learning not to take things from another child. They will hit or bite and will have trouble controlling themselves in all areas. They may need extra protection while crossing streets, while handling objects. They will behave inappropriately with other children and adults.

It is crucial here that the family disappointment not result in a turning away from the child, who still needs love and support. It is a parental obligation to find the best training and place for this child. Although retarded children will be less interesting or varied at this age than their normal brothers and sisters, they still are ours, their emotional life is still vivid, their capacity to love and be loved is as strong as any other child's. We as individual parents and as a culture as a whole have to find ways to meet their needs without destroying our own well-being. Most communities have support groups of other parents that are connected with special schools, hospitals, or churches.

These groups are enormously helpful in guiding mothers and fathers, leading them to the best schools and activities for their child as well as offering crucial friendships at a time when parents feel battered and isolated. Many parents of older retarded children speak of the special qualities of love they have known because of their damaged child, and describe the personal growth and moral enrichment they have experienced as they struggled to accept their child's handicap.

Nevertheless, many marriages are threatened by the burden of extra work, guilt, blame, and grief that such a child brings, particularly into the homes of ambitious parents. These are all normal reactions to the unfairness and indifference of biological error. Parents often feel as if they are being punished. They feel ashamed. They feel as if they have failed each other. The first few years after the diagnosis has been made are certainly the most difficult. After that, most families have absorbed the shock and found ways to live with the situation. They have found community support and discovered means to retrieve honor from the ashes of tragic disappointment.

The child who learns letters and numbers slowly may be not retarded at all but suffering from discrete learning problems which can afflict a child with normal intelligence. Good testing can separate the retarded child from one who is learning-disabled. In either case there are special programs that should be entered as soon as the correct diagnosis is made.

Tics and Tic Disease

Many children between three and six will develop tics of the face or body. These are muscle spasms that seem beyond the child's control and come and go at random. Most of these tics will be outgrown in a year or so. They represent some immaturity of the central nervous system as well as some tension that the child is experiencing. There are many natural sources of tension in a young child's life, and we ask a great deal of them in matters of control and delay of their wishes. They are also under pressure from their internal thoughts, fantasies, and fears. No wonder some of them have passing tics.

Long-lasting tics, tics that persist for more than two years or so, may make their way into the child's psychological system and become hard to dislodge. These do represent some level of emotional disturbance, and often will be found in children who have other symptoms —excessive fears, problems with aggression, nightmares, or insomnia. Even so, without any treatment at all some 50 percent of these tics will be outgrown by puberty.

At around the age of four or five a small group of children will begin to develop serious tics, or Gilles de la Tourette disease, named after a French psychiatrist who first identified the illness in the 1800s. Children with this affliction first show several tics of the shoulders and limbs. Then sometimes around five or six years they begin inarticulate noises that are brought about by spasms they cannot control in the diaphragm. The next step in this illness is an uncontrollable urge to shout out obscene words. The utterance of the obscenities helps the child to reduce some of the other more violent ticing activity of his limbs.

Of course this is a very disruptive disease. The child may be teased or ostracized by other children, and may have to be removed from school. Children suffering from tic disease are often mournfully sad, alienated from friends and parents. This is an ailment that needs immediate psychiatric treatment. There are medicines that have been found effective for some children. In addition, the child needs support in maintaining and regaining some sense of self-worth and hope for the future.

This is not a common illness like the winter virus. Most practicing pediatricians have never seen a case. So when parents first see tics appear in their children, they should not jump to the conclusion that a serious disease is brewing. In all likelihood and for the vast majority of children tics are just one of the minor troubles of childhood, like diaper rash in infancy or acne in adolescence.

Hair-Pulling, Hair-Eating, and Self-Induced Baldness

Hair is of great emotional importance to children, who often fondle, twist, stroke, and twirl their locks as they once fondled their mother's hair and face when they were small infants. Touching hair for the little child becomes a way of remembering the closeness with mother and of easing separations.

For some children, this normal and usually temporary habit can become caught up in the brambles of anxiety and lead to an excessive self-mutilating act of long duration. Some children pull at their hair until it comes out, leaving bald patches on the scalp. Psychiatrists call this trichotilomania. While there are no reliable statistics on the exact frequency of this disturbance, we do know that it appears in little girls far more frequently than in little boys, possibly because in our society little girls are more apt to be forced to control their angry feelings and are given less leeway in open physical expression.

We do know that the symptom, which can start at anywhere from two and a half years old to the beginnings of puberty, is often seen in children who have experienced either the real loss or the threatened loss of one of their parents. Some instances have been reported in which the hair-pulling began just after the death of a brother or sister.

It is easy to see that sexual conflicts can be transferred from the penis and the vagina up the body to the more socially acceptable hair. Some children who have been too forcefully and harshly prevented from touching and exploring their own genital areas may instead turn to the wisps and strands of hair to comfort themselves and ease tension. Children who are angry at their parents for leaving them, for neglecting them, or even for some kind of actual abuse may turn their anger against themselves and pull their hair until it comes out. Some come from families in which the parents do not allow any kind of direct, immediate expression of anger. The fact that the baldness is considered unattractive can play into the young child's feeling that she is ugly and deserves to be punished.

Some children develop the habit of not only pulling out their hair but then eating the strands that they have harvested. This is a disgusting act for most adults to watch and can become a major source of additional friction between parents and a child who persists. This habit is seen only in children who have a strong need to establish a missing closeness with their mothers, or who are disturbed in other ways. They may be retarded, psychotic, or children at the edge. They may also be more normal children dealing as best they can with overwhelming amounts of anger and sadness.

This is a symptom that usually does not appear in isolation; other trouble spots in the child's life will surely be there. Eating of the hair is perhaps a desperate attempt to nourish the self with a symbolic part of the body that is associated with closeness to the mother. It is a symptom that needs the prompt attention of the parents and of pediatricians and psychiatrists. While the symptom itself will likely disappear in time, it warns that important connections are in trouble.

Feeding Problems

There are some children who present feeding problems that are more than just temporary and go beyond the normal fad eating common to this time of life. Fussy eaters, picky eaters can go to unhealthy and dangerous extremes, and sometimes do. They use the meal as a battlefield in which they really have a winning card: You can bring a child to table but you can't make him swallow. Some children will eat so slowly that they drive their parents wild. They will select among the items on their plate the few that are acceptable and they will mush, delay, and fiddle with even those. Some will not eat if there is something unappealing in color or texture on their plate or on the table. Others will not drink milk and will make an afternoon's activity out of lunch before they give in on the point.

Where battles over food have gotten out of hand, threatening the child's bone growth and necessary nourishment, we often find that the mothers themselves had feeding problems in their own childhoods. Food has become a kind of symbol for the will of the parent. The domination of the parent and the resistance of the child can become a dangerously drawn line, where the child holds on fiercely for fear of being totally crushed by the steamroller of a feeding parent.

The subtext of these meals might be the child's clear statement: "I am the only one in charge of my body and my mouth." The mother's counter-theme, which continues as she cooks and offers, cajoles and bribes, commands and stares at the full plate, is: "I am the one who tells you what to do. If I say open and eat, than you must open and eat. You are the extension of my mouth and your body belongs as much to me as to you." Naturally, this chorus is not heard by human ears; nevertheless, it resounds off pot and pan, spoon and fork.

Often these four- or five-year-old finicky eaters are very good in every other area. They are docile and quick to follow commands, careful to hide and disguise any frustration, anger, or disappointment they may feel; but they have found a way to take their revenge over the soup and nuts. If the pitch of the battle gets high enough, it can be quite frightening.

Parents can try to ignore the temptations the child puts in their way to fight over food, to make it an issue. Parents can try to offer appealing food and genuinely leave it up to the child to take what she wants or not. This is a game easier to play on the printed page than in reality, but worth a try. If this doesn't work, parents have to examine their whole relationship with the child. Perhaps they have not allowed her to express anger in other ways. Parents need to express their own anger at the child openly and allow the child to complain back. A child with feeding problems needs room to claim control and explore freedoms in other places than the kitchen or the dining room. It would be a good idea for a parent to back away from the table with the child altogether. Let the other parent stay with the child for the main meal. Let babysitters and other relatives do a lot of the feeding for a while. Let the child have snacks that he takes for himself and give up on offering balanced full meals until the battle is over.

Perhaps the toilet training was too harsh; or perhaps the child has picked up the fact that the parent really is often very angry at her just for being there. Perhaps the child, feeling unloved, grows angry and frightened, and expresses through food the mother's wish that the child would shrink and disappear. In order to live you must eat. As soon as the child learns that she can pretend to follow the mother's partial wish for her death by play-acting at dying, she may try it. At the same time she can take revenge in a way that she cannot quite be punished for by tormenting her mother meal after meal.

Children's attitudes toward food are very much a part of their feeling toward their mothers, who offer them the mixture of physical closeness and actual nourishment that permits them to survive. If a child rejects the mother's food in a serious and ongoing way, we know there are ugly distortions in the relationship, and that the problem between them will not automatically go away as the child matures. Rather, it will increase in intensity and spill onto other areas of life. Although it is difficult to do by oneself, a determined mother can examine her feelings toward her child, allow herself to think out loud some of her own angry thoughts. A mother might be able to reestablish a more loving relationship with her child by ignoring the food battle for a while and concentrating on doing things with the baby that are pleasurable and happy for both. One mother we know took a painting class with her toddler, another began to swim in the pool with her child, and a third spent more time over storybooks and records than she had before. These simple acts brought the mother and child closer. A period of time in which food was never allowed to be the subject of a fight between them ended the feeding problem. Another mother realized that her marriage was in trouble. When she and her husband began to solve some of their problems, her own anger and need to control her child subsided and the fights over food gradually ended. Some parents may need a objective eye to help them resolve the complicated tight spot they are in with their child. A therapist, an educator, or a wise friend can be a big help at this time.

Overweight

Even at three, four, and five, some children become overweight. They are constantly concerned with food and eating, preoccupied with when and what the next meal will be (especially the dessert). Some children are overweight because the whole family simply eats too much; heaviness in this household is considered normal, and the amount of food considered healthy is calorically higher than the body really needs. These families may respond to nutritional advice from their pediatrician. Far more worrisome is the child who turns to food for reassurance, for comfort, in moments of stress, exhaustion, separation, or minor wounds. We worry about the already overweight child who uses eating as a way of restoring an inner balance, a way to remove a variety of discomforts that have nothing to do with real hunger.

We may find that such a child has not completely separated himself from his mother and eats constantly to regain that sensation of closeness that belongs to the sucking infant. Such a child may have been pushed away from his mother too soon. He may have been offered cookies or juice or milk at every cry, whether he was actually hungry or not. He may be trying to take into himself the part of the mother that he cannot have. This is a cause for concern not only because obesity is physically dangerous and has side effects in a child's life that can become unpleasant and damaging, but because it signals some error in the child's system. He is eating instead of finding healthier ways to relieve inner strain, such as creating a fantasy, painting a picture, playing a game, learning a sport. Often he is eating instead of expressing anger or fear.

With such a child, parents can try to increase the amount of exercise and physical activity they all do together. They can encourage the child to cut down on sweets and offer rewards or bribes for weight loss. They can help the child to be independent of the mother in whatever ways are realistic and to be close to both parents in age-appropriate activities. But if a child is very overweight at five and this is not a family pattern, we would suggest that a physical examination be given to rule out thyroid or other difficulties and after that a psychiatric consultation be arranged. Early intervention can prevent a lifetime weight problem by healing the other dislocations that lie just behind this symptom.

Wetting Clothes and Bed

The psychiatrist's word for this troublesome failure to maintain control of the bladder is enuresis. Different societies and different social classes within communities have their own timetables for the child to accomplish the complicated task of staying dry during both the day and the night. In general, we would begin to expect a three-year-old to maintain control, with occasional accidents when some unusual separation or other event has altered the child's life. We know that roughly three times as many boys as girls seem to struggle beyond the sixth year to achieve dependable control. While there are no exact statistics to be found, most experts feel that a Swedish study of 9,600 boys and girls in which 5.8 percent of the children were still wetting themselves at age seven is a decent gauge of the extent of this provoking difficulty in the general population.

This is a fairly serious problem for a child because it creates a flock of additional burdens. He will surely feel that there is something wrong with him, that he is babyish instead of grownup, bad instead of good. His young pride will be wounded and he will feel deeply ashamed of himself. He will have a host of concerns about being discovered, being ridiculed by other children. He will avoid sleepovers and visits with playmates. Because he feels not quite as good as everyone else, he may either become too aggressive or withdraw and isolate himself.

An extremely small percentage of four- and five-year-olds who are wetting themselves do suffer from some organic problem. Pediatricians should be alerted and will check this out very carefully. They will look for some anatomical obstruction in the body or some metabolic or chemical disorder. Another very small percentage of bedwetters have fathers who had the same difficulty in their own childhoods. These wetters by inheritance are male children from three to nine, who may also walk and talk in their sleep. There seems to be some neurological difficulty for these children in the transition between the first hours of deep sleep and the lighter sleep in which we dream, called REM. Some pediatricians have found that antidepressant drugs help, but the symptom will be outgrown anyway as the child reaches puberty. If the child can be helped to handle the social effects of the wetting, we would of course prefer not to use drugs to end a problem that will disappear in its own time.

However, the vast majority of children who wet themselves do so because of difficulties in their relationships with their parents. There are two separate kinds of problems. The primary one is shown in children who never achieved adequate toileting and from the beginning were unable to follow the parental wish for control. The secondary kind of problem is seen in children who had achieved toileting for some time but lost it, because of some frightening event such as the loss of a parent or the birth of a sibling or the move to a new home.

Among children of four and five who have never established real bladder control, we see several factors at work. The child may well be caught up in an unhappy struggle for self-determination in opposition to her parents. She may feel that to give in to the parental demand for dryness would be to abandon her sense of being a real self. With these children, we often find that the mother has been overly harsh in her reaction to accidents. This harshness and the implied threat of loss of love create both anger and fear. The child may insist on releasing her urine as she pleases because she is afraid of losing her independence if she complies. Mothers and fathers should try some months of substituting encouragement for threats, and offer praise and rewards for achievement. At the same time parents should make less of a fuss about the entire matter of using the toilet. This will often solve the problem, as the child's natural desire to please her loving mother and father will reassert itself once the battlefield has been removed. If after some months of changed parental attitudes the child is still not dry, we suggest consultation with a psychiatrist. This is one of the childhood problems that can rather easily be vanquished with professional guidance.

Some children get caught up in sexual conflicts that affect their willingness to use the toilet. Boys involved in a dramatic sexual rivalry with their fathers may be so afraid that their fathers will attack them for their bad wishes that they retreat to babyish ways. Some children do not achieve bladder control because they have been too severely rebuked for touching or rubbing themselves or showing signs of sexual arousal. Everything about the genitals then becomes frightening and "bad." Such children may prefer to wet themselves unthinkingly rather than focus on sensations in the "forbidden area." Urinating into the toilet either standing up or sitting down is a mark of sexual identity, and some children who are confused or unwilling to accept their gender may avoid the issue by wetting without using the toilet at all. Many of the children who do not achieve bladder control are very compliant and good in other areas. They may use wetting as a means of expressing the angers and bad feelings they are otherwise afraid to reveal. All of these are possible reasons for the lack of control and are signals of real trouble, signs that the family needs some help.

In the Swedish study, two-thirds of the untrained children lost bladder control when a major separation occurred in their lives, such as going to school for the first time, or to summer camp, or there was an impending or actual divorce in the family. Although many of the children appeared to deny the seriousness of the problem, they all felt deeply ashamed and upset. Many of their mothers were threatening and punitive, and made a big issue of the child's sudden failure, insisting on a great deal of time being spent in the bathroom. Here, too, parents should try a period in which rewards are offered and encouragement given, and the actual wetting played down in importance. If this does not work after several months, psychotherapy is recommended to help the child achieve the separations maturity requires without retreating to baby ways.

It is rare that a long-term lack of bladder control appears as the only problem in a child's life. Often such children are also overly fearful, have tantrums or anxiety attacks, are clinging or too aggressive or too quiet. The bathroom and the body functions that occur there are a crucial thread in the weave of mental health; a child who is failing at four, five, or six in this area is expressing a core difficulty, a real and serious interruption of forward growth.

In moderately and severely mentally retarded children, and in children with the serious mental illnesses of childhood, bladder control is usually lacking. In these instances the symptom is only one of many that help us to understand what is happening to the child. The problem is our major concern only in those children for whom most things are going well and who have a sufficient sense of themselves and of reality to suffer from their own inability to conform.

Failure in Bowel Control

It is crucial for the pride and well-being of the child that bowel training be successfully completed. In our society we generally expect this to be accomplished some time after the third birthday. This is one of the important milestones in development; it is a minimum requirement for a child to be accepted by his peers. It shows that he is no longer a baby, and signals his ability to control other impulses and to delay satisfaction when necessary. Failure to achieve bowel control is called encopresis by the professionals. Following the parent's request to deposit the B.M. in the toilet means that the child has mastered some sense of what is a part of his body and what is not. He has demonstrated that he is confident of his separate identity and is not afraid of losing a part of himself. These children have found it possible to please their parents while pleasing themselves. They have taken the parental command into themselves and made it their own, saying in effect, "I do this because I want to." After the usual struggle, they have accepted the parental point of view about B.M.s. Of course the three-, four-, and five-year-old is still fascinated by all things having to do with the toilet, but now the interest has changed primarily to an enjoyment of bathroom jokes. Nursery schools are overflowing with young comedians howling at the mention of making "poo" or "kaka." Having achieved control over their body functions, they now find it all a laughing matter. These jokes about the bathroom are like the jokes of a soldier after a battle is over.

* * *

Samuel is a five-year-old with red hair and freckles. He knows all the Dr. Seuss books by heart and can tell you the name of every quarterback in the NFL, but he has trouble making friends. He tends to push other kids around, to boast about everything he has. He wakes up often with nightmares and his mother is worried about him because he so often hides under his bed and falls asleep there. He's forever punching his little brother and although in his games he plays at being a superhero, he still hasn't learned to ride his bike and he won't go near the water.

Samuel has a real problem that just doesn't seem to go away: he still soils his pants. Not every day, not all the time, but often enough that he doesn't feel like everybody else. His secret, his shame, the one that no one but his parents knows, is affecting every part of his life.

The Swedish study of 9,600 children mentioned earlier found that 1.5 percent of them had marked bowel control problems lasting past the age of six. This figure includes three times as many boys as girls. This symptom may appear in children who have experienced a severe illness during the first three years of life or had a mother who was depressed or otherwise inadequate or unavailable. For these children it is particularly hard to let go of something they conceive to be a part of themselves. They have experienced a great deal of anger, which makes them both less willing to accept the parents' wish and more anxious about losing a part of themselves. Their fragile sense of being a separate person needs extra defending, and so they may become defiant over this issue. They may be expressing their anger at their parents indirectly by refusing to use the toilet. The bowel movement can become a tool in a struggle for power or dominance or revenge. Some few children will develop long-lasting and uncomfortable constipations rather than comply with the parental wish.

We can pick a child up and place him where we wish; we can use our greater size to force him to give back a toy or to go to bed. But we just can't force a child to have a bowel movement or to have it where we want it.

Many little girls at three or four will confuse the bowel movement itself with the baby that also comes out of a special opening. The bowel movement then becomes for the child the baby that they hoped Daddy would give them. For these children, constipation is common as well as soiling. They do not want to give up their symbolic baby, to be flushed away. Boys who are unduly afraid of their father's retaliation (because of their own fantasies about harming their father) are sometimes afraid that something terrible will happen to their own bodies. The B.M. can become equivalent in their minds with their valued penis. If they are frightened enough, if their father is really severe or cruel to them, they may soil themselves rather than willingly give up the B.M. to their parents. The witholding of the bowel movement can also become a kind of disguised masturbation as the anal area becomes sensitive, giving the child erotic pleasure. Children who are not permitted to touch themselves genitally may discover the anus and find it hard to give this secret place in themselves over to social control.

All of this sounds a little unbelievable to adult minds, trained as we are not to pay too much attention to our bowel and bladder functions, and aware as we are of the biological realities of eating and eliminating. But remember that for the child, the emergence of the B.M. is still a magical process. Our disgust with it is new to him, and our demands are impositions on his natural impulses. He is not so sure what parts of the body come off and what stay on. If a child is soiling past the age of three and a half, then we know he has not solved some of these basic questions, and that is cause for some concern. A rather high percentage of children who soil themselves had achieved adequate control for a while and then lost it, because of a divorce in the family, a long illness, a separation such as going to school or going off to summer camp. Many children will have accidents for a short while after any upsetting experience, but some seem unable to regain their former control. They will rarely have accidents at night and rarely at school, but will often soil themselves at home or on the way home. Once the symptom is established, it can be as hard to remove as if it had always been there.

Mothers of children who are soiling also experience some public shame and some private guilt. Toilet training the child is one of those accomplishments that mothers use to prove to themselves and others that they are doing a good job or as good a job as everyone else in the neighborhood. This embarrassment adds to the anger a mother feels toward her non-compliant child and heats up the battle between them. It certainly can make a mother feel a lot less loving, a lot less like reading a story to her child or playing a game with him, if she has just had to wash out his pants or clean up his bed. She will surely feel frustrated and inadequate, and her child's failure will become her own. It is extremely painful for parents at any time to be forced to admit that something is not going right, and that the failure might be the result of something they have done or the way they have done it.

There are several furies that accompany this symptom and damage the child's well-being. Pride is diminished and shame follows, making it harder for a child to like himself. Clearly, he is not as good as other children who do not "make" in their pants. We rarely see this symptom in isolation. Usually a child who is soiling is also nail-biting, presents odd feeding problems, may have speech disturbances or frequent unexplained stomach aches. These children will appear tense and frightened. They may have trouble sharing with other children. Some will be very quiet and have only a rare temper tantrum; others as they get older may begin stealing and lying. They may be demanding and dependent on children and on adults, and some may find themselves ostracized by the group.

Mothers of children who are soiling tend to be harsh in their methods of toilet training and to have begun too early. They have violent reactions to their child's accidents and express extreme disgust about the B.M. itself. Parents can try to tone down their reactions to accidents, to encourage with praise and reward rather than shame and anger. If this change in approach is not effective within a few months, we strongly recommend psychiatric help. The results of psychotherapy are usually very good. This is a symptom that can be removed and the child's spirits restored by a return of smooth relationships with members of his family and playmates. While the symptom of soiling will itself disappear at puberty without any treatment at all, it will have left permanent scars on the development of the child and make the tasks of the teen years more difficult to achieve.

Constipation and diarrhea also occur in children who are disturbed or in conflict in other areas of their lives. The birth of a new baby, divorce, the death of a parent, some difficulty in school or in controlling or expressing anger, all may provoke bowel disturbance. A child who is struggling with the difference between the sexes and has fears that his body may be harmed will sometimes become constipated or have diarrhea. The bowels are a sensitive pathway that responds easily to the child's total emotional life. If constipations or diarrheas are more than passing episodes and pediatricians can find no organic cause for them, we would recommend consultation with a child psychiatrist.

Problems in Nursery School

Beth's mother was surprised when Beth said she didn't want to be anything for Halloween this year. Beth said she hated Halloween and wanted to stay home. Just the week before they had picked out a costume, so this change of mind seemed odd. As Beth's mother questioned her further, Beth began to cry, telling her mother that she was the only girl in the class not invited to Marion's Halloween party. Those things happen. Beth's mother wasn't too concerned until she remembered that the three children that Beth had asked to come over after school had all declined for one reason or another. Beth admitted that she had no friends. She never had a partner when they lined up to go out to play. No one wanted to sit next to her during juice and cookies. Beth said she hated nursery school. Beth's mother couldn't sleep that night.

We all want our children to get along well with both teachers and other children. We all want our children to be "popular" and successful in school. It is always an upsetting experience for a parent to attend a conference with the child's teacher and learn that qualities such as shyness, aggressiveness, withdrawal, babyishness, or demandingness are making it hard for our child to make friends. But these reports do come and many children have some degree of difficulty in school.

Some children, particularly only children, may have a hard time in a situation in which they have to share the attention of the adult and do not receive what they want the minute they want it. Time may erode their demandingness, and after a year or so they begin to make friends and settle into a group situation. For some, the other children, instead of representing possible friends, represent possible threat. Some children are slow in controlling their aggressive feelings and will strike out at other children at the first bump or the first sign of holding on to a wanted toy. Some children are more babyish than others. They may talk badly, retreat from active games to thumb-sucking or rocking activities. They may wet or soil in class, causing the other children to shun them. Some children will play happily and quietly by themselves but avoid contact with the others for a long time. They do not join in circle games and they do not build a tower with a friend. They are loners, who are absorbed in the activity of their own minds and do not need or want outside contact.

It is in the nursery school that we see our children as citizens, as one among many, as separate from ourselves and on their own. Many of the difficulties that appear in the first months or year of school will disappear as time passes. The aggressive child can learn to control himself and the withdrawn child can eventually become tempted to join the play of others. Children between three and six play games that often involve excluding someone or being cruel to someone. The child who is now consistently the victim may one day change roles and become a leader, and the child who is a bully may calm down and learn the value of sharing and caring about another.

We can help by giving the child who is teased some clues as to what provokes other children about their behavior. We can tell her not to whine, not to talk baby talk, not to tattle-tale on the others. We can help her by telling her not to cry when someone says her dress isn't pretty. Teach her to ignore cruel remarks. Very often if other children feel her strength and independence, they will stop teasing. Most importantly, we must make a special effort with a child who is having trouble with others to make sure that she feels loved and admired at home. Help her to find the things she is good at—drawing, sports, music, puzzles, words—and give her every opportunity to feel happy about her own accomplishments.

Self-confident children are never teased. But sometimes they are the teasers. If your child is more than ordinarily cruel to others, you must talk to him about this. Make it clear that you want him to respect the feelings of other children. You want him to be the kind of person who protects others and does not hurt them. Don't make him feel guilty for being a bad person, but insist that he control this behavior. Talk to him about how other people feel. Share your feelings of pleasure, pain, and sadness with him about all sorts of other people in the world. He will soon identify with you and feel pity, sorrow, and empathy; and out of these grow kindness and consideration for others. Perhaps he needs to be able to express his anger at you more directly. Allow him to be angry sometimes but not to hurt other children, their feelings or their bodies. Let him know that this disappoints you.

Parents can learn from these early school reports which areas of their child's development need watching and perhaps some extra care. Such early reports should not be taken as the handwriting on the wall. The child who is slow to do puzzles at three may be a math whiz at seven; the child who is friendless at four may be the leader of the pack at eight. Listen to the teacher, watch your child in a group, help with weak behavior, give your child plenty of opportunity to be with other children, but do not despair if things don't go perfectly smoothly. Normal development includes a lot of trial and error, especially error.

There are, however, some children who will not talk easily, and who resist all attempts to draw them into the activities of others. If this persists for many months, we would suggest consultation with a psychiatrist. This could signal the beginnings of real illness or it could be a simple slowness in social response. It could be the sign of a child who cannot separate from his mother and is frozen without her company. Persistent isolation needs attention.

Some children will be so aggressive and uncontrolled in a school situation at three, four, and five that they place real strains on the group. In the process they begin to think of themselves as bad and not loved, which only further angers them and aggravates their behavior. Consistent reports of hitting, shoving, taking things, being unresponsive to requests to share and to do things quietly with others are a sign of a child in trouble with impulse control. Perhaps it would help to have a professional evaluate either the extremely aggressive child or the overly withdrawn one to see if the source of the anger or the nature of the disturbance can be identified and its direction altered.

The Running Child

By the time Andrew was five, he was a real pain to be around. He had been born in Germany, where his father had been stationed as a sergeant in the Army. There had been some bad arguments and the marriage fell apart. His mother came back to the States when he was two and left him with his grandmother. She picked him up again a year later and took him to California, to the home she had made with her new husband. Now Andrew had two half brothers and a third was on the way; his overwhelmed mother was thinking about sending Andrew back to his grandmother. Andrew smiled at everyone and hugged anyone who would give him a kind word, but he never stayed in one place long enough to hear instructions, much less follow them. His well-meaning mother was exhausted chasing him, yelling at him, trying to get him quiet long enough for dinner and a bath. The many changes in his life had affected Andrew and he became a "running child."

Some children without any physical brain damage just can't sit still. They seem to be in a kind of perpetual motion that causes parents and nursery school teachers to despair. They knock into things; they concentrate only briefly. They interrupt conversations and they move from game to game, from activity to activity, unable to persevere, to see things through, to put all the pieces of the puzzle in place or to listen carefully to instructions. They are forever leaping off high places and jiggling their feet and hands. This kind of activity is seen far more often in boys than in girls. It seems to be caused by floating anxiety exploding in their minds almost constantly. We see this kind of hyperactivity in children who are unduly afraid of their parents' anger, who have been abused, neglected, or rejected. It appears in children who have been frightened by witnessing some violent act or have been moved around from home to home so often that they are afraid of losing all connections to loving people.

Hyperactivity can also be a symptom of the child at the edge or of the retarded child who cannot make order out of his impulses and desires. If the hyperactivity is temporary, it could be a response to the arrival of a new baby or a move to a new city or a new school. Hyperactivity that is caused by anxiety coming from the outside world will subside when the child feels safe again and in place. A child who has no particular immediate cause to be frightened but who is still in constant motion may be suffering from inner tension, some distortion of reality, some anger, and some fear. He may need professional help in calming his excessive worry.

A different kind of hyperactivity is organic and stems from damage that may or may not be measurable in the child's brain. A child who is in perpetual motion may be suffering from attention deficit disorder, which may or may not be accompanied by learning difficulties. This problem must be separated out by a professional from the hyperactivity caused by anxiety alone. It can be treated when the child reaches school age.

Attention Deficit Disorder, or Trouble Learning and Trouble Sitting Still

These are children who have major difficulties in one or more areas of learning. Forty percent of them will behave like small tornadoes, knocking things over, moving constantly, fidgeting and breaking things and bumping into people. It is hard to be a child who can't learn as easily as the others and it is hard to be a child who needs to move all the time when adults are always asking you to be still. These children often have other emotional problems that follow in the wake of the storms stirred by their disorders of learning and are the product of the engines of the body running all the time at breakneck speed.

This illness affects approximately six times as many boys as girls. For those who are hyperactive as well as learning-disabled, the signs may actually have appeared before birth; their mothers often describe endless kicking in the womb. These are babies who squirmed in our arms and rolled back and forth in their cribs. They are said to have run before they walked and to have been in constant motion since birth.

Children with attention deficit disorder are apt to be clumsy while walking, running, or riding tricycles. They may have been slow to learn to use a pencil; they may not speak clearly, or they may speak well spontaneously but if asked a specific question have trouble organizing their thoughts. At three or four they may not be able to do simple sequences, such as: *dog cow cat; dog cow —*. At four or five they may have not learned the letters correctly and confuse *d* and *b, p* and *q*. These early signs of learning disorder may be outgrown around five or six with the maturation of the nervous system. But for some children such confusions of letters and words, of left and right and up and down, signal a learning disorder that will need prompt care in the early school years.

Children with attention deficit disorder will show a wide scatter of performance on their I.Q. tests. They will be normal or above average in some areas and deficient in others. Most normal children score roughly the same on all parts of the I.Q. test. In the years between three and six this disorder can only be suspected, not confirmed, because some naturally outgrow these symptoms as their brains mature and the learning lag and the hyperactivity disappear. We would suggest that an overly active child be watched carefully. Mothers can learn ways of helping their children to calm down. Mothers who suspect that their child may have some organic problem can try to keep their child's day as unexciting as possible. They can try not to blame the child for behaviors he cannot really help. He will do best playing with only one friend at a time. Movies and circuses are not necessary and prove overexciting. It is very important that this kind of child have enough rest, and that things be quiet and calm just before bedtime and around meals. Perhaps with an overly active child it would be best to wait a while before insisting on good table manners and instead concentrate on good feelings at the table, despite spilled milk and other inevitable disasters.

Mothers who are exhausted from trying to contain a physical whirlwind of a child can take some comfort from the fact that in adolescence their nervous system will likely return to normal. If their child should prove to have learning problems connected to attention deficit disorder, this can now be eased through special education. The activity that is so disconcerting can with the proper medication be contained and channeled in the right direction. Medication should be offered only after a careful diagnosis has been made by an experienced clinician. We would suggest second opinions on such an important matter and careful testing should be done by a psychologist. The important factor in this illness is early detection. Prompt action in the early school years should be taken to prevent the child from feeling stupid and angry at himself and others.

Some children will have learning troubles without the accompanying hyperactivity and some children will be hyperactive without the learning difficulties. Nevertheless, the two are often connected and represent some error in the nervous system.

253

Learning Problems

If you ask five-year-old William the letters of the alphabet, he can say them quickly and easily. But unlike many other children, he can't recognize them when they flash across the TV screen or appear on the printed page. He doesn't like to draw very much, preferring to turn the crayons or the pencil into an imaginary bulldozer and demolish the articles on the table. He learned to talk on time but often mixes up words and sounds. Sometimes his mother worries about his hearing; other times she worries about his memory. Other children his age have learned songs or stories but he seems to pay little attention and to care less. William may be a late bloomer, or he may have a real learning problem.

The child with learning problems can be tentatively identified in nursery school, but the diagnosis is uncertain because children do have a major forward leap in brain development during these years and often problems that appeared in the three-year-old are outgrown by six. Teachers look for children who have not established hand dominance, left over right, or right over left. Teachers are somewhat concerned about four-year-olds who cannot tell any of their letters apart and who confuse the shape of numbers. They are also alerted to the possibility of learning problems in children who lisp or stutter or talk without full grammatical play; who have tiny vocabularies; or who frequently mix up words.

Children with learning problems will have difficulty in making sequences out of words and they may have trouble with puzzles or with building constructions. Children who have difficulty sitting still or listening quietly even for a short while, who are disruptive and burst out in action and sound all the time, may eventually show learning problems. We would suggest that these children all be watched very carefully so that if they have any difficulty with the beginning months of first grade, they can be immediately tested and evaluated by a professional in the field of learning disabilities and offered whatever remedial help is necessary. In nursery school we would consider starting some kind of extra preventive work for those children who show a marked language problem: coming up with the wrong word, speaking in sentence fragments. We would intervene if a child with normally verbal parents has an impoverished vocabulary.

Lack of drawing skills and the inability to hold a pencil well do not indicate trouble in the child under five and a half. Inability to tell left from right is common in children up to the age of six or so. In fact, learning problems occur in only 6 percent of the population and most children can be successfully helped to overcome this handicap. We will discuss learning disabilities further in our next section.

Fears

For the child of three to six, fears of giants, witches, dogs, dark, closets, water, and thunder are as common and normal as mayflies in May and June bugs in June. We have seen that the child has fantasies of replacing the parent of the opposite sex and is afraid that she will be punished or attacked by an enraged parent. It is too hard for a child to be afraid of a mother or father whom she also loves and needs, so the child invents the convenient enemy in the dark closet, the witch who will poison her cereal, or the dark that holds goblins and ghosts. The danger is then placed onto these creatures of the imagination and the parent continues to be seen as loving and good.

As the turmoil of this age settles down and the child accepts her defeat in her first erotic passion, and gains a greater knowledge of reality and her place in it, the fear of retaliation for bad wishes against the parent gradually fades and finally is abandoned in the locked closet of early childhood memories.

But for some children, these fears can become excessive and they can spoil a child's enjoyment and vitality. Then we become concerned that something is not going well. A few children will become so afraid of dogs that they will not go outside to play. Some children are so afraid of the dark that they cannot sleep at night even with a small light by their bed. Some become so afraid of so many different things that their freedom to explore or learn or play with other children is limited. How serious are a child's fears? Only a parent can really judge whether his child is being undermined by his own terrors. Parents must weigh the number and intensity of their child's fears, how far they interfere with daily life, and see if they appear to be of tolerable quality and amounts.

When a parent is really angry at a child, or dislikes that child, or has not given that child reason to love and trust him, then fears may grow out of proportion and attack the child's well-being. When a parent is abusive or neglectful, a child may become so enraged at that parent and so afraid of her own rage that anxiety and fearfulness dominate the day. If a parent of the opposite sex is absent or has left the family through death or divorce, it is possible for a child to become frightened of revenge from that parent because the child is left alone with the person she wanted for herself. When a child is too fearful we know that her angry thoughts are great and that she is having a harder time than usual in working through the romantic and sexual tasks of her age.

Parents of an excessively fearful child should check to see if their discipline is too harsh or if more positive attention and care are needed. Parents can try to avoid sexually arousing play because that excitement only heats up the child's fear of retaliation. Children do become sexually stimulated by a lot of roughhousing, tumbling around with parents, or bathing together. This kind of sexual excitement can contribute to a child's fearfulness. If after some months the changes in the family life do not reduce the child's anxiety, we would recommend professional consultation.

Although fears of giants and witches will subside as the child grows older, excessive fear signals us that something is wrong in the child's basic relationships. We worry that his resolution of these important normal conflicts will not be solid and that he will enter the next phase of development without having successfully completed this one. Help and guidance from a psychotherapist can restore the child's forward direction and prevent difficulties later.

The Child Who Believes He or She Is of the Other Sex

Michael's mother and father consulted their family doctor when he was four; the family doctor referred them to a child psychiatrist. Michael's parents told the doctor that they were worried because if you asked Michael if he was a girl or a boy, without a moment's hesitation he would tell you that he was a girl. Naturally his parents had corrected him thousands of times. He remained convinced that they were somehow in error. Lately he had said that he was a boy who was really a girl. He wasn't interested in trucks or cars or balls; instead, he loved his baby doll, his stuffed poodle, and his coloring books. He would dress up in his mother's clothes and keep them on for hours even though she had begun to object and to forbid him access to her room. Michael was a sweet, bright, lovely child. His father said wistfully, "He would have been a perfect girl." These parents had cause for worry.

A few children are convinced that they are really children of the other gender. They feel totally comfortable with the role of the sex they are not. They are biologically of one sex and psychologically of another. Psychotherapists call them transsexuals. We see three- and four-year-old little boys intent on playing house, fond of dressing in girls' clothes, interested in their mother's activities in the kitchen or the house, and uninterested in any of the rougher games of the other boys. We see little girls who refuse to wear dresses, who are interested only in the activities of boys, and who will tell anyone who stops to listen that they really are boys. Today's society is more tolerant of girls who wish to be boys than of boys who wish to be girls, but in this illness the problem is one not of wish but of conviction. The children really are convinced that they are members of the sex they appear not to belong to.

This is a tragic confusion, because the child will be forced to behave in a fake or artificial manner in order to conform with the expectations of others. Often at school age this child will be ridiculed and ostracized. Feeling always fake and never genuine or whole is the fate of these children. The transsexual operations that appeared to offer solutions to adults with this problem seem now to be less desirable both physically and psychologically than was at first thought.

Transsexuality is an illness that has been with us since the beginning of civilization but has been identified only in the last thirty years. We do not know the causes or the cure. In some cases the mothers of these confused children have been found to be very depressed and have themselves had occasional homosexual feelings. The fathers have been often absent physically or are emotionally distant from their children. But at this point we do not know whether this is true for all such children. What role does biology play and what is the result of uncertainties in the environment? Many children have depressed mothers whose fantasy life may be homosexual and distant fathers but they still do not become transsexuals.

From three years to six, transsexual children will appear quite happy and contented. They are simply convinced of their gender identity no matter what the grocer or the neighbor down the street may say. Only when they enter school are they thrown into conflict and distress because other children will not accept this cross-identification and will make it cruelly clear that it is not acceptable. Transsexuals will learn to deceive, and to hide their real interests and real feelings about themselves. But no matter which way they turn, they will feel non-authentic and uncertain of how to behave and what to be.

Psychotherapy has helped some children to resolve the conflict and to reidentify themselves with their biological sex. It has not helped all such children or all such families, but at this time we have no better approach and no certain cure. The earlier the difficulty is recognized and dealt with by the family, the better the chances are of reorganizing the child's sexual identity. All children may sometimes claim the social role of the opposite sex, but the transsexual child will consistently think and state that he or she is really the other gender and behave that way.

It is very difficult for us as parents to face and deal with such a confusion, which threatens our own sexuality, and frightens us with its strangeness and its promise of disaster in the future. To listen carefully to the child, to see clearly even those things we do not want to see, this is part of the discipline and the obligation of being a parent. Fortunately, this illness is extremely rare and parents must be careful not to become alarmed if their child simply does not want to stay within our arbitrary lines of strict sexual stereotyping. Males and females are both entitled to enjoy the experiences and pleasures that society may have deemed the exclusive property of one or the other sex. That is not illness; on the contrary, it is creative human growth. All people have aspects of their soul, interests, and capacities that are both male and female. This is normal and does not signal a disruption in core gender identity. Only the child who truly over a long period of time believes that he or she is of the other sex is an ill child, one for whom we would recommend psychotherapy.

Dressing in Girls' Clothes

Many little boys will from time to time dress up in their mother's or sister's clothes. They will parade around, clowning or joking for friends, or just experimenting with the feel of female articles. This is natural and normal. Boys have an identification with their mothers, who are so important to them, and will try on their clothes to play out their feeling of sexual oppositeness, to see if they could be girls or women. But this play will be discontinued sometime after five years of age as they become more interested in protecting and asserting their masculine roles and their permanent possession of a masculine biology.

For a very small number of boys, dressing in girls' clothing becomes an habitual and significant part of their play activity. It takes on a deeper meaning and is a signal of real trouble in claiming a masculine sexual identity. Psychotherapists call these children transvestites. Such little boys always have had a hard time in the first three years of life. They may have suffered long separations from their mothers, or they may have been ill, or their mothers may have been depressed or unavailable to them. They are constantly afraid of being abandoned or of coming apart and dissolving into nothing.

When they become three or four, these little boys experience the same erotic desires for their mother as all other boys do. They get erections and may masturbate with fantasies of having the mother all to themselves, but then they become especially fearful that the father may harm them in retaliation for their incestuous desires. They are afraid they will lose their penises. They are afraid they will lose their mother's love, and they are afraid that their bodies will be destroyed. This is more anxiety than they can bear and so they give up the erotic desire for their mother. They give up all fantasies of having her to themselves; instead, they identify with her, making themselves like her, a person to be loved by the father. They will feel safe and happy in her clothes and will fantasize about the father's love for them.

We do not know exactly why one child will react to his mother's depression by confusing his sexual identity and another child will choose a different solution. We do know that when a boy turns in the direction of cross-dressing, his sexual identity is badly compromised and he may well have a homosexual orientation in his adult years. We would suggest that parents who see their sons dressing up as girls frequently and over a long period of time, seek professional psychiatric advice. This is a problem that can be more easily helped when the child is young and sexual identity is forming. The child's feelings and thoughts are reachable and acted out in his play and can be put into words by him. We cannot undo the child's babyhood experiences that have left him vulnerable to this path, but we can help him to feel safe and secure as a male and to identify himself safely with his father.

Some parents find the cross-dressing cute and appealing. All our lives we find men in women's clothes interesting, funny, and somehow titillating. This shows that there is a residue of the problem in all of us—no one is a simple sexual creature. However, in small children cross-dressing is not charming and it tells us of a child who cannot tolerate the anxiety of the sexual drama belonging to his age. He will come out of it with a difficult masculinity if we do not intervene. Psychotherapy will not change the sexual direction of all affected children but it does help many and will certainly be of support to a child who is apt to have trouble with his school mates in the following years.

Dressing in Boys' Clothes

When little girls insist on wearing only pants they are showing some desire to be boys, some wishful thinking (clothes determine gender), and some dissatisfaction with their role as girls. But for almost all girls this is just a passing phase, a way of working out the mystery of biology and the oddness of social patterns. Little girls whom we would call tomboys are well within the range of normality. If left alone, most all of them will find solutions, ways to be female that they can accept while growing to appreciate their own anatomy and to accept it. Little girls can refuse to wear party dresses or mary janes for months or even years without our becoming unduly concerned. At this age the problem of cross-dressing applies to only the male child. Female sexual confusions are not usually identified until adolescence.

Homosexuality

The erotic love of man for man or woman for woman has been part of civilization at least since the beginning of recorded time. Some societies have been more accepting of it than others. But even in those communities where it was considered an offense against God and nature, homosexuality, secret and shameful, continued in a certain percentage of the population, generation after generation. We do not have any evidence to prove that the choice of a same-sexed person for romantic or sexual love is in and of itself an illness, or a disorder of sexual development. Homosexuals come from a variety of kinds of families. Although many will lead troubled lives, it is impossible to separate out the painful social effects of making a homosexual choice from the sexuality itself.

Heterosexuals too have a wide range of difficulties in making commitments, in sexual functioning, and in finding happiness. Being a heterosexual does not guarantee a good life and being a homosexual certainly does not condemn one to a life of mental pain or suffering. Sigmund Freud, when writing to a guilt-ridden mother who had sought his advice about her homosexual son, expressed his conviction that homosexuality may well be genetic. Its precise causes are unknown and at this point in our knowledge of the weavings of mind and body inexplicable. Because of the many homosexuals who have told us something of their childhood experiences, we do believe that some potentially precipitating situations can be identified. We assume that these special family conditions must have been assisted by a strong genetic tilt toward homosexuality. Other children with similar life stories did not develop a homosexual orientation. Perhaps in some instances particular childhood events caused the homosexuality while in others a homosexual orientation would have developed no matter what the history of the child. The best guess today is that genetics and environment, working in some double helix of their own, produce the homosexual.

Some children arrive at the age of three or four without a clear sense of themselves as having male bodies with male genitals, or being female with female genitals. Babies who have had severe illnesses in the first three years of their lives, who have had surgery and experienced a lot of pain, may find it hard to get a clear picture of their own bodies and of their sexuality. Babies who have lost their mothers or had disappointing mothers who were either angry at them or especially depressed may also be unclear about their maleness and femaleness. Infants who have been excessively nervous or moved about from home to home or abused or neglected also are at risk for gender confusion.

All these children, on entering the next phase of development, may not form an erotic love for the parent of the opposite sex; instead, they may anxiously cling to the parent of their own sex. They may do this because they are so frightened by their original sexual fantasies and afraid of retaliation or destruction that they give up their first heterosexual impulses. Boys who have suffered too many separations from their mothers may identify with them because they can't tolerate being different from their mothers in any way. They cling to their mothers and recreate them within themselves by denying sexual difference.

In the years between three and six, when the child is working out his sexual identity and experiencing sexual feelings, usually for the parent of the opposite sex, homosexuality may follow if a child is badly scared by operations, by a bloody accident, or by an especially cruel and punitive parent who makes the child give up his secret sexual wishes for the parent of the opposite sex in hopes of keeping his body safe and intact. The loss of a parent by death or desertion also can turn a child to identify with the remaining parent in an attempt to avoid any more pain and loneliness. But remember, many children have these experiences and do not become homosexual. Many others become homosexual without this history.

Homosexual tendencies are noticed only by parents of those three- to six-year-old little boys who have become what society will call "sissy boys." These are boys who play with girls' toys most of the time, who may dress in girls' clothes frequently, whose arm and leg movements and whose basic interests seem to follow their mothers rather than their fathers. Parents correctly worry about boys who spend a great deal of time dressing up their Barbie Dolls and avoid roughhouse games, war games, and other sports.

Studies done on groups of these sissy boys have shown that two-thirds of them grow up to be homosexuals while one-third seem to outgrow their gender confusion and take an apparently heterosexual position. So far no one knows why one boy changed and another did not.

Parents who are concerned about the female behavior of their male child can wait and hope that their child is in the group that will grow out of it, or they may seek psychiatric consultation. Therapy is by no means a certain cure, but some children can be redirected and those fears that caused them to make the female identification can be examined, explained, and perhaps abandoned. A good child therapist will do no harm and might be able to help. The sissy boy will be bruised by the cruel remarks of other children shortly after entering first grade. He will be ostracized and ridiculed by our homophobic male children and this will be very painful for him. Parents can help by continuing to love and accept their child no matter what his final sexual orientation may be.

Some homosexual male children are identified as males and are therefore invisible to the parental eye. These boys are ones who may have been so upset by the sexual difference and the possibility of loss of their own penis that they simply cannot be sexually attracted to a female who lacks the penis. This kind of homosexual male will eventually find effeminate men to satisfy him; in this way he maintains his male identity while avoiding a confrontation with female anatomy. In the years between three to six, this child may have had some violent or bloody experience that frightened him. He may show a great fear of being hurt, or anything being broken or any part of a doll or toy falling off may cause him to panic. Parents should always reassure their children that the boy's penis cannot come off and that girls are made with vaginas. It is particularly important at this time that little children not be exposed to menstruating mothers. They will have a hard time understanding the bleeding and it may frighten them badly. Of course no one factor such as accidentally coming upon the mother changing a menstrual pad will cause homosexuality. The precipitating factors we have mentioned above are only part of the story; they work together with many other forces, mostly unknown at this time, to create the homosexual response.

Homosexuality in girls is not apparent at all in the three- to six-year-old although it may already exist in her fantasy life. Looking back we can see that if she is so afraid of separation that she cannot turn away from her mother long enough to permit the sexual feelings to emerge for her father, she may attach those feelings permanently to females. If her father has deserted her, if he has been brutal or neglectful, if her mother has not given her sufficient support to feel confident of survival when she turns away from her for a while, or has angry thoughts sometimes, she may not be able to turn her sexual feelings toward men.

Some children who have been neglected, abused, frightened by major operations, or deserted by their parents do not show any signs of sexual confusion. Naturally they will have other problems but they do not seem uncertain in their sexual identification. Other children will have only a mild history of these problems and they will quickly develop difficult-to-reverse homosexual positions. Parents along with psychiatrists have to learn to respect this mystery and respect each child, no matter what his or her final sexual orientation becomes.

Conclusions

The character, the personality, the life quality of all children is determined by two kinds of climate. The outside world has its own weather and each family has its own way of being close, of making separations, of demanding or allowing, of loving and supporting and respecting —or not. The inner world of the child has a second climate. There the changes in weather, the force of the winds, the heat of the day, the dryness of the air, the storms with their lightning, thunder, and rain, are determined by the child's age and by the child's own biological nature. These two climates together shape the child into the person we will call Bill or Dora, Eileen or Carlo.

From the third to sixth year of life, the inner turbulence in children is so high that we normally expect to see signs of stress and difficulty. As parents we are fighting against the child's primitive instincts. We are teaching him delay, control, detours. We are teaching him disgust at the waste products of his bodies. We are teaching him to hide his sexual feelings from us, but simultaneously we open up to him the marvelous world of civilization, of language and reason, place and time. Children of this age change from day to day: last week's terrible monster hiding in the closet can become this week's game. But forward direction is always marked with backward slips. An earache, a stomach ache, or a stay with grandmother can make the most cheerful of children prone to passing temper tantrums.

If Mommy takes a job, or Daddy isn't home on Sunday, the most reasonable of children may suddenly want a nightlight or have an accident in their beds. If a baby sister or brother is born, a child may insist on having his precious blanket returned to him or he may wake every night for weeks with nightmares. Children at this age are learning so fast. Their vocabulary increases each day. Their capacity to listen, to look, to understand is certainly one of the true wonders of the world. Their absolute joy in physical pleasure, in running, in swimming, in jumping is a reminder to all us adults how much we've lost by growing older. Their ability to love us and each other, to imitate and invent, is nothing short of miraculous. They also have a great capacity to heal themselves when trouble appears. They may get off the track and then by themselves, just given support and affection, find their own way back.

For some children, of course, the troubles are more than they can handle alone. In some families the lines of affection and control have gotten tangled and the children show problems that need professional help. Therapists work with young children by listening to their words and understanding their play. They can help the child and the family to understand what is wrong. Therapists release the child from old binds and encourage a forward leap.

Like every physical problem, every psychological problem is not curable. Some of the severe diseases caused primarily by genetic error or severe neglect or abuse cannot be reversed even in so a young a child. Parents will need help from family, from church, from friends and professionals, in finding out what best to do, and in mourning the child they had hoped to have. Everyone is profoundly depressed and grieved if his child is psychotic, autistic, or retarded; but it is possible to pull out of the depression, absorb the blow, and continue with one's life. Parents deserve support from others. They have to fight not to let their own lives, their own marriages, go under with the grief that accompanies a severely damaged child.

Many difficulties that children might develop later cannot be identified in the three-to-six age group. The problems of character, of personality, of wrong solutions to inner tensions that spoil learning or play or sexual pleasure have to wait for identification until the child is older and his behavior has settled down into recognizable patterns. The formation of the continents of the soul must be completed before we can begin to look at most of the instabilities of inner structures that cause so much human misery. This we will do in the following section, which describes the child from six to ten.

Part Three

SIX
to
TEN

Section I

The Remembered Childhood—Growth from Six to Ten

In books, in stories, in the classical children's adventure tale, life appears to begin at six or seven. In children's books this may be because of the age of the reader but in adult books from *Huckleberry Finn* to *The Member of the Wedding*, from Dickens to Tolstoy, from Louisa May Alcott to Truman Capote, childhood memories are those of the child old enough to observe the world with some judgment, some distance, some sense of himself both as a part of and separate from the events around him. Although vulnerable to the cruelties and failures of adults, literary children are rarely totally helpless.

If we think back into our own childhoods, we begin to gather the greatest consistency of ongoing memories after the age of six. This is not a coincidence or merely a demonstration of a more highly elaborate and capable memory. It is a sign of our greater understanding of, and participation in, the world beyond the one of our inner fantasy life, beyond even the walls of our own houses. It is a sign that after six we are no longer being blown about by the emotional storms of jealousy, fear, and rage that chase away reason and create a bad climate for realistic observation. It is a sign that we have absorbed the elements of time that mark our days and have become aware of a larger universe that works by laws of logic and reason beyond our immediate control.

At six the child is by no means a finished product, a shrunken adult, a dwarfed version of the real thing. A lot of important growing unfolds in the following years. But the inner climate has definitely changed. The child is no longer concerned with the boundaries of self, no longer fears being cut off or abandoned by all-powerful, all-knowing parents. The six-year-old child is rather like that primordial fish that came out of the ocean for the first time, balanced gingerly on two stumpy gills, and gasped for air while looking around at the wonders of tree and grass, sun and star. What a vision that first fish must have had. What a vision all of our children are sharing as they celebrate their sixth birthdays!

It's not just the start of real school, of learning in a disciplined steady way. It's not just taking your own lunch and perhaps going back and forth on the school bus. It's not just being able to walk the dog every morning or actually being able to catch a ball or hit it with a bat. Those things are wonders in themselves, but the really exciting part of a six-year-old's life is the whisperings in the playground, the sharing of a secret, the capacity to lose at Monopoly to a child who remains your friend, the wearing of a team uniform, the learning to ride a bike around the corner so you can go to the store with a playmate, the clubhouse in the back of the garage, and the language you invent to keep out the unwanted and despised. To love your parents is wonderful; to love a friend or a group of friends is sublime. This is the beginning of a childhood that the mind retains a lifetime long.

Sexuality and the Five- and Six-Year-Old

The child of five or six does not suddenly change from one day to the next. Slowly over a period of a year or so the fears that were stirred up by the child's jealousy cool down. They do not disappear entirely. We can see their trail in the way children play with each other, inventing games in which by design one person is left out or called out, in which murder and mayhem may be play-acted. The child is most often the hero who rescues, the doctor who cures, the nurse who tends, the builder rather than the destroyer. The child of five or six suddenly has a new interest in board games in which one wins or loses, another example of the leftover use of the competitive feelings now channeled into safe games with shared rules.

War games and little boys go together as the proverbial marriage and baby carriage for little girls. This is so because we live in a world of sexual stereotypes, which persists despite our best attempts at change, and because little girls in this culture spend a lot of time imagining themselves as loved and exclusively cherished grownup women, and in this way postpone the satisfaction that they cannot gain from their own fathers. Little girls play dress-up. They play at taking care of others as doctor, nurse, or mother. They play at family life, imagining future chores and future successes as tamers of the unicorn, regents of the realm, dancers on the stage, movie stars, objects of love and admiration, healers and nurturers.

Little boys turn instead to pretend combat, to sport, to physical prowess, to a love of the details of cars and the making of little model nuclear subs, because they have drawn away from the competition with their fathers. They are no longer erotically in love with their mothers. Now their interest turns toward those activities that they consider specially male. They imitate their father. They have chosen to be like him, not to be in competition with him. The signs of competition now appear only in a disguised form, as boys begin to root passionately for their team to win over the other guys. The imaginary good guy–bad guy battlefield is not only a reflection of the human obsession with destruction; it also serves as a way of channeling the aggressive feelings that had been previously evoked in the competition with the father, and of acting out and reinforcing the pleasures of identification with him.

Little boys of six or so turn away from their girl friends and seem to prefer the company of other boys. They no longer want to kiss a girl in the coat room or to play any kind of imaginary or other games with girls. They have temporarily lost interest in sexual explorations. Girls, they seem to feel certain, are other creatures, not like them, not to be wooed, not to be treated as companions in sport, best either left ignored or teased. The extremeness of this response is a kind of compliment to the female sex, admittedly in deep disguise. The little boy doesn't want to wake in himself any of the previously disturbing sexual feelings that were directed mostly toward his beloved mother. He knows that girls have a kind of power, like his mother, and for the time being he doesn't want any of that. He bands together with other boys at school and at play just as at home he watches his father and soaks up from him whatever interests him, what a male is, how he should move, and how he is supposed to behave in this male world toward other people, toward women. Most of the information is stored away for a time when it will be useful. In the meanwhile there is clearly a male sharing as the Saturday football game gets turned on on the TV and the boy is given a fishing rod by his father and taught to use it, or given a watch that belonged to his grandfather, or taken along on a business trip.

For the little girl, the ages of five and six bring a matching dislike for and disinterest in the opposite sex. They continue to love Daddy but no longer have fantasies and dreams of replacing their mother and gaining their father's actual sexual love. Now they turn to the work of learning to read and to do math. At the same time, they are taking in the ways and manners and habits and expectations of their mothers the way a thirsty athlete drinks down the offered water, the way a plant soaks up the rain. The actual interests of boys and girls will probably become more similar as society makes less and less of a fuss about distinctions between male and female behavior; but differences between the sexes are certain to remain and find new ways of expressing themselves as biology determines.

What has happened to the six-year-old's sexual feelings? They don't disappear like baby fat or diaper rash. They are simply pushed out of the part of the mind that we can easily reach, the part we know about and can talk about. They are sent into the dark recesses of the soul, where they wait to be remembered and transformed into sexual feelings for someone their own age at another more biologically appropriate time of life. They surface only in disguise now, as when a little boy develops a crush on his first-grade teacher or a little girl begins an intense love affair with horses.

Masturbation continues but not as frequently as before. It is now used more often as only a nighttime comfort, and the fantasies that once accompanied the rhythmic movements have lost some of their lurid and spectacular quality and become vaguer and far less provoking of anxiety. Physical motion can take the place of direct sexual arousal. Jumping, horseback riding, running, can all be disguised forms of masturbatory pleasure for the young child. For the boy, the external organ and the many opportunities he has to rub and excite himself continue. But now the boy will pay less attention to his own erections and will experience shame if they occur in a public place. His physical pleasure will be separated off from his rich fantasy life, in which he will take many kinds of prizes that do not appear to be directly sexual.

From the ages of six to nine, sexual feelings mostly rest, as when a flower goes into its dormant season, as when bears hibernate. In this, biology is working with society, or society is in total harmony with biology, because the lowered sexual thermometer permits the spring season of civilization, knowledge, and reason to take root and establish itself.

Right and Wrong—Good and Bad

For the young child under six, the rightness of sharing a toy, the goodness of kissing one's baby sister, the badness of stepping on your mother's new hat, and the wrongness of taking a playmate's bike are perfectly apparent. The child over three will know right from wrong, but she will correct or alter her behavior only because the actual voice of the actual parent will soon call out in approval or in protest. She can anticipate how Mommy or Daddy will feel about her hiding the baby's pacifier and she can judge how they will probably respond if she eats all the cookies waiting to be served the company coming for tea. The child between three and six can't always pay attention to the future responses of the all-powerful parent. Sometimes the impulse to commit a minor crime is just too powerful and sweeps the small delinquent up in the pleasures of immediate satisfaction. The control comes from the outside, not from the inside of the child.

For the three-year-old, the voice of conscience is heard as if it comes from a loudspeaker placed in the outside world. But as the child settles some of the sexual turbulence of the fourth and fifth year, the parent's voice becomes a part of the self, is taken inside. The loudspeaker in the room is dismantled and replaced by an inner sense of good and bad, right and wrong. This is done by a complicated process of identification with the parents. The inner voice is no longer a mere obedience and desire to please. It has a structure of its own, existing inside the mind of the child, and is a crucial part of identity. Freud called it the Superego. We speak more plainly of a good or bad conscience; we speak of a sense of innocence or guilt. It amounts to the same thing. A good six-year-old has taken his parents' commands into himself. He now expects himself to behave like and to think like and to be a certain kind of child. If he fails, he may need no admonishment from parents or teachers; he may punish himself. A six-year-old conscience is not as subtle and flexible or graceful as it will one day be. It is rather like the child's early hand-writing: large, bold, and rigid. But six-year-olds know when someone has broken the rules. They know that when a person has lied or stolen or harmed someone else, he is bad. The normal child strives to please his inner voice, to be good, to live up to the set of expectations that now have become his own.

Pain, and anxiety, and discomfort are created when the child attempts to break away from his inner voice. Guilt and a feeling of being less than wanted—of loving oneself less—follow the six-year-old and plague him with a sense of being out of joint, of being cut off from his usual place, unbalanced and disordered. The seven-year-old who steals money for candy from his mother's purse may be visited with nightmares of a gruesome and violent sort. The six-year-old who spilled nail polish on the rug and then denied it, blaming her friend, may find herself vomiting up dinner and weeping when her Daddy comes in to kiss her goodnight.

The early conscience of children is very like the early law systems of ancient societies. It is hardly acquainted with concepts of mercy, understanding, forgiveness, and proportion. If you ask a class of six-year-olds what should be done to the child who knocked all the coats on the floor, they might answer that that child should be thrown out of school, should be beaten with a big stick, should be hung by the thumbs in the gymnasium. If you ask a class of seven-year-olds what to do with a classmate who made up a nasty story about another child, they might suggest that no one in the second grade ever talk to that child again for the rest of the year. These are courts that do not believe in tempering justice for themselves or for other offenders. If they had their way, little bodies would swing from the gallows on the crossroads of the entire nation.

There are valid explanations for their harshness. Early consciences have to be strong and excessive because they are fighting against the equally strong desires of the child to do and have just what he wants. Conscience has to control the child's normal aggression toward others. It has to work hard to keep the undesirable, most desired wishes of the child from affecting behavior. A harsh superego is necessary at first to help the child resist the powerful impulses of greed, cruelty, and rage.

Conscience is not only an internal set of commandments, it is also a kind of secret safe deposit box in which the images of an ideal self are stored. The child is constantly opening the box and checking the reality against the ideal, which has been created through the parents' attitudes toward dozens of small and large matters, and glued together out of the parents' behavior toward each other and people in the community. The parents' expectations for the child become part of the picture. These ideal self-portraits are usually benign friends, a means of checking up on oneself and leading oneself gently forward.

Some children, however, use these images to make themselves feel unworthy and without quality, bad and unlovable. Conscience is a double-edged sword. For most children it becomes their guide and their educator, a harmonious part of the whole; for a few it can be a weapon carried inside the mind and used in a destructive, punitive way against their most primitive desires. The younger child of five or six is easily controlled by threats of shame; he doesn't want to be ridiculed or made ridiculous in front of others. The eight- or nine-year-old is less susceptible to shame, but he is more vulnerable to guilt as the inner voice becomes a more and more powerful and elaborate part of his soul.

Discipline

The child from five to nine is normally both eager to please and eager to learn. His need to assert independence and autonomy has settled down and will cause few conflicts between parent and child or teacher and child. Now the problems are more often in the relationship between the two groups, adults and children. The individual child, while still dependent on parents and on teachers, has discovered another source of strength and support in his playmates, a group which has certain antagonisms and quarrels with the adult world that can cause difficulty. The child now perceives that the code of morality and the code of good behavior demanded by the adults may not always be in his best interest.

To begin with, other children hate a goody-goody. They want to know that a child is on their side in the kind of low-key cold war they are waging against the authority of school or home. A child who always does what he is told and who appears to buy totally into the adult way of seeing things is going to be in the soup with his friends. Michael may shock his parents by stealing a pack of baseball cards from the local store. Mary may bring her mother to tears because she refuses to wear her sneakers to gym. Harold may insist on turning in his excellent math papers with peanut butter smudges on the corners. Most children will sneak extra television when parents aren't looking, will delight in the forbidden candy bar just before dinner, and will stay up after they have been told to turn out their lights. They may lose their library books, or they may lie and say they practiced the piano the required hour while in fact they were watching cartoons on a friend's television set. These minor infractions can seem to parents as if the child is seriously challenging their authority. They may feel they have to react with the full force of a state that believes a little rebellion in the provinces might just bring the entire nation into the streets. Handle such minor infractions firmly, calmly, and with a sense of proportion. Punishments should fit the crimes. There is no need to assume that parental authority is really being challenged; it is only being nibbled at in a quite normal and even healthy way.

In truth, children of this age are more interested in proving their allegiance to their friends than they are in overthrowing any parental senate. They almost have to express attitudes disapproving of school and showing resentment of teachers and homework, even if on the whole they rather enjoy their academic life. They just can't be seen as too loyal to the world of grownups. They have status to maintain in a group of their peers, which requires a certain opposition to the daily demands of the adult world and an equally intense loyalty to the secret and not-so-secret goings-on of their friends.

Most children who are not seething with extraordinary amounts of anger at their parents and who have found ways to express and relieve the tensions that competition and work bring will not develop

276

into delinquents or saboteurs. They will from time to time talk back. They may use language they have learned from one another that offends the adult ear. They may refuse to do a chore or follow a request to stop what they are doing and come for dinner. They may test the family requirements for cleanliness. These signs of resistance to adult rule are best met with humor, tolerance, and avoidance of a major battle of wills. For most children a simple disapproval, a definite "I don't like that, I don't want you to do that," will suffice. In most instances of disobedience the child will have some guilt of his own that when matched with a clearly expressed disappointment from the parent prevents a repetition of the incident, at least for a while.

Sometimes it is necessary to let a child know that your disapproval will be backed up by action. A child in a bad mood may defy or provoke a parent to the point of lost tempers and ruined afternoons. It is best to send that child to her room, or to deprive her of a shared family treat such as going to the movies or out for an ice cream. Children actually prefer and respond better to a punishment of definite time and duration than to a potentially endless period of alienated affections. A real punishment, a real display of immediate anger, is sometimes the only way a parent can show the child that the household is not a Third World country in a state of civil war, but an ordered, controlled environment in which the adults are in charge and the children follow.

This is the most reassuring of all universes for the six- to nine-year-old. It is what they really wanted to know. They are still not certain that they can control all their angry competitive feelings and that reason and harmony will determine their actions. Just as the supports for the great cathedrals in Europe are essential for the dizzying heights the architects were able to reach, parents serve as buttresses for their children. So your demands, your insistence on clean hands at dinner, on homework done before play or the garbage taken out, the dog walked, or the baby brother treated with care, all work with the child, not against him. They help him to gain your approval, which is what the normal child wants above and beyond anything else.

Sometimes children will call down anger and punishment on their heads for reasons that are not clear to the parents but are very important to the child. Sometimes a child will be feeling ignored by the family. The older sister has been chosen for the lead in a play; the younger brother has made the soccer team. Father has decided to teach the older sister how to use his calculator and mother has planned to pick up the brother after school and take him for new clothes. The middle child, the one who at the moment feels ignored, might just choose the dinner table to spill his milk, pull his sister's hair, and call his brother a fag.

This child needs to be put in line. He needs to know that his parents will not let him get away with havoc, mayhem, and rudeness. But at the same time we as parents have to learn to read the behavior as a message that says: "Help. No one is paying any attention to me!" This kind of peculiar, negative, upside down, inside out bid for attention is not a sign of serious disturbance. It happens to almost all children at one time or another. Parents have to be alert not only to the immediate behavior of their children but to the reasons why the child acted up.

After the age of five or six, some children can't tell their parents very much about what is happening to them in their school and play groups. A little girl might begin tormenting her younger sister, using every possible moment to tease and wound the younger child because her own best friend has deserted her for someone else and the child is angry, hurt, and desperately alone with her unhappiness. A busy parent may see only the bad behavior and think that her daughter is developing a mean streak, an evil disposition, when in fact the child is simply struggling with a pain too great to be contained.

When children suddenly break rules, erupt into rudeness, or create endless incidents of hostility with their brothers and sisters, we have to stop their unacceptable behavior while trying to find out what in the child's life is creating the strain that we see in the unpleasant events in the home. It isn't as easy as we would like to think to have our children talk to us and tell us what is really going on. If they feel that what they might say is disloyal to another child, they may not be able to do so. If they feel that by telling us what's wrong, they are retreating to a more babyish, less independent state, they may also not be able to confide in us. Sometimes if we sense that a problem is going on for a while, we may have to talk with our child's teachers or the parents of their friends. Children sometimes have higher expectations of themselves than are reasonable. Sometimes they feel so disappointed in a bad grade or a sports failure, that they act badly in order to provoke us to punish them.

Unlike a younger child, for whom behavior problems are matters of insufficient control or indicate a struggle for self and separation, the misdemeanors of the six- to ten-year-old are caused either by group trouble, group loyalty, or by some other unmanageable demand on the self from the inner or outer world. It remains our job as parents to be in control and at the same time to attempt to find out the reasons for consistently bad behavior. We cannot assume that a spouse is spoiling the child or that the neighbors' kids are a bad influence or that the child needs to be hit or spanked. Physical overpowering of a child this age leads to such frustration, rage, and a sense of helplessness that it damages the child far more than it educates. An older child learns how to behave from our own behavior; if we resort to physical attack when angry, they too will strike out at those who frustrate them. The more powerful parent may force a child into submission and make that child afraid of him, but he will not be helping the child to gain better control over his own behavior. He will not be helping the child to see the adult as an ally, a person to be admired and imitated. He will lose the trust of his child, and no amount of conforming behavior is worth that enormous loss.

A parent's job at this age is made easier by the child's natural tendency to want to do those things that the parent would approve of even if the parent is not physically present. The child now has his own conscience, which directs action and hands out approval or disapproval. When we disapprove of ourselves, we feel guilty and uncomfortable. For the most part children will do things to avoid that discomfort and will try to live up to their own inner ideas of right and wrong, good and bad. Out of a desire to love themselves, most children will not seriously break rules, cause disruption, or jeopardize their good opinion of their own souls.

The savage beast inside the child has not shriveled up and gone away. Impulses to destroy those one doesn't like, to take everything one wants, to smash the child who laughed in math when you made a mistake, to drown the little brother mother thinks is so adorable paddling around the pool, to cheat on homework, and to steal money to buy an expensive toy are all there. These impulses are controlled by the child's own conscience. For the most part they are so horrifying they are even pushed out of the mind and buried down deep.

They appear only in nightmares, in enjoyment of violent television shows, in descriptions of dreadful, unacceptable other children.

In groups, however, children like grownups can let their consciences sleep a little and their behavior slip. Together, they can do things that they would never do alone. For most children, this means that they can be cruel to each other in ways they would not be able to square with their own feelings of justice and mercy. Cruelty to the scapegoat is the major outlet for the destructive impulse in these years of childhood. Children are shockingly mean to the child who is less capable in sport or learning. They shun the weaker child as if the inability to throw a ball or to learn letters was catching. Perhaps it is this great fear of being the outsider oneself that explains such chronic and almost universal meanness. Children are also obsessed with not being different from the others. They are determined not to wear the wrong kind of socks or to carry an odd kind of lunch box. It is here perhaps that we see the real roots of group prejudice, based in adults on such flimsy excuses as religious or racial differences. Not dressing strangely, not having parents whose looks or profession or manner differ from the neighbors', not having a home that distinguishes itself in any way—sadly enough, these are the common ambitions of childhood.

The child at this age finds identity and strength in being alike, in having a best friend wearing the same shirt or reading the same book. The world of the child from six to ten has suddenly grown much larger. Perhaps it is the very knowledge of infinite space and infinite places in the human community that causes the young child to gain such security from being a member of a particular group. It may be the Boy Scouts or the church choir or the school baseball team, or perhaps just a little group of girls who made a club and don't allow someone else to join. These groups give the child the courage to move away from the family. They serve as a kind of Teddy bear or precious blanket that no longer represents the smell and the feel of the mother but does carry the magical power of safety, protection, belonging. We spend a lifetime struggling to be an individual, yet we do not want to be all alone. Groups for both children and adults serve to help us leave our mothers and find substitutes in the human community that become like the arms of the protective parent, preventing us from falling into empty space. In the child of six to nine we see this drama in its clearest and most pristine form.

Learning

During the fifth and sixth year, the nerves and tissues of the brain reach their final form. The eye and hands will work together as they never have before. The child is physiologically ready to read and write and reach out into far corners of thought, to reason clearly, and to order things with beginnings, middles, and ends. Now the child can tell the difference between a dream and reality. She will tell you the contents of her dream and recognize that it was only pictures in her head. Now when children draw people, they include necks that separate the body from the head as if they now believed that the mind and the body were distinct but connected parts. At this age a child learns to solve problems in his head. He can imagine how to work his way out of a maze instead of having to literally move through it. He can find his way through many problems by imagining the solutions and no longer relies only on trial and error to get results. This new capacity shows itself as the child learns to tell time. When she can understand that the clock with one face represents two twelve-hour time periods, at once the world of multiple meanings has opened.

Reading and writing do not come with the same ease to all children. Some just mature a little later than others and move more slowly toward the organizing of letters and sounds into words and sentences. Handwriting varies from child to child, and girls usually achieve neatness and control months or years before boys. While children do learn at different rates, we begin to see a division between the child of high intelligence and her merely normal age mates. Now the speed of learning and the richness of texture of question and interest will mark out the more gifted child from her sister.

The essence of the learning change that takes place after five is the shift to a view of the world larger than the home, larger perhaps than the community. It includes some sense of historical time and place —gradually through the first grades of school a child learns of distances that are both geographical and historical. She learns that there are laws of reason and season that determine the way we live and what happens to the outside world, its weather, its tides, its shape.

Many children, particularly boys, have trouble sitting still and listening to instructions in the first grades of school. But gradually most children are caught up in the excitement of learning. They enjoy it. They derive deep pleasure, satisfaction, and pride from the victories over the multiplication tables, the reading and spelling skills. They become conquerors of new vocabulary, of new orders of cataloguing and arranging rock collections, of memorizing the names of all the dinosaurs, learning the routes of the first explorers. They revel in the workbooks and textbooks that are their tickets on the train traveling toward their adult lives.

All this activity is made possible not only by the human intelligence, which is of course a primary matter, like water to the fish, but also by the gifts of energy shifted now from sexual and body interests into the workings of the mind. The child who once watched his B.M. disappear down the toilet with some alarm may now turn into a little collector of insects, pebbles, fall leaves arranged by size and color. Collecting and cataloguing is a new place for the interest that once was attached to the body. The child who stores his dinosaur stickers in a notebook is a civilized version of the child who expressed such interest in the toilet.

The child who finds the places on the map from the list her teacher has given her and who learns the names of every capital city in America is the same child who peered under the skirts of her mother and her mother's friends and who insisted on getting into the shower with Daddy. The curiosity that was first brought to life about sexual matters, about the places and the functions of the body, has changed to a curiosity about the real world and all the names and places in it.

Learning requires a sense of responsibility and a capacity to maintain order or neatness. The child who once wanted to put his hands into his own B.M. now becomes a child who doesn't like erasure smudges on his pages, who likes a clean sheet for each piece of work, who separates out the subjects in his notebook and is careful not to lose books or papers. This does not happen overnight and is not the result of walking in through the front doors of the school; but the interest in neatness and order is fostered by the school and is gradually made a part of the child's own demands on himself and others. It happens as he turns away from his early interest in the bathroom, becoming increasingly private about his body and filled with disgust about the messiness and smelliness of functions that had once absorbed him so intensely. After a stage of bathroom humor that is usually outgrown toward the end of the sixth year, he takes on an adult view of the subject: the less said the better.

Messiness

Some children remain messy and disorganized longer than others. They may refuse to clean up their rooms and have to be forced each day to put away toys or to put clothes in a laundry hamper. These children, too, are reacting to our earlier demands for body cleanliness. They are still insisting on their rights to some baby behavior; they still take some pleasure in making a mess and claiming it for their own. For most children this is within the range of normal resistance to adult demands and firmness. Consistency and a sense of humor can help a parent bring a child to a tolerable level of neatness. It is best to avoid constant fights over straightening up a room or putting away toys. Try rewards, try bribes, try encouragement and general approval. The child of six or more really wants very much to please. If the problems of messiness are not blown into full-fledged wars, where they get caught in old problems of independence and self-assertion, they will die down in time.

The child who inclines to messiness may do so to some degree his entire life. Such a child will probably not be a biochemist. He will be more apt to lose things rather than collect them. In all likelihood he will not grow into a tax accountant or an academician who creates files and footnotes. On the other hand he may have large amounts of creative freedom. He may have an advantage over his neater sister when it comes to spontaneous thinking, inventing, and acting. We would not want to make any large generalizations about a child's future based on his degree of neatness or messiness at age six, but some character trends, some possible directions can be hinted at by watching how carefully or indifferently a child orders and gathers his things.

Reading

Reading opens up a wonderful way to satisfy old longings for the parent of the opposite sex without causing any new anxiety. Through stories, the child can become a princess, a heroine, an inventor, a scientist, or the winner of the greatest of prizes. A boy can overcome dragons, thieves, shipwrecks and feel himself a victor, a man like other men deserving of a lady. Boys like adventure stories in which the hero does in the bad guys and survives to claim rewards. Girls like stories of female triumph over illness, over the wilderness, over cruel witches and wicked step-parents. They love stories about orphans who are finally reunited with their long-lost fathers or who win the love of the prince over the evil doings of ugly sisters.

The imagination, aided by the power of the written word, takes the child into places where victories and triumphs abound, and the present real state of the child's relative helplessness, inferiority to the parent of the same sex, is forgotten. The years from five to ten are years in which learning is directed toward the real world and in which imagination helps the child to feel as if his most secret wishes will one day be satisfied.

As children start school, parents should openly express their interest in and approval of the child's work. Parents who think school is important will give that message to the child. Homework, no matter how simple the level, should always be treated seriously and with respect by the parent. That work, school work, is a necessary and crucial part of life should be an accepted fact in the household. Most children will work because of their desire to please parent and teacher. They will increasingly enjoy the rewards their own efforts bring. Some few children are resistant—they leave books at school; they find a million excuses to avoid the tasks they have been asked to complete. Parents must make it clear to such a child that work is not an option. While play, or television privileges, may be withheld until work is completed, such a child should be encouraged and admired for what he does. Parents can try working with him for a while, giving approval and expressing their own interest in what he is doing. Most children will soon adopt steady work habits; while pretending to dislike it all, these children quickly gain satisfaction from their learning. They will come to expect it of themselves. They will see that other children do it. They will not want to be different from the others.

For those few children who after some months still resist doing work, we would suggest an evaluation by a professional educator. Perhaps the child has some learning difficulty that he avoids confronting by avoiding work. Parents should be careful not to turn school work into a battlefield. They do better by avoiding punishment and scorn, and by encouraging the child to try to be like them, to please them in this all-important matter.

Television

Television is fine for an exhausted child. It gives him a chance to relax and refuel. Television also has a great deal to teach our children about our values and about the world around them. Children who see programs set in other cities, in other kinds of families, in other time periods, can learn a great deal. But if the television set is overused, it becomes a narcotic. The television can think for the child, can be his imagination, can be his major friend. This is dangerous. The solution is to monitor it. Permit only a certain amount each day. Make sure that the programs chosen are ones you think good for your child. Except for a child with a fever, we would never let the television run on and on. At least once in a while parents should watch with their children. They can correct the images on the tube. A parent who is there can say, "Isn't that silly? Indians aren't like that at all," or, "Most women don't giggle all the time," or "Lots of fathers like to cook."

We can protect our children from the stupid stereotypes and the false information that television brings by watching with them. But television violence is a part of our children's lives. We cannot screen it out completely. Children enjoy the brutality of cartoons, of chases, of crashes and murders, because all this material is in their imagination anyway. We would not suggest that children should watch whatever they want, but we would not get too excited about the images of mayhem that the child absorbs. They are not going to turn your child into a delinquent.

Recess

Children from six to ten have an enormous need to let off steam. They can control their behavior for increasingly long periods of time, but they still need to use their whole bodies to express and release the tension that builds up through the effort to control themselves, to concentrate on the outside world. Children need the physical release and opportunity safely to play out their angry feelings that both organized and unorganized physical games allow. A school yard is a noisy, confused, whirling, twirling place where it seems nothing stands still and everything turns or moves in different directions. This is how it should be. The young child desperately needs the recess, just as the baby needed to be rocked to sleep, the colicky infant needed to be walked around the house till the stomach pains subsided, and the hungry baby needed to wave her arms and kick her legs to release the tension that discomfort forced on her.

Recess is the time when the child works out his place in the pack. He makes decisions about how cruel he will be to another. He chooses his friends and he asserts his power or suffers from his powerlessness. Adults can only guess at what really goes on in recess. Our children are in their own pressure cooker at this time. Some inevitably get hurt. We do see differences between the sexes in their play at this age. How many of these differences are innate and how many created by cultural pressures, we don't yet know. Girls become interested in talking about each other as early as age six. Boys are more accepting of one another and make their judgments more on a basis of physical skills than anything else. Boys are more apt to talk about sports, collections, and games, while girls begin to discuss feelings and learn how to manipulate each other, jockeying for friendships, excluding and including one another as if social relationships were a round robin tennis game.

Girls in our present culture will play pretend games longer than boys on the average. They will become challenged by jump rope and jacks and other skill activities that involve moving the body in just the right way. Yet in the midst of their enjoyment they are always watching the social scene, who is with whom, who likes whom best.

Boys at recess are more apt to be blowing off steam, practicing ball games whose skills they take very seriously. They will respect the athlete far more than the scholar, whose day will have to wait until adolescence. If they notice the girls at all, it will be to tease them, frighten them, or tell them they are no good. These are broad generalizations and many children cross over the sex lines at one time or another. We think the more boys and girls share play styles the stronger and more interesting people they will one day be.

But it remains true that without recess this important work of childhood—to play, to be one of a group, to make someone else feel left out—would not be possible.

Play

Five- and six-year-olds will eagerly learn games with rules. They enjoy board games that involve counting. They love games of strategy like checkers and they will enjoy a good puzzle on a rainy afternoon. They are beginning to learn how to play physical games with balls and bats and can lose themselves in team fervor and excitement. At first they will have a hard time obeying and understanding the rules. You can't hit the other guy in the face. You're out if you don't touch all the bases. You can't throw the bat. You must get the ball over the net not under it, etc. Their increasing capacity to play with each other and play by the rules accompanies a new willingness to be part of a group, to gain strength from the group. Children will have fierce loyalties to a team, to their school, to their classmates. All this signals the change from home to society, from a single self-centered way of being to a more sociable, communal kind of life. Games are the means used to travel together. The games of childhood are the teachers of social codes, the initiation rites into the larger society.

But children of five, six, and seven are not suddenly transformed into rational group animals. Most of them maintain their childish abilities to invent and pretend, to imagine adventures and situations in which rational thought is diminished and magic and the illogical poetry of the dream can still take over. If one listens to the six- or seven-year-old in school as he answers questions his teacher asks in class, one might think he was well on his way toward a law degree, capable of deduction and rational thought equal to most adults. But listen to the same child in recess when he and his friends are planning an attack on a superpower with a rocket ship they have imagined, and listen to the way they smash and crush their enemies, and listen to the appearance suddenly in the midst of the battle of Dracula, who bites the opposing general on the throat, and listen to the accounts of banishment to Mars of the defeated soldiers, and watch the resurrection of the dead in a sudden counterattack. You'll wonder what happened to the reasonable child who just an hour earlier saw that water was made up of two parts hydrogen and one part oxygen.

The child's mind can easily slip into magical thinking, irrational and primitive constructions. The imagination of the child is not entirely tamed, and in those few of our children who go on to become artists of one sort or another, the ability to let go of reasonable thought and slide into the chaos and jumble of more primitive thinking remains through a lifetime. Professionals call this kind of thinking primary process thought. The artist uses both secondary process (rational) thought and primary process thought as he creates. For most children the last years of early childhood bring a farewell to irrational, imaginative, associative mental activity, at least while awake. Children who are six and seven can write a line of poetry of startling beauty and insight. Sadly enough, as they learn more, as their rational processes develop and take control, this special gift falls away with the baby teeth, in most cases never to return.

Girls and boys gain great pleasure from their increased physical coordination. Girls will play jump rope for hours. They will learn to roller skate and bike-ride, and with each new accomplishment they will feel more secure about themselves, more confident that they are not helpless or dependent beings. Little girls also will begin to play jacks. This game involves fine eye–hand coordination and some of course will be more skillful than others. The pleasure in this apparently mindless activity is one of both mastery and completion. Going from the ones into the tens and back again makes a kind of order and sense of a world that is often beyond the child's control.

For boys, the games become more organized and follow the sports that are seen as masculine on television. Boys will wear the hats and jackets of their favorite teams as a way of associating themselves with powerful men, with victors. If we think back to the Indian tribes that organized themselves around a variety of totem animals whose powers and prowess the members of that totem group were thought to possess, then we see that the baseball or football teams of today serve a similar purpose. They bring the little boy into a masculine culture and lend him the attributes of strength and force that he must wait for his adulthood to actually attain.

Boys and cars take on a special closeness in these years that puzzles most mothers. Many boys can recognize the make and year of a car several blocks away. Their interest is clear if we remember the boy's desire to have a powerful, fast body like his father, like other men. The car, the train, and the plane are all favorite play items because they express the boy's own yearning for force and speed and strength. The car and the other toy vehicles—whether they hurtle through imaginary space or down pretend highways—become symbolic extensions of the boy's own body, expressing aggression and thrusting power in a way that on one level relates the child to the real world while on another it enables him to satisfy his need to be as invincible as the rocket that splits the clouds.

Friendships

The world of the child in early elementary school years is not so idyllic or easy as we would have it. Her happiness depends on her acceptance by friends. Being a part of a group, having a best friend, being like everyone else, and being liked by those one considers important—this is the hard stuff of childhood. It is in this matter of belonging that even little children who have just started to subtract in two columns or begun to learn the rules of spelling are apt to be bruised by the passing cruelties of a sometime friend, or a would-be friend, or a group of friends who have suddenly made it clear that their circle has closed and someone is left outside.

Loneliness and alienation are thought to be sophisticated problems of the modern age. But loneliness is suffered most severely in the playgrounds of schools, in the backyards of children who can't yet reach the top shelf of the icebox and who have never heard of the latest rock group. Fortunately for most children this loneliness, this state of the outcast, is a temporary matter. In a few days, in a week, in just hours, the social scene can reverse itself and the bully of yesterday become the pariah of today. Children do lose their best friends to another. They do, perhaps because they have for one moment or another appeared different from the crowd, lose their status as one of the "in" group. They are terrified of being left out, so the more dominant among them may organize matters so that someone else is ignored or despised or whispered about.

Boys increasingly judge each other on the basis of physical ability. They may well choose their friends the same way they would pick players on a baseball team. Boys are not so interested in character or wit as they are in aggressive, active body dominance. A little boy who is small for his age, plays a good game of chess, and prefers the violin to the basketball may have trouble for a while with the other kids. A little girl who is shy or who is taller or shorter or whose dress or habits are different from the others may also have trouble. The world of childhood groups is a world of conformity and brutality.

For both boys and girls there is the subtle but real fact of charisma. Some children just have a kind of special energy and outgoing force that attracts others to them. Other children who are more reserved and reflective are not as immediately appealing to their age mates. These personal qualities are always in rapid flux and the child who controls the group for one six-month period may be pushed back the next. Children are also involved in imaginary life, and the child who is able to invent and sustain games of adventure is a much sought out playmate. The timid child is at a disadvantage; children will often either ignore or torment the child who seems afraid of the others. The child who holds himself aloof from the fray is also an outsider and can become the butt of the game. Each child is so afraid the pack will turn on him or her that they eagerly join in or initiate an attack on someone else.

But children are also capable of loving friendships and surprising acts of generosity and warmth. The pains of a best friend can easily be suffered as one's own and the extent of the love of one child for another is often amazing.

The boy who is naturally clumsy and awkward at sports needs to be reassured by his parents that physical skill will not always be an important factor in how a child makes friends or is respected by a group. Parents can offer the child some extra practice time and perhaps find a particular sport at which he may excel; but for many children the comfort has to come in a promise of future friends. The parents of such a son must make a real effort to help the child find other areas of competence in which he can gain self-confidence. Perhaps he can collect stamps or play a musical instrument, or learn all about the Civil War or make the most glorious kites in town. Parents must be inventive, follow the child's interests and supply their own, and fill his life with materials that will in later years earn him respect and friendship among his peers.

Sexism or Stereotyped Roles

The bonding of the six- to nine-year-old in same-sex groups is normal and common enough. The different kind of play each sex enjoys seems to promise an adult life for these children in which each will be firmly contained within the borders of clearly marked sex types. There is no doubt that children of this age act in sexually stereotyped ways. If this became a lifetime pattern, reinforced by strict social standards, both sexes would lose some of their potential and a large part of their humanity. The biological differences between the sexes and the different paths of development taken in early years do not necessarily validate a lifelong division of roles, or a social or intellectual arena that belongs to males instead of females or females instead of males. Most boys will be more interested in sports and most girls in imaginary games at six or seven years. But the intelligence of girls and the intelligence of boys is equal, and the work of doctoring or engineering, design or business is not performed with the genital organs.

As children mature, they become more and more capable of transcending the rigid positions of their biological givens, more and more able to use the full range of their capabilities, which are not organized on sexual principles but rather on questions of mind and character. The early sexual differences that we see are based on the child's closeness to his anatomy. The little boy has both pride and fear for his penis. The little girl begins to see herself as a mother, the possessor of a womb and the nurturer of future generations. But this is only the beginning of learning about the self and its varied possibilities. Girls and boys need not rest in the divisions and separations nature has imposed on them as they learn to share interests in music, math, or politics. If the society does not remain as unsophisticated as its six-year-olds, if it is able to pass on to another stage where male and female can share the same concerns, the same ambitions, then the sharp divisions of the early years will be forgotten just as the earlier attitudes toward the toilet underwent major transformations.

We do not believe that giving little girls trucks to play with or insisting that little boys make muffins will really change matters. Some little girls will like to push around trucks and some little boys will like to mix and bake (which if not taken to extremes is fine and healthy). But most young children will be busy establishing their gender by whatever simple means the society makes available to them, be it dress, toys, or games. Boys are apt to tease one of their own who plays with the girls and the girls will despise a girl who tries to be one of the guys. If the adult world does not take these early statements of sexual identity as more than a mere claiming of anatomy, then the children will be able to expand from their basic sexual natures into the full variety of human experience. Girls can become astronauts and boys can become nurses, men can cry and girls can make a killing in the stock market, and we can all be comfortable with our biological reality without having to wear stereotyped masks of one kind or another.

Feminist parents have been disturbed at the macho attitudes of their sons and the play with dolls they may see in their daughters. If we understand this as only a child's view of the world, a young attempt to make sense of sexual difference and to feel secure in the mysteries of the body, we can indulge our children in their sexual divisions knowing that in time they will outgrow the need for them.

The Bully

If your child is continually being cruel and leading the pack in cruelty to other children, you can express your disappointment very clearly. You can tell your child how sad it makes you feel that he should hurt another human being. Tell him that you want him to help others, not harm them, and that this is an important part of being the kind of person you want him to be. Help him to imagine how the other child feels. Take special care to express to him your admiration for his powers of leadership and strength, making it clear that these qualities can be used well or badly and that you expect him to use them well. Praise him for thoughts and acts of consideration and kindness. The chances are that he will want your approval enough to change his behavior. He will take inside himself your image of a good person and follow it. We will discuss the child who cannot stop being cruel in the next section.

The Victim Child

Some children are so desperate for friendships that they will allow others to be cruel to them just to be a part of the group. Some are unsure of themselves, shy, or perhaps just different in minor ways from the pack and so get picked on. Parents can help such a child by urging him to stand up for himself, to fight back with dignity, and to walk away from hurtful situations. Parents can also help by finding new friendship groups for them where they can start afresh, such as Scout troops, dance classes, or sports programs. A boy or girl who has trouble in a particular group may do quite well if their class at school is changed. Consultations with teachers are a good idea. Perhaps the child is ignoring other children who would be good companions. Perhaps he or she is behaving in some way (crying frequently, not sharing, not listening) that provokes the others.

It is usually hard for parents to see such behavior in their own children and children themselves rarely have any idea why others are picking on them. A teacher or an adult neighbor may be of help in clarifying the situation. With reassurance and some practical guidance, continual victims will eventually find new friends and become a happy part of another group. This is, however, a situation that should be watched carefully and should not be permitted to continue year after year. If a child is the victim in group after group despite parental support, we would suggest that consultation with a psychiatrist might be a good idea. We will discuss this further in our next section. In the years between six and ten all children need to belong to a group, to have at least one good friend, to be accepted by others. This is as important to their growth as adequate nutrition.

Brothers and Sisters: Fighting and Biting

The six- to nine-year-old knows perfectly well she can't push her little sister into the pool or pour paint over her big brother's stamp collection. She knows the boundaries of decent behavior, but (and this is a very large but) the pressures of jealousy do not diminish at this age. In fact, they increase in scope and in variety. Since the children are now aware of each other as separate people, with different skills, they become even more concerned that they will lose some imaginary battle in which only one child will be judged the favorite and the most loved. The rivalry with the parent of the opposite sex has been abandoned, but the rivalry with brothers and sisters takes on a new and terrible dimension as it becomes clear that this brother has a gift for the piano and that sister learns to read without even trying.

Children begin to compare their skills, their competence, their accomplishments. They are often afraid of being left behind. The older doesn't want the younger to catch up in skills and the younger one will often fiercely strive to go beyond what is expected in order to compete. There are bound to be disappointments in this contest; there are bound to be resentments and angers that follow in the wake of this vigilant watching of the other, the steady fear of not being as good, as approved of, as loved.

It can drive a parent crazy to hear the constant bickering in the back of the car: He pinched me, I did not, He did too. It makes most of us wild to listen to endless complaints: He stole my record, She took my sweater. I set the table yesterday, it's her turn today. She won't let me play with her friends. She twisted my arm. She's a poor sport. He won't pick up the pieces of the game just because he lost.

These noises and countless unpleasant others are the normal background hum of the pre-dinner hour, the rainy Saturday, the long vacation. They occur in part because all human beings who live together are constantly rubbing against each other, trying to dominate, to get their own way, to prove their superiority, or simply to release tension by making someone else feel bad. These arguments also are reflections, echoes in our daily lives of the continual struggle between children to win the larger share of parental love for themselves. It does no good to explain that the pie like the sky is infinite and cannot be divided into equal or unequal pieces. Rivalry and hurt feelings, anxiety about the success of the other is as natural as can be.

Families, of course, have different styles and permit different amounts of expression of this rivalry. They insist on different ways of suppressing or expressing these feelings. Difficult as it is, it is necessary for parents to permit a certain amount of verbal nastiness between children. Some of the arguing is a letting off of steam, a jockeying and negotiating for position and respect. Parents prefer all this to take place in another room. If children insist on carrying on a loud and unpleasant fight in front of parents, most will and should insist on silence, separation, and peace.

Of course parents have to stop physical violence between siblings. Children have to learn that hitting, hair-pulling, biting, and bruising are simply not allowed. We tend to get angry at the older child, who can do more damage, but don't forget, the younger one is aware of your protective feelings and is equally capable of inflicting physical pain or damage. This must be clearly, strongly, and absolutely forbidden. You can tell your children that anger is all right, words are permitted weapons, but physical harm is always, under all circumstances, unacceptable. Children will feel relieved that you feel this way. It will help them eventually to control their anger and change its expression into a verbal one. Don't try to settle arguments; it's a hopeless venture. Don't try to figure out who started it. Today's victim probably did something rotten yesterday. A happy home is not one in which no feelings of anger or spite are expressed. A happy home is not a harmonious melody; at best it is one in which the cacophony is not constant and individual voices can be heard above the din.

A child will feel guilty if a brother or a sister falls ill. She will feel guilty if she succeeds too well in the competition. She will feel anxious if a parent actually favors her over another child. If you can love one better, admire one more, then your taste may change and she is in danger of losing the advantage. It sounds simple enough to distribute your affection fairly between your children but most parents find this tricky. One child will be easier to talk to while another will fulfill your ambitions to be a fantastic tennis player. One will act just like your hated cousin Sue and a third may always remind you of your own difficulties as a child, a fact which causes you to ignore him when he most needs your attention. We try not to have preferences among our children, but while our loyalty and commitment to all of them may be the same, the fact is that some children are easier to get along with and bring more pleasure than others. If this gets out of hand a family is in trouble.

There has been some talk about the ideal spacing of children in an ideal family. We would feel that competition and comparisons exist no matter how wide the age difference. Children close in age have greater and more immediate problems of envy and jealousy but they also have the compensating pleasures of companionship and support. The age difference is not the important factor in a child's life. The way the parents distribute their love and the mood and tone of the home determine the quality of life for all members of the family. We would like to see at least twenty-two to twenty-four months before another sibling is born just because babies require so much attention and care, and an overly exhausted mother has trouble giving all that is needed. There is, however, no ideal painless moment to introduce a new sibling. There can be no family life without some kind of competition and hurt feelings.

Yet competition is only part of the story of brothers and sisters and the childhood experiences they share. Along with the rivalry, jealousy, guilt, and anxiety come loyalty and commitment and a greater sense of security because of the connection and caring of family members. In the years between six and nine we see siblings playing together for hours, enjoying secrets, enjoying television, enjoying going places together, sharing possessions, sharing friends, bringing each other treasures of all kinds, and protecting each other from the possible harshness of the world. Sometimes the fights between brothers and sisters are caused because one loves the other so much he becomes jealous of friendships that do not include him. This image of brothers and sisters is neither sentimental nor romantic if one remembers that the other picture exists as well.

If the husband and wife are managing well enough together and if the children are not suffering from some outside pressure, it is most likely that as the years pass they will find more ways to depend on each other and to enjoy each other. When marriages are in trouble, we often see children who sense the tension and are frightened, bitterly fighting with each other in imitation of what they sense is going on in the adult world. In the school-age child, we often hear fighting when one child or the other is under pressure from teachers or friends. Sometimes we can be alerted to trouble in our child's life because there is a sudden upsurge of fighting in the home.

The Fantasy of Being a Twin

Some children after age five enjoy the fantasy of being and having a twin. This invented sister or brother is usually an identical twin and has many important meanings to the child. The twin is always there, a companion who never threatens to go away, to choose another friend, to abandon the creator to loneliness and isolation. The invented twin blunts the pain of being alone, no longer a part of mother, no longer the baby who is cared for and protected at all times. He can through imaginary games carry the voice of angry thoughts and disobedient wishes. The twin can suggest the unthinkable. He can either be more helpless than the real child or more independent. The twin is the companion who understands everything and with whom there need be no mask, no pretense, no behaving well.

This invented twin is not at all like the real twin experience. It does not contain the rivalry and competitive aspects that are unavoidable with real twins. It is only a fantasy of the perfect companion, the Teddy bear or blanket now brought to a new and more complicated stage, where it can remain in the mind and enter through the imagination into the game life of the child where conflicts and problems, fears and troubles are acted out and mastered. If a child has invented a twin, he has invented a new way to love himself. It's not a bad temporary solution for the aloneness, the disconnections all children this age must feel. As the growing child comes to accept his separateness, this fantasy fades.

The Family Romance

Many children develop a fantasy we call the family romance. In it they decide they were taken home from the hospital by the wrong parents, that if the birth records ever came to light they would be revealed as the son or daughter of different parents. These fantasy parents are either very rich and powerful or very poor and miserable. The choice reveals something of how the child feels about himself. The fantasy of being the scion of a royal family indicates a good sense of oneself, if temporarily a little out of proportion. The opposite fantasy, of being the child of gypsies or beggars, can tell us that a child is accusing himself of unworthiness.

The frequency of these fantasies shows us that children must find ways to release the anger they build up against the control of their own mother and father. In their fantasies, they banish their real parents and instead adopt a new set that will be ever so much better. The child is struggling to move away from his home and is at the same time aware of how needy he still is. Therefore he invents parent substitutes, and since he is the creator he can mold his imagined set of parents any way he likes.

Adopted children have a variant of this fantasy; it lasts longer and remains more important to them. The fantasy is less of a game for them and we will discuss it further in our section on adoption.

Rituals

Because the child has to make a large effort to push away undesired thoughts and feelings, as well as impulses for destruction and sexual urges, many children develop habits that can appear quite peculiar. They may insist on walking on the right side of the street; they may wear a sweater in all kinds of weather; they may pile their coin collection up in a certain way and continually check to make sure that the order has not been violated. Some children grow insistent about washing their hands after every activity and some will demand that the window shade rest at a certain height in order for them to be able to sleep. These rituals are magic formulas designed to keep the child safe in a world in which he perceives danger coming from unexpected sources. The danger he really fears is an eruption of his own feelings —his own anger and his own sexuality. While at this age the sexual drives dampen down, they do not disappear entirely. The child still needs to use some of his invention and some of his energy to keep his sexual feelings at bay. The rituals serve to help the child stay in control of himself and to feel less threatened by the world.

Only if these rituals become intrusive in the child's life do we feel that they deserve professional attention. If the child becomes so caught up in his way of dressing or eating that normal procedures can't continue or his work or play life is affected, we become concerned. This would tell us that the child is trying to contain a massive amount of anxiety and anger and is having trouble. For most children, the ritual aspects of their behavior are normal and gradually lighten and disappear.

Don't forget that much of religious practice is a transformation of these rituals, designed to protect us from powerful evils. When we share these acts as a culture, we take our private magic and invent the decorations and the styles of civilization. This not only is a common human activity, it even seems to be a basic necessity.

Illness

During the years six to ten, many children will show signs of stress through passing body symptoms. Hives and rashes of all kinds are common. Headaches and stomach aches of no known cause serve as an outlet for the child's struggle to remain in control of his behavior, to push away unwanted sexual and emotional conflicts, and to keep from his conscious knowledge some of his worst fears and angers.

Vomiting and pain are real events in the child's life, whatever the reasons for their arrival. Most of these symptoms are transitory and disappear as the child regains the upper hand in his battles against disturbing feelings. The fact that such a conflict exists and shows itself in the occasional physical symptom is not a matter of concern for parents or doctors. It is a normal part of the coping capacity of children at this age. If it is not prolonged over a period of weeks, and if physical symptoms do not interfere with the child's school life or friendships, then we can watch the rashes, the aches and pains (in other generations called growing pains) come and go with calm and understanding.

Divorce

During the years six to nine, a divorce in the family is just as deeply disturbing and threatening as it is for the younger child. But there are some important differences in the response that are crucial to our understanding of the child's experience.

The older child will have worries about the divorce that are related to reality. Will there be enough money? Will we have to move to another city or to another neighborhood? Will I be able to go to the same school and have the same friends? The child from six to ten will still be afraid of being abandoned by one or another or both parents; he will still be afraid that his own jealous feelings or occasional bad behavior has contributed to the parents' unhappiness. But the older child is able to more quickly understand the explanations that are given. He is less apt to feel the guilt of the potential fulfillment of romantic fantasies toward one parent or the other. He is better able to use the supports outside of the family to give him a sense of security, continuity, and self. Since his school life, his teachers, and his friends now occupy a major part of his attention, he is better able to reassure himself that the divorce has not caused the sky to fall on his head and the ground beneath him to open up. But despite his improved ability to see the reality of the situation and to use other people in his life for support, the child at this age has other difficulties. He finds it nearly intolerable to be different from other children. No matter how many divorces there are in the immediate area, each child will feel marked and stigmatized. Divorce is not the way it is supposed to be, and the child at this age, with his enormous investment in being like everyone else, suffers from a fear of being outside the normal.

Children at this age are more acutely aware of their parents' feelings. They are apt to overhear or to be parties to conversations that involve recriminations or expressions of depression and grief. By now they are so identified with their parents, are so busy learning from them how to be a person in this world, that when parents are in a stage of upheaval or a state of siege, the child suffers all the confusions, the tears of loyalty, and the bleakness of mood that so often pervade a house at the time of divorce.

In the event that one parent deserts the family, the child will feel that she has done something to cause the desertion. She will feel helpless, enraged, and alone. Her sense of herself as being lovable and wanted will be diminished. If the parents fight for custody in either a full-blown battle or merely the kind of hassling and irritable unpleasantness that can accompany visits from one parent or another, the child may try to push both parents out of mind, and will concentrate her energy on friends and teachers, sports or school work, hiding away from conflicts that she can neither resolve nor comfortably live with.

Most children of divorcing parents will show signs of stress. These may range from an increased aggressiveness, a drop in school performance, nightmares, or fears of animals, to a new set of neatness habits that determine the way the child dresses, a new disregard for appearance, and a wide variety of misbehaviors or withdrawals. These may include a loss of interest in music lessons, a sudden fear of swimming, a general constriction and tightening of the child's exploration of the outside world. These signs of pain will die down slowly after a year or so, if the parents themselves adjust to the divorce and begin to make new lives. If they can find a way to incorporate the children into their new lives, if they remain steady and consistent in visits, and if they are not overwhelmed themselves with either economic or social problems, children will regain their balance.

Schools should be informed when there is a divorce in the family so that teachers can offer support and can understand possibly erratic behavior. Children should be told what has happened and what will happen as soon as the parents are clear themselves about their next actions. It is better if both parents talk together with the children about the divorce. This is a painful conversation but it is the responsibility of both parents: the presence of both at this moment reassures the child that she is not about to lose either of them entirely. Parents should respect the child's desire not to talk about the divorce with anyone, or equally, understand the desire to talk about it with everyone. They should also be open to questions and ready to answer with truthful answers whenever possible.

The parents should try not to continually express bitter or angry feelings toward each other, but they must admit to the feelings they really have and be ready to share them with the children, sparing them of course the painful details and endless recriminations. "Mommy has fallen in love with someone else and I feel very hurt but there is nothing I can do about it" is enough. Each parent should try to preserve the child's respect and love for the other parent. Despite the obvious difficulty that some circumstances cause, each parent should avoid trying to enlist the child on their side or involving him in any decisions that would force the taking of sides or the making of judgments. In the early days of a divorce parents should not be panicked by a child's anger, silence, or symptoms of disturbance.

These will subside in time. Parents should try to keep life going as normally as possible with as few changes as possible. Skating lessons, visits with friends, chores, routines should all be kept constant. In time the child will be reassured by the ordinariness of life. Extra presents, extra treats are unnecessary; and convey the message to the child that something awful is happening to provoke the parents' guilt.

Eventually children will see that divorce is so common in our culture that they do not have to feel like lepers. They will understand that the important people in their lives remain important and caring, and that the changes that have occurred have not resulted in their own destruction. With each passing year more and more the child's sense of self-worth is determined by his performance in the outside world; more and more of his necessary nourishment comes from friends, counselors, and teachers. This, too, helps the child of divorce find his own center.

Parents can guide their children through the difficult first years after a separation by minimizing their complaints about the other parent, by accepting the new partners of the other parent, and by creating as little tension between the values and styles of the two homes as possible. Parents can help their children by not including them in their new social lives until the relationship appears to be deep and long-lasting.

Mothers seem to have some trouble with boys in matters of discipline. Boys, who need their fathers and who miss the opportunities for identification, imitation, and companionship, seem frequently to act up against the single mother. Often these boys must protect themselves from sexual longings for their mothers by creating tensions and extra distances between them. There is no easy solution to this problem, but a mother who is aware of its causes may not react with panic at signs of hostility from her son. Mothers must remember that it is important not to use the child for substitute male companionship or to pretend in any way that the boy has become the head of the house or the male in the family. Nudity and other kinds of physical intimacy are best avoided in these years, especially if a divorced mother is living with her son.

Fathers have found that their daughters seem to withdraw from them after a divorce. They may no longer permit the kind of cuddling or hugging that had been common before. A father must respect his daughter's way of avoiding sexual competition. He should not be insulted by this withdrawal but find new ways to be close to his child. Fathers should not allow a daughter to act as if she were a woman in the father's life. She should not cook for him, choose his clothes, or in any other way take on the mother's role. A father can best express his love for his daughter by remaining a father, ignoring or gently discouraging any attempt on the part of the child to assume a woman's role with him.

While it will appear to a busy parent that the six- to nine-year-old child is absorbed in baseball cards, collecting stickers, or playing with the other children on the block, these children are watching out of the corners of their eyes everything that the divorced parent is doing. Their eventual attitudes toward the opposite sex, toward trust and love and relationships generally, are being affected by what they see and hear. We cannot remake their world, but we can try to protect our children from the extremes of hatred, disappointment, and financial war that so often follow the breakup of a marriage.

Divorce itself is not a cause of illness in children; too many happy and successful people have been the product of divorced families for this to be seen as the single cause of later mental trouble. Divorce is very painful for a child and affects many aspects of his life, but in most instances it can be rolled with, accommodated, adjusted to, used to gain new personal strengths. However, parents must remember that at best the divorce will cast a shadow over the child that in some way will last a lifetime.

At the back of their minds, children keep on hoping that parents will reconcile. Remarriage and the birth of half siblings do nothing to alter this powerful wish to reunite the original family. In hurting ourselves, we hurt our children, which grieves us even more. Make no mistake, the wound of divorce does heal but the scar remains.

Remarriage—The Step-Family

Three million American children live in families with a step-parent. Since over 75 percent of divorced people remarry within five years, large numbers of children are visiting and living in homes with step-parents and half brothers and sisters. This fact is encouraging, in that it tells us that families are in some way indestructible. They may be forced to change shape, to add hyphens to names; but family struc-

tures continue through the chaos of changing values and social disorders that are part of the modern American way.

Children will not instantly love or accept a step-parent. Even if the
step-parent has been the companion of their father or mother for a
long time, the fact of the new marriage is experienced as frightening,
a threat to the relationship the child has with both biological parents.
There are questions of jealousy: Will the parent love the new spouse,
the new siblings more than me? There are questions of loyalty:
Should I love this new parent as much as my own father or mother
whom I see only weekends, or monthly, or on summer vacations?
There is the question of name change: Who am I really? There is for
the child a period of resentment: Mommy or Daddy is happy with
their new mate but they have bought their happiness at the expense
of my old home, of my former happiness.

These real questions in the child's mind will not go away quickly
or easily. The step-parent with the best will in the world must endure
a trial period, a time of testing, of coming close and withdrawing
again, of being compared to the real father or mother, of being
denied authority, intimacy, or even the necessary privacy with his or
her mate. There will be a time of raw jealousy, fighting, and bitterness between the brothers and sisters, natural and step. Children
often find it easier to take out their fears and distrust and dislike of
the new situation on one another than directly against the new step-
parent.

A new baby born to the new marriage may be a delight for its father
and mother, but for the step-child the unwelcome intruder is another
sign of the inevitable division between his natural parents. The new
half sibling is a symbol of a family joy that the child feels always
slightly outside of, to the side of, and threatened by. Children hang
on, despite all realistic evidence to the contrary, to some fantasy that
one day their own parents will return to each other and their family
become one again. The new marriage assaults this fantasy, although
it doesn't extinguish it; the child, although comforted by the fact that
his mother or father is not dependent on him alone for warmth and
support, feels also a deep level of betrayal. If the mother or father
loved the child enough, then there would be no need for all these new
people to come crowding into a house that was managing well
enough without them.

If the step-parent can move slowly toward the step-child, a little like the way one might approach a frightened and wounded puppy, the chances of good things eventually growing between child and adult improve. There can be no sudden love between these strangers brought so close because of their intimate connection with a third party. The best that can happen is that the new step-mother or new step-father, behaving always with respect and deference to the child's real parents, stands quietly near as a potential friend and ally in a larger world.

Time will knit many of these remade families into durable structures, with traditions, values, and memories of their own. But there is no easy route to instant community. The ghosts of the real parents, whether dead or divorced, whether living on another coast or across town, are always a part of all the happenings in the family. A step parent may well find that after four years of picking up a child after soccer practice and taking him to clarinet lessons, doing the laundry and helping with the homework, cooking a million meals, staying up all night through bouts of asthma, cleaning up after stomach viruses, and soothing anxiety attacks over final exams, the moment of graduation will come. The child, given only two tickets, will invite his biological parents—and the step-parent may be left waiting at home for the ceremony to end. This is to be expected in the step-parent relationship. It is not a role for those who need to be appreciated or rewarded on this earth.

Step-parents, while not as wicked as legend would have it, do often resent the financial burden that the step-child places on the new family. It can be painful to spend precious funds on a child who has expressed dislike or disdain for you. Even if the child is angelic, the step-parent may find it hard to give generously of spirit and money to the stranger, who is after all a reminder of the earlier marriage and an intruder in the present husband-wife situation. Step-parents can naturally feel jealous of the child their new mate loves so intensely; step-parents can feel competitive about their own natural children in comparison to their step-child. This is the stuff of nasty stories such as *Cinderella*. There is some truth in these old myths.

Step-parents need not accept the image of themselves as monsters but it may be necessary to admit that sometimes you do have bad feelings toward a step-child. These feelings are normal and can be balanced by hosts of good feelings and connections in time. If such bad feelings are totally denied or ignored, they become potentially explosive and can make the well-meaning step-parent increasingly guilty, which only adds to the tensions and complications of the situation.

Certain basic things a step-parent should never do include criticizing the biological parent and complaining about money spent on the child in front of the child. Step-parents should not express negative feelings about the child's manners, religion, taste in music or food; these will be heard as an indirect criticism of the other parent. It is best, whenever possible, to leave matters of discipline up to the natural parent. Don't be provoked, don't be teased, and don't try to assert your authority until it has been won by a long period of happy association. See what the child needs and offer it. Perhaps you are a good tennis player or a card shark or a history buff. Offer the child something to do with you that he would not get from his natural parent. Don't be insulted if he seems to ignore you for a long time. Allow the child plenty of time alone with his own parent. It may seem as if you are being forgotten, but by being generous and unobtrusive you are building a sense of trust between you and your step-child. In time that will be the bridge to a real friendship.

Patience and a little touch of saintliness may bring a step-parent the wonderful present of a really special kind of friendship and love with a child. We have as yet no untainted word for this friendship, which goes beyond the sort of respect and pleasure people of the same generation can have for each other. It is far more profound than what one might experience in a good student–teacher situation, and it can be as important as any other loving connection that will occur in life. It can be a companionship that contains respect, affection, and deep knowledge of one another. When it happens it is wonderful, and it can happen in the step-family if not too much is expected at first, if parents are aware of the child's basic primary loyalties, and if they can slowly with trial and error (forgive the errors, they are inevitable) grope their way toward a commitment that becomes mutual and dear to both.

Sex Education

Most schools begin their sex education programs in the sixth or seventh grades, when the children are eleven or twelve. Most children, however, begin to learn the basic facts of reproduction before entering school. Many parents have told their children about intercourse and the way the baby grows and arrives before the child's fifth birthday; children have usually asked the right questions and received the basic answers from parents or friends before they learn to read. Sexual activity as a source of pleasure and sin has usually been understood by most young children. The biological facts of physical sexual growth, including menstruation and puberty, are generally known to children from friends if not from parents by their eighth or ninth year.

Children respond to the idea of sexual intercourse with both excitement and disgust. They cannot clearly imagine the how of it and they often have trouble seeing the why of it. Their own sexual feelings after the age of five or six have usually been dimmed or excluded from awareness. They respond to the information given with their own versions of sexual matters that often include distortions of some sort or another. Many children just push the whole matter out of their minds for a while, becoming puritan in their disinterest and dislike of sexual talk, and private and modest about their own bodies.

Eight- or nine-year-olds would prefer not to think about the biological functions of the other sex. They will absorb the scientific rational explanations of sexual activity that are given, but they try to hide from themselves the personal implications of this information. The biological facts of menstruation are alarming. The young girl is concerned with controlling her impulses, with being neat and orderly, and with not allowing just anything at any time to exit from her body. Then she is told that she will bleed for a few days each month and that this is necessary for her to be able one day to have a child. Most little girls push this information away from their thoughts until they begin to see the bodily changes that anticipate puberty. The first signs of nipples budding, of figure changes, which may occur as early as nine years, do bring a return of thoughts about menstruation. Little girls may become afraid of scratches; they may become excessively insistent on washing their hair or body; or they may ignore their bodies, allowing layers of dirt to accumulate, knees to be scabby, and fingers to be streaked or stained.

Many primitive cultures have elaborate taboos that separate the woman while she is menstruating from the rest of the tribe. The first period in particular may be surrounded with elaborate rituals and long seclusions. In primitive cultures, men are often afraid of being touched by the menstruating woman and assume she has some evil power at that time which might harm them if they didn't isolate her. Rituals have been discovered in which men and women will deliberately prick themselves at this time or will go to great lengths to avoid combing their hair or cutting skin or clothes. These magic rituals remind us of the familiar story of Sleeping Beauty, who had been cursed. Her parents were told that she would prick her finger on her first grownup birthday and bleed; then she would fall asleep for one hundred years, until her prince came to offer her love and marriage. The fable reveals how dangerous menstruation appears to us, how anxious we are about female sexuality, and how uncertain we are whether biology has cursed or blessed us. Looking at the way cultures across the globe and throughout man's history have reacted to menstruation gives us a sense of how hard these facts are for our children, both male and female, to absorb and accept. We can help them only with the truth, along with a sensitive response to their need not to hear what we are saying until they can come to terms with it in their own good time.

Some time around six or seven, boys and girls hear about homosexuality. This is especially frightening information at a time when most friendships are between children of the same sex. Children are disturbed by the idea that sexual feelings might erupt in themselves and they are afraid that their own new roles as male or female might be shaken. The factual knowledge that homosexuality exists tends for most children to lead them to exaggerate their maleness or femaleness along simple traditional lines. While the tomboy is more acceptable socially than the sissy boy, both are in some trouble with their age mates, who view as a threat anybody who challenges their own rather rigid ideas of sexual identity. That's the cause of much cruelty and intolerance among young children, for whom the word "fag" is the most dreadful epithet in the universe.

We feel it is fine for parents to talk to their children of seven, eight, or nine about the facts of menstruation, puberty, wet dreams, and even homosexuality. Children will hear talk about this from other children anyway, and you want them to have their facts as straight as possible. Some children are too anxious to listen and will avoid or distract you from real communication; others will be willing and eager to talk about sexual matters with you once, but never again.

Each child has his own style of dealing with the rush of excitement and fear that the sexual information evokes. As parents we do best to respect their wishes on the matter, to provide information and wait for questions. We have to be understanding about the child who pretends indifference or who denies any interest at all, as well as the one who claims to have heard it all and doesn't need our help.

Drugs

It is a terrible indictment of our society that in writing about six- to ten-year-olds we feel it necessary to include a section on drugs. But the children will learn of them from older children, from each other, from television. We need to prepare them for their encounters with the drug culture, encounters which in some parts of this country are occurring routinely in junior high school.

Children don't need too much information. We are not called upon to give them a chemistry lesson or to alarm them about the evils lurking in the playground. What we want to do is to tell them clearly that we do not want them to smoke, experiment with drugs, or make friends with others who do. We want them to know that drugs, far from being exciting or interesting, lead to a loss of enjoyment, a loss of potential for learning, and a destruction of the quality of life. Our warnings, our clarity of position may help our children form their own judgments when the time comes. Between the ages of six and ten they are not in rebellion against our teachings, so they are more apt to agree with us and to assume that our thoughts will be theirs. So we want to reach them on this subject before their deepest loyalty turns toward their own age group.

We cannot predict accurately which children will become drug or alcohol abusers, but we do know that the more vulnerable children, those with the most difficulty in school and in friendships, are at risk. We know that being able to control his anger and his desire for immediate satisfaction gives a child the capacity to avoid major trouble. As parents we can't play ostrich and assume the drug pushers will all depart for outer space. Unfortunately, we will continue to share this planet with them, so we must alert our children to the hazard of drugs, just as we warned them about speeding cars and not talking to strangers in the park. Parents who themselves drink more than they should or who use other chemical substances cannot be surprised when their children follow in their footsteps. By eight or nine years of age a child can distinguish between what you do and what you say, and he may jump on the back of the discrepancy and ride it all the way to hell.

Sleep-Away Camp

Children are ready for camp at different times and parents should wait for the child to respond eagerly to the suggestion before packing the trunk. Most children will have some trouble with a long separation from home before the age of nine, but of course this varies from child to child. A child should not be sent away to camp who has not shown that he makes and keeps friends within his home community. Parents sometimes think that a summer away will heal a child's social problems. It never works that way. The one who is left out at school will be left out at camp; in fact, the child will suffer more because there is no escape from the peer group. A child who is overweight, shy, timid, too aggressive, whining, who wets the bed, has nightmares, is not a good athlete, or has not yet made three or four close friends is not a good candidate for camp.

Some children have none of those problems and still have a hard time. The separation from home may have come just a little early and they may, under the strain of being independent with their peers night and day, find themselves lonely, outside the group, and homesick.

Camp at the right time and for the right child is a wonderful experience. It can offer enriching friendships, learning skills, the feeling of being part of a team, the pleasures of cooking out, learning about nature, adventuring. These are the benefits, the happiness of camp. At the end of a good summer a child will be more confident about himself, have learned something about other children and demonstrated that he can get along without his parents for a while. This is a major growing experience and one we would wish for all children.

However, some child at the camp will fail in friendships, will fail in skills, will long for home, and will return less confident and more determined to cling to his parents than before. If a child at camp calls within the first few days, and sounds miserable, and wants to be rescued, we would suggest you wait a week, talk to the head of the camp, the child's counselor. It is probable that with a little time the adjustment can be made. The child's victory, if he can be happy in a situation that started badly, is worth the few extra days of difficulty. But if after a week or so the child has not bounced back, made friends, does not feel connected to his bunk mates, his counselor, his team, his activities, then go get him. Nothing is to be gained by a summer of isolation and pain. He can try another year when he may be older, readier to leave home, and more capable.

Try to find out from your child and from the counselors why he had this difficulty. Sometimes it's just a matter of bad luck. A bossy, dominant child takes a dislike to yours and turns the group against him; in another cabin, another place, the child would have been fine. Sometimes you and your child have to work on his social skills, on helping him to feel independent from you and close to his age mates. If your child leaves camp before the end, find out what went wrong. Homesickness can be a sign of a child in difficulty, needing some extra help to make his way.

Even though it is tempting, don't send a child away for his first summer at camp if you and your mate are in the middle of marital difficulties. Don't try to distract a child from a divorce or a death by sending him to camp. He may not be sure enough of his home to leave it easily. Don't send him away just as he is getting used to a step-parent or the birth of a baby brother. Don't send him to camp if he has had a serious illness or hospitalization within the last year. It is better for a child to be bored at home than to leave too early, or in the midst of trouble.

Pick your camp carefully. If friends or neighbors have been there and can recommend it, so much the better. Don't be fooled by shiny brochures. Make sure you talk to parents of other children who have attended the camp. Find out where the staff comes from, how old they are. What kind of a camp is this? Does it have the kind of activity your child likes? Don't send a quiet artist to a soccer camp, nor an athlete to a crafts camp where they talk about building individuality through pottery. Don't send your child automatically to the camp you went to as a child; it may have changed. Or your child may have different needs than you did at the same age.

Camp is a kind of icing on the cake of childhood. Nobody needs it to grow up and be a happy, productive person. While for most children it provides wonderful times and growing experiences, for others it undermines their confidence and weakens their independence. There are risks in sending a child off to camp. Do it, but do it carefully.

Differences Between the Six-Year-Old and the Ten-Year-Old

Most professionals divide the years six to ten into two parts, early and late. The late section begins as the child turns eight. At this age the child is given greater freedom from his parents. In cities, children are often permitted to cross streets by themselves and to travel alone or with friends on the bus or subway. Children of eight are allowed to move about in groups of age mates and are often permitted weekends away or even summers at camp. This greater distance between the child and the parent is a sign of the growth the child has made toward independence.

The child of eight or so has gradually changed the content of her fears. Previously she was afraid of monsters, demons, ghosts, witches, or zombies. Now the evils that may still lurk in the closet, hide behind trees, or attack in the dark are more human and realistic: robbers, kidnappers, and muggers. This shift, while of no particular comfort for the child, does show an advance in contact with and knowledge of reality. The dangers have a human face. This is intellectual progress toward a time when the child will be able correctly to judge her margin of safety in any real situation, and the irrational fears of childhood will have been banished.

The child of eight shifts her interest away from stories of good guys and bad guys and black and white situations. The cartoon heroes who were so satisfying several months earlier now become boring and predictable. Children become interested in more complicated ethical questions and are able to understand that bad and good often shade to gray. The most popular stories still have heroes and villains, but the world around them is peopled with real folk whose struggles with good and bad may be elaborate.

With this intellectual shift comes a new view of parents, who are no longer seen as all-powerful and all-perfect, but are gradually reduced in size by a more realistic appraisal. Naturally no child is ever able to see his own parents in the clear daylight of pure reason alone, but the eight-year-old is more apt to notice that father doesn't know anything at all about computers and that mother is as musical as a stone. At the same time children are making these not-so-flattering observations, parents are discovering all kinds of things about their children. Bob is a fine athlete but a terrible sport about losing. Frieda is a wonderful mathematician but a disaster at learning foreign languages. All the tiny facts about the character, skill, and special personality of each child begin to become apparent as the eight-year-old turns nine. What is happening to both parent and child is that the abstract idea of mother and baby, the universal of father and child, is busily turning into the particulars of individual people, each with troubles and triumphs of their own.

Conclusions

When everything is going well for the child of six to nine, we know that certain important changes have taken place in the very structure of that child's soul. We know that she has developed a capacity to control her own behavior, not just in one instance but in all similar instances. The child can sit through a long math class without getting up and running around in the aisles. The same child can be taken to her first concert, and even though her mind may wander and she may twist her hair or bite her nails, she will not move from her seat until the final applause has finished. We know that the child can be trusted to wait for the green light and to return the change from a purchase at the grocery store. She can wait patiently in line at the post office and can bring a book back to the library.

This capacity for delay of impulses, this willingness to act in ways we consider grownup, not to cry for food in a restaurant or insist on being served the first or biggest portion, are signs that the child is accomplishing the difficult and amazing emotional tasks of this age. Sexual feelings are being pushed into the back of the mind, where they can be better controlled and create less guilt and anxiety. The child has developed a rich fantasy life, in which the problems of anger and fear, of helplessness and desire for revenge and power, can be acted out, imagined without threat to any of the real relationships in the child's actual world. The pushing away of sexual feelings plus the pleasure in fantasy combines to make a space in the child's mind where objective learning can take place, where there is no anxiety or fear blocking the new information or the new skills, which are now built on facts and realistic perceptions.

The child of this age whose inner life is advancing just as it should will probably have some irrational fears and some peculiar rituals. If they are not excessive, these are a good sign that the child has learned how to control her own inevitable anger that arises naturally out of the events of the day. If a child is afraid of monsters or kidnappers, she has learned how to take her anger and separate it from her own image of her own goodness and place it outside. While it may sound odd to say that the child who fears a giant in her closet is showing a fine adaptation—has coped very well indeed—it is still true.

The child who has become modest, who shows disgust at the very body functions that so fascinated her a short while ago, is also doing well. The child who can be shamed, who has a sense of guilt, is doing fine. The child who shows some odd habits of cleanliness or collecting, or arranging things in one particular order or another, is putting up a decent battle against the opposite impulses to mess, to create chaos, to destroy.

At about five or six most children will begin to forget their infancy, to forget their toddlerhood. They will no longer remember the name of their first nursery school teacher; they will not recall the passionate love they felt for their mother and their father; and mercifully enough, they will forget the terrible feelings of competition and jealousy they had experienced. They will forget, along with the names of their favorite Teddy bear and doll, their old fear that an angry mother or father might take revenge on them. This forgetfulness allows the child to pay attention to the tasks of the day, to the rules of the game, to the words and feelings of friends and teachers. Only the remnants of all those baby wishes, all those rages, and all those hard times last, revealing traces of themselves in the fantasies and games that children play generation after generation.

It is odd that in writing about the normal development of the child from six to ten, the description of his inner mental life leads us into far fewer mazes than the same kind of description of the younger child. Yet the children themselves are becoming increasingly complicated, interesting, and varied. Character and personality, taste and style, gifts and liabilities are all becoming clear. The child of this age is already a unique self—a self that defies grouping or easy classification. This apparent contradiction is only one of the many paradoxes of the human condition. The healthier the child, the more unique and individual he is. The less we have to say in describing his emotional life, the more hues it carries, the more it satisfies.

Section II

The Troubled Child: Introduction

Sometimes the normal patterns of the child from six to nine never have a chance to develop. Sometimes these patterns, which are really helpful defenses against anxiety, fear, and sexual impulses, break down because the outside world attacks—as when a child suffers from physical sickness, abuse, death of a parent, or seduction by a parent. Sometimes the child's defenses were just not strong enough to contain the emotional storms that had originated in earlier stages of development, as we may see in the neglected infant, the toddler not given a chance to gain some measure of selfhood, the four-year-old who couldn't learn to use the toilet or play with a friend. Some children cannot get on with their tasks of learning, playing, and turning to groups their own age because they are still struggling with such intense feelings for one parent or another that they cannot push those feelings away, leaving the necessary neutral space and time for other activities.

Each stage of a child's life requires new ways of learning, offers new pleasures, and demands new accomplishments. Each stage means shifting away from the one before, and each depends for its success on the sturdiness of the stage that has just preceded it. While children have enormous capacity to make the world anew for themselves, they also cannot erase their short but meaningful histories. Like all organic life, their present and their future spring from their past.

It is at this age that parents and psychiatrists begin to see a host of peculiar and harmful behavior patterns. Some children will have the kind of conscience that punishes too harshly while others will have one so weak that it allows the kind of freedom which evokes rejection from the world of teachers, parents, and playmates. Some children will have so many fears that they can't join others in physical play or in normal outings. Some will develop so many rituals and habits in attempts to control their own sexual and destructive outbursts that they will appear odd, weird, unacceptable to others. Some will be so dependent that they seem inappropriately babyish, while others will be so independent that they seem unattached, unreachable, marching to some dangerous drummer, beating a tune just for them.

Many of these troubles will hamper the child as she moves into the first years of school and on. They may bring learning problems or troubles with friendships, or they may simply prevent a child from gaining in independence, from liking herself, from feeling comfortable and confident. These problems will affect the quality of the child's life now and in the future but generally do not cripple the child totally, do not exclude her from many of the joys of these years. Most of us, in one way or another, have experienced some kind of problem, some kind of unresolved conflict that follows us about and shadows our lives. This seems to be part of the enormously complicated and sensitive work we do to become adults, as well as a reflection of the society we live in, which sometimes presents us with hurdles too high for us to leap over or too low for us to crawl beneath.

As parents, and as psychiatrists, we have to decide which of these conflicts are serious enough to require intervention and which will fade away in time. This decision is based on the degree of suffering the child shows and the degree of impaired development that the conflicts have caused. A child who cannot imagine or invent is missing a tool to solve his own problems. A child who is having too many upset stomachs may miss an important time in his life when he needs to be mixing with others instead of home in bed tended by his mother. Whether or not to bring a child to psychotherapy depends partially on the distance the child has come from infancy; has he come far enough? Is he suffering? Unfortunately, children do suffer when they are so sad they cannot play, when they are so frightened they cannot explore, when they dislike themselves too much and stagger under too heavy a burden of guilt. We want to weigh each child's own enormous powers of recuperation and renewal. Many children will alter by themselves directions that seem dangerous and will regain capacities that had been temporarily eclipsed. We do not want to burden the child or the family with unnecessary interventions when time itself will bring about a happy change.

During the years six to ten, a few children do break down entirely: the chaos and emotional disorder of their minds overwhelm them. Parents through cruelty and neglect may have caused this to happen. But it may occur because the biological mental structures of a particular child simply couldn't carry the weight of life, the stress of being human.

Even in the matter of the more moderately troubled child, the parent is not necessarily at fault and should not take full responsibility. Biology has its own designs. We cannot yet explain why one child suffers the trauma of, let's say, being in a car accident and recovers with minimal psychological damage, and another child in a similar accident begins to have night fears that threaten his emotional balance. We may find explanations in each child's family history, but then again we may not. Therapists do not know the causes of everything. Genetics and constitutional make-up are powerful, little-understood forces that have great effect on the fate of our children.

It hurts a parent to see his child hurting. It hurts a parent to recognize that he may have failed in some way. Yet we will feel better if we can put aside our wounded pride and arrange a consultation with a qualified therapist if necessary, so that the child can continue to move toward the best possible future. As parents we want to know that we have done everything within our power to give our children their chance to find happiness.

The Child Who Breaks Apart: The Psychotic Child

While insanity in a child does not break out suddenly, like the measles or the mumps, it does appear to have a rapid onset. A child will begin one day to show symptoms so strange and disturbing that parents and teachers, relatives and friends know something is wrong. These symptoms may range from a sudden constant fear of dirt to a strange whiney voice and an unwillingness to leave the house. There may be a return to wetting the bed, an inability to play with other children, and a bizarre pattern of movements of hand and body. A child may suddenly lose speech or have a crying rage attack every time mother tries to leave the room. There are many difficult unmistakable symptoms that tell us that the child has lost rational control. His fear, his impulses, and his guilts have triumphed in some inner battle, and destroyed his capacities for defense, for living with others.

This does not happen to a child without some other milder signs having been there all along. Some of these children will have shown a peculiarly erratic pattern of growth from infancy onward. They will gain and grow and then stop as if on a plateau for a while. They may exceed other children for a time, then fall far behind. They may have been irritable babies who couldn't be comforted by any of the usual means, or they may have been remote, listless babies who seemed unusually uninterested in events around them. They may have had odd eating habits or frequent unexplained stomach aches and headaches. Speech may have developed slowly or been unusually precocious. They may have had difficulty entering nursery school and been dependent on their mothers a long time. Gestures of babyhood such as hand-shaking or finger-twirling may have been long retained.

Such children may have been intensely involved with complicated rituals of cleanliness or ordering of their toys. They may have been struggling with the tasks of school because they found it hard to pay attention to the teacher. All of these symptoms can be part of a childhood with difficulties yet without eventual madness. We identify the child who falls apart after it has happened. We can then go back over the history and say, Yes, the signs were always there; this didn't go well and that might have warned us. But the truth is that we can recognize this illness and distinguish it from its less malignant cousins only when it reveals itself in full bloom.

These children will develop wild and terrible fears of commonplace objects such as the family toaster or the door to their room. They will begin to carry around with them other objects which they may have endowed with magic protective capacities. One such child was inseparable from a Coke bottle, another insisted on clutching to his chest an old sneaker. Such children will often give up speech as a means of communicating something to someone else. They may use a jumble of words that follow some inner thought association that is very hard to understand or to track. Or they may abandon speech altogether, or only echo words they hear around them. Often they will lose the sense of normal rhythm in the language so that the words they say come out flat or strangely pronounced.

Some of these children hold their bodies in particular rigid ways; they may begin to move clumsily as if their muscles weren't working well. Others may begin to rock or bang their heads against walls or start strange shaking, trembling motions that are part of their magic designs. Some will be unable to sleep while others will wake with constant horrible dreams. They will appear to have forgotten the proper uses of things; pieces of puzzles may be put in the mouth, toy airplanes used as earmuffs. They may turn wheels on trains or bang together blocks, but nothing is built and the trains are never going anywhere. They may show panic with each bowel movement or ignore their body signals altogether. They may wet and soil at will, as if they are not inside their own bodies.

Only as these children become eight or nine years old do some of them show the conventional adult symptoms of schizophrenia. They then may feel that someone or something from the outside is trying to control them or to destroy them. They may begin to hear voices that tell them what to do or that mock them constantly. One child thought an alligator lived in his throat and encouraged him to bite other people. Another thought that Martians were eating at his fingers and toes, causing him great pain. One child was convinced that her mother had eyes on the palms of her hands and could see through walls. Some children see apparitions that talk to them, others carry on conversations with creatures of their imagination that have become real to them.

It has been estimated that this is an illness that affects six times as many boys as girls. Since we cannot assume that so many more boys than girls are exposed to neglect and cruelty, it seems clear that a biological weakness must play an important role in triggering this illness. While statistics here are not certain, it appears that approximately one in ten thousand children breaks down in this way. With hospitalization, with the medicines available today, many of the symptoms seem to abate and the child can return home and live a comparatively normal life for a while. Often the upsurge of feelings and anxieties that accompany puberty again causes these children to break down.

As adults, many of them are frequently hospitalized and are dependent on their families for constant care. Many spend most of their lives in institutions; the others who may reach some fragile balance are profoundly compromised in their capacity to find meaningful love and work. Childhood madness is a tragedy—a tragedy for the child and a tragedy for the family that must bear the financial and emotional burdens. In the 1950s it was fashionable to blame the mother for this failure of her child. Now we see a much more complicated pattern of biology and environment creating this illness, and in fact biology alone can often take the blame.

For the parent, the task is to protect the rest of the family, to recreate the sense of hopefulness and purpose in family life that every sick child undermines. The marriage itself is threatened by the child's emotional failure. Each parent may try to fault the other; each feels a bitterness that tends to separate rather than to bring them together. It is a hard human task to have to mourn a child who is still alive but whose potential as one first dreamed it, is forever destroyed. This is a prime example of the unfairness of life and the brutality of nature, whose subjects we all are.

The Child at the Edge

Children at the edge have a long and constant history of trouble. Whether or not they first come to the attention of professionals during the years six to ten, they do not experience a sudden worsening of behavior, a sudden breakdown in reality sense, or a radical change in their relationships with friends and parents at this age. These are children who have been flooded with aggressive feelings, with fears and panics, from their very earliest years (see the description of Children at the Edge, ages three to six, pp. 229–233). Because of their inability to deal with tension and frustration, because of their intense fears of separation and loss and their high level of guilt and rage, they come into the years six to ten without the necessary capacities to accomplish the emotional and intellectual tasks of that age.

They will have trouble paying attention to a teacher. Their inner life will dominate their minds, pushing out the objective voices describing the kinds of dinosaurs that once walked the globe or the list of all the capitals of the United States. They will have difficulties making and keeping friends because they will not be able to play by the rules—they will not be able to control their need to be first, to have more, to do things immediately. They will be slow in learning the skills of a sport or a social activity. Their inner world will constantly make demands on them that distract them from the reality other children are beginning to enjoy. They lack the capacity to push away their sexual urges and guilts and to turn that sexual energy into learning energy. They cannot direct it easily outside of themselves.

This means that these children cannot use their fantasy life to make symbols of their feelings, to overcome their fears, to play out their inner dramas. While indeed they may have a rich fantasy world, it does not help them to dampen the primitive destructive urges and impulses that flow in and out of their thoughts. Their sexual feelings remain high and the fears increase. Since they have so much difficulty with the outside world, they have a very poor opinion of themselves. Their self-dislike awakens more fear and more anger, placing them more and more outside the company of their age mates.

They do not have an inner voice that guides them in matters of right and wrong in quite the same way that other children have. Because they feel so much anger at their parents, because their sexual feelings have been so strong and so uncontrolled, because they are so frightened of the harm that a parent might do to them, they sometimes become overly harsh with themselves. They feel they are unworthy and deserving of punishment. At the same time they can't use the inner voice to guide them because so frequently that inner voice is overwhelmed by the strength of their impulses. This kind of child cannot be depended on to behave well in any particular circumstance. The fact that on Thursday he was able to concentrate for twenty minutes on a piano lesson does not guarantee a repeat performance the following Tuesday. Most children at this age are able to put together the bad and the good in one person. They begin to see their parents more realistically. They begin to know that Daddy is a good provider but stingy with money and given to temper now and then. Their love for their parents survives and is even deepened by a realistic recognition of them as special and unique flawed human beings. For children at the edge, the merging of good and bad into one person remains difficult. The angry feelings are so strong that they remain projected outside onto monsters, robbers, and other terrors. The need to be loved, the need to hold on, to cling to mother or father, remains so strong that they are unable to bring together a realistic picture of their parents.

During the years six to ten, these children are somewhat less turbulent than before or after. They are helped by the natural growing process and will make every effort to conform to expectations appropriate to their age. Unlike children in whom the structures of the mind have crumbled, they maintain good contact with reality. They may develop special gifts in one area or another. They may with a great struggle conform to some of the demands of school. But the defect remains.

Most professionals believe that this defect cannot be cured. It is a given of the child's mind and will last a lifetime. Most professionals try to lead such children to a closer understanding of their own flaws, helping them devise ways to head off difficulties, to recognize when some experience will be too much for them, suggesting ways to drain off the excess fear and anger that they so constantly experience. Parents can help by offering therapeutic support. Parents will be able to help their children more as they understand how their child perceives the world. They will be able to alter their expectations of behavior and achievement to those that are more realistic. The parents of such children need a lot of support and guidance, but with effort and care they can help their own child enormously and can at least keep the bond of love between them strong.

We do not have statistics that tell us how many children at the edge make up our adult addicted, alcoholic population. We do not know how many end up in prisons, in hospitals, or living out in the world always feeling that something is wrong with them, never able to find peace in work or love. We do know that this illness is another biological cruelty. Right now we can sometimes help a child to work successfully around his handicap but we cannot yet create a complete cure.

The Child Who Must Do Certain Things Over and Over or Else

There are some children who at age six or so appear to be very, very good. They are pleasing to adults and gratifying to teachers. Their homework is never eaten by the dog and their hands are always washed long before dinner. They follow requests and instructions to the letter; often, sadly enough, no one complains about them at all. They may have temper tantrums every once in a while, which surprise and puzzle their family. They may indulge in a single act of rebellion like wearing the same pair of dirty underpants week after week or losing library books time and again. But for the most part they are caught in a desperate striving for perfection, for approval, for goodness. They will have developed certain ways of doing things that must be repeated in just the way they want before they can feel safe and in charge. They will arrange their pencils from the largest to the smallest each time, or they will place the soap back in the soap dish always at the same right angle. They will open the window exactly six inches from the sill each time, and they are apt to count, constantly, the number of steps up to school, the number of buses that have passed in a half hour, the number of mailboxes on a given road.

These children have given up the pleasurable messiness of the days before they used the toilet. They have stopped being demanding, sloppy, impulsive, and greedy. They have conquered all those unpleasant, undesirable whims. Instead, they have reacted with disgust to dirt, with disgust to their own body and its products.

They are trying to please the harsh voice inside of their heads that demands that they be high achievers, good boys and girls, clean and neat, smart and cooperative, unselfish and kind. They try so hard they make themselves anxious. They try so hard that they are cut off from real friendships with children their own age. They are so busy pleasing the adults that they can't do anything with spontaneous feeling and eruptions of joy. They are too busy counting and ordering and being good to really join their age mates in the rough and tumble of play. They can't be angry and punch a fellow in the stomach. They can't be mean and exclude another child or whisper about him behind his back. They are too busy creating an ideal out of themselves.

The temper tantrums they are apt to have long after other children have abandoned them are a clue to what is really going on behind such a facade of perfection. These are children who have all the normal angers and resentments at being controlled that beset other children, but they have learned not to express them because they are afraid of the loss of parental love that might follow. They are driven to a state of goodness even at the loss of their own selfhood, their own independence.

Very often the parents of such children are themselves perfection-ists, high achievers, people who want everything they do to be just right, and this includes the behavior of their children. Parents of boys and girls who cannot ever talk back, or be bad, or just not do some-thing they were supposed to, are apt to have allowed their toddlers very little chance to make their own mistakes and correct them. They probably asked too much of their children before they were truly ready to achieve. They may have toilet-trained them harshly; they may have pushed them into intellectual achievement before their time.

The striking fact about all these children is their emotional isola-tion. They are not really close to anyone because they are always hiding their real selves. They are so afraid of some bad feeling or bad act breaking through that they place these bad thoughts outside of themselves and practice protective magic to keep the dogs, robbers, monsters from attacking. This is normal for all children, but for these very good children the fears become increasingly intense and the ability to take them inside, to remake the image of the self, comes late if at all.

Too good children have a kind of brittle quality. They may thank the doctor for giving them a shot; they will withhold tears if they fall; they are apt to draw very straight lines and neat boxes. Their imagi-nations are often impoverished as their interests turn to counting and ordering of objects rather than to free imaginative play.

All children have some tightness, some inhibitions, some places and times when they are fake. All children want to be good and they pay some price in spontaneity for the conformity they give to the adult world. All children between six and ten may have some exces-sive rituals, controlled ways of doing things. Many children enjoy counting and collecting and will have habits that seem too orderly. But the healthy child will also have real friends, real moments when he can laugh or cry or defy the adult authority. The healthy child will have a rich fantasy life and a real capacity to express a wide range of feelings. The child who is too good has paid a high price for his membership in our civilization. If parents see that their child is too good, is practicing too many rituals, seems isolated from friends, and hardly ever expresses any anger, they might want to consult with a child psychiatrist who will help determine if the behavior is within the normal range or not. Therapy will enable this child to shout and invent and communicate freely again.

Personality Disorders

Some children have a distinct way of reacting to their world that we can identify and name. Psychiatrists have grouped these reactions under the heading "personality disorders"; we will describe these below. However, these very same personality disorders are not disorders until they become extreme and take over the child, hindering normal growth and pleasure. In most of us, adults and children, these clusters of behaviors and tendencies are observable but do not cause any particular trouble. Some people do tend toward neatness and orderly precise activity while others are dramatic, imaginative, and quite likely very messy. These differences in character are not labeled or even noticed by friends or relatives. They meld easily and comfortably into the many other shapes and designs that form all our personalities.

In some instances, when experience has marred development, personality structures can become caricatures of themselves, parodies of what a person can be like. Then we have personality disorder. Each of these disorders has a group of symptoms attached to it that signal its presence. The symptoms may be excessive fears or excessive collecting habits or overreactions to dirt or an indulgence in messiness. But every child who practices rituals does not suffer from a character problem and every child who loves to act and dance for company is not a petri dish breeding disease. It is only when these directions become hardened and disruptive, when the child who counts his steps to school can't stop counting to enjoy a story or the child who loves to work with puppets can't keep his math homework together, that we have trouble. Children tend for the most part to have character traits similar to those of their parents. These are learned not by study but by the constant process of identification that goes on all through childhood, night and day, week in week out, binding the generations together whether they wish it or not.

In the discussion of personality disorders that follows, we want to be clear that only when the cluster of symptoms has hardened and persisted over a period of time would we consider taking a child to a therapist. It is not the character direction of a child that would

327

concern us. One way is not better than another; a single isolated symptom does not invite therapy. Only if the child's ability to grow and enjoy, to learn and to love, are affected over a period of considerable time would we suggest professional consultation.

The Very Sad Child

Professionals argue among themselves about the nature of depression in children. Some feel that children do not suffer from the same kind of life-destroying bleakness that affects adults, while others claim that the same illness is present although often in disguised forms. Whether in the exact form of adult illness or not, the truth is that some children do indeed suffer weeping bouts and a severe loss of appetite and energy. At the same time they will show various kinds of school difficulties, from excessive daydreaming to disruptive behavior. One day they may cling to their parents like little babies, and the next hit them or scream at them. They may well have a great deal of trouble sleeping, and when at last they do fall asleep they wake frequently from bad dreams.

These children have a fantasy life that is rife with defeat, hopelessness, helplessness, and stories of loss and death. If such a child imagines a trip to the moon, it ends with the rocket ship losing its compass and drifting off into outer space. In his imaginary trip to the zoo, the tigers all escape from their cages and eat the child and his companions for dinner. If the child dreams up a battle between a good and bad knight, the good knight is given a poison drink by his lady-fair and dies in great pain. It is always dusk in their drawings and the children in their stories are always small and afraid, trapped in burning buildings or caught in the crossfire of opposing armies.

There are really very few children who openly show this extreme degree of sadness. But a much larger group appear to be hiding their helpless and hopeless feelings behind a lot of activity. These are children who may have trouble concentrating or sitting still, who are always in motion, as if they want to flee from their own feelings, which unfortunately like their shadows follow them everywhere. Some sad children may be cruel or brutal or aggressive toward others while hiding from themselves their own sadness. Other sad children may have stomach aches, asthma, colitis, rashes, or headaches that distract them from their own grief-filled centers. Some children may steal or lie or run away from home or camp, getting in constant trouble with authorities to create a false sense of drama and action in their essentially lonely and hollow emotional lives. Although all these children may appear different, they have in common the same kind of fantasy life, which reveals a black and heavy mood of despair.

One of the major causes of sadness in a child is the sudden loss of a loved and crucially important person in that child's life. The death of a parent or loss through divorce or abandonment could begin this sad mood. If a family has moved away from a grandparent who was close to the family, this massive sadness could grow.

After a loss, children will reattach themselves to someone else if that someone else is there for them. But sometimes in our chaotic and confused adult world, a child is left to mourn alone. Drastic loss makes a child feel as if he is worthless, as if he must have deserved punishment in some way, and these feelings of being no good only aggravate the pain and despair already felt. Then small events such as leaving a teacher at the end of the semester or having a good friend move away can trigger a sense of great sadness. Some of these children may grow up to be adults who have to repeat the patterns of loss again, always picking romantic partners who leave them, or always changing jobs.

Another cause of sadness is frequent separations from loved ones during the first five years of life. The child who is moved around from house to house, who has loved and lost and loved someone else and lost again, is likely to become distrustful and aloof and also to suffer an inner grief of enormous proportions. This extreme sadness is evoked in children when a loved person suddenly becomes unavailable to them. A mother might have fallen ill or remarried or given birth to a preferred baby. A father might have lost his job and turned to alcohol. An older sister who has been very active in the child's life might find a boyfriend. A reaction to loss, sudden or chronic, is behind all these childhood despairs. The loss itself evokes a great and usually unmanageable rage, and the anger that sweeps the child makes him feel guilty and unlovable. Often the anger is turned inward—the child hates himself instead of the painful outside world.

Depression in young children can be tragically created by a parent who expresses his dislike of himself or his lot in life by belittling his child. Some children truly are rejected by parents who tell them that they are bad, not worth the food that they are given, or that everything they do is wanting in some respect. These children will use their parents as mirrors of the truth and see themselves as worthless. Their diminished pride and continual experience of guilty failure translate into an almost intolerable grief.

Some children who carry around sad feelings are identifying with their mothers or fathers who are themselves sad and hopeless. It is hard for a child not to absorb the mood of the parent, not to take the parent's world and personal view as his own. Children of chronically despairing parents are at risk of losing their natural childish hope and buoyancy, and becoming withdrawn and prematurely gray, at least in mood. This is particularly probable if the child is tightly bound to the troubled parent and has not been permitted to find and develop a separate self. In several studies, a huge 37 percent of the children of depressed parents were themselves suffering feelings of loneliness, hopelessness, and despair.

Suicide attempts are very rare in children under the age of fourteen, although thoughts about suicide and death are common among these sad and defeated children. Unlike adults, children do have a natural growth push which seems to bring enough optimism and joy to sufficiently balance the bleak feelings and stay a child from suicide. Children have a great capacity to deny reality, to use their fantasy life to act out feelings that they can then keep separate from their daily thoughts. Children also can deny their feelings of guilt and worthlessness by ignoring them, by distracting themselves with motor activity. Children, then, have several defenses against sad feelings: they can magically wish them away, or they can turn them into other kinds of problems that are less painful. This is why the sad child so often doesn't appear sad until you listen carefully to her stories and make-believe.

For children six to ten suffering from these sadnesses, we recommend that the family problems be dealt with in some form of therapy and that the adults in the child's world be alerted to the child's need to feel better about himself, to feel secure in an attachment to some adult, to recover from the severe feelings of loss that have so affected his life. In some instances it will be important to work with the child in individual therapy as well. The aim of all therapy is to restore the child's trust in adults, to permit a free expression of feelings including those of anger and grief, and most importantly to give the child an opportunity to experience himself as capable, successful, and worthy of love and attention. Together, all these strategies should remove the child's sense of hopelessness.

However, the child who has experienced many losses before the age of five may always be at risk of awakening his own despair and may never be able to hold on to the good harmonious feelings about himself that are necessary for a healthy, happy life. The roots of adult depression certainly wander back into earliest childhood, when we are least capable of withstanding the pain of loss.

In Europe, doctors use drug therapy with young children. In America, most physicians are cautious about medicines because their long-term effect has not been studied and because the drugs themselves have potentially damaging side effects. There may come a time when the biochemistry of mental illness is so well understood that the problem of childhood grief can be safely treated with drugs. At this writing we would prefer that parents try family therapy and/or individual therapy for their child before venturing into the still uncharted territory of mind-altering chemicals.

The Technicolor Child

Some children don't get mad, they get very very mad; and they don't just laugh, they laugh very loudly for a long time. These children feel great extremes of joy and sadness, and express clearly and openly all of their passions, moods, and responses. They have a flair for the dramatic, even for the melodramatic. They have a thousand and one ways to attract attention to themselves and enjoy every minute of the limelight. They are not shy, never withdrawn, and they don't suffer silently. They love to be right in the center of the stage, be that stage in a real theater or merely the family dinner table. The trouble is that they are very suggestible and dependent on others. They are never quite sure who they are or what they should believe or do. They will play any part that might bring them attention, but then they are not sure where the play acting ends and reality begins. These are children who will do anything for approval and have trouble saying "No" to friends or being alone and enjoying themselves. They will play imaginatively and creatively long after other children have submerged themselves in the hard facts of learning, in games that have specific rules. These are children who seem theatrical and of the theater long before any idea of going on the stage has possessed them.

If children of this sort begin to show emotional trouble, their problems may appear in the form of excessive fears of animals, places, objects. Or they may show a sudden paralysis of the hand— the very hand that they had been told should not touch their genitals. They may choke if asked to believe a story they cannot swallow. They may sometimes forget what they are doing and appear to be sleep-walking while awake. They may forget the name and address of their school.

These are children who are caught in the family drama, and although they may have reached the age of six, seven, eight, or nine, they still are struggling with feelings of erotic love toward the parent of the opposite sex and have not yet identified clearly with the parent of the same sex. Such children do not have free energy for the tasks of learning that are right for their age. They are still too busy being involved in games of wooing and loving a parental figure.

Very frequently in the families of such children, the mother and father have become estranged. They may be living together but are emotionally distant one from the other. Often one parent is using the child to fill certain erotic and emotional needs—to fill in the space left by the distant spouse. One such parent continued to bathe her eight-year-old boy and to play teasing, tickling games with him. Another took his ten-year-old daughter to the movies each Friday night, leaving his wife at home to clean up after dinner.

The technicolor child is very appealing and knows how to make adults respond positively. Eventually, however, the hollow center, the sense of Who am I?, brings a really frantic behavior to the surface. Such a child will have trouble listening and concentrating and accomplishing the learning tasks of this age.

If parents feel that their child is overly outgoing, always seeking attention, and having trouble concentrating on mundane tasks, doing things alone without applause or reaction, we would recommend a psychiatric consultation. We do not want to put every flamboyant child into therapy. Clear distinctions must be made between the child who is in trouble, whose behavior is a sign of a hollow self, and the one who is merely filled with energy and charm. Sometimes this distinction can be made only by a therapist looking closely at the child and his family.

The Very Worried Child

Some children are tense, nervous, and worried all the time. You can often tell by just looking at their faces; the tight lips, the pallor, the circles under their eyes, and the joyless expression they habitually wear tell it all. These children will often have trouble falling asleep and need reassurances, extra trips into the parents' room, and lights on long past their fifth birthday. Although other children between their sixth and tenth birthday will find that they are having fewer and fewer bad dreams, these anxious children will rarely get through a week without waking in terror. At school they will daydream frequently and have a hard time paying attention to the rules and requests of the teacher. They will turn and wiggle and jump about constantly. Sometimes this kind of child is confused with a child with learning disabilities or minor neurological disorders, but the restlessness is less intense than in those children and the anxiety is far greater. They will eat poorly and savagely bite their nails. They may pull at their own hair or develop odd tapping or twiddling motions with their fingers or feet. Some of them talk too much and listen too little.

The constantly worried child is not responding to a real fear of a real danger but is instead flooded with a vague feeling of worry that something bad is about to happen. This worry is usually a warning to the child that some feelings of anger and destructiveness or some sexual feelings that are forbidden and dangerous are about to erupt into his mind. The healthy child of six to ten usually pushes these unwanted thoughts away and so can freely concentrate on learning and enjoying the world before him. The extremely worried child has trouble keeping the bad thoughts down. He is always at the edge of being overwhelmed by his own angers and feelings.

The parents of anxious children are often found to be inconsistent and unpredictable; the child has had trouble learning what is expected of him and what is permitted. Some children have had painful and disastrous hospitalizations in which they felt helpless and abandoned; some have suffered real losses of a parent through death or divorce. These wounds have made it hard for the child to develop the inner strength to keep away his strong fears and angers. He may have a parent who is also fearful and anxious, hiding angers and impulses that hover just below the surface of conscious thought. Children will identify with their parent and imitate or reproduce their dominant mood in themselves.

Worried children have developed a basic mistrust of the world outside. This mistrust echoes their fear of their own inability to control their feelings. Trust in oneself and trust in others is a basic building block of normal life. Worried children will have difficulty learning and making friends. Their fearfulness will prevent them from acquiring some of the play skills that other children enjoy and will isolate them from their more adventurous and confident age mates. Psychiatric work with the child and members of the family is advised when a child has been anxious for a long time.

The Clinging Child

There are some children who by age six appear to be clinging, dependent, whining, and demanding. This is the child who asks her mother for a toy every time they go to the grocery store. This is the child who still fusses and complains and perhaps throws a small tantrum if her parents hire a babysitter for the evening. This is the child who resists zipping up her jacket and tying her shoes and won't wash her own hair and is always asking for a special treat—an extra candy or another dessert.

This kind of child will be non-athletic and non-competitive. She won't want to win the game as much as she wants to sit on someone's lap. She won't like games that involve learning skills or learning rules; she will prefer the games of younger children that involve pretend and imitation play. Naturally she will likely be ignored or picked on by her age mates, who will be further irritated by her habit of bursting into tears when thwarted. She will use tears as a method of gaining the teachers' attention and protection. It would not occur to her to fight back, to hide her upset, to master a difficulty, or to try harder at any given task. Her first thought, if things look dark, is to whine and complain that she isn't being treated fairly. Other children will call her a "cry baby," but she will find this less of an insult than they do because she is not in such a hurry to give up the perceived privileges of infancy.

Clinging is usually created by overprotective parents who have not allowed their child to take the necessary first steps toward independent self-confidence. They intervened before their child could suffer even the slightest bruise or the most minor of bumps. These parents put food into mouths long after the children were eager and competent to take over for themselves. These parents encouraged and admired those activities that kept the child close at hand. They discouraged climbing rocks and scaling jungle gyms. They did not let the child bike to the corner alone.

These children may be longed-for only children, or they may have been sick with chronic illnesses, such as asthma or diabetes. It is easy to understand how realistically anxious adults may begin to overprotect a frail child. Some parents, however, have to keep their children close and cannot tolerate signs of their growing separateness and individuality because of their own sense of weakness and loneliness in the vast world. Some parents feel an anger toward their children that is mixed with love. They are so afraid this anger will harm their children that they keep them close, seeing danger everywhere in the outside world. These children will be in trouble at every stage if the parents cannot be helped to see that it is time to fold up the umbrella of parental protection and let their children get rained on a bit.

The Rebel in Disguise

There is a kind of child whose personality is most difficult for parents and teachers because he never says, "No, I won't do that." Instead, he agrees pleasantly to most anything but then just doesn't do it. This is the child whose mother placed him on the potty and he sat there for hours quietly not doing anything. He appears to be willing and eager to please his mother, so she can't really be angry with him; yet he has resisted her and so she is angry. Sometimes the resistance will spread into all activities of life and spoil the child's pleasure in learning and playing.

The child will forget his homework day after day; he will lose the book that he is doing a report on. He will dawdle getting ready for school and miss the bus time after time. He will promise to take out the garbage but then forget and when reminded will cheerfully promise to do it later. He becomes a master procrastinator. Everything will be done later.

This child rebels against all demands that he do what others want. He doesn't rebel in an outward, nasty way, but in a hard-to-figure, constantly ignoring, avoiding, undoing method that effectively sabotages teachers and parents. He will accidentally spill the milk he didn't want to drink and take so long eating dinner that his parents give up trying to get vegetables into him. He will delay so long on each chore that someone else usually takes over to reduce the hassling.

He feels all demands on him are excessive and unfair. Finally he is in danger of ruining his own life by becoming a failure at school and at play because all activities require work, attention, the capacity to stick to it through hard or boring times. All rewards in learning and in friendships come through some capability to do what others want, what others ask. The child who puts up such a strong resistance ends up sacrificing everything to his resistance, and missing out on those important experiences of discipline that give each of us a chance to master our environment and eventually to take over for ourselves.

He will come to the attention of the professionals when schools become frustrated and parents are at their wits' end. This is a difficult disorder to treat because the child has become clever at avoiding responsibility for his own actions. But if he can be helped to see what is going on, and how he is actually hurting himself, new paths may be taken. Families have to learn different ways to treat him that prevent his getting away with procrastination but at the same time offer other rewards if he gives up the satisfactions of his absurd but oddly triumphant rebellion.

Parents must let the child suffer the consequences of his own procrastination. If he misses the school bus, he stays home. If he doesn't clean up his room, he doesn't watch television. If he delays getting ready for a family outing, he stays home. At the same time parents can offer the reward of a new hockey stick, of a trip with Daddy, or a late-night treat if he does what is asked of him. The important thing is for parents to be aware of how angry their child is making them. It helps to bring into the open the passive resistance so that it cannot be ignored by either parent or child.

The causes of this disorder are not really known. It is possible that toileting was begun too early and was too pressured, but it may also be that some few children have a biological constitutional bent for this style of resistance. Such children may feel that to follow instructions means abandoning their identities, a frightening loss of self. In some children this trait is so crippling and extreme that professional help is required to alter the behavior and aid the child to express his anger openly and non-destructively, allowing him to join others in their learning and in their play.

The Withdrawn Child

Some children are so quiet that we worry about them. They are so shy that they will not talk at all in front of strangers, or only in whispers. They stand as if sunk in cement at their mother's side. These children did not run off and explore the playground when they were three or four. Now they do not go up trees and around corners and they don't take their bikes as fast as they can down the block. Rather, they walk quietly at their parents' side. Very often they don't speak much at all; they prefer to gesture to what they want and are content to wait silently until someone turns to them. They enter first grade without ever having made a friend and they don't make friends in school. They don't reach out. They don't talk up in class. They don't join jump rope games and they don't play catch. They stand outside the other children and look on.

Such children would really like to have a friend. They would like to join in the games. They would like to ride a bike and learn to swim, to laugh at jokes with everyone else. But they just are too fearful and don't know how to go about it. Very often they come from socially isolated families, where the parents have developed a great mistrust of the outside world and have let their children know that they are safe and comfortable only inside the family house. These are parents with few friends or relatives, who avoid contact with others as much as possible. Since their children are lonely and sad, they may develop other symptoms.

School authorities can reach out to these families to help them bring their child into the social community. Therapy with the adults in the family is probably the best way to break the fearful bonds that tie the child. Parents can try to broaden their own social spheres and join in church or school activities, making new friends and bringing them home to share with the child. Parents should encourage the child to invite others over and can help the child by urging that he attend Scout groups, dance classes, or sports activities that require cooperation with other children. They should also encourage independence by sending the child to the store to make purchases, by leaving him with relatives for a weekend. Once they are aware of the life damage such a high degree of timidity and withdrawal creates, parents can work with the child to alter the situation.

The Fearless Child

Certain children at around age six will find themselves out of touch with their age mates and always in some kind of trouble with adults. These children have never given up the idea that they are all-powerful and can control the way the world works. They are fearless about physical danger, convinced that no harm could possible come to them. As younger children, they would dive into the deep end of a pool before learning to swim. Now they will climb too high in a tree, cross streets without waiting for lights, challenge larger and older children to fights.

They don't listen to reason, or to warnings about electricity, sharp objects, fire. They are enthusiastic about everything and full of motion and energy. Yet these children are somewhat out of touch with reality: they lack normal caution, healthy fear, and a keen sense of observation of the behavior and concerns of others. They are not liked by other children because they are particularly insensitive to the feelings of others. They have a babyish need to do things by and for themselves and are not involved with or caring of either other children or other adults. They won't go along with the rules of a game or the rules that determine behavior in the classroom. They consider themselves something of an exception.

Parents frequently let this kind of child walk all over them, treating him with deference and respect out of proportion to his age or his knowledge. Such a child has not had an opportunity to learn that the world is not always his oyster and that at any rate he would be better off with a friend and a humble hamburger. He needs limits put on all his behavior. But the lack of judgment about what is safe and what is not may indicate that the child is flooded with impulses that he just can't control. His use of magic thinking, "I will be all right no matter what. I can jump or run faster or avoid all danger," is not a good sign in a child over six. If it continues over a period of time, we recommend that parents arrange a consultation with a qualified therapist, who may be able to search out the root of the problem, restore the child's sense of reality, and improve his relationships with other people.

Sometimes fearless behavior shows up in children who suffer from some chronic illness, or who have experienced some really frightening life-threatening accident. Then the fearlessness and the self-centeredness represent an effort to overcome the extreme feelings of helplessness and weakness they have endured. They have been close to danger and know it all too well. As a result, they may deny reality with a vengeance that is abetted by parents who have trouble saying "No" to a sick child. The child is now denying how afraid he really is.

Parents can sometimes help by talking about being afraid with the child. Tell him that mommies and daddies are sometimes afraid, and that once in a while it is sensible to be scared. Parents should see if they can't get the child to talk about what has frightened him so badly that he will never let himself be scared again. Talking about it, sharing his feelings with his parents may change his behavior and reduce his need to deny his vulnerability by acting like Superman. This situation may change as the child become physically healthy or has many reassuring experiences.

The Child Who Is All Alone

There is a kind of child who shocks adults by his extreme aloneness. He will be distant, distracted, detached, and cold. He doesn't care if the hero of the TV series saves the girl or not. He doesn't care if the family pet runs away. He doesn't respond if his parents get divorced. He avoids games and groups and conversations, being much more interested in things. He may collect stamps or pieces of wire or yogurt tops; he may spend contented hours building model airplanes or playing video games. He is uninterested in competitive sports and he won't participate in spelling bees or tugs-of-war. He likes to be alone.

Unlike the withdrawn child, who just doesn't seem to know how to join up, these children are truly loners. They prefer their own company. They are not concerned about being left out—they don't notice that they are. Their pleasures and satisfactions seem to come from a very aggressive fantasy life, in which they are the heroes and rather dreadful bloody things happen to everyone else. Occasionally such a child will break out in some unexpected viciousness like throwing a cat out the window or destroying a sister's favorite doll.

Some of these children will lose their hold on reality and begin to behave in bizarre ways, showing the symptoms of real madness. Then they may spin their bodies around, shake their hands in repeated odd gestures, lose language, or begin to confuse words and shout, whisper, or laugh inappropriately. In their teen years, some will hallucinate and others will become frozen like zombies; they will be hospitalized off and on throughout the rest of their lives. Others manage to stay isolated but not out of contact with reality. They will live long lives in single rooms, always alone, untouched and untouching, but able to finish school, hold jobs, and have bank accounts, to take vacations and wear a mask of normality until they die.

Aloneness is a severe illness that remains without a special name. We do not yet know whether neglect, abuse, or loss of loved people causes this condition, or whether it is another biological misfiring, a matter of infinitely complicated chemicals of the brain causing overload, broken connections, with tragic human results.

If a parent feels that her child is isolated and teachers echo the fear, a consultation with a psychiatrist should be arranged. When the aloneness is deep in the character, parents cannot by any particular behavior of their own alter the direction of the child's life. Therapy can occasionally reach into the mind and rebuild and reawaken the capacity for affection, love, vulnerability. But for most children the severed connection is as irreversible as the snapped spinal cord and for now remains beyond our capacity to mend.

The Child Who Won't Go to School

The reluctance or out-and-out refusal of a child to go to school is a serious problem that demands immediate professional attention. Some children develop a sudden fear of a particular teacher, or of other teasing children, or of the janitor, the toilets, or the dining hall. Some don't explain what frightens or upsets them about going to school, but each morning they wake up with nausea and vomiting, sore throats or leg pains, symptoms that seem magically to melt away if they are permitted to stay at home. These children, who range in age from six upward, may show a terrible panic and erupt into wild screaming or helpless tears if they are physically forced into the school bus.

Some children experience a brief and unimportant kind of school fear if a baby brother or sister has just been brought home or if they themselves have just recovered from a severe illness or an accident. A few days are all that are needed to reassure them that the angers and anxieties recent events have stirred up will do no harm. But if the fear of school lasts for as long as a week or two, parents should be concerned. School is a necessary intellectual part of a child's life. It is absolutely crucial that a child be able to leave home and feel safe in the outside world.

The child who is afraid of school rarely becomes a truant in the usual sense. Truants are not interested in learning. Truants avoid their homes as well as their schools, whereas these children want only to stay at home with their mothers. They want very much to join the world and feel ashamed and deprived of learning and playing activities, but still they are unable to remain in school.

Some children become resistant to school for realistic reasons. They may have a mean, vindictive teacher who has humiliated them, or may have, for one reason or another, become the victim of some sadistic fellow students. They may have learning problems, which make them feel bad about themselves when they are in school. These reasons for a school fear can be eased by a change of teacher, a change of class, or academic help. But other children are afraid of being in school for sad and unhealthy reasons. They are afraid that while they are away from home, something terrible will happen to their mothers or fathers or themselves. They are scared that they will die if they are not in the company of their parents, or that their parents will die if they themselves turn away and enter the school.

The causes for this fear of death are deep and troublesome. The child will show a clinging kind of attachment to the parent, and the parent will often show the same kind of feeling toward the child. Frequently we find school fears in children of mothers who would never leave their babies with babysitters, who felt angry at the constant demands of their infants but were unable to show their anger. Instead these mothers became overprotective, over-fearful, unwilling to let the child explore and grow on his own.

A child with a fear of school has many bad feelings about his parent on whom he depends so much. In the unconscious soul children expect that their angry thoughts can actually create harm, and so angry feelings produce a fear that something will happen to the parent, that death is really coming. The parent, too, will have angry feelings toward the child, which make that parent unduly fearful that something will happen to the child. The jumping to aid the child at every moment of distress so often seen in these parents is a disguise for anger. Both parents and children are afraid of being abandoned.

The child is not really afraid of school, nor of the cafeteria or the teachers or the other children. She is afraid of losing her mother. She does not recognize or accept her feelings of anger toward her parent, and so places those feelings outside of herself, turning them against herself and her mother. She is afraid her mother will die because of her rage. Only in the company of her actual parent can she feel that they are both safe. She needs to see the parent all the time to be sure that nothing terrible has happened.

If a child is suffering from a school fear, we know that she is still thinking magically. She is afraid that her thoughts or wishes may come true and that harm can come from her angry feelings. This child has not created for herself a self, secure and independent of the actual arms and voice of the parent. She feels the world away from the parent is filled with danger, and so she wants to control the parent at every pass, ensuring that they will always be safe together. Often the parent is involved in exactly the same game, holding tightly on to the child so that she can be sure that the child is safe. The more closely they stay together, the less air and space they permit to come between them, the angrier and more afraid each becomes.

Sometimes children with school fears come from homes in which either the father or the mother is behaving in a seductive way with the child, using her to fill certain sexual roles that have been vacated by their mate. Too much sexual excitement can result in a child's great anxiety and fear of retaliation by the other parent. These fears make it hard for a child to go off to school and trust that all will remain well at home.

By refusing to go to school, the child exerts control over the family. She shows them that she is not just an appendage but an independent person, even if independence is purchased at the price of real freedom, growth, and selfhood. This symptom is so destructive because it prevents the child from growing up while allowing her to vent at least indirectly some of her anger at her parents.

School fears need to be treated right away, but professional therapy for the child is only part of the answer. The family itself, the mother and father, must learn what has caused the response and how to change their ways of living with the child. The initial school fear will disappear quickly after the onset of therapy. It is important that the relationships of each member of the family to the other be looked at carefully, and that everybody in the family grow and change so that the fear of hovering death that grabbed the child so dramatically can be put to rest forever. Family therapy or individual therapy with both parents and child can release the father, mother, and child from the ever-tightening binds of this difficult, sad, but very human situation.

If a school phobia appears suddenly in a child of eight or nine, there is some possibility that it is a forewarning of a more serious break with reality to come. In some children, severe mental illness announces itself by a refusal to go to school. In these children school phobia is a part of increasing withdrawal from the real world. This is rare of course and parents should not jump to the conclusion that worse things are yet to come. Most school fears are treatable and can even be considered positive. They are signals of distress that lead families to work together to create better and happier homes for all their members.

The Overly Active Child

We have discussed the hyperactive child in earlier sections, but some parents do not become concerned about their children until they enter school. At this age they can be clearly identified and helped.

Some children can't sit still. They jump up and down when they have no place to go. Even when they are sitting in a chair, their arms are jiggling and wiggling and their feet are tapping on the floor. Their constant motion goes beyond high spirits and normal childish energy, turning into a destructive problem that makes it hard for them to concentrate on the words and instructions of others. It makes it difficult to learn the rules of a game and obey them; it gets them into constant trouble with teachers and playmates.

Hyperactive children often have trouble controlling their emotions. They may laugh suddenly and too loudly. They may easily become angry and aggressive and then be hard to calm down. The wish to punch someone in the face may be quickly followed by action, or the desire to own the calculator in a friend's hand leads to a grab

343

for the prized possession. Such children often don't sleep well, and when they are tired, their impulsiveness and activity become even more marked.

Hyperactive children may have normal or superior intelligence but they can easily think of themselves as stupid. Everyone is always yelling at them. Other children often don't like them and exclude them from their play. Teachers are exasperated because their papers are messy or lost, their attention has wandered long before the instructions were finished, and their fidgeting and fooling around distracts others in the classroom.

Many of these children will also have specific learning difficulties, which will be discussed in the next section. The combination of excess energy and frazzled nerves makes it very hard for a child to achieve in the usual way, and feeling himself to be "bad," or "weird," such a child can hide his defects behind constant rebellion and anger, leading to truancy, school failure, delinquency, and social alienation.

The hyperactive child is not to blame for his behavior; neither are his parents, who have not been either too strict or too permissive. This problem is not created by errors in child rearing. Its origins can be traced back in the child's life to the earliest days of infancy, when often these children will roll over in the crib, wave their arms and kick their legs constantly, and be hard to comfort, hard to still, hard to put to sleep. This problem is one of biological error, of chemical imbalance. Although it is usually outgrown by early adolescence, it can leave deep and open wounds in the psyche.

We do have medications that can help the child calm down, pay attention, and get along better with other children. Stimulants seem to work in reverse in children, producing a calming effect on the child's nervous system. The medication must be prescribed by a doctor and only after a thorough examination has been given so that parents and physicians are certain that the illness has been correctly identified. The child must be monitored and cared for by a trained and experienced doctor while on medication. Doses have to be checked and side effects guarded against. No parent should try to medicate his own child.

Hyperactivity is sometimes a symptom of other emotional problems not caused by a biological imbalance. A frightened or upset child, one who has been abused or harmed or suffered severely, may also appear to be unable to stay still. Hyperactivity that has been caused by anxiety or fear will not be reduced through the use of stimulants. This child needs other kinds of help and should not be medicated. Hyperactivity sometimes accompanies other severe emotional problems such as childhood psychosis or borderline psychosis. In these instances, too, the treatment plan would be different. Only a trained physician can distinguish pure hyperactivity from the other illnesses that have hyperactivity as one of their symptoms.

For the truly hyperactive child, medications do frequently have a magical and wonderful effect, allowing the child to gather himself together, to listen, to sleep, to play well with others. Since many of these children also have learning problems, the medication allows them to absorb the special instruction they will need, and grants them the inner peace required to work hard at overcoming the obstacles to learning that stand in their way.

We have to be careful not to use medication wildly. We should not use it to change the lifestyles of children in the inner city and we cannot use it to insist that boys be quiet and conforming. Medication should never become a tool of social control, but rather fulfill its potential to better the lives of some biologically imbalanced children.

Some doctors have suggested that food additives and preservatives cause allergies in children that lead them to become hyperactive. This theory has not been scientifically demonstrated. Some grand claims are made for it, but we would suggest that while there is no harm in experimenting for a few months with diet, parents should be aware that this approach has not been proved effective. The idea of giving a child mind-altering medicine is disturbing to most parents. We do not know everything about the eventual or residual side effects of these drugs and parents are of course concerned and worried. However, when hyperactivity does present a clear and unmistakable picture to the specialist, we would accept the risks of medication in order to help the child calm down.

Parents of hyperactive children also have to learn how to head off trouble with their children. Trips, many friends, exhaustion, overly exciting television programs all have to be carefully watched with this kind of child. The more ordinary the days are, the more things are the same, the fewer new places and people introduced, the better this child will manage.

Given medical help, time, understanding, and the continued support and love of their parents, hyperactive children can emerge at childhood's end with their self-confidence intact and all their strength and capabilities ready to take them on into a happy and fulfilled life.

Learning Problems

Learning problems are not clearly identifiable before the age of five and a half or six, but they appear in some 4 percent of our children. About six times as many boys as girls have learning difficulties. Some children will show symptoms that may later develop into learning problems in their nursery school years, but many of those children will spontaneously outgrow the difficulty as their nervous system matures.

Children who have trouble establishing dominance of one hand over another may be reflecting difficulty in the brain spheres. Children whose eyes are crossed sometimes have additional troubles with mental functions that require processing information through the eyes into the mind. Learning-disabled children may have trouble reading letters from left to right, distinguishing between *p, b,* and *q.* They may have trouble doing tasks with their hands that require guidance with their eyes, judging relative sizes, and doing puzzles that require a sense of space and direction. Such children often have trouble seeing the object in the foreground and confuse it with the background on a picture. Frequently they have depth-perception problems, misjudging distances of hand to glass, body to door. They may find it hard to catch a ball, hammer a nail, get a pencil to go in the correct direction.

Some children with learning problems will have difficulty distinguishing close sounds in words like "blow" and "bell"; sometimes they will confuse words. For example, you might ask a little girl, "How are you?" and she might answer, "I'm eight years old." She will have confused the word "are" with the word "old." Some learning-disabled children have trouble keeping the orders and sequences of numbers and letters straight. They may add $2+3$ and give you an answer like 23 or 32—they confuse the direction of the numbers. Spelling is challenging because they will confuse the direction of the letters, so that *dear* becomes *daer.* Some will have trouble with abstract thoughts. If the teacher has told a story about a ghost, the child

346

will only be able to think about that particular ghost and not see that the teacher is talking about other things that might frighten you at night. Some children may be able to remember things that happened to them several years ago but be unable to recall the spelling lesson they mastered only an hour before. It can take such a child a long time before information is properly stored in her mind and becomes a permanent part of memory. Some have trouble with language only when they have to speak or respond quickly. They are all right if given time to organize their thoughts and find the right words.

Teachers first identify learning problems in the first or second grade when failure to read on time and to do simple arithmetic becomes obvious. If the problem is not recognized in the first months of the first year of school, most children develop other disturbances that follow on their initial difficulties. They begin to feel they are stupid—they know how much longer it is taking them to catch on than the child at the next desk. They begin to avoid the pain of feeling inferior by clowning around, pretending they don't care, or disrupting the class. Some children will just withdraw into daydreams in which they imagine themselves as heroes or heroines, happily victorious in everything they do. Some children when faced with school failure and parental disappointment will begin again to wet the bed or have temper tantrums, to talk baby talk, to eat with their fingers. They are attempting to return to a less stressful period of their short lives before things were asked of them they couldn't achieve.

Learning-disabled children will quickly begin to have trouble with their age mates. They will not easily learn or obey the rules of a game and may have a hard time playing jacks or baseball or following the rules of Monopoly. Since they do not perform well academically or athletically, they will have trouble gaining the respect of their classmates, and their own feelings of being worthless will place them in situations where they may be either bullied or ignored. Some will become overly aggressive, as if to assert some accomplishment, while others will become so afraid of failure they will refuse to try anything new, taking refuge in the television set and their own fantasies.

Learning-disabled children may become afraid of school. They may develop a special fear of a child who has teased them or they may have frequent stomach aches, headaches, cramps, and diarrhea. The physical complaints are used in part to avoid going to school; they can also be body responses to the stress the child feels in a situation where he cannot succeed. Learning-disabled children sense that there is something wrong with them, that they are different. Often we hear them say that their head hurts, or that their knee hurts, because they can't explain or understand what is really wrong. Some children get angry and insist the teacher or the classmates are out to get them. They feel isolated and bad, and they often toss those bad feelings back out on the world and assume that everyone is mad at them.

Fortunately, there is help for learning difficulties (which are called dyslexia when applied to language problems). There are many specially trained psychologists who work in this field. Techniques have been worked out to help such children read and spell and write. Educational psychologists know how to teach this child to work with numbers, to read music; they understand the need for certain kinds of repetition. They use techniques of education that call on all the senses, such as having children touch letters as well as look at them. Sophisticated tests enable them to tell just which area of a child's thought process is affected by the learning disability. They can then show a child how to use his own strengths, and so give children a sense of success and accomplishment in learning.

A good specialist in learning problems knows how to make the child feel worthy and valuable. The therapist is able to help the child see the problem as partial and not the sum of himself, as accidental and not his fault. It may take several years of work with a therapist, but most children can win out over these difficulties and by their early teen years perform up to their full intellectual capacities. Children with learning disabilities have become successful writers, doctors, teachers, stockbrokers. If they are not forced away from school, if they are helped when they need it, this problem, while not a minor one, can be overcome.

Some eye doctors have offered theories that eye exercises will help learning problems. So far these exercises have not been demonstrated to be effective and the American Academy of Pediatrics and the American Academy of Ophthalmology have issued a joint statement critical of this approach. If parents wish to try eye exercises, they certainly cannot hurt, providing a parent at the same time takes his child to an accredited educational psychologist who uses the methods of working with learning difficulties that have for many years now been established as effective.

It is frightening for a parent to receive the report that her child has a learning problem and requires educational therapy. Since this is a chronic, long-term illness, it requires strong and dedicated parenting to provide the extra love and care a learning-disabled child needs. Many parents run away from the news, trying doctor after doctor to see if the diagnosis can be reversed. All parents feel in some way guilty and profoundly disappointed. Learning disabilities are often family-related. In over 40 percent of the children, a father, mother, or brother also struggled with the problem. This makes it harder to accept, not easier. We tend as a culture to judge ourselves and our children by the essentially foolish standards of grades, teams, prizes, and so on. The learning-disabled child with proper help can have all these rewards in time, but through the early years he must be valued for other qualities of the soul, for other aspects of his character. His achievements should be measured against his handicaps rather than against the boy down the street.

A child who has learning difficulties without hyperactivity should never be medicated because we do not have a medicine that will aid children to read, write, or think. However, some 40 percent of hyperactive children are also learning-disabled. For them, the medication creates the calm in which the educational psychologist can work. The hyperactive child with learning troubles is in double jeopardy: he needs help if he is to learn and to steady his internal climate.

Parents should remember not to jump to the conclusion that their child has a learning problem if he is a little slow in first grade picking up reading. Many children mature a little later than the majority and will pick up and excel in time. There is no need to get anxious if a child has not learned letters in kindergarten or seems uninterested in reading through many months of the first grade. Some children don't like to try things until they are sure they can master them. Some don't like to be pushed. Some are just naturally a little slower than others—this does not make them learning-disabled. If the school has raised the question, if you yourself are wondering about certain lags the child is showing, then arrange for testing by a qualified educational psychologist. Your school should be able to recommend one in your community.

The Bad Child

Some children are always in trouble. Their teachers are disappointed and frustrated, their parents desperate. These are children who will lie to cover up misdeeds. They may steal from neighborhood stores. They may hurt little children or small animals. Some break windows and smash lamps, others may set fires or chronically fight against any directions, any commands. They appear to be junior-size criminals and seem to feel no guilt. While they may promise never again to punch another child in the face, or never again to cheat on tests or steal money from the teacher's purse, they will, as surely as the sun comes up in the morning, commit some new misdeed, some sneaky or explosive or inconsiderate act.

Although we do not yet understand the origin of evil or why the snake was set down in the Garden of Eden, we do know something about the problems of these bad apples. They are suffering from personality disorders that can lead them into lifelong troubles with their fellow humans as well as with the laws of society. Yet while they often appear to feel guilt-free, while it seems that their conscience has fallen asleep or shrunken away to nothing, they suffer deeply from their exclusion from the rewards of working well and becoming true friends with others. They are cut off from important kinds of intimacy, love, and self-respect. Although they would be the last to tell you that they care, they will suffer from the turmoil of aggressions they can't control and the fears of retaliation that their badness evoke. When they become adolescents, some are dangers to us all. Even so, they are human beings whose development has been distorted and disrupted by weakness of their constitution as well as the frequent cruelties and corruptions in their parents. They are not nice children, but they are victims all the same.

They do not suffer from a tension between their sexual and aggressive impulses and their conscience. They do not develop symptoms of rituals and fears, and their defense systems against their own angers have not made them behave in odd or self-crippling ways. Instead, they have basic defects in their characters that make it hard for them not to grab or yell, to hit or run when they want. They have

350

very little capacity for delay of pleasure, for reflection before action.

These are children who do not trust the outside world to be fair to them. They feel that they are alone in a jungle: that any technique they use to survive is right and good. Their basic attachment to a loving parent has been cut off or aborted. As a result, they often cannot imagine how another person feels or experiences their behavior. Their only place is in their own shoes. They are without empathy and can often move through the human community the way most of us maneuver across a floor littered with wooden blocks. They can manipulate or coerce others into doing things for them; they can beat up younger children and take toys from weaker children. When the preacher speaks of the children of God, when the teacher speaks of mankind, when the boys on the block speak of "us," this child does not feel included.

Children with this defect are primarily male. They often have suffered a real loss of one parent or another in the years between three and five, when other children are identifying with their parents and learning to distinguish good and bad from them. They may hate the parent who has left them, even for death. They may learn about the bad qualities of the absent parent and identify with those. They become smart about how the real world works, but they must distort truth in order to defend themselves against any invasion of guilt. They search for immediate pleasure and try to cover up their profound sense of helplessness. Many of them do have some slight signs of brain damage. They will grow into the outcasts, the criminals, and the uneducated of tomorrow. Only the most skilled and experienced of therapists seem to be able to make headway with the "bad" child. It is hard to find a way for such a child to trust and need an adult; yet that trust and need are necessary for therapy to begin to have any effect.

Stealing

Children by two and a half have almost all learned the word "mine." This idea is stronger and far more appealing than the idea "yours," which comes a little later and much more reluctantly to most children. Accepting the fact that others may have what you want and you can't take it is a basic necessity in our culture. The childish expression, "Finders keepers, losers weepers," tells us how little we like this whole business of having to give up to others things we want.

In order for a child to accept this concept, there must be a basic fairness within the family. If one child receives much more than another, or the giving is capricious and unjust, than naturally the grieved child may take it upon himself to take what he believes is fairly his. Some young children around six or seven years of age will begin to steal small amounts of money or valued objects from either their mother or their father. They are taking from the parent a symbolic substitute for withheld affection. If father is distant, if mother is involved with other children, or work, or is just not attached to this child, sometimes stealing is a way a child uses to rectify matters. The child will often steal something that he then pretends he has been given. The child is trying to maintain to himself the all-important fiction that his parent does indeed love him and wants to give him things. Some children who steal repeatedly from their parents are in effect saying, "Since you refuse to give me what I need, I will take it." This stealing is a way of getting even, getting back at a rejecting parent. The other idea that is sometimes behind a child's theft is, "I do not need or want you to give me anything. I prefer to take it myself to injure you since you hurt me." For a young child it is natural for an inanimate thing to represent love.

Some children may steal money in order to buy things to give to their playmates. This tells us that a child fears he cannot win respect or friendship in any other way. This is a child in need of help because he feels inferior, unwanted, and without worth. Parents who find their six- or seven-year-old taking things for friends should try to help the child build his confidence, make new friends, make certain he feels loved and respected at home.

Around the age of eight or nine, we do see some not-so ominous stealing in which the child will feel that he has to prove that he is not a goody-goody. An episode or two of minor theft at this age is normal and does not signal any kind of problem. Of course, parents will want to be firm in their disapproval and stress that stealing of any kind is disappointing and unacceptable. Parents must take a firm position that the stolen object be returned. Children want to be part of a group, and want to demonstrate their fearless bravado against the adult world. If the parents are themselves not criminals and the culture of the streets the child walks does not respect the criminal way, minor stealing will pass quickly.

Sometimes a child will steal something around the time of a crisis in his life, such as the birth of a baby brother or an illness or divorce in the family. This stealing tells us that the child is upset and needs attention. But only when stealing becomes a habit do we become concerned.

For some children, stealing reveals that they look upon people as objects too and see people as if they were all like themselves, ready to use others for their own ends, unreliable and corrupt. Stealing can be a mark of a child already cut off from human connections and human affections. A child who steals is refusing to accept our standards of good and bad. In order to keep his self-respect, he must then feel contempt for the values of others. These children are easily frustrated by demands to wait, to work hard, to deny themselves any immediate pleasure. They do not expect to be taken care of and they do not have caring feelings for others. As the child's thievery continues he slips further away from reality and a sense of consequences, and he increasingly hides from himself his own behavior. He tries to deceive himself as well as others.

Stealing is itself a gratifying and exciting activity. It becomes a hard habit to give up, especially for the child who cannot trust the adult world to supply his needs. Individual and family counseling seems in order for these children and the results of therapy can be good, although the work is very difficult. If the child starts to steal from the therapist because he wishes to possess him or get back at him or make him give something, then the chances of a successful treatment are improved. The child is at least capable and willing to have a relationship with an adult with whom he can eventually identify and trust. Some children just steal randomly and do not care about anyone. It is far more difficult to treat them because they have slipped beyond the human connection and are floating alone in a void where they especially need the excitement and sense of mastery that their thefts bring.

Running Away

Running away from home is a rare act in the years six to nine, although many children in a pique will threaten to leave, pack their things, and go off to a friend or relative for a few hours. The child imagines a home where he will be better understood and permitted to do those things his parents disapprove of. This is usually a passing disturbance and most parents handle it with amusement and understanding.

All little children enjoy games that involve running away and being chased by an adult. These games symbolize the child's crucial struggle to be independent, to move away from the parents while maintaining the loving bond. The pleasure in running away is in being chased. The game is about gaining freedom without losing attachment. For some children, when they become six or seven, this game can turn into a kind of nightmare in which they must repeatedly flee. For them the problem of closeness and separation, the fear of being engulfed, surrounded, swallowed up, or abandoned, has become filled with constant anxiety. This child may well cling babyishly to his mother on Monday, insisting that she stay in the bathroom with him and help him wash his hair, and then on Friday when she asks him to walk the dog, he may get into a rage and call her names, hit out at her, and run away. The pattern may be repeated over and over.

The possible reasons for this behavior include mental retardation, which makes all stages of development difficult to master, or some form of minor brain damage that makes it hard for the child to put together the images of the good and bad parent, the parent he loves and the parent he is angry at. But the most common reason of all for repeated running away is the poor attachment a child has with his parents. He is waiting to be chased, afraid of closeness, afraid that he has already been abandoned. If one thinks of the children playing hide-and-seek about the yard and the giggles that one hears, and the shouts of joy when someone is discovered, it becomes especially sad to think of the runaway child. He is playing the game for real and there is no laughter, just the grim loneliness of a child who feels unloved and unlovable.

Parents can see if their method of discipline is too harsh, causing the child to get a message that he is a bad person. Parents should build areas of closeness with the child. Perhaps a father needs to spend more time in the house or a mother should find a way to do something special with this child. Parents can try to help the child feel independent but not disconnected by letting him join clubs or sports groups outside the home. They can help the child find some area of work or play in which he can excel and gain self-respect.

If the running away continues, the parents should consult with a professional. Perhaps the family itself needs to clear up its confusions, or perhaps it would be best for a trained therapist to work with the child. Certainly, repeated running away is a serious statement of separation conflict, even if the child does not run far and returns quickly. Parents should respond with active concern and care.

Vandalism

Breaking windows, smashing objects, spilling papers, turning over plants, and painting on buildings and sidewalks are all acts of destruction and expressions of explosive anger. Children who are vandals are angry children, afraid to express their feelings directly to parents and teachers who may have aroused them. Instead, they hit out at objects that can't possibly hit back. This kind of child is terribly frightened of his own anger and frightened of the anger of others. He sees himself as vicious, evil, and dangerous. He has great difficulty in controlling the storms of fear and rage that attack him. He has probably been treated cruelly in his infancy or has some defect in his character that makes him unable to contain and master his anger.

The young vandal needs to discover that he is likable, that he has other methods of mastering his world, that someone can reach him and stop him from acts of destruction by making him less afraid. He needs therapy, and his parents need guidance in helping him find acceptable ways to express his anxiety and in setting firm limits on what is permissible and what is not. The child who repeatedly destroys property has lost his positive connection to the adult world. It urgently needs to be reestablished.

Cruelty to Animals

At one time or another it is not uncommon for boys to treat a stray cat with cruelty or to mangle or mutilate a frog or fly. These acts are supposed to represent a kind of male dominance rather than give enjoyment in and of themselves. We can tell our children just what we think of such heedless and unpleasant behavior, but there is no need to feel alarmed. Boys are testing out their toughness and following the crowd. The occasional cruel act will be outgrown quickly as the child senses the reactions of other children and adults.

Acts of cruelty to a family pet or neighbor's pet are, however, a sign of serious difficulty. Repeated expressions of cruelty indicate that the child is having trouble feeling what others will feel. They tell us a child experiences himself as inferior and helpless—feelings he tries to overcome by hurting another. He does to others what he is afraid others will do to him. The rage that accompanies these bad feelings is expressed in the act of blinding the dog or covering the cat with glue or suffocating the bird in a plastic bag.

There is a stage in infancy when all children will bite or attack or hurt others, but this stage is quickly passed. As they identify with their parents, children will feel that cruelty is wrong. The child who ties tin cans on the cat's tail has missed some important loving connection to an adult and his value system is defective just as his capacity to handle anger and fear is weakened. Very often these children have been physically and emotionally abused by the adults who should have protected them. Sometimes they have identified with the person who has mistreated them and become like them—a beater, a violator of others.

Cruelty is a very serious symptom because it shows us that the child is incapable of containing rage. He must split off his anger at his parents and place it on other helpless small creatures. Once having done so, he loses the capacity for real love and connection to other children and adults. In order not to think of himself as evil or bad, he will think that all the people in the world are capable of his kind of act and he will consequently fear them and dislike them. Therapy is recommended for family and child either individually or together.

Lying

The innocent lying of early childhood is no more than a reflection of the three- to five-year-old's occasional inability to separate truth and fiction, to know what is real and what is not. In five- and six-year-olds we often see fantasy lying, in which the child will tell versions of events as he wishes them to have been. "I was the winner of the spelling bee in school." "I saw a flying saucer and the men from Mars gave me a present." "My mommy is mayor of the biggest city in the world." "I learned to swim this summer all the way out to the far float."

These lies are in the nature of experiments and flow out of the mouths of young children just as they drift through their minds. They will quickly disappear as the child learns that adults insist on reality and that reality should always be distinguished from pretending. Like the differences between yours and mine, good and bad, private and public, the distinction between truth and lie is important, and the child must master it on her way toward intellectual and emotional wholeness.

The kind of lying that signals trouble is delinquent lying, where a child of seven, eight, or nine will deliberately lie to gain an advantage, to avoid punishment, to achieve some kind of material gain, or to make someone else look bad. When a child continually lies in this manner, we know that she feels a sharp and painful sense of personal weakness and inadequacy. She is using the wrong tools to deal with internal and external pressures. The extensive use of denial, the I-am-better-than-I-really-am kind of lie ("I didn't eat all the candy in the box." "I didn't pull my sister's hair." "She took your lipstick and wrote on the mirror, not me"), affects the child's capacity to think logically and to understand the real world around her.

Other children don't like the liar. They will exclude her from their groups. They don't like the child who boasts that she can run as fast as a car or claims her mother is a movie star, nor the child who denies that she pinched a friend or knocked over a glass. All children are struggling against impulses to bend the truth in their favor, so they are especially angry at the child who fails at this task and lies.

Lying is rarely the only problem seen in a particular child. Usually it accompanies a whole set of actions that have to do with non-acceptance of adult standards of good and bad. Lying may be the sign of children who have rejected the adult. There may be serious defects in their inner sense of right and wrong—values that children normally drink in with their love of their mother or father. If your child lies frequently after the age of six, you should be concerned. One can try to educate the child about the importance of truth. A parent can point out to a child that lying is making the other children turn away in anger. Parents can firmly punish a child for lying by withdrawing a privilege or a treat. But if the child persists, parents should seek a professional consultation.

Fire-Setting

Fire-setting is a frightening symptom that creates a serious hazard for everyone. Fire has been mythically connected with good and bad in most cultures. People believe that fire can purify and cleanse while at the same time it is an expression of power and anger. Fire was crucial to the beginnings of civilization and has come to represent its end, the apocalypse.

Children who repeatedly set fires have almost all had parents who did not want them and have made their dislike quite clear. Children of six to eight set fires when they are under great stress at home. A parent has beaten them for a transgression, an abandonment has been threatened, a new man or woman has come into the home. Fire-setting is found primarily in little boys who have almost always suffered some unusual degree of maltreatment. They may be retarded or slow and have learning disabilities. They believe that fire has the magical power to save them. Fire will have become part of their sexual and erotic fantasy life and seeing the flames will often cause erections. It may be that these children are also bedwetters and are equally absorbed in the power of water.

Since this symptom is so dangerous and destructive, it indicates a failure of the child to understand reality, to care about others, to be free of frightening fantasies, and to imagine the consequences of an act. It is therefore a serious symptom requiring immediate consultation with a professional. Sometimes a child should be removed from the home while treatment is taking place. It is important for everyone's safety that this symptom be immediately attended to. It is important for the fire-setter himself that he find more generous human connections to support his growth.

The Child Who Is a Master at Making You Mad

Some children say "No" to everything even when they are six or seven years old. They refuse to pick up their clothes and they argue with you if you tell them to wash for dinner or do their homework or turn off the TV. Behind your back they do the very things they know infuriate you and to your face they are openly uncooperative and rude. They use the words you have forbidden. They drop crumbs on the floor you just vacuumed. They pick friends you don't like. They make a big point of liking the Red Sox if you root for the Yankees.

These children often have parents who don't know how to set limits. They don't follow through with threatened punishments, remaining angry at their children for long periods of time. Often these children have suffered some kind of neglect or abuse and the parents have failed to offer them consistent affection. It is this love and protection that woo a young child into initially conforming with parental wishes. If that affection has been absent, the child may see no reason to conform. He has not taken into himself the parents' way of seeing the rights and wrongs of the world. Sometimes such a child will need to go through patterns of crime, punishment, atonement, and reconciliation over and over again. He feels unlovable, wicked, and is afraid of his own destructiveness. He behaves badly, defying authority in order to find a way to be controlled, to atone for his own bad wishes and feelings. Some of these children are afraid of being dependent, of being swept up into their mother's arms and returned to a state of helpless babyhood. Their bad behavior is a painful way of asserting and assuring independence and selfhood.

Parents can try to increase the firmness of their discipline. This does not mean increasing harshness; it means being consistent. Simultaneously, the parent should build affectionate bridges toward his child by increasing opportunities for companionship and mutual respect. Parents can reassure the child that he is not bad but that he has not yet learned to control some of his behavior. He can be told that time will help and the parents will always be there for him to help him and care for him.

If all this doesn't change his behavior in a matter of months, the child who constantly brings punishment down on his head needs therapeutic help and the family needs guidance to restore goodwill and trust between all its members.

The Scapegoat

Sometimes one child in a family causes a great deal of concern, disappointment, and turmoil. The parents come to a psychiatrist seeking help for this child who has a host of troubles and appears to be at odds with all the important people in his life. It may become clear to the professional, listening carefully to the parents' complaints and concerns, that the child in question has become a scapegoat for all the hidden and unexpressed tensions in the family. The parents will deny that anything is wrong with their marriage or that any of their other children present any problems at all.

It seems that human cultures often take one group that appears to be different from the majority and make them the focus of everyone else's dislike or concern, attributing to them the source of all communal pain. Prejudice has its psychological roots in this desire to create a scapegoat who will be destroyed for the sins of the nation. (In ancient Greece, and in long-ago Jerusalem, there was just such a ceremony, in which a goat or ram was sacrificed to purify the tribe.)

In families we sometimes see one child who may be less able to control his impulses or different in some way from the others. By being constantly in trouble, he directs all attention toward himself and away from the real problems in the family, usually those between the adults. In family treatment we see that once the parents are helped to face their own quarrels and disappointments with each other, the sleeping, eating, or learning problems of the marked child clear up quickly. It is as if the child were expressing in a self-destructive code the angers that are hidden within the entire family.

Families in an effort to maintain the balance and status quo of their life will let one of the children act as a safety valve, causing tension that distracts the parents from their real concerns with each other. It is amazing how children understand without spoken words or open directions the innermost needs of parents and will follow these unspoken directions even to behave badly or to suffer, to keep the family system balanced. Parents with one difficult child may want to review their marriage, to try to talk openly with each other about their feelings toward each other. Scapegoating may be fairly common in families that have forgotten how to tell each other the important things. Most families who are letting one child become the focus of their discontents need an objective eye to help them rethink their family design.

Homosexuality

We have placed our discussion of homosexuality in a section on developmental difficulties because most parents will be concerned at signs of homosexuality in their children. Society pressures, even hounds, the different child, creating other painful symptoms. The scientific evidence is not clear. We do not know if homosexuality is in and of itself an illness, a problem, or merely an alternative path. We can understand some of the developmental events in the life of the homosexual child and some of the hurdles he faces. We can recognize some few conditions that seem to be conductive to homo-sexual development in children with such a genetic make-up, but explanations of first causes and final judgements will have to wait for further advances in the study of the human mind.

By the age of six, some little boys will be interested in Barbie Dolls instead of football games. They may be interested in playing with the girls in their class. They may avoid games that involve roughness or any perceived danger. They may follow their mother's interest in math instead of their father's bent for literature. The fact is that these boys are clearly identified as "sissies." Other boys will make fun of them and they will begin to feel that they are different and "not right," "not normal."

Recent studies that have followed these boys into adulthood indi-cate that at least two-thirds of them become open homosexuals. In studies done of homosexual men, the vast majority reported that they were "sissy boys" who felt themselves to be different and in social disgrace from the first grade on.

The origins of homosexual development go deep into the earliest years of childhood, where they link up with constitutional, genetic factors to spin development in the direction of identification with the parent of the opposite sex and erotic feelings for the parent of the same sex. Here we cannot yet separate apart the contributions of nature and nurture. We do know that little boys who are given no opportunity to develop affection and companionship with their fathers are at risk. We know that little boys whose mothers prefer girls and discourage activity, exploration, and independence are at risk. We know that males who have experienced physical pain and illness in the first years of life are at risk. We know too that some children are brought up in homes where all these situations have occurred and yet they are fully identified as males and heterosexuals. There seem to be no simple causative explanations. We have only hints of directions taken and opportunities for heterosexuality passed over.

What we do know is that by six years of age the erotic life of a child is clearly pointed in one direction or another. In the years six to nine most children will experience a lowering of sexual drive and an increase of disguised fantasies. The homosexual child will have a fantasy life in which he is rescued by a strong male or protected by a knight in shining armor. He will imagine triumphs for himself that have to do with some male admiring him and giving him presents. He may identify with Dorothy in *The Wizard of Oz* instead of Luke Skywalker.

We believe that a different kind of homosexuality can develop in little boys who have been frightened or rejected by their mothers. They may not lose their male identification but still turn away from girls. While at age six most boys turn away from girls and band together, some boys avoid girls permanently. These boys will be happy in male company and in male activities. Only later when the other fellows turn back toward women will they feel the discomfort of their different sexual orientation.

There are many different kinds of homosexual men and there are many different kinds of homosexual children. In the elementary school years, some of them are in jeopardy because they appear different from others and attract the unreasonable cruel scorn that grows in our nation's playgrounds. Other boys, equally directed away from heterosexual activity, will ride out their childhoods unnoticed by others and very likely not knowing themselves that their erotic energies will remain always with men.

Female homosexuality is also set in motion before the child's sixth birthday. Little girls who identify with their fathers and have erotic feelings toward their mothers will likely become among the women who choose female partners in later life. All little girls have the hard task of removing love from their mothers, where it first bloomed, and turning it toward their fathers. Some little girls never make this switch, either because of constitutional factors or because they were frozen in the relationship with their mothers. A mother who refuses to let a child go, a mother who has abandoned a child or abused and neglected her, may create such a need for mothering that the girl cannot mature, separate, and focus her attention on others.

Our society is basically tolerant of a little girl who acts like a tomboy (most tomboys later identify as females) and through the early school years the homosexual girl will go unnoticed. Her fantasy life may be different from the girl down the block but her behavior will probably not mark her out for ridicule. She may pretend to herself that her future lies in marriage and child rearing while at the same time she will be building a method to distance herself from these unwanted roles. She may also have wild crushes on female teachers or fellow students that stimulate her fantasy life and allow her to imitate the interests and values of one woman after another.

These crushes in girls after ten are common enough; but for younger girls, they may have a special energy and are not preambles to a dating life. They are in fact the beginning of the real thing. Since crushes are so common they should not be any cause for concern by parents. It is only later, in adolescence or adulthood, that retrospectively one can identify the beginnings of homosexuality in the female child.

Psychotherapy for these children and their families may redirect some of the fathers to spend more time with their sons. It may help mothers to see ways in which they are leading their sons and daughters away from good feelings about their own bodies and about their mates. The children themselves can learn to feel better, safer, less overwhelmed by their fear that they will be harmed in revenge for their own anger. But changing sexual orientation is a long and difficult matter that cannot always be accomplished even by the most experienced of therapists.

Biology has its own claim—and genetics certainly play a significant role in sexual orientation. Events of early childhood that affect sexuality are grooved deep in the layers of each soul, the chemistry of each body, and are hard to alter. While it would be a very unusual thing to find a parent who was pleased with the homosexual development of his child, some of us must come to accept that this is the only possible direction for a particular child. If a child feels unloved, unwanted, and unaccepted because of a sexual orientation that has become obvious, then all kinds of secondary symptoms are sure to develop. The child who might have been strong, creative, and productive in many areas of life suffers unnecessary crippling emotional pain. This, at least, is within the power of every parent and therapist to avoid.

We also have to remember that all human beings have wishes and thoughts that are potentially homosexual. We all have moments when a homosexual erotic feeling or fantasy emerges. Children can alter the direction of their sexuality again in adolescence, when the emotional turmoil of that period permits new solutions to old problems. Studies have shown that over one-third of boys who had extreme effeminate behavior at age six developed heterosexually later. It is then possible that all by himself a child who appears to be headed for a homosexual life choice will shift energies and focus in the teen years.

When considering therapy, parents and therapists will question the entire life experience of each child. Does he have friends? Does she work well in school? Is he suffering from other fears or is she too quiet or too aggressive? Does he seem sad or angry too much of the time? Sexual misdirection is often accompanied by symptoms that will cause the child a lifetime's troubles no matter where the final sexual destination lies.

Therapy should not be started if the child is happy, doing well, and only shows signs of sexual identity confusion. Remember that our society still creates overly rigid sexual designs to which it expects everyone to conform, and our most imaginative, inventive souls may have difficulty staying within these lines. Venturing across those lines should be applauded, not cured. Some children have a genetic predisposition toward homosexuality: if their parents support them well, they can mature into self-confident and loving human beings. Therapy is only for the child who is unhappy, slowed down in his emotional development in several areas of his life, and imprisoned by his own anxieties and fears. Many adult homosexuals are happy with their sexual partners and content with their lives. If society did not harass them, many more would surely be so.

Stuttering

If a child is stuttering by the time he enters first grade, there is little chance that the difficulty will be easily outgrown. The child who stutters develops odd mannerisms to cover up the stutter and to break the word blockage. Some children will take deep breaths and open their mouths wide or move an arm or a leg in a sudden peculiar gesture. These mannerisms, coupled with the difficulty in speaking freely, make it hard for a child to feel comfortable around other children. Stutterers tend to be shy, quiet, and often withdrawn. They speak in class as little as they can. Other children of course pull away from them because they appear different, wounded in some way, and alien.

The stutterer is not in control of his own speech, and therefore he is apt to feel helpless and weak in many other areas as well. He feels unequal and bad. Stuttering appears to affect four times as many boys as girls. In many instances it will spontaneously disappear as the child matures; in others it can be a lifelong handicap. We do not yet have an organic or psychological explanation for this problem. It has been suggested that the stutterer is a child who has trouble letting go and holds on to his words as a much younger child might to his bowel movements. This child has simply changed the part of his body in which the struggle to give up or to retain takes place. Although this is a nice theory, we don't have any hard evidence for it. Some psychotherapists have suggested that the stutterer has an unusual problem with expressing anger and that this anger has gotten caught in his speech and turned against himself. Others have pointed out that stutterers seem to have a confusion of sexual identity and that their uncertainty whether they wish to be male or female leads to an unwillingness to complete words or sentences. These, too, are interesting but unproven theories.

When one thinks about the intricate and complex nervous system actions that are required for normal speech, it doesn't seem so surprising that sometimes the multi-millions of cells, connections, and electrical impulses might go astray, resulting in the interrupted, beleaguered speech of the stutterer. We do not yet know the interaction of biological and psychological cause but we do know that there are unavoidable emotional reprecussions for the stutterer. It is with these that psychotherapy can be of help, and it is to the understandably anxious mother and father of the child who stutters that psychotherapists can offer support and guidance. We would certainly recommend speech therapy with a qualified speech therapist. Speech therapists have many methods of helping the stutterer to deal with his handicap. Some children will be cured altogether. However, both psychotherapy and speech therapy, while helpful, frequently do not succeed in creating a normal flow of words.

The Child Who Chooses Not to Speak

There are a few children who will not speak to strangers and may maintain a vow of silence in school for many years. This is a very serious problem because it cuts a child off from the outside world and ties her ever closer to her family. The symptom is a reflection of some severe disorder in the child's capacity for independence. It can also be an awesome measure of the depth of a battle between a parent who wishes the child to speak and a child who stubbornly holds back words. In some instances it accompanies the beginning of a severe breakdown of all the child's relations with reality and is part of a package of madness.

As we've seen, many small children around the age of three or four will turn their backs on strangers and hide behind their mothers. Many of these shy children will be silent for several weeks on entering nursery school and will be totally quiet in any new situation, be it at the dentist or the birthday party of a friend. But normally this shyness, which is a kind of continuation of the separation anxiety normal in infants and extended in some particularly sensitive children, fades in the first months of school. While these children may never be among the most outgoing of their group, they will after several months speak up and speak freely.

If a child fears being abandoned if she moves away from her mother, if a child feels that the outside world is threatening and her only choice is to cling to her parent, if she is so angry at that parent that she is afraid any move away might result in her abandonment, then she may choose to protect the closeness with her mother by remaining silent. Keeping speech from others becomes a form of power, a form of holding on, getting attention, and frustrating others' intentions. A child who has not had enough chance to assert herself, who feels overwhelmed with demands and controls, might just resort to silence as a means of self-assertion.

Some children who refuse public speech experienced a great deal of pain or shock just at the time that speech was developing in their lives. They may have lost a parent or been hospitalized for painful surgery. These children may associate speech with their pain and avoid it as a way of undoing the terrible thing that happened to them.

Often children are caught in some battle between their parents, who are using the child, giving her the message that other people are to be avoided, tying the child close to them as the marriage is threatened.

Behavioral therapy sometimes can help remove the symptom but psychotherapy has a better chance of getting at the structural causes of the problem. Some children cannot be treated at home. Only in a hospital setting, when new people and new ways of reaching them are tried, does the symptom fade away. Often psychotherapy is successful in that the child will speak to everyone except the therapist. Since it doesn't matter if the therapist is forever cut off from communication with her, the work is considered complete. Except for those children in whom this symptom is simply part of the disintegration of mind that comes with madness, it is a treatable although alarming condition.

The Child Who Has Too Many Accidents

There is no hard evidence showing that some children really do have accidents over and over again for psychological reasons. Studies that have been done have been disproved by other studies and the assumptions made several decades ago about self-destructive behavior in children have not been easy to prove. However, accidents do remain the major cause of death in childhood, and it does seem likely that for some children who suffer from guilt and fear of punishment, the temptation to climb too far out on a limb, to chase a ball across the street, to take a turn on their bike a little too fast, may well be there. Some children are just more active, curious, and explorative than others; they will have more accidents than their more cautious, sedentary brothers and sisters. On the other hand, if a child does seem to be in constant peril, repeatedly breaking bones or spraining ankles, then a parent might want to investigate the possibility that this child is in some kind of emotional trouble and is experiencing anger and guilt in uncontrollable proportions.

If the accidents were caused or encouraged by the inner drama of the child, other signs of disturbance would surely be there. The child might have learning difficulties or sleep problems or trouble making friends; or he may indulge in a package of rituals meant to ward off the impulses that might break through on a bike ride or a tree climb. But it would be ridiculous to jump to the conclusion that an otherwise symptom-free child is causing all his mishaps because of misdirected anger. He may just be unlucky or clumsy or have a slightly immature sense of judgment.

The Fat Child

An overweight one-year-old is a candidate for lifelong obesity. The child who has somehow mixed up the signals of hunger with those of fear and anger is at great risk of eating too much, too often. We don't know exactly how the infant and the young child confuse stomach contractions, which indicate biological hunger, with other sensations of fear and worry and rage. But we do know that these can become tangled up with the soothing, happy feelings that accompany eating, provoking long struggles over food and weight.

Some parents are perhaps too willing to substitute a cookie or a bottle for the attention that a child requires. A baby needs to be held in one's arms, talked to, played with, or touched. If that baby only gets juice or sweet crumbs in his mouth, he may confuse his own biological and psychological wants, and learn to use food to satisfy needs and feelings that are far better soothed by conversation, by contact. At a certain stage of development all children may bite, but most go on to learn other more effective ways of expressing their feelings. For some the biting response, the chewing, and the nibbling continue to be a way to drain off anger and to keep hidden the bad feelings they may have. The proverbial jolliness of the fat person is not just a disguise but reflects an absence of the irritable, cranky, self-assertive behavior that most of us can't avoid merely by consuming a box of Oreos.

The fat child is in trouble with his schoolmates, partly because he looks different and all differences mark a child as vulnerable. The fat child is also apt to be less competent in athletics, which is the arena in which children create their pecking orders between the ages of six and ten. The fat child is apt to withdraw from competitive play and by exercising less become even fatter. The fat child looks in the mirror and does not like what he sees: he thinks of himself as less handsome, less beautiful, less worthwhile, less admirable than his age mates. These bad feelings about himself stir up anxiety—and the way to dampen anxiety is another trip to the icebox. The cycle is a hard one to break. Bad feelings also make the child angry and he may not know what to do with that anger, whom to punish for his despair. He may turn the anger back against himself by letting himself get fatter, a punishment that fits the crime.

Some heavy children become masters of the social situation. As clowns, they make a place for themselves in the group by acting outlandishly. Some children learn other skills such as music, chess, or art, and turn their energy toward mastery of things that they can control, unlike their eating, which is controlling them. Some children, however, will show other symptoms of disturbance that follow their bad feelings about themselves. They may suffer from nightmares, bedwetting, fears of animals or robbers. They may become afraid of new situations and reluctant to leave their mother's side.

Excess weight in a child, although an indication of trouble, is not in itself a reason for psychotherapy. We would look at the child's overall happiness, his capacities for friendship, for work, for pleasure. We would see how she was sleeping and how independent she was for her age group. Sometimes something within a child's soul does get out of kilter and then, given time, corrects itself. Some children suffer from pudginess or even real obesity in the elementary school years, then later manage to make adjustments themselves that bring them back to the proper weight and a stronger psychological balance.

For other children the obesity is a loud and clear alarm, accompanied by other problems. For these children an evaluation by a trained professional would be an excellent idea.

The Very Thin Child

Some few children get themselves stuck in battles with their mothers over what, when, and how much to eat. These children may actively resist food and will certainly become picky eaters. Mealtimes can become the focus of an endless battle, with an increasingly anxious parent trying to ensure adequate nutrition and a fierce child determined to assert herself and resist as long and as much as possible.

When this battle has continued into and after the child's sixth year, we see a very skinny child. We also see a child who is not enjoying food in a normal way. The things that go into the mouth have become enemy objects, emissaries from a mother who wishes capitulation. Taste, texture, sweetness, the joys of pizza and the pleasures of M. & M.s escape this child.

This behavior in a young child does not usually lead to the dangerous kind of self-starvation that one sees in the early teen years. But the child will in all likelihood eat so little that she may lose a few inches in height she might otherwise have had. Because of her skinny legs and small frame, she will be less able to participate in sports and physical activities. She will look upon food as potentially dangerous stuff that might be forced down her throat at a friend's house or at a school cafeteria. Her puberty may be delayed. But she will still eat enough to survive and mature.

This problem is usually seen in otherwise compliant children who do everything else to please and delight their mothers. Such children are often too good, having learned that their safety depends on expressing not too much independence and no anger. They have mothers with high standards and ambitions who insist on excellent performances from their children at all times. Only the table expresses the tension between the pair. The child soon learns that she can get back at the mother, frighten her by not eating, control her by forcing her to fix those few foods on her menu that are acceptable. Mother and daughter become locked in a kind of duet about what goes in the mouth, which can be a replay of those battles that may have taken place around the toilet.

This, too, is a symptom that may disappear as the child moves further away from the mother's orbit and wants to be accepted among friends as an equal. Undereating reflects some disturbance in the mother–child pair, some struggle that is going on for dominance and freedom. But without other symptoms such as night fears, bed-wetting, school failures, social isolation, excessive fears of dogs or the dark, one would watch such a child and see if a balance can't be achieved by the child for herself. The eating battle may subside as she joins the school newspaper, as she spends two weeks at Girl Scout camp, as she becomes a champion jacks player and no longer needs the attention her eating habits have brought. Her desire to be one of the group, just like the others, may lead her to munch on potato chips, widen her menu, and gain so she will be more like her friends.

Very often the parents of skinny children have themselves had eating struggles with their own mothers. Feeding is one of the areas where patterns of family behavior seem unfortunately to repeat themselves generation after generation.

Illness

Asthma, allergies, and colitis are the most serious of the illnesses of childhood that some professionals consider caused, partially caused, or aggravated by emotional factors. Many children suffer at one time or another from stomach aches, rashes, sneezing fits, headaches, or bone pains that seem to have no physical basis. We know that the mind and body are by no means separate entities and that emotional stress has its reflections in increased heartbeat, tissue strain, meta-bolic changes. On the other hand, such illnesses have not been con-clusively linked to psychological problems. While teasing hints of connections between repressed anger and specific symptoms remain, no absolute evidence has been offered showing the pathways and the direct effect of mental disturbance on body health. We would assume that there are some connections between emotional balance and physical health, but we would never dismiss the importance of the physical approach. We would insist that all children affected by a psychologically implicated illness always be treated with the full arse-nal of appropriate medicine.

When medicine alone seems unable to cure a child, and when the emotional climate of the home seems to be damaging, we would recommend a psychiatric consultation. We know that infants left for even a few days by their parents tend to come down with viruses, rashes, and other minor illness. We also know that widows and widowers almost all become sick within the first year of mourning and that widowers in large numbers die in the year immediately following the death of their wives. The pains of the body originate occasionally within the mind.

Therapists working with asthmatic children have observed that frustration and anger, unwanted feelings threatening to surface, tend to precede asthma attacks that take place in the therapist's office. Children in therapy will have episodes of diarrhea, stomach cramps, nose bleeds, or headaches in the midst of therapy sessions when the subject has become too painful for the child to tolerate. These will quickly subside as the therapist is able to help the child understand his feelings and express them in words.

Psychosomatic illnesses have a way of working with the child to control the parents. Asthma is one of those childhood plagues that force the child's mother to pay close attention to him, to be concerned and connected. Asthma has been thought by some professionals to be related to a child's inability to separate himself from his mother. The first separation in life is after all the newborn baby's act of drawing his first breath into his untested lungs.

Asthmatic children can easily become overprotected and can consider themselves helpless and in mortal danger beyond the actual handicap of their illness. It becomes hard for the casual observer to untangle the cause and effect of the child's anxiousness and the mother's worry. Some asthmatic children have improved dramatically when they have been hospitalized far from home without access to their mothers. Other children have not been helped at all by physical distance from their parents.

There is no simple relationship between emotional disturbance and the progression of asthma. The connections have proved to be more complicated than was first thought. At this point we do not know whether allergies, stomach ulcers, or colitis are truly expressions of rage turned on a biologically weak spot or are random attacks on a particular child's body, followed by emotional problems that the illness creates. Either way, families of children with these illnesses may want to seek some help. They need to find ways to protect their vulnerable child without binding him or being bound by him in a suffocating relationship.

Allergies such as hives and eczema, sneezing attacks and coughing fits, are possibly related to emotional distress. A child who suffers from these symptoms severely should be evaluated by a psychiatrist. Some children have been dramatically cured of these troubles by psychotherapy. However, we are still not able to say that hives, eczema, or respiratory failures are caused directly by a specific emotional problem. Through treatment of many affected children we have learned that anger and fear that cannot be openly expressed tend to make their way along underground paths. When children have understood some of their inner conflicts, come to terms with their sexual urges, and are in trusting relationships with others, many but not all of these rashes, sneezes, and coughs disappear.

All this is equally true of the unexplained stomach aches that affect as many as 10 percent of school-age children on any given day. Harold has pain each morning before he goes to school; the pain clears up in an hour if his mother lets him stay home. Mary has violent cramps every time she is expected to visit her divorced father; the cramps subside if the visit is canceled. These children experience real physical pain. If it persists, we would want Mary and Harold seen by a psychotherapist so that they do not develop the habit or the pattern of attacking their own bodies when they feel under terrible pressure or distress.

Arthritis

Some people have suggested that rheumatoid arthritis, a disease of childhood that leads to frequent fevers and muscle weakening, is also caused by emotional distress. There is no clear evidence for this, although it is true that any child who experiences pain, crippling, and hospitalizations is at risk of developing emotional disturbance. His trust in the world, sense of worth, and safety have all been violated. Naturally he will cling longer to dependent childish ways, naturally he may be afraid of expressing anger, expecting worse punishments to fall down on his head. Prolonged physical illness must leave some mark on a child's soul and such a child needs special encouragement to reach out and explore. He may need special help in reaching for a healthy way to express his fury at an unkind fate.

Diabetes

Diabetes is a disease of childhood whose cause has not been connected with psychosomatic problems. While the child is being treated, however, many emotional problems can arise. The diabetic child has to endure so many injections, has to learn how to inject himself, and is therefore in some danger of becoming erotically attached to the giving and receiving of pain. The anger that a child in this situation feels can grow too large for the child to comfortably contain. He may then do destructive things to himself, such as break his diet or skip his shot.

Wheezing and Hyperventilation

Some very anxious, fearful children do clearly express their agitation with wheezing and with hyperventilation. They may feel dizzy or faint, they may feel that they can't get enough air, they may feel a tingling in their arms or legs. They may feel numb and sometimes they actually faint. These symptoms are not diseases in the usual sense. They are clear physical signs of fear. If a child hyperventilates when her best friend has just told her she no longer wants to be best friends, we understand what has happened. If a child begins to wheeze when asked to spend the night at her grandmother's house so the parents can go off for the weekend together, we understand. Wheezing and hyperventilating are not serious problems. The physical difficulties clear up quickly as the anxiety level subsides. A child who is having frequent trouble with breathing may very well have too high a degree of fear, too anxious an inner atmosphere. Only if such a child had several other problems as well would we suggest a psychiatric evaluation.

Hysterical Symptoms

Some physical symptoms are directly produced by certain kinds of emotional conflict. These we call conversion symptoms. A little girl is suddenly unable to move her legs and the doctor finds no organic cause for this dramatic and terrible paralysis. The psychiatrist, however, finds that the child wants to be wheeled around like her newborn baby brother. When the jealousy of the baby is investigated and brought out into the open, the paralysis disappears as magically and as instantly as it arrived. A little boy has been told by his mother that if he plays with his penis, he will go blind. One morning he wakes up and cannot see. The doctor finds nothing wrong with his eyes but the child truly cannot see. A psychiatrist finds that the child has decided to blind himself because he was guilty about his nighttime transgressions. When the mother and child both come to a more reasonable understanding about masturbation and guilt, the child immediately is restored to the sighted world.

These physical symptoms were far more common in Victorian days than they are now. They stem from the process of pushing away bad feelings mixed with a lot of sexual ignorance and fear. Today, these conversion symptoms are less common. In Western culture, we have learned for the most part to live more comfortably with our children's anger and their sexuality.

The Hypochondriacal Child

Some children become frightened that something is wrong with their bodies. They are always producing symptoms of one kind or another that bring them to the pediatrician's office. They miss a lot of school and their fears make them cautious with other children. They will spend a lot of time thinking about illness. They may have frequent headaches and stomach aches and leg pains, or they may become frightened of germs and begin to cry if someone near them on a bus coughs or sneezes.

This child is using physical illness to ensure continued attention from his mother, who most probably has her own excessive concerns about health. Through his hypochondriacal symptoms, the child expresses the fear that he might be damaged physically, that he is not as strong or as safe from harm as other children. He probably is somewhat babyish and clinging, and likes to have his mother look at and tend his body in ways another child his age has long abandoned. He may be feeling guilty because of his continued erotic feelings for his mother. This guilt makes him afraid that somehow he will be damaged or hurt for his forbidden thoughts. He may assume that his body should be punished for his secret thoughts.

We are all vulnerable to fears about our health: every child and adult will have a hypochondriacal thought or two each week. But if the concerns get out of hand, if most of the time we can't push our fears away and live each day as if we were never going to fall sick, then something has gone wrong. The hypochondriacal child suffers from unruly feelings that need professional evaluation. The sick child receives some extra babying, some secondary attention that all children crave. We must be sure that our children do not buy that attention at too high a cost to their natural vitality.

Sleep Disorders

Normally the child of six begins to have an increasing number of dreamless nights. The nightmares that woke her frequently in the earlier years seem magically, wonderfully to have vanished for the most part. At this age children will report dreams that are more and more elaborate. They tell us that they observe themselves dreaming while they sleep, and have a clear sense of what is dream and what is reality. The nightmares they have reflect earlier developmental struggles. If these nightmares continue until the child is eight years or older, we know that they are signs of inner conflicts that have not yet been properly resolved. A child of nine who dreams of robbers kidnapping him and killing him or of witches boiling him in their soup is still caught in the triangular love affair with one of his parents, still concerned about retaliation and guilt.

An occasional nightmare, a slip back into old conflicts triggered by a move, a new school, the birth of brother or sister, or a divorce, are quite normal, but constant nightmares at this age are a cause for concern. They mean that the emotional work of the earlier period has not gone well and the child is still plagued by guilt and fear that will show itself in other areas of life. A child of eight with frequent nightmares will certainly have other symptoms of disturbance; he may have trouble making friends or trouble learning. He may have many daytime fears or endless rituals that prevent him from enjoying himself freely. Sleeping well, like eating well, is an important accomplishment on the path to adulthood.

Night terrors are a form of dreaming in which a child will partially wake after experiencing in deep sleep a terrible fear which has no remembered content and no recall in the morning. These night terrors tend to be outgrown by most children around the age of eight. They are thought to be caused by massive amounts of uncontrolled anxiety that have broken into the child's mind at stage 4 sleep. This happens because of some some immaturity of the central nervous system, which has failed to keep the lid on the terrors we all carry within us. Although the child may wake screaming and frantic, these night disturbances are not signs of trouble. They are most often outgrown and unrelated to the general stress that a child is under. The nervous system matures at different times and in different ways for many children. Night terrors, while alarming for parents, are not symptomatic of emotional or neurological difficulty.

Sleepwalking, too, is an odd symptom that appears to be a disturbance of the nervous system. It sometimes runs in families and is most often outgrown before a child reaches his twelfth birthday. It will occur when the child is under particular tension; a fight with a best friend, a swimming meet the next day, a move, or an impending separation can set it off.

Sleepwalking frightens parents because the children look like zombies and appear to be only half alive as, glassy-eyed, they float through the house. This is not a symptom of a disturbed child and the parents need not make any special fuss about it. Very often it happens to sons whose fathers also walked in their sleep as children. It is perfectly safe to wake such a child gently and lead him back to bed. Children usually do not seem to hurt themselves at these times. A child should not be teased or made self-conscious about the symptom. He can be told that this is the way his mind works and that in time he will no longer walk in his sleep. If parents react calmly, sleepwalking will disappear, leaving no more effect on the child than early teething pains or diaper rash.

Part Four
SPECIAL SITUATIONS

Twins

Everyone has special feelings about twins. In some primitive cultures, their birth was considered a sign of the goodwill of the gods. They were given special privileges, worshipped as reflections of the deity. In other cultures the birth of twins was considered a sign of evil triumphant, an omen of coming disaster. The second twin was often put to death; if a boy and girl were born, the girl was killed.

In modern America, parents show vestiges of both responses. Some mothers will be delighted and proud to have produced two babies at once, while others will feel there is something unnatural and freakish about the event. They will feel insulted, demeaned, marked out by the special birth. Many mothers have both sets of feelings simultaneously.

There is no question that the economic and emotional burden of parenthood is doubled with the birth of twins. Parents who would struggle valiantly with one baby are overwhelmed by the responsibility and constant work of two. Mothers must make endless decisions as to which baby is more in need of food, dryness, cuddling, talking to; at any given moment the other must wait. This apportioning of time and affection creates guilt in the mother and amplifies fears that she is not serving her babies well. In our society there is, however, a lot of excitement and pleasure taken in twin babies. Whenever the new mother takes her babies out in the carriage, strangers and store-keepers, passing grandmothers and the postmen, will all come over to wonder and beam. We are all fascinated with the idea of a double image, of a self that has a mirror, or a shadow that keeps us company and protects against the loneliness of each unique existence. For some mothers the additional attention they receive fuels their capacity to carry the double burden. They sail through the first years of their babies' lives with the pride of a new Nobel Prize winner.

There are dangers for twins that place them at greater risk than single babies. They tend to be smaller than average and frequently are premature, which leads to their spending weeks or months in incubators out of their mother's arms. This slows down their intellectual and emotional growth. The death rate for twins is higher than for the general population of newborns. One in six twins will die at birth or in the following weeks. We know that the average I.Q. for twins is slightly below the national norm. Eleven percent of all twins begin to stutter before their seventh birthday. Because of the workload on the mother, the continual guilt she feels from choosing one baby over another, and the extreme exhaustion the care of two babies provokes, mothers of twins are in danger of becoming depressed and withdrawn. They may lose emotional contact with their babies while still providing adequate physical care. This depression places the babies at risk of emotional malnourishment and the disorders of infancy that follow the mother's failure to connect to her baby.

Twins constantly vie with each other for maternal attention. But as they become aware of each other, around the sixth or seventh month of life, they begin to use each other as comforts, as always available Teddy bears to reassure themselves that they are not abandoned or alone. They begin to copy each other. They may develop a secret language, which excludes everybody else including their parents. The need to communicate with other children comes slowly; they tend to lag behind in matters of self-assertion, will, and the capacity to do things on their own.

There are two kinds of twins: the monozygotic, in which two infants have grown out of one fertilized egg; and the dizygotic, in which two separate eggs were fertilized at the same time in one womb. These create either identical or fraternal twins. Fraternal twins are no more alike than other siblings but identical twins have exactly the same genes. Biologically speaking, they are two of the same person. This always arouses some fascination and envy in other children, who fantasize about their own lost twin, the loving companion they would have liked to have. It also evokes a kind of fear, since other children become confused over which twin is which, and become uneasy that their own identity might also be duplicated or disappear.

Whether the twins are identical or fraternal, it seems the best idea to give twins non-alliterative names; to dress them differently; and to place them in different classes in school as soon as possible. Twins need to grow separate identities, to make different friends, and to find out ways in which each is a special and unique person. None of this should violate their unquestioned special bond with each other. Twins will often think the same thoughts, have similar experiences even though they are miles apart, repeat in their own lives the patterns and choices of the other. This seems natural.

We want to help twins to avoid the lags in growth, the intellectual and social limitations, that come from a parental assumption that they are the same person, or from a prolonged period of isolation with each other that encourages the fusion of one twin into another instead of the separation into distinct selves. Parents of twin babies must find the time to talk to and play with each one separately, encouraging their interest in the world of adults and other children, and providing them with tempting activities and pleasures outside the twin relationship.

It is hard for parents to forgo the charm of twin children dressed in matching sweaters, gloves, and scarfs. The parents of twins, who have worked twice as hard as other parents, seem to need and deserve the additional attention this brings. But in the long run the parents' pride and pleasure in their children will be enhanced when they can see that they have nurtured two separate, wonderful people.

The Blind Child

The child who is blind or nearly blind from birth onward suffers not only from the deprivation of sight but often from the effect that her blindness has on her mother. The tragedy of a blind child is compounded by the mother's grief and depression, and by her consequent inability to feel the warmth and love that babies require for their survival. Mothers are often repelled by their blind babies' faces, which seem blank and odd. They are guilty and ashamed of these feelings. This shame only increases their anger and intensifies their dislike of the baby. Many mothers of blind babies feel that they will be unable to give all the extra care that a blind child requires. They feel they have been unjustly chosen to bear this terrible weight. All the normal feelings of anger at a dependent infant affect these mothers three times over. They are entitled to their feelings; there is no question that the birth of a blind child is a cosmic injustice, worthy of the deepest of rages and the wildest of cries.

Blind babies show the same social smile that sighted babies develop around two to three months. Their smile appears in relation to the mother's presence, but it is a pale smile and often disappears after a short while. Since the baby does not see a smiling face in return, this all-important gesture of human communication is lost. For the mother, this unsmiling face increases her sense of alienation and estrangement. The baby's face remains impassive no matter what she does. Blind babies stay alert only in a quiet, passive, listening posture most of their waking time. They do not reach out for objects that they cannot see and they cry less than other babies. Until they are nine or ten months old they do not use sound to orient themselves, to turn toward a voice, or to reach out for a object that has a ringing bell on it. All this time the mother feels useless, cut out of the baby's life, angry and disappointed at the damaged child she has received.

Because blind babies appear to be content to be left alone, they often are ignored for long periods of time. The care they are given is hurried and without tenderness or expressiveness. As the child receives so little stimulation from the outside world, her attention returns to the inner workings of her body. Blind babies keep their hands in their mouths, place their heads on the floor listening to vibrations, or touch themselves in order to become oriented to the world. After nine months of age, blind babies will begin to use their hands as expressively as other babies use their faces. If you watch a blind baby lovingly finger the nose and lips of her mother, you will see the equivalent of a joyous smile of recognition.

The mother's capacity to recognize that the baby is using her hands to reach out to her is crucial for the relationship between them to survive and flourish. The baby does not reach up when the mother enters the room the way a sighted child will after three or four months. But if the mother can see the baby's fluttering fingers as communication, as connection, she will encourage the baby to touch her and she will feel needed and wanted. These feelings in turn will make her even more sensitive to her baby.

During the first two years of life, children experience many intellectual challenges, involving both things and people, which encourage the growth of abstract thought and creative invention. The blind child necessarily is cut off from much of that experience. It takes him a long time to conceive of the idea that a ball is still in the world after it has rolled away from him.

Blind babies rarely crawl. They do not see objects they want that would stimulate them to move forward or backward. They do not seem to express the kind of normal anger we see in infants fifteen months of age and older. They do not tend to bite or tear or scratch. It seems as if the effort to feel safe each moment drains all the energy of the soul away.

Many blind children, if encouraged and cared for by parents who are alert to their special needs and who have made a caring, loving connection to their babies, will walk at about two. They will talk also at about the same age, but they are very slow learning the pronouns "I," "you," "he," and "she." Clearly, it is harder for the blind child to understand the concept of a single self, of another person, of male and female.

Most babies will begin some time in the second year of life to play with symbols: "This doll is my baby and this carriage is a real carriage and we are going to the zoo." "This block is my hammer and I'm building a big rocket that is going to the moon." Blind children are slow to use one object to represent another and to invent and pretend. They spend a great deal of time checking on the whereabouts of their mothers and holding on to them for safety. They are understandably more afraid of abandonment than their age mates. They naturally have greater difficulty in achieving self-sufficiency—they can't tie their shoes and put on their coats as well as the sighted child.

Most young blind children develop a series of habits known as blindisms. They will knock their head continually against a chair or a wall; they will rub their eyes constantly. They may rotate their head in some rhythmic pattern, or stretch out their arms at shoulder height and wiggle their wrists or fingers in odd ways. These habits are thought to be the blind child's way of discharging tension and anger that other children release by running around, jumping, knocking things over. The rigid movements the blind child shows are evidence of the inner constrictions, the fear that holds the blind child as still as possible.

There are now experts trained to help mothers prevent the intellectual and emotional retardation that has often accompanied blindness. Mothers can be taught to find ways to keep their blind babies involved in the world around them. This requires more attention and concentration than we would give a sighted infant. The results for the blind child are so rewarding, however, that we are certain every parent would want this opportunity for their child.

We may not be able to cure blindness but we can dramatically alter the quality of life for the blind child by insisting that he play with us, by working with him on his crawling, by watching his hands and learning to read them as we can read our sighted children's faces. Recognizing that certain stages of independence must be delayed for the blind child, we can nevertheless teach the child as many accomplishments as possible in order to foster the independence and self-discovery that are the glories of human life.

Mothers and fathers need support in the special care of the blind child, and they need time to recover from the shock, grief, and loss they have experienced. Groups of other parents are enormously useful in sharing their experiences and expressing their common pain. We suggest that all parents of blind infants immediately involve themselves with programs that will aid them in building an emotional closeness to their child and lead them in ways of enriching the baby's life.

Blind children at about age three or four become aware that other people have sight and they are damaged and unable to do what others can. This bitter discovery is often followed in the child by a period of mourning, of anger at his parents, who seem to have permitted this injustice. It is a hard time for parents, who understand their child's shock and disappointment. There may be a kind of regression at this time. The child who had achieved toileting may revert to soiling; the one who was walking without holding anyone's hand may suddenly insist he can't move alone. But the period of mourning seems to pass. Children accept their handicap and struggle on to find their own path.

Parents do best to share their sadness with the child and avoid statements that are unrealistic or too cheerful. The facts will have to be lived with. As the child masters more and more of his environment, his mood, his intelligence, and his social skills will all depend more on the quality of contact he has had with his mother and father than on the effects of the blindness on his soul. It is important that parents not wait to get help until their child is school age. Schools for the blind will be able to refer parents to a local center where, even in the earliest months, with the guidance of trained professionals, parents can begin intelligently to aid their child to use his own resources and his own wit. This early attention can prevent a permanent slowness of mind and can give parents a way to be with their child that will allow them to find the specialness of their baby and the joy he can give despite his handicap.

The Deaf Child

It is a severe sorrow for parents when a child is discovered to have a profound hearing loss. They have taken a baby home from the hospital who appeared normal; only gradually have their anxieties grown. The diagnosis must cut deeply into their pride in their child. Very often the bad news is followed by a period of real depression in one or both parents. This frequently strains the marriage as each partner blames the other and feels responsible themselves.

Deafness can easily be mistaken in a small baby for mental retardation. It can also look very much like an emotional disturbance in which the child rarely responds to the parent. Pediatricians tend to delay in the diagnosis out of a hope that the problem will disappear and out of a natural wish to avoid giving pain to the parents.

Deaf children lose a large part of the meaningful communication that fills the day of the hearing child. They miss the exchange of play with words with their mothers. They miss the chance to influence what will happen to them with their own words. Naturally, it is hard to explain to a deaf child why she must not do something or why she can do something later but not now. Without language, children tend to be pushed and pulled and poked. Without language, children are slow to learn to delay pleasure, to postpone action. As they grow into toddlers and enter nursery school, they tend to be way behind other children in distinguishing between wish and reality, fantasy and fact.

They are dependent on their mothers, who are protective of them but not always proud of them. They are often immature, impulsive, quick to hit or bite or strike another child. Some of them are just too good and hardly move without permission; they seem joyless and lack spontaneity. Deaf children seem to be less creative than normal children even with materials such as paper and crayon that do not depend on hearing.

As they reach school age, many deaf children whose intelligence is perfectly normal still seem to show lags in thinking abstractly. Their imaginative pretend life lacks energy. Many hold themselves rigidly and have developed all sorts of rituals to control their frightening world. Often they arrange objects in set orders and become very upset if something is out of place. Many of them seem to be unable to feel what another child feels long after others their age can do so. Unlike hearing children of the same age, they seem caught in their own world, in which they remain at the absolute center.

Professionals who work with deaf children seem to feel that there are two drastically different types. One is too good, too controlled and stiff in every way; the other behaves like Attila the Hun, attacks, has temper tantrums, and falls apart all the time. Both types of deaf children are slow to understand complex thoughts.

The major disagreements between professionals working with deaf children is whether or not to teach sign language. The argument for avoiding signing is that without this aid, the child is forced to learn to repeat sounds and to develop some speech. If they do sign, they may resist learning speech. Learning to speak without being able to hear is hard work for the young child. It requires hours of drill and these hours of drill seem to inhibit the creative play life of the child, but without the acquisition of approximately normal speech, the child is forced into the ghetto world of the deaf.

Most hearing parents are especially anxious to have their deaf child join the mainstream. Deaf children of deaf parents are more often taught sign language early and permitted to sign with their parents. These children seem to be much stronger emotionally than the deaf children of hearing parents. They do not show many of the inhibited, immature, depressed qualities of the usual deaf child. Clearly, signing early keeps the communication with parents open and increases opportunities for pleasurable contact. However, the improved mental state of the deaf child of deaf parents may be the result of less grief and disappointment over the child's handicap. Signing, while frightening and strange for the hearing parent, may be worth while if it enlivens the child's mind in those all-important early years.

It would seem that whichever form of education a parent and doctor decide to follow, the crucial factor remains keeping the love, affection, and communication between parent and child as rich and multitextured as possible.

By eight years old all deaf children seem to understand that they are handicapped and that their ears don't work like other people's. They can suffer from a loss of self-esteem; they can feel unworthy, guilty, and unlovable. It is at this point that the sensitive parent must help the child gradually to accept himself and find qualities to admire that do not depend on either hearing or speech. Residential or home education is a choice each parent must make. Some studies have shown that deaf children in a residential setting, seeing successful deaf people all around them, are more contented, learn better, and feel better about themselves. But this is a decision that each family must make in terms of how much support can be given the child and how well a particular child is able to endure the initial terror of separation from home.

Parents should not try to educate their deaf child alone. There are many specialists who have worked hard to develop techniques and methods that can make a difference. The important role of a parent is both to find the right help for her child and to give that child as much love and approval as possible. This means that parents cannot mourn too long for the perfect child they wished to have—they must take action to keep their own lives vital. This will be a major gift to their child. Most communities have support groups for parents of the deaf, which are extremely helpful both with practical advice and in healing the pain.

The Hard of Hearing

Some children are born hard of hearing, possibly losing as much as 30 or 40 percent of all sound. This deficit is frequently overlooked by parents and pediatricians. While some children will have loss in the higher frequencies only, others will be limited at all levels. Being hard of hearing makes it difficult for a child to learn well, to play with other children, to feel confident and capable. The constant effort to understand what others are saying requires special energy and concentration, leaving the child irritable and exhausted.

The hard of hearing child will have particular difficulty when there are several people talking at once or there is a lot of background noise. These children often let their minds wander away and lose the context of what is going on. They then have trouble picking it up again and may just withdraw.

Early identification is extremely important. Parents should be alerted to a possible hearing problem if their child does not respond when called unless he is looking at you. Parents can see if their child habitually turns the television set on louder than the rest of the family finds comfortable. Some children will have learning problems in school and seem friendless. Investigation will show that they have trouble hearing the teacher and the other children clearly and consistently.

Lip reading is an enormous help to these children. Many of them, if well taught, can use it to bring their hearing up to a normal level. Hearing aids are not as perfect as we would like. They may bring in too much background noise, confusing and disorienting the child. Children resist wearing the hearing aid because it marks them as different and damaged.

In all major communities there are groups for the deaf and the hard of hearing. It is crucial that these children are taught lip reading professionally as soon as possible. Groups will provide information for parents as well as support and guidance. We strongly suggest that wherever possible parents use these organizations for the valuable help they can supply.

Parents of the hard of hearing child must be alert to other developmental problems that may grow out of the child's hearing difficulty. Some children become excessively shy or withdrawn; others have trouble controlling their anger, which is understandably high in a world that so often is a puzzle to them. Parents need to watch these children and support them with extra care in their social endeavors and their school work. If there seem to be some emotional difficulties, the advice of a child psychiatrist should be sought.

With care and prompt intervention, the effects of this handicap can be kept to a minimum. The child can develop many skills, accomplishments, and satisfactions in areas unaffected by hearing loss.

Choosing a Therapist

Parents who have decided that their child needs help beyond what they can give are usually upset and concerned. Often they feel responsible, guilty, vulnerable, and unworthy. They know that something has gone wrong despite their best intentions. They are severely frightened for their child's future; suddenly many of their important decisions in life are up for reevaluation. This naturally creates additional strain in the marriage as each partner blames the other and both experience themselves as inadequate, as probable failures. In such a tense atmosphere it is hard to think logically and coolly about where and how to get help.

Behavioral therapy is a form of therapy that works to change the child's symptoms by training him to overcome fears, to condition him to accept certain controls, or to reward him for proper behavior. It does not look for reasons or explanations but rather quickly and in some instances effectively can remove the symptom that is disturbing the child. Behavioral therapy offers a quick solution for some symptoms that are fairly isolated and whose easy removal will restore the child onto a forward track. But sometimes removing one symptom only leads to the formation of another; the symptoms themselves were responses to inner tensions and struggles that do not go away by the simple disappearance of the bedwetting, the fear of dogs, the dread of school.

Before taking a child to a behavioral therapist, it would be wise to have a thorough psychological evaluation done by a trained psychologist so that you have a clear idea of where your child is in difficulty and how complicated or simple the problem appears.

Most child therapists work with the child and the family to uncover the child's misperceptions, to allow a release of feelings, and to create understanding where confusions had been. Child therapists will work from a knowledge of where your child should be in his development and what detours or false directions he may have taken. Referrals to child psychiatrists or child psychiatry clinics can come from your family doctor, from your priest, minister, or rabbi, or from a trusted family friend. In small towns or rural areas parents may have to travel great distances or settle for the one therapist working in their area. Check your nearest hospital for referrals. Consult with school principals or guidance counselors. Do not use the phone book or go to a therapist who has advertised in local papers. This can be dangerous, as he may not have the proper credentials or training.

It is very hard to make the call for the initial appointment. We have been so indoctrinated in codes of independence, of family privacy, of keeping a good face on things in public, that many families delay making that first call long after they see the necessity for it. They are ashamed; they deny what they know as long as they can because they are frightened of the bad news they may hear if they go to a doctor. In fact, making that call is one of the most protective, nurturing, courageous acts that a parent can ever perform for his child, putting his child's well-being above his own discomfort and embarrassment.

Once the connection to a therapist is made, many parents become awed and intimidated by the process of their child's therapy. They have the sense that the doctor knows something they don't know, that they have failed and the doctor has a right to take over, that doctors are powerful and magical. This is of course nonsense. Therapists come in all different stripes and some are excellent, sensitive people whose work with children combines the best of science with the best of art. Other therapists, perhaps with equally acceptable credentials, are clods who go by the rules, hide behind the authority their degree gives them, and move through the interviews with parent and child without imagination or enthusiasm. Some therapists without fancy diplomas from recognized schools are far more gifted in this work than colleagues with more training and more impressive papers on their wall.

Parents when they are upset and guilty have a hard time seeing that a particular therapist is unappealing, or slow-witted, or too rigid, or sloppy. When talking to a potential psychiatrist, parents are so easily made to feel wrong that they tend to hold back any judgments or bad feelings about the therapist. Other parents swing the opposite way: they are belligerent, defensive, and angry at the therapist for placing them in such a awkward position. They may dismiss a good doctor, a good social worker, out of misplaced anger and anxiety. It is very important to choose a good therapist for your child, one you can trust and work with and basically like. You should feel that the therapist likes you and your child. It may be worth seeing several people before deciding on one. It may take courage to turn down a particular therapist and break your next appointment with him, but this is a crucial choice. It is very important for the outcome of the therapy that you feel good about the person you have chosen. He or she will become a big part of your life in the months to come.

Make sure the therapist has been specifically trained to work with children. It is also important that when you are in his office, you feel free and comfortable to say what you want. Perhaps this person makes you feel shy, guilty, ashamed of what is going on with your child. Does she explain things to you in a way that is clear and open, or do you feel that she is hiding something from you?

It is also all right to have a personal, not entirely rational dislike of a therapist. Perhaps you hate the style of furniture in his office—you find it overly pretentious or stuffy. Perhaps you don't like the way the therapist is dressed—too flirtatiously, or like a frump. Perhaps you don't like the way they didn't answer your questions directly. Whatever the reason, don't dismiss it as unimportant. You have the right and the responsibility to choose the therapist for your child who will fit well with you and your family. In that first interview it is important to remember, no matter how upset you feel, that you are choosing the therapist; you are not applying for a job or for college, nor for admission to a club.

If after a year of therapy you do not see some improvement, do not feel that the goals of treatment as they were outlined to you initially are in motion, then you have every right and even obligation to consider a consultation with another therapist, and to make a change if that should prove to be a good idea. Every therapist is not equally effective with every child. You don't want to wait five years to find out that this particular relationship was not blooming. On the other hand if the child is over six, the therapist may wish to work with him alone, keeping the child's confidence and respecting his privacy. This may mean that the therapist will not talk to you very often and will not tell you much of anything about what is going on in the treatment. This can be frustrating for an anxious parent who now has to share her child in a most intimate way with a stranger. Many parents understandably find this difficult. They feel excluded from the relationship and distanced from their own child. But if the parent can see real improvement in the child after a year of so, and if the child is truly connected to the therapist, the parent must step back, giving the treatment time to work.

Parents tend to look upon the therapist as either a savior or a villain. The truth will lie somewhere in between. Parents must try to be as clear as possible about the value and the work of the therapy. They must support it and follow through on suggestions, and they must help the therapist in her work from time to time. But parents must also remember that the final authority and responsibility are their own. If they don't like what's going on with their child, if it seems as if nothing is happening or too much, they must bring these concerns to the therapist. At all times they are entitled to a consultation with another therapist.

Family therapy is a kind of psychotherapy in which the entire family, parents and all children, meet together and discuss their problems with each other. The child who has the symptoms is not necessarily the only one in the family in trouble. Therapists working with the entire family at once have found ways of changing the structure of that family. Who is distant, who is always wrong, what are the real quarrels, what can each member do to make himself and the others happier? Family therapy may be suitable for certain kinds of symptoms, such as eating problems, delinquency, or school fears. It is particularly helpful when the child's symptoms are disguising an unhappy marriage.

Whether one chooses family therapy or individual psychotherapy for the child, the whole family needs to be involved. Sometimes one parent or another will seek therapy for himself as he understands more about what is troubling his child. Sometimes the child with the symptoms is only expressing the troubles that mother and father, brothers or sisters are feeling. Hidden problems in a marriage, hidden withdrawals of parent from child or partner, may be revealed and resolved in the course of therapy. The therapy of the child can and should open the adults to new and better ways of being with each other, enriching family life at all levels. This should be one of the benefits of therapy no matter what the orientation of the therapist or which kind of therapy you choose.

The office of a child therapist is really a playroom. The therapist will paint with a child, play with figures in a dollhouse, allow the child to invent collisions with toy cars and to arrange the stuffed animals any way she likes. The therapist joins in the games when asked or just

394

watches the play. As the therapist understands the meaning for the child of the constant car wrecks, the black circles drawn on the page, or the doll who is always thrown in the play toilet, he will talk about the child's feelings and real experiences. But before he can do this, he must have won the child's trust and friendship. The child will have been told that the doctor will help her with her worries. After a while she will understand that playing is a form of talking about problems. Some children will sometimes talk directly with the therapist without the use of toys, paints, or pretend games. Others will always communicate indirectly.

Therapists are trained to interpret the hidden meanings of the child's play, in which desires and fears are acted out, imagined, fantasized, and embroidered. This is not as hard a science as molecular physics nor is it akin to the reading of tea leaves. Many years of training have enabled the therapist to understand the development of the child as well as the messages coded in the child's action and play. The therapist can reassure a child when he knows what really frightens her. He can correct her misperceptions of reality. He can help her to trust adults and to like herself better. He can allow her to express and explore her angry and destructive feelings, which are not permitted in the real world, outside the therapy room. He can help her to tame those feelings without hiding them so far away that they cause her trouble.

Children seem to understand that there are things you can do and say and feel in therapy that are not proper in the real world. Children working with good therapists will find that their excessive fears, their burdensome rituals, their inability to make friends, their babyishness, their loneliness, their jealousy, their stomach aches or rashes, all fade away, to be replaced by a greater freedom to be themselves, to learn about the world around them, and to be comfortable in it.

Danger from Strangers: Protecting Your Child

Every year in America some thirty thousand children are taken from their homes and abused, raped, and often killed. This appalling fact terrifies all parents. We see the distraught faces of grieving mothers and fathers on our evening news or in our morning papers, and we feel sick with reflected pain and fear. We know that there are perverse, sick, homicidal people walking our streets, sharing our buses, shopping in our stores, and going to the movies with us.

We want to protect our children from the dangerous stranger. But there are problems. We don't want them to believe that the entire adult world is treacherous and murderous. We don't want to stir up our children's own exaggerated fears. We all want our children to feel secure as they walk down the street, as they go into the grocery store, as they play in the yards or the playgrounds of our communities. Children afraid to let go of our hands, afraid to smile at the postman, afraid of the construction worker and the saleslady would be children robbed of a childhood.

While the statistics are disturbing, it would be an overreaction to imprison or to unduly frighten our children. Children up to the age of six can be calmly told not to talk to strangers, not to go anywhere with someone they don't know. But parents must understand that the problem with this instruction is that children do not always remember your rules. They may think that the man whom you said good morning to yesterday in the parking lot is not a stranger because you spoke to him. They may feel they should give someone directions because you have also told them to be helpful. They may think that if someone knows their name, that person is a friend, not realizing that their name is printed on their T-shirt or their lunch box. We would feel that the best protection for the child under six is not to be alone on a city street. They should be accompanied by an adult when they are outside or they should at the very least be with a group of children.

Above the age of six, children begin to need to go places and do things on their own. By eight or nine most city children have gradually learned to cross the street, to go to the store and make a purchase, to take a bus, and to go to a friend's house. This independence is important to them. We would tell the child who is allowed to go to the corner by himself for a candy bar that there are some very few grownups who do harm children and that he must not go anywhere with anyone he doesn't know very very well. He must not go over to a car if any grownup calls to him who isn't a close friend of the family. Children will be afraid when you tell them this. They may have nightmares for a few weeks after this conversation, but in time as they return home safely day after day they will be reassured.

We would not let children go into unsafe neighborhoods alone or even in groups of two or three. We would not let children play in isolated areas. You can tell your child that if anyone he doesn't know approaches him on the street he should run, call for help, or rush into the nearest store. However, the terrible fact is that some child abductions occur in situations no one could have predicted or protected against. We can take some precautions, but we must recognize that as with precautions against disease, flood, earthquake, and hurricane, to a large extent we must rely on luck. The police and the organizations formed for missing children advise parents to have their children's fingerprints taken and their dental records kept up to date. Parents can certainly do this. Clearly, once such information is necessary, the disaster has already occurred and the records in themselves do not serve as a shield to protect our children. The fact is that the statistics, terrible as they are, tell us that 99.9999 percent of all children are never threatened by the stranger we fear.

Sexual Abuse

The sexual abuse of children is one of the hideous facts of our culture. It leaves scars on the souls of each of its victims and it is hard to detect or prevent. We do not have exact figures on the numbers of violated children but we know that they are not as low as we had once hoped. Some researchers are claiming that as many as one child in ten has been molested. Many children have been sexually attacked by older children, young teens who are in the neighborhood or are used as baby sitters or are friends or relatives. But the overwhelming majority of children who have been so badly misused have been harmed by members of their own family: fathers, uncles, stepfathers. Most child abuse is then a flag on a tragic family situation in which all the bonds of caring and nuturing have been twisted or broken. It isn't possible to protect a child against sexual abuse by a member of his own family. The child must follow a parent; frightened and upset and guilty as he may be, his only path is acquiescence and probable silence.

It may however be possible to alert children so that they can avoid the advances of a teacher, counselor, music instructor, casual friend or acquaintance. We can tell children around the age of four or five, when they have already learned of robbers and kidnappers and bad guys, that no older person outside of the family should touch their penis or vagina or anus. We can tell children that these parts of the body are special and private and to be shared only when they are much older with someone they love. We can tell them that if anybody should want to touch them in such private places they should tell us immediately. Then the subject should be dropped. We don't want to harp on it or frighten children, the vast majority of whom will never meet a molestor. We do want to give them a way to understand what is happening if an adult should approach them. We want to give them the words to tell us what has happened or might be about to happen.

Some psychologists have suggested telling children that there is good touching and bad touching, but this can be confusing for a child and we don't want to inhibit normal expressions of affection and warmth between human beings of all ages. It is best to be specific about what shouldn't be touched and by whom.

We do not know whether the forewarned child is really better able to report abuse to his parents or not. We are not sure that he can avoid it any better than his less informed classmate, but it still seems a good idea to give your child the frame for such an experience; this may help him resist the pressure from an adult or older child.

Parents must be alert to changes in their child's behavior. If a child is suddenly not eating, having nightmares, acting up, being sullen, hitting his sister, or having bowel or bladder accidents or losing all his homework or staying alone in his room for long periods, or is unable to tolerate being alone, the parent should question the child. Something is wrong. That something could be that he had a fight with a friend, is angry at his teacher, is having trouble with math, or is upset at his lack of baseball skills. Or it could be that something especially bad is happening to him and he can't come right out and tell you. It is a parent's responsibility to try to get to the bottom of any sudden change in a child's behavior. As parents we cannot totally protect our children but if we keep a watchful eye on their days we can know if something is happening and move to stop it.

If a child tells you he has been molested by an outsider, believe him. This is something children do not make up. Help him to understand that this is not his fault and you are not angry at him. Help him to feel safe and secure and loved. He may need some extra babying or care for a while. Watch your child. If after several months you are not satisfied that he has overcome this frightening episode, then you should consider bringing him to a therapist. If he is not sleeping well, eating well, playing well, studying well, enjoying the things he had always enjoyed, he may need some help to restore his forward development. Some children can manage this kind of dreadful episode well enough and given time will balance themselves again. Other children need some assistance and therapists are well trained to intervene in such an instance.

Muggers

Many city children between the ages of six and ten are attacked by larger children, who will take bicycles, bus passes, money, and watches. It is a common urban experience, happening more often to boys than to girls. Teenagers and older children from troubled neighborhoods tend to assert their own power by attacking males from another class or another ethnic or racial group.

Children are vastly upset by these experiences because they feel helpless and enraged. Boys tend to feel that they should fight back. They worry about themselves if they have docilely handed over their property; they are ashamed of how frightened they felt. We must reassure our children that being strong does not depend on punching someone bigger or more dangerous. We must stress to them that fighting back in this situation is foolish and stupid. We should tell our children this as soon as they are moving around the city by themselves. We expect them to fight back, to stand up for themselves only in situations in which they have an equal chance, in which their attackers will not have knives or outnumber them. Despite the messages given by TV heroes, manliness is not defined by the use of fists. We must be sure our children know we feel this way before they are confronted with a potentially damaging band of hoodlums.

We can explain to a child of eight or more that some children are angry they don't have things. In many ways the world is unfair, but a good person fights the criminal by helping to make his city a better place for everyone to live. A child needs to feel that one day he can do something about the injustice of what has happened to him. Tell your child that one day he can help see that justice is done, that bullies are punished, and that people learn to treat each other with kindness. You can explain that manliness is far more than mere brute strength, encompassing moral values as well.

Expect a child who has been mugged to be difficult and ornery for a brief time. He may have nightmares or tease his younger sister cruelly. Mugging is a common situation in our cities and children learn to take it in their stride. Allow your child to be angry at the particular boys who attacked him, but help him to see that all people of the muggers' group are not his enemy or responsible for what has happened. If he learns to contain and focus his anger, he will have emerged from the experience with his human dignity enriched.

Movies

It is hard for a parent to deny their child the right to see a movie that all the other kids on the block are talking about. Ratings as they stand now give us little guidance. They don't reflect most parents' feelings about violence. Movies can be scary, brutal, and gory. Children can have nightmares from a particular scene, and they can become fearful of the dark, of robbers, of kidnappers, of things from outer space, as a result of an afternoon at the films that was intended as entertainment. Children up to the age of seven or eight are still struggling with what is real and what is not. Their fantasy life is rich and scary enough, without our further terrifying them with explicit pictures. Up to the age of seven children are still struggling to control their own angry impulses. Film violence can undermine their own efforts to push away bad thoughts, to live in the real world. We think it is worth fighting pressure from the child. We think you will be protecting your child by avoiding all but the gentlest of movies.

After the age of eight, we would relax some. Then the child can have real pleasure in being scared. There is a delight in the horrible. The child's fantasy life will no doubt contain scenes at least as grisly as those thought up in Hollywood. The latest adventure film is a must for a child who wants to take part in the games of his friends. While we wish that the movies could restrain themselves from literal violence, we don't feel that for most children over eight the scary film will have more than a passing effect. Our children understand pretending perhaps better than we do. They will not turn into snake eaters or bank robbers because they saw it on the big screen. Children have a way of closing their eyes, of turning away, of going to the bathroom or getting popcorn when the tension gets too great to bear. Parents should use some discretion and not let a fearful child attend the latest horror flick. A hyperactive child or one with problems in self-control can be overexcited by movies. For these children we would monitor the fare, steering away from the worst of the offerings.

Some movies are sad and show death or disease to children. We think it is best for a parent to go to such a film with their child so that it can be talked about. There is nothing wrong in children's experiencing sadness in the movies. They can enjoy it for the same bittersweet reasons that we do. But some films, not meant for children, present too bleak a view of the world. If a child sees one of those, you need to be there just to offer a hand to restore balance.

Don't forget how much a child learns by going to the movies. Places, facts, history, politics, anthropology, sociology are painlessly absorbed as plots unfold and scenes change. The view of the world through film may be bizarre but plenty of important information is gleaned from the silver screen. It is not very likely that your eight- or nine-year-old will think that James Bond is the all-American male or that the Pink Panther represents good police work. On the other hand, he will have seen Paris, the ski slopes of Switzerland, the dances of India, and the marketplace of Cairo. In today's world, a child without movies is like a child without books.

Common Errors of Everyday Parenting

Ambition

Some parents begin to feel as if the achievements of their children are in fact their own. These are usually remarkable, energetic people who for one reason or another have experienced some personal disappointment; while they may appear to be successful to the world at large, they harbor regrets for missed opportunities and lost moments of glory. Such parents may place an enormous burden on their children to achieve for them.

There are stage mothers and football fathers and parents who drive their children to practice hours on the violin or just to get straight A's and enter medical school or learn perfect French and join the diplomatic corps. Whatever the form of the ambition, the child becomes a tool for another's fulfillment. Then he has lost his opportunity to make a person out of himself. Children of course base their identity on their parents' characters, interests, and expectations. They add to this their own combinations of gifts, curiosities, habits, skills, tastes, and experiences. For overly ambitious parents, the child's self-discovery represents a threat. Such parents often over-control their children, insisting on perfect behavior. Often they don't allow their child to make the kind of mistakes necessary to gain independence. These parents treat their children as if they were their own good right arms, their own good legs. This is a dangerous situation and can result either in excessive rebellion during the teen years or in total submission, and neither direction is good for the child or, indeed, for the parent.

We are not talking about the natural ambition most parents share in which we hope our children will do well in school, be good athletes, enjoy music or art, and succeed in whatever they care about. Americans in particular are given to hoping that our children will have a happier and more comfortable life than we have had, excel us in our place in society. These ambitions are normal. They give spice and direction to our days. Only when we drive our children in a competition we have created for them are we going overboard. It is natural to want your son to be as good a swimmer as he can be. It is unnatural to insist that he spend six hours a day practicing for the meet if it means he can't play the trumpet, which he also loves to do. It is natural to want your child to bring home excellent grades but unnatural to expect and insist that he be the best in his class all the time, or to give him the feeling that you love him because of his academic achievement.

There are children who will become whatever their parents want at the sacrifice of their own feelings and instincts. These they have to hide because so many of them might be unacceptable to the perfectionist parent. The hiding is done at a terrible cost: the child loses himself and his own ability to see and choose and feel clearly.

Parents should check themselves to see if their hopes have turned into whips that drive their children on in a direction they might not necessarily wish to go. Parents should make sure not to attempt to win, through their children, some prize for themselves. This is an act of contempt for the child and robs him of his dignity.

Creativity

Some parents are so anxious not to stifle their child's imagination or artistic impulses that they miss the child's obvious need for order and control. Such a parent might allow a child to paint on the floors, to interrupt grownup conversation at will, to demand attention at all times, to leave toys strewn about, and to say whatever she wants without regard for other people's feelings, all this in the name of creative life.

Imagination is given to all children. Why it lasts for some into their adult years we do not know. We do know that the imaginative response, the creative drawing, the poem are not products of confusion and unbridled anger. They are, rather, the results of control over desires. Making order for your child is not going to stifle artistic capacities, but permitting chaos to overwhelm the child prevents the ordering and forming work that is the basis of all creative effort. Artists are probably born, not made, and they rarely come from families that expect them; but children can be limited if limitations are not placed on their behavior.

Overpraising a child for his drawing, his poem, or his first song can be destructive. Children recognize how important their work is for you and they can become frightened that they will not continue to please you or that they are not really as good as you say. This can make it hard for them to produce freely and happily.

Parents can help their children best by sharing their own pleasure in art in ways that are appropriate and accessible. Children will enjoy a short trip to the museum to see just a few items. They will appreciate listening to music with you from time to time. They will relish all the stories you tell them and many of the pictures you look at with them. Some children are more original in their responses and perceptions than others; some are more conforming and lack an ability to play with form in color, words, or sound. We do not know why this is so and have to resort to an explanation that rests on the genes. Parents should not worry about the creativity of their child. For most children it is as natural as breathing, not so long-lasting as we would like, but wonderful and satisfying while it is there.

Power

Some parents feel angry and unhappy if their authority is questioned by the child on any point. They must have their child obey them immediately and without question in all situations. It is possible with enough threat, force, and power to ensure that kind of "good behavior" from a child, but we feel that in the long run the good soldier, the totally accepting subordinate is neither a strong child nor a healthy one.

Parents do better to allow the child a little space to talk back occasionally, to protest a command or an order, to complain and sometimes disobey a little bit, in small ways. This is not to recommend that parents allow a child to run all over them and control the day, but simply to point out that the child needs an occasional victory in order to feel independent, vital, and in control of himself.

Perhaps another half hour of TV would not be a disaster one Sunday night. Perhaps allowance could be increased by a nickel a week. Perhaps it would be all right to go to the movies with Jane and her mother after all. Perhaps a mother or a father can say "I'm sorry" to a child if they have lost their temper, or accused them of something that they haven't done, or reacted badly to one situation or another. Parents do not have to be perfect, nor have the last word all the time. They do not have to run their families as if they were totalitarian states in constant fear of the slightest rebellion or sabotage. Moderation, flexibility, permitting oneself human error in the long run create a better disciplined child, who, like the willow tree, can bend with the winter storms and survive season after season.

The Child as Best Friend

Many parents find that they are isolated in the world. Divorce or marital troubles or distance from one's own mothers and brothers and sisters can tempt a parent to make of the growing child a confidant, a friend, a needed ally against the difficult world. Children are always there and will respond lovingly and caringly to all your troubles. In this sense they are ideal best friends. The problem is that they have a right to a parent, and a parent must be the one who is in charge, who appears as strong as the dike against the floodtides, as the walls of the house against the wind that blows outside. If a parent shares all his trembling, that parent can no longer be seen as the caring, protecting one and the relationship with the child goes off balance. In a sense the child becomes the caretaker and the parent the child.

We have to walk a fine line between hiding ourselves behind the parental role so that our children never know us as we really are, and telling them too much, too soon, so that they are forced to worry about us and to feel that the responsibility for our welfare lies with them. The balance, especially for parents going through hard times, is not an easy one to achieve, but the price of failure is to fail as a parent.

Estrangement from the Child

It can happen that a child appears to turn away from one parent. A little boy can light up when his father returns from work and barely smile at his mother when she follows. He can cry if his father goes out and pay no attention to the comings and goings of his mother. A girl can tell all her secrets to her mother and seem unresponsive when her father tries to get her attention, to talk or play with her. Children will, for periods of time, appear to prefer one parent to another. This happens because the child is struggling with a need to be independent of the parent they seem to be ignoring. Sometimes a child is angry with one parent and takes refuge in closeness with the other.

Parents can get pretty upset about this, feeling rejected by their own child. "He just doesn't like me," one mother said sadly. "I guess I'm not his type." Parents should know that their child has no choice. By definition he needs and loves both of them. Unlike other relationships, it is impossible for one of you just not to "like" the other; the bond is permanent, too much is at stake. He may turn away at one stage of development or another and seem to focus only on the other parent. Let it happen. The child has reasons and none of those reasons has to do with his dislike of you. Most likely the period of banishment from his open affection will last only a short while. He may be angry because you brought a baby home. He may be angry because you went on a trip. He may ignore you because he wants so much to crawl into your lap and feels he's a bigger boy than that and would jeopardize his independence if he comes too close. Whatever it is, it will go away soon. The patient parent will find a loving child, a few days, a few months, down the road.

Epilogue

Having a baby is the one creative act that belongs to us all. There are very few Rembrandts or Shakespeares or Mozarts. But like an artist, we can all find our immortality in the making of the new. Like all creations, babies require more hard work and drudgery than pure inspiration. Our babies survive because we give them our energy, our selves, because we make the loving connection to them that pulls them day by day into the human community, into speech, movement, desire, expression, affection. Without our eyes looking directly into theirs, without our arms letting them sink close into our skin, smelling, feeling, holding us; without our smelling, feeling, holding, cooing at, and stroking them, our babies would be only empty shells. Without our work and our attentive minds and souls, there would be no more humanity. We are the makers of the miracle. It is a true wonder the way the baby seems programmed to elicit from us just the response he needs for survival. It is an equal wonder that we for the most part so naturally, so eagerly, so unquestioningly give ourselves over to the new life we have created.

We exhaust ourselves and we worry. Is everything all right? Are we doing things well? Is there a better way? Are we communicating our worst selves with the mashed bananas or is our best good enough? Is that best revealed in our hands, in our smile, in our methods of saying no or saying yes? We worry, yes, but we also feel satisfaction, pride beyond anything that has happened before. "My son learned how to ride his bike today," one woman reports to another. "My daughter can tie her own shoelaces," one man tells his neighbor. The accomplishments are ordinary and yet for each child, for each parent, each time, they are significant, even gorgeous moments. We are proud of our children, we are proud of ourselves for having made our children.

As the child grows, we come to respect and enjoy the special, unique original person he is. We know his faults better than anyone else. So often they are our faults, too. We also know the way he goes to sleep, with his fingers in his hair and his woolly lamb arranged just so. We know how he looks when an illness is brewing. We know how he sounds when he is scared. We know how hard he works to stay within the lines when he colors. He is ours and yet he is himself. This is not the easiest paradox in the world to live with, but most of us manage.

How amazing is the resilience of the child! We must never forget how much they learn, how fast they learn it, how they can correct and control and rearrange their behavior, their perceptions, their inner emotional structures. It is their gift that at each stage of development they find new resources to strengthen themselves. If they have hit a snag, if they appear to be in trouble, they can so often amaze us with a leap forward months later. Children are vulnerable. They need to be treated with understanding and respect; yet they are tough as the new weeds that push themselves through the hard-packed soil of a dry spring. This is both a contradiction and a fact.

When you have a ten-year-old child, you look back and think that time has been stolen away, gone so fast. When you are in the middle of it all, it seems as if childhood will never end. On bad days you may wonder where your own life is going, where the person is who once went to the movies at will and ate chocolate cookies at two in the morning and swam to the lighthouse on a dare. Gone, of course, only to be reborn in our new selves. We grow up with our children and in discovering them we discover ourselves. It is a rare parent who hasn't unearthed a fault or two in his own character as he studies himself with his child. It is a rare parent who hasn't stumbled upon some wonderful new skill, some great satisfaction he never knew before as he takes his child fishing, or bowling, or walks along the path by the penguin pond in the zoo. It is a rare parent who doesn't surprise himself with his endurance in the middle of a long night of illness or continual bad dreams, who isn't amazed at his patience as he reads the same Dr. Seuss book again for the hundredth time. It is a rare parent who doesn't look back over his child's childhood and sense how much richer he is for having rushed to the emergency room with that bad earache, for having taken the Scouts on a trip to the science museum, for having tempered his pride the night of the school play, for having searched every store in town for a small enough tennis racket.

You will always remember the smell of baby skin, the look of a bleeding elbow, the feel of a body hurtled, welcoming, against your knees, the weight of legs dangling from your shoulders, the soggy warmth of a sleeping child curled in your lap. It is odd how much we learn from our children, about what is important to us, about what we believe, about who we are, and how much pleasure it gives us to have made so many lunches, so many dinners, to have purchased snowsuits and bathing suits, to have saved and sacrificed for our family.

We have created our children out of the everydayness of everyday events. We have probably had very few dramatic moments but we have endured the daily work, the discipline it required. We have shared ourselves and our resources. We have, by piling small acts together, created ourselves as parents. We have by now been humbled. We know that we are far from perfect and that, like our neighbors, we are only human. As we steel ourselves for the amusement park of adolescence, we can draw strength from our accomplishments and deep happiness from our children. Uncomfortable as they have so often made us, we are grateful to them for being—for being themselves, for being with us.

Index

father(s) *(cont.)*
  son's love for, 165, 167
  toddler's need for, 93–94
  see also parents, single
fearless children, 338–339
  characteristics of, 338
  discipline of, 338
  sense of reality in, 338
  therapy for, 338–339
fears:
  of abandonment, 52, 55, 88, 90,
    112, 155, 214, 259, 270, 300, 354,
    366, 385
  anger and, 87, 256
  of being different, 280, 300
  in boys, 136–138, 165–166, 174, 263
  of broken objects, 137, 138, 139, 263
  of dark closets, 255
  of death, 341
  divorce and, 206–207, 300
  of dog bites, 182
  emotional illness and, 145
  excessive, 255–256
  of father's anger, 165–166
  of ghosts, 182, 212, 312
  of giants, 255
  in girls, 136, 138–139, 171, 307–308
  of losing parent, 256
  of losing part of the body, 54–55,
    61–62, 96, 112, 141, 216, 259
  of loss of penis, 61–62, 66, 136–139,
    165, 174, 216, 263
  of menstruation, 66, 263, 307–308
  of minor injuries, 137, 165, 174, 307
  of needles, 215
  of new siblings, 87
  of noises, 30, 87
  of parents' deaths, 341–342
  for premature baby's survival, 107
  in pre-schoolers, 151, 155, 165,
    181–183
  in psychotic children, 320
  rituals and, 298
  of school, 340–343, 347
  in school-age children, 270, 280,
    294, 300, 312, 314

  of separation from mother, 30, 34,
    52, 71, 94, 131–135, 155, 263
  of sleeping, 36–37
  of shampooing, 202
  of strangers, 29–31
  therapy for, 256
  of thunder, 87, 255
  of toilet training, 53–55, 112, 141
  usefulness of, 230, 255
  of vagina, 136–138
  of water, 255
  of witches, 255, 312
  in worried children, 334
fears, irrational, 181–183
  causes of, 182
  examples of, 181
  overcoming of, 182–183
  parents' treatment of, 182–183
feeding:
  bottle, 70–71
  breast, 18–19, 69
  weaning and, 71
  see also eating problems
feet-stamping, 37
fingerprinting of children, 397
fire-setting, 358
flirtatiousness, 170, 171
foster homes, 116
freedom, loss of, following childbirth,
    11, 25, 102
Freud, Anna, 2
Freud, Sigmund, 38, 140, 164, 261, 274
friendships:
  of pre-schoolers, 152, 153, 248–250
  of school-age children, 289–290

Galenson, Eleanor, 2
games:
  boys' preferences for, 286, 288–289
  clinging children's preferences for,
    334
  girls' preferences for, 286, 288
  for pre-schoolers, 154
  school-age children and, 287
  as teaching tools, 77–78, 287
Garden of Eden, 74, 350

talking, by babies, 32–33
teasing:
  in pre-schoolers, 161, 249
  in school-age children, 280, 286, 293
  in toddlers, 58–59, 76
technicolor children, 331–332
  characteristics of, 331–332
  erotic parental love of, 332
  parents of, 332
Teddy bears, children's attachment to, 35–36, 67
teething pains, 109
television:
  as disciplinary tool, 194
  pre-schoolers and, 159–160, 193–194
  school-age children and, 285
  violence on, 285
telling time, 281
temper tantrums, 325
  bladder control and, 244
  of borderline children, 229
  of learning-disabled children, 347
  of psychotic children, 226, 227
  of toddlers, 49–51
testing, for nursery school admission, 158
testosterone, 160
therapists, 391–395
  behavioral, 391
  child psychiatrists as, 391
  family, 394
  initial contact with, 392
  parents' relationship with, 393–394
  referrals to, 391–392
  selection of, 392–393
  techniques used by, 394–395
thin children, 370–371
  enjoyment of food in, 370
  mother's relationship with, 370–371
  puberty in, 370
thumb-sucking:
  divorce and, 206
  by newborns, 20, 199

  by pre-schoolers, 199–200
  tooth damage and, 199
thyroid problems, 241
tics, 235–236
  causes of, 235
  frequency of, 235, 236
  as serious disease, 236
  treatments for, 236
time, understanding clock and, 281
toddlers (one-to-three-year-olds):
  aggressive behavior of, 57–59, 87
  anger of, 37–40, 91, 132
  asthma of, 145–146
  bladder control of, 138
  broken toys feared by, 137
  cautiousness of, 32, 35
  clinging behavior of, 131–135
  conscience of, 89–90, 95
  curiosity of, 76
  depression in, 117–119
  discipline of, 40–49
  divorce and, 92–95
  dreaming of, 84
  eating problems of, 46, 48, 68–72, 113–114, 148
  emotional sensitivities of, 116–117
  erotic feelings of, 44, 58, 64–65, 66, 96, 135
  father's importance to, 93–94
  genital touching by, 60, 63–64, 96, 135, 137, 172
  hospitalization of, 90–92, 110, 139
  incessant questioning by, 76
  independence of, 35, 39, 50, 58, 59, 95, 131
  lack of growth in, 115–117
  learning capacities of, 77–79
  masturbation by, 172
  mental resilience of, 101
  minor injuries feared by, 137
  new babies and, 85–89
  overdisciplining of, 48–49
  overprotection of, 133
  nudity and, 64–65, 138
  overweight, 368
  in parents' bed, 67–68, 111